This Woman's Army

D0879952

The Dynamics
of Sex and Violence
in the Military

Marie deYoung

Hellgate Press
Central Point, Oregon

Published by Hellgate Press/PSI Research
© 1999 by Marie deYoung

Managing Editor: Kathy Marshbank
Editorial: Eric Hansen
Cover Designer: Steven Burns

Please direct any comments, questions, or suggestions regarding this book to:
Hellgate Press/PSI Research
Editorial Department
P.O. Box 3727
Central Point, Oregon 97502-0032

(541) 479-9464
(541) 476-1479 fax
info@psi-research.com e-mail

Library of Congress Cataloging-in-Publication Data
deYoung, Marie
    This woman's army: the dynamics of sex and violence in the military /
Marie deYoung. – – 1st ed.
        p. cm.
    ISBN: 1-55571-507-9 (pbk.)
    1. United States. Army – –Officers – –Biography. 2. United States. Army – –
Women – –Biography. 3. United States. Army – –Women – –Sexual behavior.
    4. Violence – –United States – –History – –20th century.
U53.D47 A3   1999
355.0082 – – dc21   99–04743
                                                                                CIP

Printed and bound in the United States of America

First Edition 10 9 8 7 6 5 4 3 2 1
♻ Printed on recycled paper when available

Acknowledgements

I wish to acknowledge my family for their patience and support while I wrote this book. I want to especially thank my mother, Alice deYoung, my sister, Lucille and her husband John Puccio, and my youngest sister Alice for their care and support over the years.

I would also like to thank my mentors and friends who encouraged me to write about the issues addressed in this story: Bob Kimball, Ron Cook, Alicia Forsey, Rev. Harry Scholefield, Rev. David Hubner, Kathy Burrus, Tom Molino, Ed Tucker, Curt Pedder, Ed Kelley, Jimmy and Valerie Shears, Tom Culleton, Forrest Church, Cheryn Swanson and John Fasano, and all my friends in the 363rd CSG, 4th ID, 44th Engineer Battalion and the 2nd ACR.

I could not have completed this project without the many helpful suggestions offered by media specialists including Mike Wallace, Tom Anderson, Laura Belt, and Arnold Diaz. In the editing process, I received excellent feedback from my assistant, Jolinda Campos and from students at Our Lady of the Lake University: Yvonne Villegas, Stephanie B. Thomé, Lorely Ramirez, Delilah Martinez and Elena Tijerina.

I am grateful to some of my colleagues at Our Lady of the Lake University, particularly Dr. Francine Danis and other members of the Women Writers Group, and Dr. Howard Benoist, then Vice-President and Dean of Academic Affairs who supported not only this project, but all of the empowerment projects undertaken by faculty and staff at the Center for Women in Church and Society.

The kindness of our sisters from the Congregation of Divine Providence will never be forgotten. In the last stage of writing this book, the sisters invited me to rent one of their trailers to shorten my horrendous commute. I discussed several chapters over many a pistachio pudding with Sr. Dorothy Ann Vrba and Sr. Martha Vrba (who taught at a boy's military academy for 19 years). The late Sr. Margaret Ellen Gallatin expressed great confidence in the book as we collaborated on another historical project.

Finally, I must thank Emmett Ramey, and his editorial staff: Kathy Marshbank, Steven Burns and Eric Hansen for the respect and attentiveness they have shown my work. The responsibility for errors is completely mine, but I am grateful for their technical support and their enthusiasm as we finally bring this message to the American people.

Contents

Preface

In an article dated July14, 1997 the *Army Times* reported the Army is having great difficulty recruiting infantrymen. As recently as February 1999 the Army announced severe recruiting shortages, leading Secretary of the Army Louis Caldera to consider aggressive recruiting of Hispanic high school drop outs. Why the difficulty? Surely, our young men are not afraid of being maimed in battle, or sent off for a dangerous stint where they could be left to die. American infantrymen hardly ever die in combat anymore. Not since Vietnam have we suffered huge casualties on the battlefield.

Fear of ground combat could not have been the deterrent. The Gulf War was dramatized on television almost as tidily as a *Star Wars* fantasy. Laser-guided missiles were touted as the be-all technology to contain third world bullies. Cameras angled on radar screens and aerial photos of military targets. The worst American casualties depicted had no more horror or physical mutilation than our young people are accustomed to seeing in their broken down ghetto neighborhoods. The fact that the Gulf War was so physically unthreatening to so many troops is still joked about, especially by those who want to end combat exclusion for women. The urban American woman's secret: American women are safer with peace-keeping troops in Bosnia or Korea than when we walk alone in South Bronx neighborhoods or the Watts section of Los Angeles.

We know fear of mortality does not faze the youth of America. The high rates of homicide, AIDS, and drunk driving accidents as leading causes of death for young males should obviate the point. Given our youth's participation mystique with the culture of death, what could possibly be deterring them from turning to the Army as a disciplined Profession of Arms that would instill honor, pride, integrity or the satisfaction of knowing one's service contributed to world peace and security?

Perhaps, just perhaps, young men are reluctant to join because of the gnawing perception that young people just don't matter to the military anymore. To matter, to have a sense of ultimate purpose and meaning, our young ones often waste their lives to an auto crash or hail of bullet fire to gain their fifteen seconds of glorious public recognition on the nightly news. On the other hand, young studs today know that they will not be valued for their military service, even if they rise to acts of heroism. Media coverage of the Gulf War amply illustrates the point. The soldiers who sweated, tasted sand for six months at a time, drudged through their tactics, hardened their bodies, sharpened their minds, gritted their teeth and pushed their souls to the heights of discipline, camaraderie, and skill - these soldiers are and will continue to be nameless, disenfranchised beings.

Who did we forget? The media seldom put a human face on the men and women who served on the ground in the Gulf War. Who were these men and women? What were there backgrounds? What problems did they bring to the Army? What life concerns did they wish to address during their formation as soldiers and citizens? Who do they vote for? What do they believe in? As consumers of a narrowly focused news industry we have only ourselves to blame for the denigration of combat arms as a form of laudatory public service. American society has become estranged from the men and women who serve in the combat arms professions. What do we know about soldiers today anyway? Who joins the service? What kind of training can we expect for young men and women who volunteer as combatants and support personnel? Are they stable? Are they intelligent? Do they care about anything besides their paychecks and their benefits?

If your opinion of Army soldiers was formed by the recurring media slant, you would most likely conclude that men who join the combat arms profession to fight are bigots, killers, rapists, and mass-murderers.

Consider the stories that have governed the international press for the past two years:

- Timothy McVeigh, born and raised Irish Catholic, turned white survivalist. His bony jaw, protruding with superior anger, McVeigh would have remained faceless as the Gulf War hero. Not until he executed his rage in a retaliatory and murderous protest of the federal government's handling of Waco did his boyish yet cold smile become a household memory.
- Two white soldiers killed blacks as part of a secret rite of passage in the 82nd Airborne.
- A black marine raped a young girl on the island of Okinawa, sparking international protests and the possible permanent expulsion of American troops.

That McVeigh and these other criminals are a reflection of military life should not be discounted. As General John Sheehan alluded in his talk to the Navy Chaplain school, on 30 October 1995, there are plenty of Timothy McVeighs and John Nichols still on active duty today. We must learn from the Oklahoma bombing. Without intimidation or accommodation to this cowardly act, we must heed the volcanic anger that seethes in the young who believe themselves disenfranchised, without a future. That mega-event is no less tragic than the 20,000 black youths who kill each other on the streets of America each year. It is no less tragic than the weekly murders of family members by active duty soldiers. These are the screams of the young men in our nation, both in the military and out, who beg for healing, nurturing, and positive leadership in their lives.

We must see the larger picture, however. Although there are plenty of McVeighs to go around, as General Sheehan asserted, most soldiers are not like McVeigh or the other men who express their anger in criminal violence. There are professional soldiers, decent human beings whose stories need to be told. In another era, men from the 82nd or the elite Marines serving in Southeast Asia would have made the news because of their daring adventures in the sky or the jungle. Such stories have no countenance in the press today. After all, if our 70-year old ex-president can jump from a military airplane and land on his feet as former President Bush did, there must not be very much daring to the existence of today's airborne paratrooper!

But the only way a soldier can dominate the air waves today is to mimic the civilian underclass, who only achieve notoriety when their violent acts are grotesque enough to draw media attention. The time has long past for us to contrast the criminally violent military men who dominate the nightly news with the vast numbers of real people who serve their ungrateful country as soldiers.

- Do we know the names of the soldiers who spent their Saturday mornings rescuing flood victims in North Dakota in the winter of '97?

- Who were the National Guard firefighters on the West Coast who saved lives and homes each summer when California fires stormed beyond their "managed" boundaries in the national forests?

- What would possess a young man to learn Hangul as he soldiers beside a Korean soldier guarding the DMZ?

- Why would an American soldier spend his Saturday mornings teaching basketball to a Korean orphan instead of sleeping off a massive hangover?

- What would it take to make these unsung military heroes as sexy and appealing to our youth as the men who conform to the media requirements for international coverage, short of the formula that guarantees primetime coverage: rape, pillage, plunder?

I would argue that the Aberdeen Trials and most notoriously, the trial of African-American Staff Sergeant Delmar Simpson hastened the demise of America's appreciation for her fighting men. These trials were never about rape or sexual assault. History will prove the Aberdeen story was about the American Sexual Revolution and the American news media gone amuck. With nominal investment of intellectual effort, social policy research, or engagement with the people who lived outside of the medium, the O.J. Simpson trials provided massive chunks of superb ratings for the major networks. During much of that period, the

This Woman's Army: The Dynamics of Sex and Violence in the Military

military was granted a reprieve from a largely negative press hound. Sooner or later, the O.J. Simpson trials had to end, and when they did television and newspapers had an elephantine vacuum that soon became the subject of media self-critiques. The void didn't last long, however, because a soldier named Delmar Simpson soon provided all the titillating sexual, violent and interracial rape fantasies required for consistently high media ratings.

Aberdeen provided the stage upon which men and women enacted soap opera rape fantasies, a racially tantalizing rendition of *Dangerous Liaisons*. In a contorted maneuver, women's advocates used the Aberdeen trials at once to stake out the territory of women soldiers as a victim class, while simultaneously using the tragedy to push for women in combat. Perversely, public advocates who insist that female soldiers are incapable of moral judgement about such issues as participation in fraternization and adultery, simultaneously argue that the best remedy for sexual harassment is to place women even further forward on the battlefield. These powerful lobby groups grandstand that women must be protected from equal standards of physical labor, personal conduct, and professional competence, yet, though lesser qualified in every professional respect, they must be placed in combat positions to lessen the hostility of men to their presence.

The media delivered the final blow to the honor and appeal of America's fighting man with the national spectacle of Sergeant Major Gene McKinney's ruin, despite his acquittal of sexual harassment and sexual assault charges brought by six white women. From McVeigh's act of terrorism to the McKinney tragedy, the prototypes for GI coverage on the nightly news, would not inspire self-respecting young men to join the United States Army. Most of our young men know quite well they can achieve infamy, a criminal record, a destroyed reputation, a cameo on nightly television without a tenth of the effort, gritty discipline, loneliness or personal sacrifices required of a soldier. The odds are one in four that a black man will be entangled with the justice system, anyway. Uncle Sam would only increase these odds, if you believe everything you read or see on television.

How did the Pentagon attempt to fill the personnel shortage? How did we recruit enough men to cover the incessant deployments and training duties for our fighting infantry soldiers? We didn't. We decided we could fill the masculine void by recruiting women. Were women able to take up the gauntlet for the infantry grunt? No! Once again, the media tells the story.

While Army men have been lionized in media accounts, women have been exalted as a victim class. Staunchly propped up by congressional advocates for women in combat, female soldiers have been granted promotion and advancement opportunities based on a double standard that grants women promotion and test points based on their effort rather than their ability. When I began this book, the only female sergeant major to make national headlines in American History was Brenda Hoster, a retired, white, 120-pound public affairs officer. Her claim to fame? Rescuing a soldier from the hands of the enemy? No. Gunning down advancing tanks or enemy planes? No. Carrying soldiers out of fiery bombed-out buildings? No. Parachuting behind enemy lines to gather intelligence that could turn a war to our favor? No. Flying a helicopter behind enemy lines to rescue wounded grunts? No.

Not a single act of heroism, yet, Sergeant Major Brenda Hoster is a household name in America. Her act of courage? Hoster accused the highest-ranking African American sergeant, Eugene McKinney, of kissing her, and soliciting sex. Hoster made these accusations on ABC, the national network that employed the spouse of her feminist attorney, Ms. Barnes. She repeated the accusations on subsequent national television programs. But asked later to testify at the Article 32 hearing that resulted in McKinney's court-martial, Sergeant Major Hoster cowed to her fears. She refused to testify in court because she feared her reputation would be tarnished by revelations about her own sexual adventures in the military, many of which were in violation of military laws.

Sergeant Major Hoster, who as a senior non-commissioned officer should be an example of the tough, uncompromising standards practiced by our leaders, allowed herself to be portrayed as a victim — incapable of holding her own in a man's world. Hoster used the national media to smear the reputation of a man who was renowned for his care of young soldiers. She had no success story of her own to persuade America of the importance of women's participation in military life.

While the Aberdeen and McKinney trials dominated America's media stories, Joan Rivers interviewed me on her WOR radio program, just after a 25-year sentence was handed down to Sergeant Simpson during the Aberdeen Trials. A caller referred to Brenda Hoster as the Army's "darling poster child" for its ill-begotten campaign to stem the flow of sexual misconduct accusations from outside feminist organizations. As the caller pointed out, once the Army had affidavits revealing that Ms. Hoster's own behavior was not above reproach, Ms. Hoster was encouraged by her high-powered attorney to avoid media contact. Sadly, Sergeant Major Brenda Hoster has become the poster girl for all of the women in the Army who have hidden their own professional incompetence behind bizarre allegations of sexual misconduct or sexual harassment. These women have done nothing to further the cause of equality or to secure the place of women in combat, unless we are willing to agree that women can defeat the enemy soldier, who would foolishly touch them inappropriately in battle, with million-dollar lawsuits.

Meanwhile, what is life like for real women who joined the Army to prove their abilities as soldiers, leaders and great citizens? What would it take to encourage our commercial producers to ask the right questions so we can get a real glimpse into not only the hardships, the struggles, but the very real triumphs and joys women experience in the military? What would cause a woman to forsake her family to spend six months in the Saudi Arabian desert as a fuel handler? How are the children of soldiers enduring the separations, their fears of parental loss due to death or divorce? What kind of woman would learn how to change tires on a five-ton truck, so that she could do heavy wheel maintenance with her mostly male buddies in the freezing cold winter down in the dusty, barren valleys near Camp Casey, Korea?

What problems do women bring to military organizations? How many women are like Sergeant Major Hoster, incapable of completing their missions on equal terms with men — forced to resort to political gender tactics to survive? Or unplanned pregnancy to avoid deployment? Women are four times as likely as men to be excused from assigned deployments due to "unplanned" pregnancies. Most alarming, however is how many women tender false allegations of rape or sexual harassment to deflect attention from their own misconduct, or to obtain post-coital birth control. These gender-based problems occur more often than we realize. Gender-based conflicts are in need of serious attention if the active duty Army is ever to become a vital, positive alternative for young men and women in the next millennium.

Fortunately, as this book is being written, a public outcry on all sides of the gender issue continued long enough to force the Secretary of Defense, Mr. William Cohen, to attempt reconciliation between the standing factions that have survived the first lobbed missiles in the military's Gender War. The sexual revolution spun out of control in the Army because of the contradictory and competing concerns of the legal sexual harassment industry against the claims of minorities and men who have made lifelong sacrifices for the sake of military readiness. Cohen appointed a number of panels to determine the efficacy of the legal codes concerning sexual conduct in a mixed gender military, and the appropriateness of placing men and women together in mixed gender basic training, near combat, and combat situations. Be assured, however, scandals will continue to erupt and policy will be challenged until serious reforms are effected.

Since Aberdeen, the tangential military readiness issue, the role and place of women in the military, has somehow once again managed to dominate the public policy discussion about military readiness. Tragically, this most important issue may be swept under the linoleum to appease powerful women's lobbies. The most important question is not what role women should have in the military, but really, what role and place should men have. How can we restore the esteem, the dignity, the authority that is worthy of America's fighting man, in a world where the privileged, the educated classes can exempt themselves from the obligation of defense by constructing, in essence, a mercenary force?

In this memoir, I hope to draw a portrait of military life that encourages the reader to take a deep interest in the institution of military training as a rite of passage for our young citizens. Military training is a process of transformation. Feminists and traditionalists can agree that "Women's Ways of Knowing" are fundamentally different from that of men. The Army honored gender differences long before feminist theory considered the importance of gender socialization. Sadly, the move to integrate women into unisex training and combat roles compromised not only the readiness of the units but the well-being of the women who serve in them. And, unisex training has been most damaging to the military man. As I recount experiences and observations about the trials and triumphs of the men and women with whom I served, I have come to gender-differentiated conclusions about the value of military service for men and women. These conclusions were the motivation for witnessing to the experiences of men and women in this book with whom I have been privileged to serve. My story may help ardent feminists realize that, as studies are proving, the secular learning process is gender differentiated, so the process of military socialization for women must also be different.

I would like to reaffirm the traditional view of the value of combat arms training for the socialization of young men as leaders, providers, and protectors in their families and communities. Paradoxically, I believe it is progressive to acknowledge that only some women will find military service highly valuable or beneficial in their lives. Most women's lives will be far more enhanced when policymakers draw upon the Title IX provisions to create far less expensive and more suitable community service and training opportunities for women to make laudable contributions to society, as well as to develop their potential.

By peeking into the gender issues through the differently refracted lenses of the real lives of the men and women who serve, I hope we can rethink some of the situations that have led to a great decline in voluntary enlistments in the Army. It is my hope that we can achieve some measure of reconciliation between those who make the greatest sacrifices to ensure the security of our nation and those who reap the benefits of privilege, access, and power, whether they participate in the required sacrifice to achieve this privilege or not.

Chapter 1

Be All You Can Be

What could possibly induce an educated, middle-class woman to join the Army at the age of 28? Back in the fall of 1982, I was comfortably settled in a safe community. I was not athletic. Never jogged, did a push up, or pumped iron. I attended Catholic schools back when the sisters associated athletic prowess with lesbianism and when mothers associated physical strain with barrenness. I didn't know what a lesbian was when I was in high school, but I knew it was bad. I didn't intend to have any children, but I knew it was a curse to be barren. I avoided both fates in my youth by remaining a good Catholic girl: a physical weakling. Why in God's name did I join the Army? Personal circumstances. Economics. Anger. Most of all, an irrational belief that women would never be taken seriously as leaders unless they participated in the right of passage that automatically conferred images of strength, heroism, and authority to men.

The circumstances? My world literally cracked open when my husband asked me for a divorce at a time when it was impossible for me to find self-sustaining work. Our country was slumped in an excruciating recession. Remember the layoffs, the huge jumps in oil prices? The prime lending rate reached 22 percent. Middle-class executives were laid off by the thousands. Magazine cover stories warned executives and their families about prevention techniques to stave off depression and suicide in this dire economy.

As a college educated woman, I wasn't an unemployed middle-class executive in perpetual fear of layoff. But as a married woman of child-bearing years with a newly earned degree in Music, I was considered high-risk for full-time employment, and often characterized by hiring authorities as someone who would "take a job away from a sole family breadwinner." The anger I felt at being deprived of a chance to work because I was a woman was ugly enough to be a weapon.

My parents taught me that education was the only route to success in our society, and I was naïve enough to believe them. Since the eighth grade I worked at night to scrounge my way through Catholic school, and later, college. Even while married, I worked for all but the last two years, to pay for my college as the expenses were incurred, believing there would be a handsome payoff — a good, secure job. For the first time since the New Deal, our society's promise that education would guarantee every American a good job was ringing false.

Equal opportunity laws were in full force, but in that horrible recession, executives and managers treated women as secondary breadwinners. We were regarded as poor candidates for management and leadership because we lacked experience in sports and the military training that develops the toughness, leadership, endurance and focus required to beat out competition or other threats to institutional success.

My belief in the American Dream was radically altered by the rejection I was repeatedly experiencing as a token female both in school and at work. I came to believe that all of the equal opportunity laws in the world would not help women gain real access to the upper echelons of management, leadership positions or political power. At some deep level, I believed women had to earn our place by taking the hard jobs, just as men did. Unless we participated in the same rites of passage as men, we would not earn their respect as leaders who are capable of enduring hardship, sacrifice, and personal pain to accomplish higher goals or to bring a team of people through hard times.

So, one crisp day in October of 1982, I responded to an Army advertisement: "Be all you can be: a Russian translator." I naively thought I would sign a contract that would help me to buy a little time for the continuation of my Master's program in orchestral conducting, which I started before my husband asked me for a divorce. I was already able to translate all the German, French and Italian markings in orchestral scores, but I did not understand the Russian alphabet, let alone the tempo and dynamic markings of Stravinsky, Mussorgsky or America's favorite: Illych Tschaikovsky. If I wanted to study authentic manuscripts for these Russian composers, I had to learn the language. Why not let the Army teach me? My professors, Dr. Pogemiller and Dr. Luedeke were always telling students they would learn how to handle any professional stress as musicians if they served in the Army. The Army would teach us how to cope with anything.

Recruiting offices looked the same in 1982 as they look today. A few metal desks were lined up with a crisp, jovial sergeant sitting behind each one. Sergeant Jay Metcalf was the recruiter who took my first inquiry at the local recruiting station in Kansas City. All of the recruiters in his office were African American. Odd, because their office was in a white segregated neighborhood. They were surprised when I asked for an application to be a Russian translator. I looked pretty un-athletic. Still do. Sergeant Metcalf tentatively gave me the preliminary screening test, which measured a recruit's ability to analyze electrical, mechanical, logic, mathematical, and verbal problems. He laughed at my self-deprecating jokes about my mechanical ineptitude, which turned out to be all in my head. Upon scoring the test results, Metcalf's jaw dropped. He picked up the phone and called his recruiting commander.

The World I Left Behind

The late Patrick Hughes, Marie deYoung and Al Doeve sing together for the last time at Al and Marie's wedding celebration. (Boston Center for Adult Education, June 12, 1976.)

I do not recall the captain's name, but the recruiting commander immediately came to Sergeant Metcalf's office, and proceeded to explain that my scores were unusually high, a positive indicator that I could successfully complete Officer Candidate School. He began to discourage me from pursuing the translator's class. He would revert between glancing at my scores and then gently peering into my eyes.

"I don't think you would be happy as an enlisted person," he said shaking his head.

"Will I still be able to go to school for Russian translation if I agree to OCS?"

"No, the Army doesn't pay for officers to attend translation school unless your particular assignment requires language training."

"What kind of jobs can I do as an officer?"

"You would specialize in administration, personnel, logistics, maybe military intelligence..."

"What do I have to do to get through Officer Candidate School?"

The captain looked at me with frank sternness.

"Listen, I am not going to snow you. This will be the hardest challenge you ever had in your life. You will have to run five miles every day. You will have to do push-ups morning, noon and night. You will march 15 miles, maybe even 25 miles. You will be harassed. Yelled at. Pushed to your absolute limits. But when you are done you will feel the greatest sense of accomplishment..."

I told the captain I had never done a pushup, a sit-up, or run more than 20 feet before walking into his recruiting station. How in God's name would I know if I could succeed?

"What if I can't do these things? What will happen to me? Will they send me home?"

"Of course not, but you should not sign this contract until you do three things. First, start exercising. Right now! Go home and do sit-ups. Learn how to do a push-up. Start running."

"I don't know how to run."

"Start by walking 50 paces, then jogging 50 paces. Go back and forth for two miles every day. Then increase it to 100 paces. Then go to 500. Before you know it, you will be running two miles without stopping..."

Up to this point, Sergeant Metcalf sat quietly at his desk. He was lanky and slender. He projected the rock solid sergeant toughness often seen in the movies. For a moment, Metcalf softened and smiled at me.

"You know, there's nothing that the Army asks you to do that can't be done by an average person," he encouraged me. "Your scores say you are way above average."

"Yeah, but those scores test my ability to think. I have never had to do physical training in my life. Everyone will tell you I am no good at team sports."

"You know, your body will change," he retorted. "It's been proven that if you do what the captain says for six weeks, you will develop new capillaries and the ability to handle all the oxygen that you have to take in when you run. You can do this. We'll help you."

The captain looked at me harshly. He was only about 30, but he had the conservative demeanor of a 40-year-old executive.

"I'm not going to snow you," he repeated. "You have to think this over. As I was saying. First you have to start exercising. Second, you have to watch two films, Private Benjamin, and An Officer and a Gentleman. You won't have a clue about the Army unless you watch these two movies. Third, you need to talk to every man you know who served in the Army. Let them try to talk you out of it. Make them tell you the gruesome training stories, the horrible experiences they had in 'Nam."

I confessed my friends were already trying to convince me that I was insane to consider the Army. "A close friend is trying to persuade me to go Air Force."

"Why don't you?"

"Because my family has always served in the Army. My husband volunteered during the Vietnam War. My uncle served in the National Guard. My dad served in the Korean War. I feel like I would be more comfortable in the Army. It is part of our family history..."

"Listen," the captain said quietly, nodding with approval as he gave me his card. "Do the things I told you. Sergeant Metcalf will do everything in his power to help you to prepare. If you have any questions that he can't answer, call me. When you're ready to sign the contract, we'll get you into Officer

Candidate School (OCS) and on your way. You can do this, but only if you really want it..."

I left that station feeling exuberant and hopeful for the first time since I realized my private world was imploding. My husband didn't want me. The academic world treated me like a dilettante. The business world didn't want me to apply for a management job until I was a crone — beyond childbearing age. But the Army, Uncle Sam, had just said, "I WANT YOU!"

Sergeant Metcalf and the other recruiters made me feel I was needed. I was hooked. The salary they offered was pitiful. The working conditions unpalatable. The future assignments unpredictable. Yet, they won my heart. They insisted that I was needed, valuable, capable, and most likely to be successful. How could I refuse their appeals?

I began a physical training regimen that same day, after I finished my two-mile walk from the recruiting station to my home. Soon, I was able to do enough sit-ups to pass OCS. Running was an alien adventure for me. In my Catholic schools days girls were not allowed to run distances for fear our reproductive organs would be damaged by the constant pounding. On my first attempt at running, I waddled through the neighborhood as I counted 50 paces, then attempted to run 50. A few weeks passed before I could run two miles straight. Whenever I reached a plateau, I would visit Sergeant Metcalf. He would smile, recite a few training slogans and teach me about running shoes, stride, pacing techniques. After six weeks I could run five miles, but not fast enough to survive at the Infantry School. Sergeant Metcalf and the other recruiters encouraged me to "stay with the program: NO PAIN, NO GAIN!"

Within three months, Sergeant Metcalf helped me to present my application packet to the Officer Candidate Board. The panelists grilled me about my motivations, my ability to transition from academic life to the military. How strong was my desire to take care of soldiers? They probed for a natural ability to lead. I still have the board's graded comments, which Sergeant Metcalf sent back to me after I was commissioned a lieutenant. Their affirmations gave me a greater feeling of esteem than I ever received from a big pay increase or medal or trophy. After the board grilled me, the sergeant who processed my packet whistled when he saw the date of my application. When I asked him what was wrong, he shook his head. "Usually, it takes us a year to process a packet for OCS. From the time you walked into your recruiter's office to the date of your acceptance at OCS — three months..." He whistled again. That was the first of many experiences that made me realize the Army was almost zealous in its efforts to recruit and keep capable women.

Before signing the OCS contract, most of my friends and relatives tried to dissuade me from my plans. They could not imagine how I could swing a rifle after so many years limited to cerebral baton-swinging during orchestral rehearsals.

My soon-to-be-ex-husband, Al, arranged for me to dine with one of his attractive co-workers. She had long, perfectly painted fingernails, the body of a goddess, and a bleached smile that would be the envy of any cable newscaster. She gently related stories about her field duty. She giggled while retelling her struggles with military gear that disabled her as she hopped in and out of jeeps.

"You know Marie," she said with the coy smile of Lamb Chop, "I finally wet myself while I was trying to get my gear off to go to the bathroom in a porta-potty. They sent me to a psychiatrist. He asked me what I wanted, and I told him I was tired of the Army. He wrote that I was unfit for military service, and I was discharged." She laughed as she daintily consumed an Italian roll. I seethed with resentment. This woman exulted that she got her way using all the tactics that made civilian employers reluctant to hire women.

Whenever my husband asked me to rethink military service, I dismissed his concern. I saw the efforts of my ex-husband and his co-managers to discourage me as, perhaps, regret that they missed their own opportunities to complete OCS. Al and many of the executives with whom he worked were selected for OCS during the Vietnam War. They declined the wartime "promotion" opportunity, preferring survival instead. In the Vietnam era, non-commissioned officers believed that lieutenants were targets for fragging. Enlisted men were more likely to come back from the war messed up with drugs or alcohol, but alive. OCS lieutenants, on the other hand, were likely to come back in body bags.

My sister Lucille, the wife of a military pilot, tossed a number of harsh realities into our discussions. She opposed my desire to become a soldier. But when she realized I would not be deterred, she became my strongest ally, helping me through every phase of basic training and OCS by writing cheerful letters, chanting motivation during my whiny phone calls and just being there at my basic training graduation.

Once I met with the board, all I could do was wait for the Department of the Army's (DA) decision to accept or reject me. Until the DA finally approved my OCS packet, I took no chances. I continued to run in the snow, the rain, the brutal Kansas City winds, to be sure I could stand any discomfort thrown at me down at Fort Benning's "School for Boys." I stretched, carried heavy bags and boxes, learned calisthenics, and finally, learned how to do Marine pushups. When I demonstrated these to Sergeant Metcalf at the recruiting station, he smiled and nodded. "You're in!! You don't have anything to worry about!"

Finally, DA sent the notice of my acceptance to Sergeant Metcalf. He was so excited, he drove to my house and left a sweet handwritten note on my door. I still have that loose leaf paper. Sergeant Metcalf was expecting a child at that time. He treated my acceptance just as importantly as the birth of his new baby. I do not know if he got a bonus for getting me through this process, but I always hoped he did. If I ever have a chance to thank him personally for his help, I will.

Sergeant Jay Metcalf was a great sergeant, the first of many to teach me how to be my best as a soldier.

On March 24, 1983, I reported to the MEPPS station in Kansas City. I was sworn into active duty. I said goodbye to my husband for the last time, knowing that when we next saw each other, our divorce would be finalized. Our last day together at the MEPPS station was filled with endless procedures, ritual farewells and new beginnings. It was the most definitive transition a person could ever experience in this life. Half-way through the day, Al went home. After several hours of lectures, testing, waiting, eating, waiting, eating and more waiting, we were told we could make one last phone call before our departure. Just before I got on the plane to Fort Dix, New Jersey, I called Al for the last time. He said he couldn't stop crying, that he had not realized what my departure would mean to him. I was worldly enough to know that Al's crying jaunt meant nothing to our relationship. He had no change of heart, or desire to reconcile. The tears were his rite of passage to freedom. I cried, too, but my tears were of regret that I could not persuade him to stop the divorce. In retrospect, I doubt I would have survived my divorce if I hadn't used the Army as the express train away from the man I loved who no longer loved me. But survive and thrive, I did.

About dinner time, eleven men and women boarded the bus for a commercial flight that would carry us to New Jersey. We were herded onto the bus like prisoners, all but shackled as our wardens, the same recruiting sergeants who used to handle us with delicate care shouted commands to speed up, wait. Stow our luggage, grab our luggage. March on the bus, off the bus. Always with the grouse command, "Single file, single file."

The movement from the MEPPS station to the airport to the base was a calculated gradation of impersonal supervision to acclimate us to the impending harshness of basic training. We were not even allowed to have an in-flight drink, as we were on duty. Our feelings of nervousness were palpable.

The flight from Kansas City to Jersey was only a few hours. We landed in darkness. The mood of my traveling companions was just as dark. The night air was cold. The drill sergeants who met us at the airport were frigid. All the cheerful friendliness I experienced in the recruiter's station was nowhere to be found at the entry point of Fort Dix. Sergeants everywhere. Men. Women. African-Americans. Whites. Hispanics. They all looked mean. They all glared at the new recruits. They barked commands and scrutinized us as we passed through the gates onto their territory.

The Fort Dix entry point was a huge, warehouse in the shape of a Quonset hut. There were hundreds of new recruits, arriving from all over the country. The drills, as they are called, yelled at us to get moving. First we passed through the Amnesty Room, "This is your last chance to dispose of your drugs, your

needles, your syringes, your guns, your knives, your brass knuckles," a drill
sergeant boomed. It never occurred to me that anyone would be stupid enough
to bring these things to basic training. "If you surrender your paraphernalia here,
no questions will be asked. You will not be prosecuted. You will not go to jail.
But if you take your drugs, your syringes, your guns, your knives beyond this
point, you will pay a big price."

The hundred or so recruits who stood beside me perked up their ears. The
drill shouted his final message: " ANY SOLDIER CAUGHT BEYOND THIS
POINT WITH A GUN, A KNIFE, A WEAPON OF ANY KIND, A DRUG, A
NEEDLE, DRUG PARAPHERNALIA WILL BE PROSECUTED. YOU WILL
GET CAUGHT. WE WILL HUNT YOU DOWN. YOU WILL GO TO JAIL
FOR AS LONG AS WE CAN SEND YOU. DO YOU HEAR ME?"

"YES, SERGEANT!" As he directed us to move past the Amnesty Barrels,
I was shocked to watch soldiers drop their pieces, knives, and drug kits into the
barrels. My first lesson about the chasm that existed between my cultured world
and the world of the '80s ghetto kid.

A pudgy female drill sergeant bellowed that we had best get our posteriors
in gear, because we weren't going to sleep until we completed all of the in-
processing tasks on her list.

"Males to the left," she hollered. "Females to the right. From this point on,
there will be no contact between males and females. You will be divided into
separate companies. You will be billeted in separate living quarters. You are
forbidden to speak to each other, to send each other communications, to look at
each other. If you so much as look at a person of the opposite sex, you will be
charged with mental rape, fraternization, and whatever other crime I can throw
at you, do you understand me?"

"Yes, Sergeant!"

"Do you see this hat," she screamed. "I earned this hat. I am not a sergeant.
I AM A DRILL SERGEANT. FROM NOW ON, WHENEVER YOU SEE THIS
HAT, YOU WILL CALL THE PERSON WEARING THIS HAT BY THEIR
FIRST NAME: DRILL SERGEANT. WHAT ARE YOU GOING TO CALL ME?"

"Drill Sergeant, Drill Sergeant."

She did not smile. She glared at us with her pulsing angry eyes.

"That's right. Now if you keep that up, you may get an hour of sleep
tonight. But you are not going to touch your pillow until you complete every
task I ask you to do. Do you hear me????"

"Yes, Drill Sergeant...."

The drill shouted to us to move through the turnstile down to the Personnel
Records Section. When we wormed our way into the rows of student desks, a

quiet sergeant induced us to take a deep breath to shed the tightness that gripped our chests. His kindness was such a contrast, it was almost painful. In retrospect, I think he realized his forms needed to be filled accurately the first time, so he cut us some slack.

We filled out personnel locator sheets, mail distribution cards, payroll data cards, and hometown press release forms. Then, a personnel clerk had us fill out insurance papers, indicating whom our next of kin was, how we wanted our insurance policies distributed, and where our home of record would be. Some of the young recruits looked terrified as they contemplated for the first time that their military commitment could entail a death experience — their own. The clerk cracked a death joke to dispel our fear.

After we filled out nine or ten forms, we were marched off to the medical station. We marched through another turnstile. Each of us was punched three or four times by a medic holding an injection gun. The shots hurt. No needles were changed. I wondered later if the Army had a high rate of HIV infection in those days due to the lack of sterilization between immunization shots.

Finally, about two in the morning, we were marched to the linen closet, given two flat sheets, one pillowcase, one pillow and one OD green blanket. Our platoon drill sergeants met us at this point and introduced themselves. They marched us back to the barracks, if you could call it marching.

Sergeant First Class Kilianski was our Platoon Sergeant. Sergeant Stevens, the Assistant Platoon Sergeant. Other sergeants assisted with training, counseling and charge of quarters duty. From the moment Drill Sergeant K and Drill Sergeant Stevens assumed control of our platoon, I knew I would succeed and graduate. They hooted and hollered to project their authority, but all the while infused their tone of voice with an air of concern and reassurance. "NO ONE, I REPEAT NO ONE will go to bed until everyone has their gear in place," was at once a command, a threat, and a promise. They knew how to inspire just enough cooperation between the 40-or-so women to get the job done and guarantee enough sleep to wage the next day's battles.

The drills already assigned their squads, and consequently, the sleeping arrangements that would prevail for the duration of our nine-and-one-half week basic training experience. Before we were allowed to drop our suitcases, bags and sleeping accoutrements, we were required to stand at half-assed attention while the drill sergeants called out our names.

"First squad, deYoung, Smith, Jones..."

I can't remember the single last name of a trainee assigned to my squad. We had to line up in rows according to the order in which our names were called. Drill Sergeant Stevens glared at us, then softened his blue eyes.

"Now listen up, people. The first person in each row is your squad leader. Squad Leaders, you are in charge of every person assigned to your squad. You will not sleep, eat, shower or shave until your people are accounted for and taken care of. Do you understand me?"

"Yes, Drill Sergeant."

This was our first lesson in the meaning of power and authority in the Army. The greater your power, the greater your responsibility to take care of those who were in your charge.

"Okay. Now listen up," Sergeant Stevens tried to give us a harsh look, but he was too tired. It was about 3:00 a.m. "You will take the bunks that I have assigned to you. Each bunk has a wall locker next to it. You will not change your assigned bunk unless I give you permission to do so. Do you hear me?"

"Yes, Drill Sergeant!" The thought of a good night's sleep made it easy for us to comply.

"We will have squad integrity. When I count off, the first nine people will march to the first room on the left..." Sergeant Stevens divided the platoon, counted them off, and had the female platoon sergeant march the women to their beds.

"Now listen up, soldiers. You have 15 minutes to make your bed, secure your gear, wash up, and be in bed. Anyone who is not in bed in 15 minutes will be in my office doing pushups. Do you hear me?"

"Yes, drill sergeant." We were dead to the world within ten minutes of parking our suitcases.

We learned our second lesson about rank, power and authority that night, and it is a lesson that selfishly drove me to push myself to climb the Army ladder of success ever since that day. Each squad was given two large rooms where all the privates were bunked together. All, that is, except the squad leaders who were first-class privates, bound for OCS. Since we had responsibility to assign chores and discipline soldiers who were improper in their appearance or behavior, we were granted small rooms that bedded two squad leaders each.

This was a blessing for me, but also a curse. A blessing because I spent my whole life running away from that kind of sisterly connectedness, struggling against the clutches of my younger sisters. I spent the first 15 years of my life fused to my four sisters like Siamese twins. I didn't want to spend nine weeks of basic training with eight bunkmates. To this day, I sometimes rebel against the thought that life is a sisterly event, something that cannot be gotten through without sisterly consultation. To grow, at times, I had to learn to separate myself from my sisters, their perspectives, their needs, and their desires. I had to move away to listen to my own dreams, my own inner voice. By the time I arrived at

Basic training, solitude was important to me. If being a squad leader meant more responsibility, I was gratified that it also meant I would not have to sleep with the eight or nine squad members who would depend on me to get them through.

My room assignment was simultaneously a curse. My roommate was an African-American married woman. She completely upset my expectations. She was a prima donna. Her husband was a warrant officer. She expected to graduate from OCS solely because of her status as an officer's wife, not because of her own competence or effort. My life in basic training was far more difficult because PFC I seldom held her own, and I often had to pick up her slack. Just one example: Halfway through training, our KP team was required to work extra hours because PFC I called the sergeant major to complain she was being abused by the cooks. She refused to carry a box of milk to the milk dispenser because she believed the strain would jeopardize her ability to bear children. The sergeant major, his heart tingling with PFC I's charming pleas to understand her "married concerns" excused her from work. He should have excused her from the Army. The mess sergeant made the rest of us work several more hours to compensate for my roommate's absence. That kind of peer pressure is used by sergeants to instigate better motivation and cooperation among recruits. The mess sergeant and, at other times, the drill sergeants know that as soon as they are out of ear shot, female recruits will taunt the princesses who wiggle their way out of discipline or work.

PFC I, or as I secretly called her "Princess I," got away with all kinds of malingering. When we went to the field, she would get excused on sick call. I would have to pull double guard duty to cover for her. I despised her, and couldn't figure out why Sergeant First Class Kilianski just didn't drop her. She couldn't run. She wouldn't run. She couldn't do more than 18 push ups. My recruiters wouldn't let me start basic training until I could do the man's minimum, which was about 40 push ups. They insisted that no female would stay in the Army unless she could do her physical training (PT). Eventually, at OCS, PFC I, the princess candidate was humbled. She was not commissioned, because she failed to achieve the minimum physical training standards required of all lieutenants commissioned through that tough program.

On our first night as trainees, though, I didn't realize all this was going to transpire. On our first night, we were too exhausted to try to psyche each other out. The leadership laboratory was not intended to begin. PFC I and I chose to like each other that first night. We both slept comfortably as we realized we had not doomed ourselves to hell when we signed our enlistment contracts. We were in the Army now, and we would do just fine.

At six o'clock the next morning, a female drill sergeant ran through the barracks clanging a cowbell.

"Wake up. You have 30 minutes to make your bed, clean up and be in formation. WAKE UP SOLDIERS!"

Private I sat on her bunk in her pink bathrobe as I waddled off the top bunk. We both ambled to the large salmon-colored latrine. The drill put her face in my face shrieking, "Soldier, you think you have all day? Move it, move it!"

I accelerated my pace a tiny bit. There were 40 women competing for four wash sinks and four toilet stalls. We waited in line to take our turn until the drill yelled, "You think you have all day to primp and curl? Get your posteriors up to that sink. You ever heard of the three S's? Y'all don't have time to shower or shave this morning. It don't take but two minutes to brush your teeth and get the oil out of your pores.... Move it. Move it...."

Anxiety percolates in women when they are pressed to share their grooming space with other women. You can feel detachment vibrations waft in the air as women move into the minimally acceptable distance to cleanse and bathe themselves. When they must shower in a herd, women look away from each other, creating imaginary shower curtains to afford privacy. So unlike men. Often, in field conditions, I've observed the men as they shared large outhouses. Six or eight will go in and sit down together, share stories, talk about their fears, their kids, their favorite weapons or cars. The women on the other side of the outhouse would arrange to use the shed one at a time to afford the luxury of a few private moments. We would laugh at the camaraderie shared by the men, and express amazement at the things they talked about. Solitude, the feeling of private space is so preferable to women, to be given up only when absolutely necessary.

The drills barked commands as we washed up on Day One, nudging us to get our gear secured, insisting we would meet their 30 minute deadline for our first formation. Most of the women there felt naked despite being bundled in winter garb, because there was no time to put on makeup. We made our platoon sergeant's deadline, which got us off to a good start. Drill Sergeant Stevens marched us over to the dining facility in the pitch dark.

"They'll be no talking now. From here on out, you repeat what I say when we march, you here me? When I say left, you step left. When I say right, you step right... Got that?"

"Yes, Drill Sergeant!"

The dining facility had three long lines of male soldiers ahead of us. "Shoot, we're getting here ten minutes early, next time. Did you hear me?"

"Yes, Drill Sergeant!"

Drill Sergeant Stevens saved us an inordinate amount of waiting time by figuring out the traffic patterns and then marching his platoon up to the entrance point of a class, clinic, clothing store or dining facility five or ten minutes ahead of the crowds. No one ever minded when latecomers to his formations were required to do extra pushups. Stragglers cost us all a lot of boring waiting time.

After a fattening breakfast filled with southern biscuits and gravy, pancakes dripping with butter, syrup, hot coffee and fresh oranges we marched down to the clothing distribution center for our uniforms and gear. Staff Sergeant Stevens moved back and forth among the women like a mother hen, making sure that PeeWee's uniform was small enough to make her look sharp, and that the tall soldiers had sleeves long enough to touch their wrists.

"Check those seams out, soldiers. Check the colors. Make sure your trousers match your jackets!"

When we were fitted for the dress uniforms, he insisted the seamstresses ignore the instructions of the young, sexy privates, who wanted tight skirts and slacks. Our skirts had to be knee length, or one inch below the knee.

The seamstresses who tailored our dress uniforms smiled approvingly as we approached their sewing machines. Many of the ladies were immigrants from World War II. They boasted of their GI husbands. They did not disapprove of our presence as female soldiers. For the most part, they wanted to mother us. Their affirmations soothed, but the woman who altered my skirts and slacks was frustrated.

"You ain't got no bubble back there," she whined, despairingly.

Since I had been running, I lost a lot of pudgy cushioning in my rear-end.

"A woman's supposed to have a bubble back there. Where's your bubble?"

The drill rolled his eyes and moved on. Even today, a common complaint about the woman's dress uniform is that the cut is an exaggerated hourglass figure. I imagine women from the Army of the forties filled the curves nicely. Modern athletic women can be all skin and bones.

We finished collecting winter boots, camouflage uniforms, dress shoes, the black pocketbook, T-shirts, the duffel bag, green wool socks, winter rain coat, hats, field rain gear, rubber goulashes, nametags, rank, insignia, laundry bags and whatever else they stuffed into our huge canvas duffel bag. Then, we got our first taste of military equality. We were instructed to hoist the duffel bag over our shoulder.

"Forward, MARCH!"

With all this gear, we marched two or more miles back to our barracks. Right then, I knew the difference between maxing a physical training test and meeting the physical demands of combat training. I didn't mind knowing that I would never be asked to lug heavy things or 180 pound male bodies around all day on a battlefield, just because I was a woman. Most of the women in our platoon complained about the heavy load we carried all the way back to the barracks. The drill just let us vent, knowing the odds of successfully completing our first forced march were greater if we were allowed to vent and even shed a tear or two.

Minutes after we started, the drill sergeant took PeeWee's duffel bag, knowing full well that she was too short to carry the thing all by herself. She marched quietly in gratitude.

Two or three days of orientation went by before we were locked into strict soldiering routines. All of the drill sergeants in the battalion introduced themselves to us. The company commander, Captain David Moore, gave us a briefing about his philosophy of training, his open door policy, standards of conduct, the Army's Equal Opportunity policies, and the Army's new policy against the use of "doo-doo words." Profanity was now considered unprofessional and possibly harassing behavior. Anyone caught using four letter words would be punished with extra pushups. All the foul mouthed drill sergeants I had seen in Army movies were just plain fantasies in the New Army. Our drills were sometimes harsh, but always dignified in expression.

Sergeant First Class K, the Senior Drill Instructor, was not a talker, but he was the most organized non-commissioned officer I have ever known. He would plan the day's training, activities, disciplinary actions, fire guard, details, and rewards. He would always head a formation, and then hand the platoon over to Drill Sergeant Stevens for instructions about movement or courtesy or regulations.

Drill Sergeant Stevens was a hardened chain-smoking Vietnam Veteran. He never used a foul word, and he never manipulated the soldiers. He was very working class: blunt, straight-shooting, and no-nonsense. Very easy to read, and tender despite his gruff command voice.

During our first briefing, he set our personal and platoon conduct rules in concrete.

"All right, people listen up.... From now on, you are a soldier. You are not male. You are not female. You are soldiers. From here on out, you will walk like, talk like, dress like and eat like, think like, sleep like, and dream like SOLDIERS."

"Yes, Drill Sergeant!"

"Do you see these baggy old ugly camouflage greens I am wearing? Can you tell if I am a man or a woman by the shape of these ugly things? NO! And that's for a reason! If I catch you having your battle dress uniforms tightened so that they are form fitting, I am going to send you up to the commander for an Article 15. Do you understand me?"

"Yes, Drill Sergeant."

Actually, we understood we would be in trouble if we showed off our figures by tightening up the straps, but on our first day, nobody knew what an Article 15 was.

"Now listen up! Hey, this isn't a hen house. Stop your chattering. When I say listen up, you listen up!"

We sat in dead silence.

"By Thursday," Stevens continued, "You will have all your uniforms prepared. All of your civilian clothes will be locked up. You will no longer have access to your civilian clothes, your toys, your books, or your magazines. On Thursday, you will become REAL SOLDIERS!"

"Yes, Drill Sergeant."

"In the meantime, if I catch you running through the hallways with your underwear exposed, I am going to put you out of the Army. Do you hear me?"

So the Information Briefing continued, until Staff Sergeant Stevens enumerated all of the policies:

1. Duty hours were from 5:00 a.m. until about 7:00 p.m. During those hours, battledress uniforms would be worn at all times.

2. After duty hours, bathrobes and slippers would be worn at all times on the floor, in the bathroom, and in the soldier's sleeping area until lights out.

3. Women were not allowed to go out of the training area or to an area where men were present, including male drill sergeants unless they had permission and went with a buddy.

4. No sexy attire was allowed, even when leaves and passes were earned in the final phase of training. During passes, soldiers were required to wear their dress uniform with pants only, subject to disciplinary action if the trainees were caught out of uniform or wearing the skirt.

5. No contact between male and female trainees even if you could prove they were married.

6. No smoking in the bunk areas, to avoid a fire hazard. Since the drills were chain smokers, they were not hypocritical. They provided butt cans for smokers to be used only during bonafide rest periods in the day rooms.

7. No cliques or gangs. (Our group was made up of middle-class whites, rural poor, Hispanic and African American women. Some of the women had gang backgrounds.)

8. No makeup, no jewelry, no provocative dress anywhere, anytime, anyhow.

9. Bras would be worn at all times. Failure to wear a bra was subject to an Article 15. When soldiers were allowed to take the heavy battle dress utilities (BDU) jacket off to do hard physical labor, no one would be excused from work because they forgot to wear a bra. They would be punished for uniform violations with an Article 15. They would forfeit pay and be restricted to the barracks.

10. All incidents of sexual harassment would be reported either to Staff Sergeant Stevens, the female drill sergeants, the chaplains, or to the company commander.

11. No suicide gestures, attempts, or threats would be tolerated.

This last one was my favorite. Drill Sergeant Stevens stood at the position of attention and looked every woman in the eye.

"Now listen up! I am proud of the Army, and I am proud to be a soldier. I spent two tours in Vietnam defending my country. If you don't want to be here, I don't want you in my Army. You just come right to my office, and I will send you home in 48 hours. But if you think.... If you think you are going to swallow a few pills to get out... Don't you ever manipulate me. Because if you attempt suicide on my watch.... I'm gonna just let you lie there and die!"

Drill Sergeant Stevens never had to deal with the manipulative act of a trainee swallowing pills or slashing to get out of a training problem, or a physical training test. He was good to his word. When trainees knocked tearfully on his door and begged him for a free bus ticket back to poverty and a welfare check, he was very generous. His approach was dead right, too. The Army is no place for manipulative, weak, conniving soldiers who are incapable of learning how to be responsible for their actions. I wouldn't want my son or daughter serving next to a passive-aggressive, manipulative malingerer in a real combat situation, or even in training, where my kid would wind up pulling double duty for the shirker.

Our first full evening at Fort Dix we were allowed to attend a free movie. My brain was exploding with a headache, most likely due to the fear that sets in when you realize you are locked into a three-year contract that could entail the loss of your life, limb, or pursuit of happiness. There were five women in the platoon besides me who were destined for OCS, assuming that we would all graduate. My roommate was one, but she was such a princess, so unwilling to try to do the bare minimum that I immediately decided to find other friends. Yes, I was intolerant of Princess I, but I realize now that intolerance was born of fear. I was a weakling, with no prior physical training, and a sensitive personality. If I flunked out, I had no husband to go home to. The last thing I could afford to do was to pair myself with someone like Princess I, who tried to get by doing the absolute minimum.

Sometime that day, I got to know two intelligent women who were also destined for OCS. The three of us became the D-3-3 Musketeers. Whenever we could pair off for an activity or conversation without seeming like a clique, we did. Despite my splitting headache, we went to the movies. Throughout the flick, I kept rubbing the ice from my soda across my forehead, but no relief. The laughs were good, but they didn't help either. Before lights out, a young, inarticulate, almost toothless woman from Arkansas told me that push-ups were the perfect medicine for stress headaches. All the women from my squad got down on the floor to see how many push-ups we could do before exhausting ourselves to sleep. Staff Sergeant Stevens approached our floor before lights out.

He was about to yell at us that we should be in bed, when he found us doing pushups. He looked at me with a cold, squinty, approving eye.

"Squad leader, your soldiers should be ready for lights out."

We echoed our response with a big smile.

"Yes, Drill Sergeant!"

The toothless woman, who later said I was a mean but fair squad leader, had the perfect remedy for what turned out to be a stress migraine. I went to bed, slept soundly, knowing that I could do as many push-ups as OCS would require.

Usually, Staff Sergeant Stevens led the Physical Training Classes. I was surprised that many women had not learned to do a single push-up before signing their contracts. Their recruiters were certain they would learn in Basic. Some of the older women were in much better shape than some of the 19-year-old smokers. This is still common, despite all the media hype about women Amazon warriors! Very few of the women in our platoon, the class of Delta-3-3, had participated in organized sports or intense athletic training of any kind before they signed on.

For most of us, basic training was our first opportunity to learn the value of teamwork, cooperation, and shared success. The drills made us train as buddies. No one got credit for individual success. Each soldier had to bring a buddy through. Our running abilities varied. Here I was a 28-year-old woman, who could get a maximum score on her run. There were 17-year-old women who could not run a mile. But there were a dozen or so women who could run really well.

Our best runner was a recruit named Agnes. Agnes was an African-American from New York, who had a mouth, the baddest attitude, deep suspicion of white people, but a heart of gold. During our first tested run, Agnes finished her two miles in twelve minutes, just like the average man. The Drills were thrilled. We were in awe. Agnes had been coached while in high school. In fact, her coaches prepared her to accept a full athletic scholarship for college, but her self-esteem, despite her enviable talent, was low. Agnes joined the Army, where she knew she could succeed, because her many brothers had succeeded in the Army.

For daily runs, we were placed in three running groups: slow, medium, and fast. All OCS-bound trainees were required to run in the medium or fast groups. Since I was older, the medium group was enough of a challenge for me. The medium group ran a pace of between 14 and 16 minutes for two miles. This was more than enough for me to get top scores at OCS without my heart bursting, or "bustin" as Agnes would say. Agnes was always pushing the women to run harder. She would teach us about stride, stretching, lifting your feet, breathing. She was bossy, too. You couldn't get away with the same mistakes twice if she had corrected your sloppy technique already.

There were many housewives in our basic training class. Lillian was a housewife from Puerto Rico. Some of the others were from Arkansas and Alabama. Their families were poor, perhaps on welfare or unemployment. Despite the conservative cultures these women came from, where the men were always the heads of the household, the women joined the Reserves to provide some basic support for the family. Cheap groceries, too, from the commissaries when they trained on Army bases during monthly drills. Some of these ladies had been lied to about physical training standards for passing basic training. They were not prepared. Others were part of close knit communities. They knew that if they completed basic training, they would never have to work too hard again at PT. After all, the commander of their Reserve Unit was their uncle or their husband's best friend.

Of course, part of the Army training philosophy involves peer pressure, group bonding. Drill Sergeant K was not about to let anyone fail the final PT test, regardless of what they thought they could get away with after leaving active duty. He used every trick in the book to nudge the women to support each other, but also to pressure each other to improve their PT scores.

During group runs, a pace is set that will help everyone to stay together, but also demonstrate personal endurance and fitness. I was selected to set the pace because I was slow enough to meet the Army's minimum standards, but steady enough to ensure that laggards could catch up. We would run through the streets, often past family housing singing the cadences to mask the pain, or relieve the boredom of exercise. Inevitably, Lillian, the housewife and some of the other young soldiers would fall out — stop running. The Drills, especially Sergeant K, would loop our platoon around, run back to catch the stragglers, then continue the run. By the time he used this pressure tactic three or four times, the good runners would have run three or four miles around the fall-outs.

I didn't mind, because I needed to run five miles as often as possible to prepare for OCS. I can't just get out and run five miles on a moment's notice. I have to run often to run that distance. OCS would be nothing but long distance runs. Some of the fast runners, including Agnes, hated to run that kind of distance. She ran fast and furiously for one reason only: to get it over with! After every run, the women would grumble about the pace and the dropouts. Tension built up over the weeks. Soon, there was a bit of friction between whites, Hispanics, and Blacks.

Staff Sergeant Stevens devised regular meetings to de-stress the platoon, because he knew that women were different from men. Especially when it came to griping and complaining. Men dissociate themselves from their feelings, grit their teeth, and just get through. But women don't let go of what bothers them. When women are aggravated with each other, the air smells as foul as a sulfuric fart until heavy rains push the bad air out to sea. Whenever the tension in our platoon built up to this point, Sergeant Stevens would take all of the women down to the platoon day room.

"Okay, it's Sunday afternoon," he'd say. "You are supposed to have three hours of free time to read, or write letters to your family, or to visit the shoppette to pick up some candy. You're not going anywhere until you get things off your chest. This is the time to complain, to tell each other what's really bothering you, and then, to get back on the same sheet of music.... Who wants to start?"

That first session, I thought I was back in a 70's style feminist gripe session. I couldn't believe the Army had appropriated a technique that I had so persistently tried to avoid as a young feminist.

"Well, deYoung, you just don't run fast enough. I mean, deYoung, our legs hurt when you make us run so slow..." A tall private made the first point. Stevens interjected that he set the pace, not me.

"Well," Agnes would pitch in, "if yooh legs hurt, you ain't stretched enough. Sergeant, I mean, Drill Sergeant, we be stretching wrong. I mean, when you run that fast, you need to be stretchin' at least five oh six minutes. Then yo' legs won't be hurtin'..."

"I am sick and tired of the fallouts," another lazy but competent runner chimed in. " I think the ones who fall out of each run should have to do remedial PT. Why punish us because they can't keep up? Why do we have to loop back and pick them up?"

"And I don't think you should be allowed to speak Spanish. I mean we are in America, and this is the United States Army. We should all speak English here."

Some of these complaints were invariable. But when the attack on our Puerto Rican buddies started, Lillian, the Puerto Rican woman who acted like everybody's mother, got up.

"You no treat me with respect. You not right. You think I no understand? I understand. I no speak English, but I understand. I understand perfectly... I understand everything. I hear everything you say. You say I not keep up? I help you. PeeWee, I help you make your bed. You so short. You never on time. I help you. Nobody perfect!"

Somehow, Lillian would make everyone realize that we still had feelings that we needed to tend to. From then on, the gripe session degenerated to a 60's style hippie love-in. One young black soldier stood up and philosophized.

"We all have to help each other. We're gonna do it."

Then the Anarchist would get up, "listen, nobody said this was going to be easy. We volunteered for this..."

`Then the backwoods Arkansan from my squad would stand out and bellow in a man's voice, "Yeah, like Drill Sergeant, I came here because I wanted to be a mechanic. And before I came here, I never talked to a black person or a Puerto Rican. All I want to do is be a mechanic. I'm learnin'. We're all the same here...."

Drill Sergeant Stevens would sit at the front of the circle, and let the good vibes flow for awhile. Then he would look at his watch.

"Alright. It's two o'clock. You have two hours of free time. You can visit the shoppette. No pornography, no alcohol, no books, no cameras. You can visit the day room. You can walk down to the end of the training area and back. By 4:00 p.m. be in formation in front of the barracks. If one person is one second late, you all will be docked your free time next Sunday. Do you hear me?"

"Yes, Drill Sergeant."

For nine weeks, we had very little to look forward to. No television. No dates. No freedom. Happiness was a supervised trip to the candy store. After our weekly group therapy sessions, we were released to replenish our stash of chocolates. We weren't allowed to have sex. We weren't allowed to lie in bed on Saturday mornings. We weren't allowed to talk on the phone all night. We weren't allowed to do drugs or alcohol... except for M&Ms and Snickers Bars... The old joke was true: "Things are getting desperate, send chocolate!" Drill Sergeant Stevens and Drill Sergeant K made sure their women had all the chocolate they could handle to ward off depression or PMS. I guess they figured if women would be lured to give up their first vote for a box of chocolates, they could be lured to succeed in basic training with a bottomless bag of M&Ms. The drills seemed to have a sure bet!

I can honestly say that basic training for women, back in 1983, was minimally an exposure to combat training. In academia, the term exposure is often used to describe a learning experience that has no depth, no practical value, but which helps you to understand the dimensions of a problem with which you have no real tangible experience or knowledge. The drills gave us a taste of all the basic tasks required of an infantryman. We knew from observation of the men in adjacent companies that our training was not even close to the real thing. We had no delusions about the extent of our pain and suffering. The men in the barracks next door did twice as many pushups, ran faster, lifted huge trucks filled with cargo, hoisted large tents, and ran through the woods with their rifles in the air an hour before we woke to do our genteel training. But the exposures we had were invaluable for personal growth and for learning camaraderie and cooperation. Especially the road marches and field problems.

If you gave me one chance to resolve deep conflicts between feuding parties anywhere in the world, I would take the enemies out to the field, give them tents, shovels, and primitive cooking gear. I would tell them, they could not come back to civilization until they learned how to cooperate. I don't care who you send to me for rehabilitation. The Hatfields and McCoys. Montagues and the Capulets. The Crips and the Bloods. Field duty is the great leveler of human experience. The porta-potties and the mud hugging induce humility, an acute awareness of the lowly terms by which we must all come to understand life. After humility is gained, cooperation follows.

Field problems were great fun during basic training. The drills certainly must have used an almanac to make our training pleasant. I had no sense of direction, but somehow, moonlight seemed to glow brightly during each of our field problems, guaranteeing my safe midnight crawls to and from the wooden outhouses.

Nowadays, soldiers sleep on cots, in heated tents. Then, we were required to sleep in pup tents, two women per tent. I was paired with my roommate, Private I. As in garrison, this was both a curse and a delight. Private I could not handle the cold April temperatures in New Jersey. She was from the Carolinas. New Jersey felt like Siberia to her. Every field problem, she managed to go back to the base on sick call. On the one hand, I had to sit in my foxhole and pull double guard duty whenever she feigned her little sniffles and weak spells. On the other, I had the whole pup tent to myself when I was finally allowed to sleep. Pup tents really don't hold more than one person comfortably, so once I crawled in from guard duty, I was more willing to forgive Private I for being such a wimp.

Field training has its own beauty. Moments of cooperation, like when we lined up to wash our gear in trash cans filled with hot water. Moments of natural beauty, like when flowers would sprout on a spring morning right next to your tent. It seldom snows in New Jersey, but we woke up to a nice blanket of snow after we established our first perimeter. Some of the women were from the South. Snow terrified them. They put their woolen long johns on, despite direct orders from the drill sergeants to wear cotton T-shirts, because the day temperatures would climb early to the 60s in the morning. Later that day, when we embarked on a five-mile road march, the Southern women became faint from the onset of dehydration.

When Sergeant First Class K discovered the privates disobeyed his dress code, he yelled at these women.

"I gave you direct orders to wear your cotton T-shirts. Your body is on my hand-receipt. When we get back, I'm gonna give you an Article 15 for violating a direct order. Do you hear me?"

I had never heard Sergeant K yell or even reprimand anyone in public before or after that moment. He was livid.

Drill Sergeant Stevens, ever the teacher, took over our formation and gave us a lesson about friction, body heat, and the reason why you don't need to wear heavy clothing when you are marching five miles with 50 pounds on your back while carrying 14 pounds of equipment. One of the Southern women still did not take off her woolen underwear, even after the threat of punishment. She believed she was going to die of frost. She tucked her undergarments in so they could not be seen. Stevens said nothing so long as her stubbornness did not make her sick.

Somewhere in the course, we spent two full weeks learning rifle marksmanship — another important combat exposure. Most of the time, we sat in stands, learning the five basic steps from instructors. Sometimes, we lay on the ground wherever we could find a spot not owned by a poison ivy plant, and practiced grip, sight and squeeze techniques.

I had no desire to handle a weapon. I was the last to learn, but my shot records indicate I can kill with the best of them. One tough private, Rosie, was an expert marksman before she was born. Her daddy was a colonel who taught her all the survival skills he would have taught to a son — she was his only chance! I used to think that Rosie actually spent her extra bullets creating three tight shot groups on my score sheet. The thought that I could kill so effortlessly was unthinkable to me. I knew from my years in the Midwest that women in the south were trained to handle guns fearlessly. Whether or not Rosie shot my targets for me, or inspired me to do better, I'll never know. But Rose set the standard as far as marksmanship was concerned.

Whenever we went to the field, we took M-50 and M-60 machine guns. We had classes on bolt breakdown and assemblage, and we fired the machine guns whenever we went to the ranges. It was thrilling to watch the bullets and colored tracers fly up to the targets by day or by starlight. The bolt box for the .50 caliber machine gun is quite bulky. We had four minutes to disassemble the box and four minutes to reassemble it. Because of my music background, I never expected to preserve a manicure, but I was never able to beat the time limit for breaking down a machine gun bolt without breaking a deep tear in my fingernails. The pain was worth it! I got to brag that I had mastered the .50 cal bolt box puzzle — something women were less likely to accomplish.

Most of the time allotted for weapons training was spent in limbo. The lull times were fraught with conflict. Class, race, ethnic differences could bring out the worst in the group. Whenever we sat around, the ghetto girls would cuss from beginning to end. I never used foul language until I went to basic training. Although I have developed a tendency to use a four-letter word to express my intense anger, I never could relate to the tendency of ghetto adults to substitute all intelligent conversation with profanity, as basic trainees are prone to do.

The profanities were mind numbing. At first, I thought I might lose my command of the English language. Soon, however, I befriended Jenny, a woman who wanted to be an officer since she was four years old. Jenny was bound for the same class at OCS . She was fluent in German, well read, and very intelligent. Whenever we sat cleaning our rifles, re-cleaning our rifles, and then, going over them one last time just to be sure there wasn't a speck of dust that would endanger our lives when we finally got to shoot them, Jenny would converse in German.

We were both enlivened by the intellectual test. But we made enemies. The same soldiers who resented our Puerto Rican friends for speaking Spanish resented our lapse into German. Often, they resented our lapse into literate English. I was so bored by basic training that I really didn't care. After working so hard to achieve academic honors, I was afraid my language skills would degenerate to military "Fucklish." Jenny and I agreed to ignore the resentment others had toward our German conversations. We both knew that the others in our platoon would be privates for a long time. In just a few weeks, we would be specialists. And three months after that, upon OCS graduation, we knew we would both be lieutenants.

Not only did differing language tastes jar the platoon but differing musical taste elicited deep feelings of resentment, as well. To pass the time, and to forget the pain of marching, we sang everywhere we went. We sang when we marched. We sang when we ran. When we cleaned the latrines. When we scrubbed the hallways. When we polished the General's cannon.

Singing was the most powerful tool for uniting us as a group. But there was a vast cultural divide in musical taste in our ethnically diverse unit. This same cultural chasm pulls our society and the Army apart to this day. Men solve the problem by simply buying headsets for all their audio gear. They don't expect anybody to learn to like their favorite music, and they don't try to like anyone else's. We, as women, could never be satisfied with 40 sets of headphones to shut each other out of community.

Creating a sense of harmony when it came to musical style was an unforgettable exercise. Whenever we were given the opportunity to sing solos, our fickleness showed. I had been raised Catholic, and was still a lapsed Catholic during basic training. Three women from Arkansas taught me my first Baptist hymn, "How Great Thou Art." Today, this marvelous song is in every hymnal, even Catholic missalette. But I was raised at a time when Protestant hymns were forbidden to Catholics. It took me weeks to melt my own icy prejudice to join in the singing of that hymn. I finally gave in and learned the song from my squad for obvious reasons: because "How Great Thou Art" was the greatest harmony-filled soul tune ever written.

Our Hispanic soldiers sang songs to rhythms none of us understood. I would sing folk music with a vibrato learned at the Conservatory. The black sisters would get in my face, and say, "Why you be singin' uh uh uh uh uh" grossly exaggerating the amplitude of the vibrato I had so carefully perfected at the Conservatory. I was incensed. I stopped singing harmony to the gospel tunes the African-American soldiers wanted our platoon to sing. Later, these women wanted the platoon to sing a song they wrote for their Sunday Gospel worship service. They were deeply hurt that I didn't show up to harmonize at Church. It never occurred to me that they wanted me there, with my "uh uh uh" inflections and all.

That was the most important sensitivity lesson for me. It's still relevant. Army religious programs tend to be ethnically separated because Black and Hispanic denominations allow for cultural differences that you will seldom find in bland mainstream churches. Of course, in civilian life, most of our churches are segregated, too! In the Army, there's a lot of room for cross-cultural sharing during worship, but very little tolerance for bland expression for the sake of multi-cultural gatherings. There are Black gospel worship services, Catholic charismatic and Hispanic services, Samoan worship communities, and general Protestant services. Soldiers are quite finicky about the choices available to them. They may have to wear their hair the way the Army wants them to. They may have to wear the uniform the way the Army demands. They don't have to conform to anyone else's religious expression, and so, they exercise this freedom to its full extent. Soldiers will not worship in a way that feels uncomfortable or in a style that feels imposed by military authorities.

Singing got us through the endless hours of waiting. Singing made it possible to complete mindless chores. Most of the chores in basic training were as stupid in 1983 as they will be in 2003. The chores required little attention to detail, and provided no training benefit besides exposure to the reality of war, which at some deep level we would have to admit is the ultimate lapse into stupidity. We pulled guard duty at least once a night both in the field and in garrison. We raked lawns and combed sand on the firing ranges, at field sites, and on the many dirt-filled fields where grass once grew. We plucked cigarettes off parking lots, sidewalks, and grassy plots. We shined cannons, brass plaques, flagpoles, mirrors, glass doors, our windows, our boots. We waxed floors. We peeled potatoes.

All of these mindless details caused me to believe that the expression "The devil is in the details" was born in the Army. If I've learned anything about the Army it's that how one learns to handle details will determine whether you become a Timothy McVeigh or a Colin Powell. Soldiers are paired off in small groups to perform routine tasks. Officially, the senior ranking person is in charge, but if that person is not very mature, the tasks can breed some really evil thinking. The Army attracted survivalists and separatists back in the early '80s as the Army attracts militant extremists today.

During the assignments, Leslie the Anarchist would share her philosophy as a survivalist. She expressed a deep suspicion of the federal government, maintaining that local militias were necessary to protect the people from a fascist takeover by the federal government. No amount of rational discussion would influence this woman to see the contradictions of her position. Leslie did not believe in the Federal Government, but she was seeking a commission as an officer. Well, she had college loans to pay off. She was a nice person in every other respect. Leslie the Anarchist taught me the only country song I know, "Lord, won't you buy me a new limousine.." Whenever we were paired at the dishwashing machine in the dining facility, she would lead this song as we scrubbed pots and pushed coffee cups through the automatic. Near the end of basic training, the Anarchist hurt her back during one of our monkey bar drills. She was not able to finish basic training, or go to OCS. I was saddened that she could not fulfill her goal, but in my heart, I could not imagine having an Anarchist in the officer corps, then or now. The Army lucked out when Leslie hurt her back. Too many of the male survivalists and gang members slyly work their way into discreet positions where they're able to recruit clandestine militia and gang members.

Before graduating from basic, we had to complete a few challenging obstacle courses. Mother Nature intervened on our behalf, making weather conditions too unsafe for us to actually attempt the more dangerous obstacles. But others gave a thrill I feel to this day. We were taken out to the woods, told we had to shimmy across a rope that was strung across the sky. On that day, conditions were extremely wet. A very handsome, muscular Hispanic instructor took off his BDU jacket, and shimmied across the rope. The women oohed and ahhed. A young 17-year-old trainee announced to the rest of us that she was going to "get lucky" with him before she left the post. When we first started basic training, we received a half-dozen sexual harassment briefings. The last was presented by the female drill sergeants who promised we could come to them day or night with our problems.

"Ladies, just remember one thing, though. If you are going to sleep with a drill sergeant to prove that you are a woman, then you'd better remember: real women don't tell! If that drill sergeant gets caught, he's going to jail. Now if you're going to sneak out with a married man, you're going to put a married man with children into jail. Now think about that! Nobody can harass you. We'll take care of you - but don't be sleeping with no married men, now! I know you can do it because you're on your own, but it's not right!"

To my knowledge, none of our classmates tried to sleep with the drill instructors until this weekend, when our 17-year-old hot private decided once and for all she was going to "get the drill!" Our platoon was filled with many older women such as myself. We tried to talk the 17-year-old private out of her adventure, but during graduation weekend, she "got lucky." She slept with the married drill sergeant from another company and she got very pregnant. A friend wrote to tell me that the lucky private's parents lied to protect her from disciplinary action during a disciplinary hearing for the drill sergeant. He lost his drill hat, some rank, and some pay, but he didn't go to jail because there was no way for the Army to coerce a discharged private into proving the sergeant's participation in fraternization. I saw the drill sergeant ten years later at Fort Polk. Still handsome, still tough, and still a hard-charging infantryman. The Army was much kinder to adulterers in those days. Soldiers could recover from their mistakes, and the Army kept their investment in trained personnel.

In the last week of basic training, we completed Paragon Trail. When I returned to Fort Dix for Chaplain Training in 1993, Paragon Trail was still a part of training. I completed the trail reflexively, but it was still as fantasy-filled as a Disney amusement park. The instructors create an aura, build up the tension, and simulate battlefield conditions in the most unnaturally pleasant way. Colored flares go off to simulate artillery. The trails and terrain features are perfectly sculpted. You can't get lost. The fields where you drop to avoid bullets are padded with St. Augustine grass. Not a hint of poison ivy or poison oak. The colored tracers and the rainbow of flares make the live fire exercises feel like the finale of a fireworks display. And nobody gets hurt, bloodied, or killed. At the time I didn't care, because I never expected to serve as an infantry combat grunt.

Upon completing the Paragon Trail, we knew we were going to graduate from basic training. All but the two women who became involved with instructors at the school. The rest of us happily scrubbed our gear, painted our entrenching tools black, polished our boots and brass and grinned all the way to graduation. As millions of other Americans would report, for the duration of basic training, we were yelled at, cajoled, pushed, pulled, stretched, and shrunk until the Drill Sergeants could proudly boast they had accomplished the impossible: turned 40 women into soldiers. Not all of the drills were screamers, though. Not all of the women wanted to become soldiers. But in the end, most of us — actually everyone who wanted to — graduated.

The day before graduation, with almost nothing left to do, tempers started to flare. We were done. All we had to do was turn in the tent pegs, sleeping bags and ugly olive-drab canteens. We waited at the supply distribution point to hand in our packed duffel bags. After shuffling in line for hours, I almost leapt for joy when my hand-receipt was finally cleared. I looked up, ready to shriek the D-3-3 slogan just one last time. Classic military insanity confronted me. I stood mute as two women from the next platoon, already cleared, already free to graduate were about to beat each other up. One was a middle class white woman, destined for OCS. She was so snobby to me before that day that even I did not like her. The other, a poor, undereducated, tough, but super-motivated African-American private. She was destined to be a hard-charging first sergeant.

I swallowed my shriek of delight, and slammed my body between these two bull-headed women. No question, the middle-class white woman was pushed and shoved by the other woman first, but only after she said something really condescending to the black soldier. The white woman glared at me as I blocked her return punch. "We are out of here," I begged.

"We are done! We're graduating! Don't throw this down the toilet after all we've done!"

Both women were named Linda. Lynda E and Linda E.

These women weren't even from my platoon. My squad stared at me in disbelief. I was such a wimp when it came to weapons, gangs and war games. They never said so, but I'm sure they often wondered what I was doing in the Army with my passion for opera and Brahms symphonies and my utter distaste for un-staged hardcore violence.

Linda E, the young African-American gave me a look of thanks when she realized she almost flunked basic training. She wandered off. Two female drill sergeants who were moving towards us to break up the fight just turned around and acted like they saw nothing. They walked slowly to make sure they would not have to come back.

Lynda E, the OCS-bound middle-class white girl flashed her black eyes angrily complaining.

"I am so sick of the jealousy. I can't help it that I have blond hair. I was born this way."

I suddenly realized I was just as jealous of her advantages in life as the other Linda was.

"You and I are out of here. In three weeks, we will be starting a new life. Just bide your time. Two more days. Keep cool."

She slumped into a posture of annoyed acceptance. She turned around and marched off with her platoon. That moment, more than any other taught me the importance of female bonding. If we were going to make it in a man's world, we had to transcend our petty jealousies, rivalries, and focus on what is truly important. Survival. Cooperation. Team spirit.

On our last night of basic training, all we had to do was primp and practice for graduation. Sergeant K took our platoon out for one last run as the sun set on our experience as basic trainees. We sang all the songs we taught each other, and all the songs we made up during our nine weeks together. Nobody cared anymore that we were blending gospel harmonies with operatic voice styles. Sergeant K strutted at the head of his platoon like a proud older brother. His message: we were no longer wimpy whining females. We were soldiers. We were the best! We stuck together, and we won. He wanted us to always stick together, and to remember that we were the best.

The message penetrated our hearts, but for the most part, it held no meaning after graduation. I never crossed paths again with any of the enlisted women from my basic training experience. Nor did I ever meet my drill sergeants again. My first personal encounter with Lynda E prepared me for the most difficult challenge we were about to face together. Within days of our assignment to the same company at OCS, the TACs (Teaching, Advising, Counseling Officers), Lieutenant Van Delft, intuited that Lynda E and I did not like each other at all. Without cease, Van Delft would sniff out all the petty personality conflicts in her platoon, and solve them by putting the rivals together in the same room.

At first, Jenny and I could take to heart the philosophy that our drill sergeants Kilianski and Stephens taught us. We had already made plans to stick together at OCS, to buddy each other to the end. But it wasn't going to be easy, we soon found out. On the day of our arrival at OCS, Lieutenant Van Delft's radar was highly attuned to the women from Fort Dix who just didn't seem to mesh as well as she thought they should. Van Delft threw a stink bomb into my plans to buddy Jenny to graduation. She could sense that I didn't get along with Lynda. She solved that problem by making Lynda E my first OCS roommate.

CHAPTER 2

Women Bonding

If West Point is a military rendition of hell, Officer Candidate School is the short version. Officer Candidate School is pandemoniac purgatory. The difference? Obvious to any officer who is not a ring knocker. West Point spends four years and $90,000 per student to transform bright, laid-back teenagers into starched, government-issue Army Officers. Officer Candidate School accomplishes the generic brand in 15 weeks. Just as my recruiters advised, I watched the movie "An Officer and a Gentleman" to prepare for the harshness of the OCS challenge.

Jenny and I arrived at OCS on the 4th of June, at the last possible minute. She visited with my family for a few days after graduation, then flew to Colorado to be with her dad. I stayed with my mother and sisters in Philadelphia. The respite after BT was enough to boost our self-assurance that we could push ourselves through our next trial by fire. We knew we wouldn't have any problem with the brainy training exercises because we were both college honor students. Neither of us had much brawn to spare, and if we could hang tough in the PT runs, we knew we'd both graduate.

The Officer Candidate School entrance is not forbidding or even pretentious. A lovely wrought-iron sign, "U.S. Army Officer Candidate School" graces the arch at the front gate. Though we were anxious about our impending tribulations, we were relieved to know we were not leaving all civilization behind. The battalion area was a throw back to the serene landscapes of a sixties suburban neighborhood. Two buildings the length of the street were separated by a large courtyard. Every door gleamed with fresh tan enamel paint. Window shades were pulled to exactly the same height from one end of the building to the other, just like a Catholic grade school.

On that first day endearing magnolia and oak trees promised us to be God's air-conditioners, the only natural safeguards from Georgia's brutally hot summer outdoor training. The Army was protective of soldiers almost to a fault sometimes. But you will never hear me complain about the Army's intolerance for heat casualties. Heat casualties are always considered a failure of leadership. At Benning, work stoppages were mandatory when the days got so hot and humid they were called Category 4 or 5. Those big old shade trees saved the life of many a soldier and home grown Georgian whose electrolytes couldn't tolerate even brief exposure to the blistering heat.

As soon as the taxi driver dropped our bags on the pavement, Jenny and I tiptoed through the gate, hoping not to attract the wrong kind of attention. Our first walk down the OCS courtyard was friendly. Officer candidates buzzed around in highly starched form-fitting battle dress uniforms, contradicting everything Sergeant Stevens taught us about the importance of obscuring the human form when dressed for combat. The candidates had all the glamour of Hollywood actors, exuding pride in their physiques, confidence in their military bearing and sheer joy at the challenge of this training conquest. It was obviously orientation week, too early for any of us to really fear failure.

Two gentlemen approached us, verified our orders, and politely led us to our 51st Company Headquarters orderly room. Jenny was just as thrilled as I was at the sophisticated tone the company leadership seemed to be establishing. We hugged each other goodbye, then snapped into military bearing. Surprisingly, our good byes were wasted. We were assigned not only to the same platoon, but to the same room. Jenny and I dared not show our excitement. If the TACs (Teaching, Advising, Counseling Officers) knew we depended on this crumb of comfort, they would never have made us roommates. Of that much we were certain.

Of the 250 newly assigned officer candidates, 40 were women. We were divided evenly among the six platoons of 51st Company. I had no fear that I would be treated badly. I did not ever think I was in danger of failing merely because of my gender. The TACs, we were counseled, would go to extraordinary lengths to ensure the success of women and minority students at OCS. Whatever re-mediation required for weakly qualified candidates, the TACs provided so that OCS would never be accused of the racism or sexism that haunts the Citadel's reputation even now.

For Jenny and I, remediation lasted one-half day. The TACs sniffed out our comfort levels, and keenly observed our complementarity. First lesson learned: we had to maintain lower profiles. Our stress levels would double like bread dough if our feelings were so easily discerned by our TACs.

Soon after we signed in, we sat on the floor of our new room. That afternoon was filled with piddly grooming tasks like painting our belt-buckles with EMU, that gooey black paint God created to save officer candidates two demerits every time they were caught with a nick on their subdued black rank or belt buckles. We calmed our nerves by touching up the black metal rank on our collars, burning the strings off our highly starched uniforms. That's what everybody else in the platoon was doing, so we just followed their lead. Conforming is worth blissful anonymity at schools like OCS. Just when we broke out our Corcoran jump boots to paste on a five-minute spit shine, a short mousy, buck-toothed woman from Second Platoon informed us that I was to follow her down to her platoon TAC's office. God. We had secretly congratulated ourselves too soon that we were placed with such a rational (and handsome) TAC in the First Platoon, First Lieutenant Joseph Smith. He was quiet, articulate and pretty aloof from his troops on that first day.

Down the hall, the Second Platoon TAC screeched her commands and paced back and forth in the hall in a ceaseless tirade about her desire to eliminate as many candidates as possible during orientation week. Talk about bad fortune! Within hours of my arrival, all hope of quiet gentle, humanistic, discipline was vanity. I was reassigned to one of Purgatory's loudest angels: Lieutenant Van Delft. Jenny wasn't as upset with the move as I because she was left behind to enjoy the classy wit of Lieutenant Joseph Smith. I was obviously the culprit in need of reform.

Lieutenant Van Delft was a stocky, five-foot-one OCS graduate. She swaggered with pride that she graduated from 50th company, the rough and tough working class Officer Candidate Company. 51st Company was known as the gentleman's company, where candidates were treated with dignity and respect, and at times with kid gloves.

If Van Delft was Dutch, she inherited none of the ethnic traits one might expect from a Dutch-American: straight blond hair, soft-spoken demeanor, or a calm spirit of tolerance. Lieutenant Van Delft wore an Afro hair cut although it had been a decade since it went out of style for white women. She squealed her commands in her tough soprano voice with an irritating Brooklyn accent that could shatter plastic tumblers.

Van Delft had the inflection of a Mafia hit man, but she didn't plan to kill anybody — just kick them out of OCS with no explanation. As a TAC, she was entitled to do that. Later in the course, the flaws of the exiled were usually obvious to the rest of the platoon, so there was no grumbling about fairness or due process that I could recall. But the omnipotence of her authority was a bit frightening at first.

She had a knack for exaggerating her Brooklyn accent in moments when the nerves of the platoon, even of northerners like myself were frayed beyond the ability to conceal petty prejudice. Van Delft's shrieking intonation had one virtue to us, though. Her battle cry was the glue that instantly bonded the men and women from 2nd platoon in our mutual hatred of her coarseness. We had no right to question her authority, but we had no responsibility to like her either. And so, we uniformly didn't.

After summoning me to her office for a three-minute interview, Van Delft ascertained my dislike for the women in 2nd platoon. I never said I didn't like them. All of us just completed basic training together at Fort Dix. It's just that I had no opportunity to befriend these women in basic training. They were all from Delta-3-3's arch-rival: Echo-3-3. Therefore, they were still my rivals. I had never played sports before. How was I supposed to know that after a competition was over, you were supposed to slap each other's fannies, then go out with your opponents to carouse over a pitcher of beer as men do after football and soccer games? I didn't know you were just supposed to forget the blood-roiling antagonisms you stirred up during the game. Minutes after I reported to her, Van Delft stomped out of her office. Was she planning to eliminate me? She called the platoon to attention, demanding a snappy response.

Second Platoon candidates dropped everything — their polish, brooms, personal gear, highly starched uniforms. They slapped their bodies against the wall right next to their doorways, making three points of contact, head, shoulders and rear, the classic OCS position for disciplinary encounters with the TACs. Van Delft pronounced that I would be Linda E's roommate. I was to bunk with my arch-rival from E-3-3, the beautiful, blonde, middle-class private whom every female in the Army envied. Van Delft proceeded to shout her hourly tirade. If we were to graduate from OCS we were to learn how to get along with everybody, how to set aside any personal animosity to get the mission accomplished. Van Delft paced back and forth like General Patton, shouting all the while her standards of success: "Cooperate and Graduate!" Those who helped each other, looked out for each other, encouraged each other would graduate. The self-serving lone rangers would be tossed out of OCS to become "High Speed PFCs" in the enlisted corps.

Whether Van Delft rolled the dice to cast her decision, or whether her canine pug nose was especially adept at discerning personal animosity I will never know. All I know is that once Van Delft called the platoon to attention, our fate was sealed. Lynda was as unhappy about the assignment as I was. We both read the tea leaves, though, and tacitly decided to conceal our dislikes or be subject to Van Delft's insinuation into our affairs.

Van Delft's definition of success countered most of our expectations for brutal competitiveness. But what better way to teach cooperation than to put two rivals in the same foxhole and leave them there without benefit of a shower or hot homemade meals until they learned how to get along? How could you argue with this formula of success? I couldn't, except that I wanted to learn how to make it in a man's world, and so prepared myself not for cooperation, but for fierce competitiveness at the home of the infantry: Benning's School for Boys.

In the second part of Van Delft's rant, she softened her posture and her voice. The nice Van Delft had the command voice of a fourth grade brat. A jarring contrast. Didn't matter. For the next fifteen weeks, her word was law. God was her adjutant. Her commands were to be obeyed without dispute so long as she was our TAC and her orders were legal, ethical and moral. No avenue of appeal — no matter how unreasonable or contradictory her instructions might be. Her voice crescendoed. "If I come into a room and only find one candidate's boots spit shined..." She would administer her punishment with the cruelty of a metaphorical loan shark, she assured us. Only she would break our spirits, not our legs. The TAC finished her leadership manifesto, then released the platoon for 30 minutes to get their rooms ready for inspection.

Van Delft's guidance was clear to both Lynda and I. There was not a moment to wallow in our disgust. Lynda was the first to address our political reality. When I moved my things into our room, she called a truce. Our strategy for survival was established that first afternoon. We made a pact to see each other through to graduation. Although I was a good friend with Jenny, my basic training buddy, I now had to accept Lynda as my OCS buddy. Only time would tell if we could become friends.

Our first days of setting up and maintaining our gear and training area were not much different than the last days before graduation. No matter how the barrack gleamed or the candidates strutted with immaculate uniforms, we were tasked and re-tasked to touch up our stuff. Much of our free time was spent plopped on the floor, shining boots, polishing brass, or the myriad other details required to have a STRAK appearance, the standard at OCS. Soldiers today don't know what STRAK means. I don't believe you can find the word in a dictionary. But if your uniforms are highly starched, your sleeves rolled up in perfectly flat symmetrical cuffs, your boots shine like glass with soles as glossy black as a new firestone tire, your laces are tucked inside your boots, your hair is perfectly military, your cap sits squarely on your head with a ranger crease down the middle, all the uniforms in your closet hang dress-right-dress with the unit patch showing, your Alice pack is geared up for a 12-mile road march and you consistently anticipate every bark from your squad leader, your platoon leader, your student company commander, your TAC and all the other TACs in the battalion, then you are STRAK.

STRAK candidates graduated. Second Platoon had plenty of STRAK candidates, so I had a good chance of graduating because the other candidates generously shared their time saving techniques with the naive ones like me. Van Delft's edict had its effect, too. The STRAK soldiers sat us all down and got us to work on those details that can make or break your commission at OCS.

That's how friendships are born at OCS. Sitting plopped on the floor with a can of Kiwi in your hand, teaching your clumsy squad mate how to make love to a Corcoran boot. Or sitting in the foxhole with a bag of candy in your cargo pocket, that thigh-long receptacle God instructed the clothing designers to sew onto every BDU trousers. Cargo pockets are best used to hide forbidden fruits: candy, chew, even a good novel.

Some things about military training will never change. Most OCS training and maintenance tasks are tedious, and at times, even stupid. Not as absurd as cleaning the mess hall with a Q-Tip, as Vietnam era basic trainees were required to do, but still inconsequential enough for hip college graduates to feel humiliated. For 15 weeks, though, time does not belong to you. Your time belongs to the TAC. Your life is spent the way the TAC wants you to spend it. The only way to make it go by, absent television, radios, or cassette players is to chat with your buddy. Now that's where times have changed. To a Vietnam era trainee, your buddy was your rifle. To enlightened soldiers of the modern army, your buddy is your bunk mate or your tent mate. If there's a human cell in your body, after wasting endless hours together and pushing each other to win this or that physical or emotional battle, you do become soul mates. In time, Lynda and I became soul mates.

Nobody in the Army bares their soul on first meeting, as Americans are wont to do on national television these days. First you trade goodies like candy, or EMU. As the trust builds, you trade secrets of success. Then, that moment of grace happens, and you start sharing the stories of your lives. At OCS, grace doesn't happen overnight.

Lynda was such a beautiful, petite woman that men would melt like Velveeta cheese on a grilled sandwich when they caught her glance. Her blond hair guaranteed special privileges from the male TACs, and special consideration from the men in our platoon. Or so we thought. I didn't think we would ever become friends. Her life was glamorous and was always destined to be so. I was so frumpy that my basic training squad called me Ernie, after the character in *My Three Sons*. Short dark hair, thick black military glasses and fourteen pounds of web gear over formless uniforms did nothing to make me look feminine. Military glasses are often described as "natural family planning" or "the Army's number one method for birth control." We were not allowed to wear contact lenses in basic training or at OCS. I wasn't planning to be sexually active now that I was in the company of men at OCS, but I did not appreciate the enforced ugliness, either. It made me certain of only one thing: I would have to work my way to success. I had no physical attribute that would mesmerize any of the guys into cutting me some slack.

Sounds like irrational jealousy, no? Sinful perhaps, but rooted in rock solid experience of working with men. Even male soldiers cringe when a beautiful woman walks into an army unit. Times have not changed. Somebody will usually wind up doing her job for her. Hopefully, that somebody volunteered himself with a silly grin from ear to ear. Too often, though, a superior delegates his favorite female's work to other soldiers. And the cute female and the superior disappear into a private relationship. Let's face it, every study has shown that men work much better with women whom they find attractive. And no amount of military indoctrination or religious training will overcome the tendency in men to sidle up to an attractive female and cut her a lot of slack. I admit that with Lynda's great looks, I thought I would be stuck with another privileged princess for a roommate, as I was stuck with PFC I in basic training, but Lynda proved me wrong.

Lynda's personality was a curious fusion of Shirley Temple innocent and Jane Fonda sex kitten. Those traits deceived many an officer. With her blond hair in a pony tale, her childlike voice and soft smile, the men thought she would be easy to manage as treasurer. The officer candidates voted for Little Lynda. They were a bit shocked later to find that Lynda was beyond their manipulation and control, as class treasurer and as class mate.

Lynda had really sharp business instincts, and a very shrewd ability to discern the straight path to power in any organization. In no time, she proved to me and everybody else that she was extremely competent as a manager and leader. My business acumen was non-existent, but I knew I could endlessly hike twelve-mile trails and spit shine away the red clay in five minutes, thanks to Drill Sergeant Stevens. My leadership style to that point was shaped by the arts world. If OCS could accomplish miracles, I hoped to develop a rugged, no-nonsense recession-proof business persona. That's why I was there. Lynda, on the other hand, couldn't shine a boot to save her commission. And at OCS, you don't get any points for your business acumen until you can spit shine your boots lickety-split after a 12-mile hike through the Georgia red clay. My first contribution to our survival was to teach Lynda how to make love to a Corcoran boot, how to gloss on the tenderest of spit shines faster than the speed of light.

"Ernie," The Author
Compared to Lynda, the OCS uniform and required black glasses did not afford an image of beauty.

It didn't take more than a few boot shining sessions for me to realize that I was wrong about Lynda. Lynda was not at all like Jenny, my friend and basic training buddy, except that she spoke fluent German just as compulsively as Jenny did. Jenny was innocent, child-like in her purity of mind and motive. Lynda was womanly and worldly. She was so well-bred. Upper crust. What could she possibly hope to accomplish by grubbing through the mud with a bunch of working class officers? Even the TAC officers expressed their curiosity about Lynda's pursuit of a commission. Why was she in the Army? In time, I came to value Lynda's sophistication and her language facility. Whenever Lynda switched our conversation to German, the drudgery of our details vanished. The conversations were as rejuvenating as if we had taken a Lufthansa flight far away from the drudge of the backwoods infantry to European civilization.

Once we got past the sharing of treats and maintenance skills, we found it easy to be friends. Our relationship began with a fair enough trade. I shared all the secret tips for healthy running and road marching that Sergeant Stevens and Agnes passed on to D-3-3 Officer Candidates. I really did show Lynda how to put a glassy shine on her Corcoran jump boots. At every boot shining session, Lynda would teach me how to smooth my leadership style. So, on the one hand, I contributed the survival knowledge of a working class woman to Lynda, who worked hard but found it difficult to deal with stupidity and bureaucracy. Lynda, on the other hand, proffered the middle class arts of finesse and diplomacy to help me tone down my blunt, direct speaking style. Every day she had another lesson for me. We would come back from a platoon tasking or a leadership class and Lynda would encourage me to be less pointed, more diplomatic when I spoke. Seems like the lessons from her would often end with her gentle admonition: "You are right, deYoung, but you have to find a smooth way to say it! You've gotta be smooth, deYoung! They're not going to listen to you unless you smooth it across!" She would glide her hand across the sky as if she were frosting a cake.

Not that we were having any social problems that would impede our success. Of 250 total students in 51st Company, only about 11 women would graduate from each class. Was sexual harassment or discrimination a problem in the 51st Company? Would the students suffer gastrointestinal distress from the moon's green cheese that was sprinkled on our daily dinner salads? No to both questions. The human cosmos at OCS was constructed so carefully that neither moon cheese nor sexual harassment were allowed to contaminate the laboratory experiment. I've never seen such careful prevention systems anywhere else in the military or in civilian life.

At the beginning of orientation week, Lieutenant Van Delft hauled all 40 of the female officer candidates down to the company day room for a sexual harassment briefing with the company commander, Captain Geoffrey Miller. By nature, Captain Miller was as quiet as I was chatty. He made a very bad impression on me during my first lunch at the dining facility. In what I soon discovered was atypical fashion for him, Miller moved around the dining room on our first day and yelled at candidates who were taking too long to eat. Then he criticized their food choices.

I was almost a vegetarian, and very proud of my weight watcher eating habits. Captain Miller came to my table, at which candidates were eating, as the rules required, in silence.

"OFFICER CANDIDATE DEYOUNG!"

Miller didn't seem to have much experience with being obnoxious, but he succeeded with me on his first try. " Can't you move it! Can't you see these people are waiting to eat lunch. They can't sit down until you are finished, and there you are picking at your salad, eating your peas! You don't have all day! You can't pick at your food like a bird! Where's your meat? Where are your carbohydrates???"

When Van Delft brought us down to the day room to meet with him, she was extremely quiet, soft and feminine. Extremely out of character in front of her commander. Captain Miller was also different from my first encounter with him. On my second evening at OCS, he was a perfect gentleman, and more naturally soft-spoken. Miller and Van Delft gave the first of endless briefings about Equal Opportunity, Sexual Harassment, and special concerns for women. They spoke about the special physical problems women experience during training. They emphasized that safety could be found in strict fraternization policies.

Lastly, but most importantly, they somberly talked about the need for women to be careful about their diets while at OCS. Still hypersensitive to Captain Miller's public chastisement, I seethed when he lectured the women on their need to shift from a heavy meat and potatoes diet to a heart smart diet packed with fruits and vegetables.

"Sir," I asked him. "I am really glad to hear you support this kind of diet, because I have learned to manage my weight through Weight Watchers, and they taught me to eat mostly fruits and vegetables."

Captain Miller smiled.

"I don't understand why," I continued. "these principles aren't followed in the dining facility. Just yesterday, I was criticized for eating my peas and my salad... It seems to me that we are being pressured to eat a diet that won't be good for us later on..."

Captain Miller paused and smiled. Lynda looked at me as if I had gone psychotic.

"Officer Candidate deYoung, you are right." He did not hint that I might have been indiscreet in my comment. "Our main concern is to give women the opportunity to succeed. Weight control is always a problem because women don't have to eat as much as men, even after they exercise. Your metabolism won't speed up the way a man's will, even after all the running we do here. The women's weight limit is higher, but if you exceed it from eating too many donuts or hamburgers, you won't graduate. But... neither will any man!" He looked at me ruefully. "I will make a point to instruct the TACs to avoid commenting on what you eat. There are plenty of other ways to harass candidates in the dining facility."

The women laughed. Every meal, candidates line outside the dining facility. We had 15 minutes to eat, just as in basic training. Still, the lines outside would pile up. TACs passed the time by requiring each candidate to swing on monkey bars, then do pull-ups. Most of the women could do the monkey bars, but we failed miserably at pull-ups. No sweat. Twenty-five push-ups were the minimum alternative. Just by waiting in line for three meals, women candidates pumped out 75 pushups.

After the pushups, a TAC would yell questions. From the first day, we were to memorize the daily schedule, which included the uniform, gear, time, place, event and a thought for the day.

"Officer Candidate, what is the uniform for the commander's briefing?"

If you could not answer correctly, the TAC sharply reprimanded you, "Hit the wall, Candidate and write yourself up!" Always, three points of contact against the wall. The uniform of the day included ballpoint pen and index card on which you were to record your deficiencies. After you wrote down your shortcoming — failure to memorize, string on the uniform, smudge on the boot — the TAC wrote down your penalty. It only took two demerits per week to lose your pass for Saturday afternoon. If you lost your pass, not only were you restricted to post, you marched silently with rifles in a specially prepared uniform for two hours on the courtyard. At the conclusion of each meal, candidates had to walk past five TACs who would arbitrarily challenge candidates. If called, we had to freeze in place, yell responses to their questions, and hit the wall to write up any failure of knowledge or flaw in appearance. Captain Miller was right. The TACs had more than enough opportunity to harass us during meal time.

The seldom seen human incarnations of Lieutenant Van Delft and Captain Miller that appeared to the 40 females during our first EO briefing emphasized their goal was to graduate every woman who deserved an OCS commission. It was reassuring to hear 57 varieties of the statement: You will not be harassed because you are female. You will, on the other hand, be harassed because you are an officer candidate. Any other kind of harassment: sexual, religious, racial or whatever would not be tolerated. But, neither would we get soft treatment because we were females. Van Delft emphasized this when she stated she would commission no woman who could not do as many pushups as an 18 year old infantryman was required to do to stay in the infantry. Van Delft's minimum standard was 55. Enlisted women, then and now are only required to do 18 pushups to remain on duty. ROTC lieutenants often show up at their first duty station only able to do half as many push ups as the guys. Van Delft insisted we would have to earn respect from our troops just as the men did. Therefore, we would meet the standard or we would not be commissioned.

We already knew that nobody would be handed a commission. Heck, a son of a general was kicked out in those first days because he was caught stealing a bottle of EMU from the PX. Or, if he really didn't steal it, he lied somewhere between the clerk who caught him in the act of leaving the PX with the EMU in his pocket and the company commander who handled the report of stolen goods.

Captain Jeffrey Miller's heart-to-heart talk with women of the 51st company was believable. Already, the training policies seemed protective of our right to succeed, based on merit. Best of all, the fraternization policies would protect both men's and women's reputations. Although men and women were training together at OCS, the fraternization policies strictly forbade any touching or social contact that was intimate or romantic in nature. Men and women shared the same hallway, but women were only bunked with women, and men with men. To prevent harassment, assault or plain old-fashioned hanky panky, room doors were required to be opened at all times. The only exception: five minutes to change clothes. Guards checked the rooms and hallways at night, so no one was allowed to sleep in the buff. We slept in our physical training clothes, which made it easy to race to the PT formation within the fifteen minutes allotted after the first wakeup call. In any public area, clothing was to be worn at all times.

Out in the training field, women shared tents with women. Men with men. On national public radio in 1997, I heard Captain Rosemary Mariner decry the Kassenbaum recommendation to separate men's and women's sleeping accommodations because she feared women would be subject to lesbian attacks if they lived in separate quarters from men. Funny. No one ever worries that an all-male infantry platoon or professional football team will compulsively engage in homosexual conduct — just because they live in gender separated conditions. Thank goodness, when I went through basic training and OCS, common sense prevailed. No one feared accusations of lesbianism just because women shared tents and barracks rooms, anymore than we had to fear harassment or assault from the men. Today, men and women insist on their right to sleep in the same tent, to sleep in the same quarters as men as well as their right to be promiscuous with their tent mates and their bunk mates. The penalty for this insanity is too steep. Our commanders spend inordinate quantities of time sorting out harassment and assault charges because the men and women living in these situations inevitably and invariably get themselves entangled in all kinds of messy intimate situations that end up in disciplinary actions after the flame of passion cools.

There were only four to six women in each platoon at the start of OCS, so the latrine situation was, as always in the Army, unfair to men. Four women used one latrine, and the remaining 36 men used the other one. At some point, the TACs agreed to let women from two platoons share one latrine, to provide more stalls for the men. All details, even latrine cleaning were to be done by squad. That meant men and women cleaned both latrines, depending on the schedule. This was a blessing, because the prior service sergeants had some nifty tricks for whisking through a latrine inspection after morning showers. For one, don't use all the showers or stalls. For another, scrub down the walls during your shower. The cleanup detail, all starched and spit shined only had to wipe dry the walls and stalls after the last soldier raced through the shower line.

Field duty required modifications that worked to women's advantages. Women slept in separate pup tents from the men. Always, my roommate was my tent mate. But while working on patrols, digging foxholes, or doing other heavy labor, we were teamed up by squad assignment. The squad leaders always paired a woman with a man, especially for heavy digging because we did not have the same strength to carve foxholes out of red clay turned rock. We worked just as steadily as the guys. The men just got more done in less time because they could crack deeper than we could into the Georgia clay with less effort.

Every military training experience includes deprivation of all kinds of personal comforts. OCS did not excuse itself from this manner of instilling personal stamina and discipline. Or so we were led to believe during orientation. We began running 24-hour guard duty and parking lot security, protecting life, limb and used Lincoln Continentals with our tough military bearing and trusty flashlights. The TACs, knowing we needed to compensate for the sleep deprivation and heavy running schedule with intensive midnight carbohydrate loading, initiated us into the traditional OCS version of POW camp or Hide and Seek: the pogie bait run.

Pogie runs were planned leadership reaction exercises as far as the TACs were concerned. Lieutenant Van Delft needled the Second Platoon student leadership during our second week of training. How come she wasn't able to smell or find any pogie bait? What kind of cowards were we, that we didn't try to sneak in a pizza or two? And have the pizza smeared all over your bunk mattresses that were dumped onto the floor when you were caught? Our platoon leaders did not take up Van Delft's gauntlet. She continued to agitate the leadership. Where was the courage of the platoon leaders? We were an older and wiser group of candidates, chastened by the harsh recession in the civilian economy. Our platoon leaders had families to support. A slice of pizza or a two-pound bag of M&Ms was not worth the price of elimination. We all thought we were being good children, guaranteeing our graduation by not taking a chance.

Van Delft relentlessly nagged our acting leaders. A good leader would figure out a way to get the pogie bait to his troops, without a TAC ever discovering the contraband! Right. And lose your commission for breaking the rules? Fat chance. Second Platoon was going to cooperate and graduate. We weren't going to blow it by getting caught munching on Domino's thick crust cheese pizza at two o'clock in the morning. Van Delft would not quit her taunting.

During a grass-cutting detail, where we were required to hack away at clumps of wild grass with dull-bladed grass trimmers that only closed partway, candidates from the 50th Company let us in on the pogie bait POW game. We were supposed to take up the TAC's dare, and build esprit de corps by completing this risky mission without being discovered.

At first, there was a rebellion that OCS TACs would even think about turning their candidates into lying little sneaks. But after all, saving your buddy in combat might involve lying and sneaking. Stealth was fundamental to survival. So was esprit de corps. We figured the game could have its value as a training exercise. Much safer than putting candidates through a live-fire mission to teach them the importance of unit cohesion, courage, loyalty or a host of other qualities required by leaders if they were to be respected by their troops. We could make all our leadership mistakes, uncover all our flaws without shedding a single drop of blood, blowing off the limb of a friendly troop, or inflicting "collateral damage" on the training field.

Just how far should we go with this game? We debated the risks for days. We were in the middle of a deep recession. We could not forget there were no paying jobs outside the Army's gate. Would we be punished with hours of mindless details and silent marching, or would we be tossed out of OCS on our ears? The endless details were going to happen no matter what we decided.

There were ethical dimensions, honor code questions to be considered before we acted. What was the difference between being dishonest and being stealthy? What was the difference between being disobedient and courageous? If the official policy excluded candy and pizza from our daily diet, weren't we being disobedient to consume these treats on the sly? If our captors ordered us not to feed our men, would we meekly obey, or discreetly strategize to make sure all our POWs had their survival needs met? These were questions we discussed in our classroom briefings, particularly as we prepared for our 40 hours of ethics training. Training in which the Army engaged in a massive attempt to correct the ethical deficiencies that surfaced in junior Army officers during Vietnam.

The TACs were our enemies, after all. And if we were in a real POW situation, we would be required to figure out an escape route. Escape would require loyalty to fellow soldiers, stealth, courage in knowing when to break the rules, and the willingness to deal with the moral complexity of being dishonest to one's captors for the sake of your troops' survival. If we did a run as a simulated POW experience, we could develop loyalty, teamwork and esprit de corps, and best of all, we could eat our pizza without getting caught by the TACs.

Our first pogie run taught both Lynda and me that there is quite a difference between physical courage and moral courage. Women can not always compete with men when it comes to physical courage, but we often have an edge when it comes to moral courage.

"Freedom's just another word for nothing left to lose," as Janis Joplin used to sing. We were not entrenched in the power systems of any institution back then, so maybe it was easier to take big risks. Nothing to lose by trying, everything to gain by winning. Lynda and I proved to our male platoon mates once and for all that we had the right stuff to eventually become officers and gentlewomen during that first expedition.

Our first party conformed to the classic pattern. Prior service candidates set up the first phase of the operation. They knew how to get Domino's thick crust pizzas delivered to any training site, even 30 minutes away where soldiers slept on the ground with combat buddies, their M-16A1 rifles. That night, thick Dominos pizzas were delivered to two trash cans at the end of our building. The driver picked up his payment from our tough, flash-light-wielding parking guards.

The tantalizing aroma of oregano pizza sauce announced the arrival of our pizzas as they were sneaked into the Second Platoon's male latrine. Those of us who were not on guard duty pretended to be fast asleep until we were tapped on the shoulders. We quietly tiptoed down to the men's latrine, five at a time.

When Adam and Eve nipped into their first apple, they couldn't have experienced the glee we did as our pizza slices were divvied up. Deprivation can exaggerate the taste bud's appreciation of even a jail keeper's home cooking. It's hard to imagine how anyone can feel orgiastic about a Domino's pizza, but that evening the guys licked their fingers and smacked their lips the same way Adam probably did on the day paradise was lost.

Platoon photographers snapped pictures of the hands of male candidates as they lifted their pizza slices with the reverence accorded the Eucharistic host. Emboldened, the photographer wanted to snap year book photos of our faces as we stuffed each fluffy succulent bite of mozzarella pie into our mouths. The men almost gave away our positions when they erupted with commands to stop the camera. Lynda, myself and another candidate lost our inhibitions. Supposedly, in the class yearbook, there is a picture of the three of us impishly grinning as we bit into our slivers of pepperoni pizza.

Pizza communion over, it was our turn to contribute to the mission. Lynda and I gathered all the evidence and stuffed it into two extra large garbage bags. Two men were supposed to carry the trash bags down two flights of steps, then run them to the trash cans at the end of our building. They panicked. The penalty for getting caught outside the barracks after lights out was expulsion.

None of the men would venture out with the trash. Lynda and I were determined not to get caught with pizza remnants in our barracks. We had weekend plans, and we were not about to be derailed with demerits that would limit our weekend freedom. We volunteered to run the trash out.

Were we Thelma and Louise or Harriet Tubman and Susan B. Anthony? Our feat had neither the magnitude of a made-for-movie bank heist nor that of a national civil rights act on behalf of human freedom. All we did was carry the trash bags down two flights of stairs, sprint to the end of our building, sprint back and get into our beds without getting caught. The thought of expulsion never crossed our minds. But we earned the enduring admiration of the men in our platoon for rescuing them from a fate worse than death. Most of the guys were still too new at risk taking to truly believe it was only a game.

If Van Delft knew we had that pogie run, she never let on. With the cunning of a Stalag 17 camp warden, she had her comeuppance at our very next feast. Georgia is stiflingly hot in June. Ice cream was the logical choice for our next expedition. The party was planned without a hitch. Shortly after Van Delft's office lights were dimmed, pints of peach and vanilla ice cream were delivered right to our bunks. We were individually responsible for keeping our ice cream concealed, then disposing of the containers. The absolute silence must have triggered Van Delft's suspicions. She pretended to leave the building, but she remained in her darkened office until the last pint was delivered half-melted. The hall lights snapped on.

"OFFICER CANDIDATE, WHAT ARE YOU DOING SITTING UP IN YOUR BED AFTER LIGHTS OUT?? YOU'RE EATING ICE-CREAM! ICE-CREAM!! PLATOON! ATTENTION!"

A few doors down from our room, a naïve man was discovered by Van Delft sitting atop his bunk with a spoon of peach ice cream in his mouth. Clearly against the rules. Candidates were always required to sleep under the woolen covers, even in August. Our rooms were air-conditioned, so it was not an uncomfortable rule. The requirement forced us to spend time making our beds in the morning, and therefore, was strictly enforced.

Van Delft ripped the mattress off that man's bed, then glided into our room before I got out of bed. She pulled my covers and derided me for dipping into a pint of vanilla from under my covers. Lynda was livid. Whatever punishment I was meted, Lynda would also have to serve with me because as my roommate, she was supposed to keep me out of trouble. Lynda was furious that I didn't have enough self-control to let the ice cream melt if necessary, until we were truly sure our nemesis had left the building.

Not only did we spend a couple of hours that night doing pushups with the platoon and listening to Van Delft's machinations. Worse, we both earned two demerits because I got caught. Two demerits meant two hours pacing back and forth on the Quadrant on a perfectly good Saturday afternoon that should have been spent sitting at the pool by the La Quinta Inn.

The next morning, bleary with fatigue, the 51st company hauled off to the ranges in stinky cattle cars for a day of weapons training. Lynda fumed with some of the handsome men in third platoon while we were sitting in the stands waiting for weapons instructors to give us our safety briefings. She flushed with indignation at my stupidity, the men roared with insensitive laughter.

"Hey, deYoung, I heard you got caught the other night! What happened, you got the clap from VD?"

That was a private joke between the men of second platoon who would deflect the sting of Van Delft's insults with the secret comfort code: "I'd rather have the (clap) than VD!"

"Na'ah!" I shrugged in response, still too much of a lady to even think of participating in that crude joke.

"I was targeted by a cold-seeking missile!"

The men hooted. "What flavor did you get? Gees, I hope you got to finish it." I didn't. That's what made me mad!

I'm just as sensitive to ridicule as Lynda, but just then, I didn't mind their teasing. It seemed that Lynda would never forgive my idiocy. She was a perfectionist, but unlike the rest of us, she was capable of achieving perfection most of the time. I seemed to make mistakes all over the place. The guys mediated between Lynda and myself. They spent some time explaining to Lynda that we were destined for some kind of punishment no matter how perfect we tried to be. That's just how OCS was supposed to be. The punishment was supposed to bring us closer together, or at least, thicken our skins. A shared experience of animosity and hostility seem to be required antecedents to male bonding, but women aren't raised to react this way. Thanks to the men in 3rd platoon, Lynda soon forgave me and we got back to the business of cooperating for graduation's sake, if not for the sake of our friendship.

Friday night our new OCS friends took off for the motel and the Bombay Bicycle Club. Lynda and I sat on our floor, spiffed up our glassy spit-shined boots. Polished the OCS brass on our lapels. We pressed the OCS neck scarves we would have to wear, and waxed our shiny powder blue helmets. This was the night that grace entered our relationship. We were no longer officer candidates whose sole motivation for enduring the sadistic punishments of our TACs was to climb to great heights of career success. We became friends, regardless of where the OCS experience would take us.

Lynda started to talk about her love relationships. None of us had ever been able to figure out why she joined the Army. She was just too classy to be a soldier. That night, Lynda finally shared her story. Like so many of us, she had left behind someone she loved, but whom she did not feel loved by. In college, I was known as "Mom Marie" because I was a bit older than the average undergraduate. The professors would laugh when they saw young freshmen and sophomores knock on the door of my practice room for lengthy comfort sessions during which they shared their insecurities about this or that boyfriend. I was an older, married, experienced woman. I was supposed to understand these things as well as God or Jesus. With Lynda, it was different. Lynda was almost my age, but that night she started to confide in me as an older sister. She never had a sister. So, she was used to handling her life without consulting anybody. Besides her mother, Lynda really didn't have any female friends.

Lynda talked that night about her mother, a Christian Science practitioner whom Lynda deeply admired. She read some of Mrs. E's letters. Her face was radiant as she read Mrs. E's expressions of pride in Lynda's extraordinary life choices. She really had made some great choices. She was a linguist. She loved to travel. She fiercely guarded her independence, turning down marriage more than once when she felt the love in a relationship was not true enough to respect her many gifts.

I couldn't imagine that Lynda ever had a problem with men, because the waters seemed to part whenever she approached them. That night, I realized such adulation could cause a different set of problems for a competent woman. Innocently, this problem played itself out in our platoon. There were two extremely handsome men from our platoon, Chandler and Catlett, whom Lynda befriended. Both those men worshiped Lynda as discreetly as they could manage. The fraternization policies absolutely forbade us to associate with other candidates in any kind of relationship besides that of officer candidate. We were comrades in arms. And that was all that was allowed. Not only was dating taboo. Mere touching was forbidden, and punishable by expulsion.

As far as I could tell, Lynda, Chandler, and Catlett never violated the fraternization policies. They never acted on their affections, and even went overboard to avoid the appearance of treating Lynda with favoritism. I was the curious beneficiary of this tactic. Obviously, as an older, newly-divorced woman, they weren't interested in me. But older also meant slower. The guys gave me all kinds of help in the field, and in completing classroom assignments — all to win Lynda's approval and affection.

Al Catlett, whose affectionate nickname became the "No Shit Company Commander" because he always promised us if we gave him no shit, he would see us through, was my squad leader during field patrols in woods that were thicker than the Panama jungles with tall trees and dark, swampy brush. For six years Al was a Ranger. He didn't hesitate to use a profanity to get his point across, but it was never personal or derogatory. He just used words that exploded with the truth of his frustrations at our naivete. Otherwise, he was exceedingly patient in coaching college-graduated city slickers in the art of river crossings and night land navigation. If he had been in a male-only squad or company, I'm sure he would have hauled the men through the woods with lightening speed. He was kind enough to keep me close to the front and to pace the group so that the older cadets could endure the 24-hour patrols during our Ranger week training. Once, Catlett, Lynda and myself went to dinner and to see a movie about a waif strip dancer turned glamorous jazz ballet dancer. The song, "What a Feeling," certainly conveyed the exhilaration those two felt. But Al made it known well in advance he was getting married after graduation. He did nothing to compromise his engagement but gleam with pride that he was able to dine alone with the most beautiful woman on Fort Benning. Well, not entirely alone. I was the foil that lent innocence to their brief evening together. My reward was to share in all the Hollywood fantasies sung by Irene Cara that would fuel our charge towards graduation.

Maybe I was a foil for some kind of relationship between Lynda and the many men who admired her, but I couldn't imagine they would break the rules when our professional success depended on compliance. I didn't want to know if they did.

Not that illicit relationships were encouraged or desired by students or faculty. During my first tour at OCS, if there were any sexual parties of the type that gained international television coverage in the 1990s, I never heard about them. There were never any scandals concerning fraternization between students or between students and faculty, either. Years later, friends told me of this or that relationship that began at OCS and ended in marriage shortly after we were commissioned. I was always grateful that Lynda never compromised herself, in fact, she often brought me along to her parties to protect herself and me from vicious rumors or unwelcome advances.

If any of the women in my class did participate in fraternization that was against the rules, they had the good sense not to tell. Our friendships deepened not because of any deception we colluded in, but because each of us took full responsibility for the consequences of our own private lives. This is so different from the Army of the post-war '90s, where the men and women want to indulge themselves without regard to peer or marital relationships, and take absolutely no responsibility for the troubles that follow.

Physical training would prove more of a threat to our success than any real or imagined prospects of sexual harassment or fraternization among OCS classmates. Our training regimen was packed with physically exhausting events, so I doubt anyone had time to squander on private relationships. Although I was kind of chunky, the OCS physical training demands were less debilitating for me than for Lynda. Even though Lynda was more trim, the physical regimen was grueling for her. At 4:15 every morning, an officer candidate would bang on our bunk posts with his flashlight yelling, "Wake-up. Last call for Wake-up. First Formation at ZERO-FOUR-THIRTY HOURS!"

The hour itself was not a punishment, since it would be too hot to run our five miles by the time the sun rose at 6:00 A.M. I don't think Lynda ever woke up before noon until she joined the Army. Her mood was grim every day as we were dragged out of bed, which was not in keeping with her otherwise cheerful persona. The only time she did not wear her Shirley Temple smile was when the guards banged their flashlights on our bunks to wake us up. We had less than five minutes to make our bunks, run to the bathroom, get our running shoes on, grab our flashlights and run down to the courtyard for the first formation of the day.

To get those bunks made in less than a minute, a sensible person would sleep on top. This was verboten, of course, because such a strategy removed the element of stress required for officer candidates to get a training benefit out of the perpetually overcrowded schedule. Some of our classmates were senior sergeants before they entered OCS. Their secret: train yourself to sleep as straight as a board, thereby eliminating the need to straighten out sheets, etc. We learned that trick posthaste, because it was much less stressful to wakeup with a crick in your neck than to show up late for formation, or to return to your room to find your bed tossed onto the floor by the TACs after they discovered wrinkles in your sheets. Lynda must have slept in a king-size waterbed before the Army, because she could never get a moment of pleasure out of sleeping like a mummy, which acutely exacerbated her early morning blahs.

As tiny as she was, she had a terrible time with push-ups and the morning run. This had to be a mental block, because Lynda could run her two mile PT test in 15 minutes — as fast as the average male. I could only run the PT test in 16:08, but since I was an older woman, this was considered a good score. Lynda struggled terribly with every five-mile run. I had very few problems once we hit the road and set an even pace.

After we completed our daily 80 or 100 sit-ups on the hard concrete courtyard, and God knows how many pushups, the platoon instructor would blossom into health nut fitness guru. With a sudden concern for our spinal cords, he'd demonstrate static stretches, the Army's new answer to all those PT injuries incurred on the macadam and concrete PT exercise fields. No more bouncing stretches for our smart soldiers. Long, deep bends to stretch the calves, the hamstrings, the un-nameables. We were required to pause for five full minutes of stretching before each five-mile run.

Without variation, we formed up for a run every single day. When we ran by ability groups, the runs could be downright pleasant. The pre-dawn darkness lent a bit of mystery to our daily ritual. Magnolias lined the post roads, providing a sweetly spiritual fragrance that made the run a bit otherworldly as we glided over this or that wooded hill.

Sometimes the men would confuse the scent of the magnolias with women's perfume. They'd complain that women shouldn't wear perfume in runs, because the scent made them nauseous, jeopardizing their ability to finish the runs. The OCS policy: fall out of three runs and you were out, a high-speed PFC. We weren't wearing any perfume. None of us were that dumb. The last thing you would want to do in 2nd platoon was to compromise another candidate's ability to finish a morning run. Once we figured out the scent was coming from the woods, though, some of the student platoon leaders tried to compensate by running the group down the middle of the road. No way this could have made a biological difference. The magnolias were just as fragrant to me, but the platoon leaders' sensitivity to the men's fear did have a placebo effect on those who were sure the fragrance was hurting their run.

The magnolias brought me comfort. Perhaps because I'd been taught their magical power by one of my college classmates, a composer. In the middle of our deep Kansas City snowstorms, he would sit back in his chair and shake his head. He used to reminisce that he missed his Florida home.

"Those magnolias. I miss the smells! If I could just have a magnolia in my yard, it'd feel like home."

Down at OCS, thanks to that memory, the magnolias made me feel at home, even in the pitch black early morning runs.

The hills were another story. The official route culminated in a steep hill, known to all of the candidates as "Heartbreak Hill." Once you got over this hill, guaranteed you could sprint back to the company area if you had to. But many a commission was lost by the quitters who stopped just before the heartbreak hill crested.

TACs were staked out on Heartbreak Hill the way highway patrol cops hide in the bushes at the edge of small towns. Only the TACs weren't out to trap speeders. They were pursuing slowpokes and the intolerable: the quitters. With absolutely no exceptions, the official OCS running standard was enforced. Fall out of three runs, and you fall out of OCS. Heartbreak hill was the place to catch the weak of heart. As far as OCS TACs were concerned, unless you were having a heart attack, you would RUN, not walk or crawl up heartbreak hill. PFC I, my basic training nemesis lost her commission because she stopped running. No love lost when she packed her bags.

The most dreaded runs up heartbreak hill were the weekly company or battalion runs. Soldiers either love or hate these esprit runs. For good reason. In a company run, 250 men and women would run as a large cluster. Regulations prescribe set distances between the commander and each of the platoons that are formed behind the leadership. To keep that prescribed distance, the troops endure an accordion effect for most of the run, particularly when corners are turned or hills surmounted.

Over the years, I've learned esprit runs are really ego runs for the commanders who want to strut their power all over the post. They are seldom spirited until the runs are near completion. Tall runners grumble when the platoon is squeezed together, not only because they are oxygen depleted, but their muscles get tight because their stride is so much longer than the baby steps they are forced to take to accommodate the slowest runners.

Short runners and most women suffer when the platoon formation extends beyond the normal breadth allowed. Tall guys leap forward like happy jack rabbits to re-block the formation and the shorties are compelled to gasp for air as they sprint to their correct place.

To Van Delft's credit, she never played games with 2nd Platoon during command runs. She must have grown proud of her platoon towards the end of our first phase. Amidst all the shouting of platoon slogans and cadences from the units that passed us, one morning, Van Delft burrowed in on the cadences our platoon sang during the Friday morning company run. She knew that cadence callers would strike a happy compromise for our mismatched group if the right person called cadence. The accordion effect made it almost impossible to be rhythmical as we bellowed out our charming esprit builders. Van Delft wanted to strike a solid beat that would keep our block formation in tact.

"What's the matter with this platoon? Where's your esprit?" she barked.

"C-130 rollin' down the strippa!" The cadence was called by a man, but in something like 5\4 time. The lopsided waltz, although quite refreshing in a Tschaikovsky symphony, is hardly a marching rhythm, let alone a good tempo for pacing runners.

"That's not RHYTHM! Where's your sense of rhythm? Platoon leader! Get another cadence caller out here!!" The platoon leader selected a tall runner who could keep a slow enough pace, but who couldn't sing worth a lick.

"What kind of platoon is this?? I want rhythm! You have to have rhythm if your are going to keep this formation together! DeYoung!! Where's DeYoung??"

"Here, Ma'am!"

"DeYoung! You're a musician. Get out here and give us rhythm!" That command should have ended my career, because I didn't think I would have enough energy to shout out a cadence and still make it to the top of heartbreak. I stepped out.

"C-130 rollin' down the strippa!" The pace was perfect, but Van Delft was dissatisfied.

"DeYoung! You can do better than that! Sing something different!" I hardly knew the cadences we were supposed to burn in our souls for a lifetime of leadership opportunities. The men whispered some first lines, and some sweet words of encouragement. Finally I struck up a song I knew:

"I got rhythm!" The platoon responded, "I got rhythm!"

"I got music!"

"I got music!"

"I got OCS"

"I got OCS" The platoon sniggled because it was a perfectly safe way to poke fun at our TAC officer. Could we keep it up?

"Who could ask for anything more!" The guys obviously didn't know the whole song, because they didn't wait a beat to echo their response. We hiccuped to another crooked waltz. Four or five splotchy beats and a soldier could have fallen out. Van Delft was not pleased. She wanted her entire platoon to finish together. She didn't wait two beats to axe me.

"DeYoung! You don't know how to call cadence. Platoon Leader! Get out here and call some cadence! What kind of formation is this??"

The men teased me all the way back to our shower point, gleeful that in a way, I'd gotten in a clever lick against the TAC. Lynda was pink with glee, too. Her approval in front of the men made me proud.

At this point in our training, we were realizing that Van Delft's motivations were not entirely the sadistic comeuppance of a recent OCS grad. She heartily wanted her platoon to bond in a spirit of generosity and protectiveness. This was evident a few weeks later during a defining command run that would sift more chaff from the graduating class. We were beginning to show signs of paralyzing muscle fatigue. Frazzled muscles can give way to frazzled nerves, but our platoon leaders synchronized teams to balance the weak and strong — ensuring that the greatest number of second platoon candidates would make it through.

I think Catlett was the platoon leader that week, but if it was someone else, the Catlett spirit was pulling us through the week with no dropouts. The steamy, July morning air was thick with pollen and swampy Georgia mold. Simply unbreathable. When we started the command run, groans of worry began to swell, even from the guys. The TACs signaled their intentions to sift out the weaklings. We knew we had to stay together or we were going to lose a candidate.

Actually, the running pace was not brutal. The air was simply too thick to inhale deeply, so I think many candidates began to build up anxiety and breathing difficulties. When we approached Heartbreak Hill, Lynda, of all people, began to flush red with discomfort. She muttered something unintelligible. Van Delft darted over to Lynda's side and half-heartedly dug into Lynda's emotional pain with the taunt, "Second Phase, not everyone's made for the final cut, right Lynda?"

Lynda said nothing.

Van Delft yelled at the platoon, "Cooperate and graduate. That's my standard." Then she ran back down the hill to harass the Third Platoon. Someone like Catlett yelled, "DeYoung, take care of her!" Men were explicitly forbidden to physically assist women during training runs, but no one ever said women couldn't tug other candidates over the hump. TACs assumed we couldn't, so there was no need for a prohibition. Second Platoon men closed in to cover Lynda and me as I grabbed her arm to pull her over the top. I doubt I pulled Lynda more than 25 meters. It was a struggle for both of us to get past the TAC assault at the crest of the hill without being noticed. The men in our platoon affectionately encouraged both of us to persist. They shielded us from TAC interference. For once, our student platoon leader guaranteed a 100 percent platoon finish by holding back the pace at the front of the formation. When victory was assured, we strutted in perfect formation to the finish line, flushed with pride and real affection for each other.

At that moment of triumph, we were as fond of Van Delft as we were of each other. She beamed her toothy smile in approval. Van Delft quickly reverted to wicked stepmother back at the headquarters, however, as she barked new commands and insults to drag us to new plateaus of achievement. When we were released from formation we raced back to the shower stalls to wash off the sweat, pollen and Van Delft's bad vibes. Men slapped each others' fannies. VD jokes were snorted in triumph. As the women lined up for hot showers, the chatter was unusually confident and buoyant — almost boastful for a change. Two other women in our platoon kept ribbing Lynda and myself about our group triumph. Lynda was reticent.

We returned to our rooms. She locked the door. We broke starch. Donned our fresh BDUs. Usually, we took turns venting about TAC abuse or peer misunderstandings for this five minute respite from the world. This time there was silence. When Lynda buttoned the 22 BDU buttons that were subject to TAC inspection, she pulled out her mother of pearl brush and began vigorously stroking her blonde hair.

"DeYoung," she finally fumed. "DeYoung, why'd you pull me this morning? You have as much trouble with the runs as I do. If VD caught you, she would have tossed you out!"

Lynda was beet red. I had more time to struggle with my 22 buttons because my hair was short. The Georgia heat would bake my hair dry by the time I ran down the stairs for chow.

"You'd have done the same for me, Lynda!" I felt more gratitude than a need to apologize.

"You have done the same for me."

"They were definitely pushing for quitters."

"They didn't get any, did they?"

"DeYoung, don't ever do that again. It's not worth your commission."

"Lynda," I suddenly felt no fear. "I think we did what we were supposed to do this morning. You help the guys. They help me. I help you. We made it over the hump. We're going to make it! All of us."

Her petulance finally gave way to a smile.

That confidence on my part was short-lived. Lynda and I were book smart, as Jenny had been. Jenny was recently dropped from OCS after she ruined the muscles and tendons in her knee during a pre-breakfast monkey-bar drill. Despite surgery, casts and an extensive recovery period, Jenny's knee would not heal sufficiently to run. I visited her often at the medical holding company. The visits made me feel very guilty, because Jenny had fantasized about an Army commission since she was four years old. I only considered military service when I had no other options. She was losing her lifelong dream. I was nominally succeeding at something that was not really intrinsic to my sense of self — at that point, anyway.

Besides my marriage, which was slowly ending in divorce proceedings, music was the only thing that I still really cared about. In basic training, my platoon sergeant finally accommodated this fickleness by allowing me to carry around my Brahms orchestral conducting scores, which I would sit and review whenever the stultifying idle time threatened my sanity. My ex-husband sent me the Brahms symphony that I had studied in Herbert Blomstedt's master class. That Brahms score was my real buddy out in the foxhole, especially when Princess I would take off for sick call and leave me sitting for double guard duty. The platoon sergeants cut me some slack as I tried to stay awake in the winter nights by letting me read the scores by infrared flashlight. We had no real enemy or bullets to shoot with — it was a real triumph for the women to stay outside all night, so allowing me to score read was a minor concession and my salvation — until I accidentally buried the score in a foxhole we filled with dirt. It's still there for future privates to decipher when they re-dig my old foxhole. When I lost my Brahms in basic training, I thought I would never make music again. Wrong.

OCS offered almost too many opportunities for me to indulge my passion for music. Chapel services were the first opportunity to get distracted from my main goal, getting commissioned as an officer. All officer candidates were encouraged to attend chapel or visit with the chaplain to alleviate any psychological stress that might impede success. Although I was still a lapsed Catholic, I found myself playing folk masses for Chaplain Joe O'Keefe. At Father O'Keefe's School Brigade masses, the pews were filled with airborne trainees whose faith in the Almighty grew with every tribulation they overcame during their first phase of training. Mass attendance tapered when their jump wings were assured.

If I had limited my music activities to Sunday Mass, I probably would have had no problems at Fort Benning. Like an addict, I did not know when to set aside the hobby to concentrate on my professional training. Shortly after OCS started, both Father O'Keefe and First Lieutenant Atkins, the West Point TAC from Sixth Platoon asked me to put together a choir for the joint 4th of July worship service at the Columbus Baptist Church. I assembled about 30 singers and prepared several standard choral hymns. We were excused from details on occasion, and later from non-essential training, such as non-tested classes on handling the .38 caliber pistol. Mayors from two adjoining cities would attend this patriotic service, so the OCS choir had to be exceptional. We practiced with the Army band for a few days before the actual performance, but by then, our company was engaged in Land Navigation training.

Our choir was filled with really intelligent, mostly prior service candidates. No one thought we would have trouble completing the Land Navigation Test, where we would have to run through a thick forest in search of ten foolishly placed sticks with orange triangle markers. So we continued our choir practices right up to the big concert day.

I never set foot inside a Protestant church before this event, so the experience was indelibly printed in my memory. Our Baptist hosts were insistent that we be part of their family for that day — providing a huge 4th of July picnic lunch and sweet motherly volunteers who piled chicken and potato salad on our plates and sat us down with their relatives in a huge church hall. In church, the choir sat up front, wearing immaculate white scarves and gloves and pistol belts in which to tuck our bulky starched battle dress uniforms.

The Fort Benning Army Band accompanied us. A male student named Scott was actually named the choir leader in the program, which in retrospect struck me as quite odd, because Scott never led anything during rehearsals or at the worship service. In retrospect, I suppose his name was required to satisfy the Southern Baptist prohibition of women showing religious authority in a sanctuary. I sang the only choir solo, which nobody seemed to mind. A female mayor spoke during the service, so I did not have the sense that women were expected to be barefoot and pregnant or second class citizens in that town.

Soon after the 4th of July, our class took the first Land Navigation Test. Not only did I flunk this test. Many of my choir members — men and women who had six or seven years prior service flunked right beside me. We were book smart, spit shined, lean mean fighting machines. To graduate, we had to be all those things and we had to pass our Land Navigation Test. Clearly, we erred when we skipped our Land Nav classes to prepare for a high-profile music performance.

Not to worry. We would take remedial instruction, learn what we missed in the first classes, and retake the test just before Ranger Week, the final challenge before we were virtually assured graduation. Friends like Gwen Hampton and Julius Abdullah attended make up classes when the rest of our company had free time or goofy details. We did not feel any shame that we were hauled out to the field to relearn basic orienteering concepts like the pace count, and the technique of triangulation. Our peers were wasting their hours picking up the cigarette stubs tossed by 18th Airborne sergeants outside the non-commissioned officer club. We tried to get to know mother earth a little better — her curves, her hills and valleys, the difference between a ridge and a saddle, the difference between a hardball road and a dirt trail.

Our TAC officers, even my company commander, Captain Jeffrey Miller took responsibility for the fact that our failure was seemingly due to our absence from the Land Nav training classes. The TACs, and in my case, Captain Miller personally walked us through the test format until they were satisfied that our skills were sufficient to pass the retest. Once confident, Captain Miller and the TACs asked me to prepare special music for our class picnic. I assembled a soft rock band, which we called the Not Ready for Prime Time Players. Every afternoon we were excused from grass cutting and cannon polishing to practice with electric keyboard, guitars, drums and microphones. We knew we were sounding good when candidates started to assemble outside the storehouse where we practiced.

Captain Miller actually put me in charge of all the entertainment for this picnic, which included responsibility for content as well as quality of the performances. He personally reviewed every routine to be certain we did not violate the EO standards for racial, ethnic, religious, and gender sensitivity. Both Miller and our battalion commander, Lieutenant Colonel Kauffman were insistent that the only candidates who graduated would be certified ladies and gentlemen. Not only did they screen our routines for tasteful presentation, they also gave numerous briefings about the Army's intolerance for drunkenness or lack of gentlemanly decorum in the officer corps. If we intended to wear butter bars, both Miller and Kauffmann solemnly instructed us to limit our alcoholic consumption to two drinks, then switch to coke. If they witnessed our inebriation, they assured us, we would not be commissioned.

Well, our show was acclaimed by Captain Miller, and not only for the quality of music and comedy routines, but for the esprit de corps we aroused in the candidates. Even Lynda, who seldom complimented her peers for their work told me that the candidates reacted to my singing as if we were a professional band.

The Not Ready For Primetime Players
The candidates pay attention to the saxophone soloist at the senior picnic.

"All the heads turned to your stage when you began to sing. Some of us didn't recognize you. It was great!"

The music was great, but it didn't help me to graduate. Soon after the company picnic, all of the Land Nav flunkies, including me went out to the training site for a special makeup test. By this time, Lynda's friends were my friends. They wanted desperately for me to succeed. Some of the guys had insightful advice which I chose not to heed.

"DeYoung, you'd pass this test if you would just not stop to eat the blackberries on the way!"

Actually, all of the women stopped to eat blackberries at well-defined breaks. I never told this man or the instructors that I would start to sing Beethoven and Mahler symphonies whenever I started pacing through the woods. That was my real problem. I was trying to do two things at once. The Benning woods were exquisitely packed with trees, birds, corn stalks, honeysuckle and berries. The smells and the color just made me want to sing. Whenever I started to sing, I stopped counting my paces. That's why I flunked the test. I didn't figure this out until much, much later.

Some of the other guys tried to coach me on the exact location of the sticks I would find. One Irish candidate came into my room the night before the test. He took out an index card. He was stationed at Benning for many years, so he knew the entire training field like the back of his hand. He drew a map and marked out ten important land marks, deep within the forest canopy that would help me to orient myself in the event that my pace count was off. He put the index card in my drawer and insisted that I should take this card to the test with me the next day. Another candidate discouraged me from crawling down a hairline trail when he saw me on the road at the test site.

"There's nothing down there, deYoung!"

I didn't listen, wasted 30 minutes crawling through bushes and flapping corn stalks only to discover the man was sincerely trying to save me some time. There was nothing down there. Finally, about three-fourths of the way through the test, I reached an open clearing where there was a candidate who should never have flunked the first time. His land navigation skills were flawless.

"I can help you, deYoung. Just let me help you!"

That seemed like cheating to me, although he really only wanted to make sure that I graduated with the rest of the class.

"No," I answered. "If its true you have to know how to navigate to win a battle, then I need to prove that I can navigate on my own. Besides, you're getting married in three weeks. What are you going to say to your fiancée if you get kicked out for helping me beat this test?"

He shook his head reluctantly, assuring me that he could help me pass. When the grades came back, he got a grade of 100. I received about a 71, which was not enough to pass the Land Nav test or to remain in the Officer Candidate Program. I was a washout!

Nobody told us until after our Ranger Orientation Week was over whether we passed the Land Nav retest. During our last week of Phase II, all of the candidates spent five days in the field sampling the survival techniques used by Army Rangers. We crossed streams with ropes and canteen floats. We did tactical marches. We shot all kinds of weapons. Dug foxhole after foxhole. The weather was stinky hot. Unlike basic training, where women were brought in by truck to shower every two days or so, in these extended OCS field problems, there were no bathes or showers out in the woods. Most of the women carried around tiny bottles of shampoo. Every couple of days, there would be a sudden downpour. The water would fall as thick as a sheet of glass. Our only opportunity to feel feminine. We'd take out a little bottle of shampoo, dab some on our hair, and take a quick fully clothed body shower in the company of our male peers. Now when men train seriously for war, they don't tolerate soldiers who perform the three Ss indiscreetly. But the men who were teamed with Lynda and me didn't mind at all that we tried to pretty ourselves up while living in such filthy circumstances.

For work purposes, Lynda and I were assigned to different squads, but we slept in the same pup tent. Our Army was not stupid enough to put Lynda or me into a small pup tent with those sex-starved but gentlemanly candidates. No one minded when we grabbed a couple of wildflowers and set them in our canteen cups to decorate our tent space.

I have pictures of some of the guys with whom I dug foxholes. Officer Candidate Craig, a former sergeant with a dozen years of service behind him, could hear the whistle of a CS gas canister the instant it was popped.

"Run that way, DeYoung!" he'd whisper to give me a chance to avoid the

The Things You Do To Graduate
OC Canter and the author compete in the human wheelbarrow race.

torture CS gas inflicts on those who are not properly suited up.

Ranger week was actually a reverential experience in many ways. The real rangers, to include Al Catlett were quiet, but their intelligence was best revealed when they taught us how to move, how to scan the horizon, and how to respond to an enemy threat in complete silence. They obviously were amused by some of the philosophical conversations that the candidates engaged in. One Bostonian, a Democrat, was constantly defending liberalism, and linking the Army institution to the highest values the Democratic Party stood for. The rangers who overheard this banter would spit out their chaw, grin quizzically at each other, then conclude their observations by stuffing another wad of chaw in their jaws. The Bostonian waxed enthusiastically.

"Consider the Army, now. Every private gets paid the same no matter how much or how little they work. The Army isn't just a reflection of the Democratic Party. It's a reflection of the socialist system. We practice the same economic system in the Army that we are fighting in our enemy... Now wait. Consider... The larger the family, the larger the living space. We bring privates into the Army and provide their medical care, their child care, their housing. That's communism! We don't want socialized medicine in America, but we have it in the Army!"

This economics lesson went on for a day. Another rainstorm struck while our Bostonian classmate persisted in demonstrating the appeal of the Democratic Party's platform for guaranteed housing and national healthcare, to soldiers who seemed to think such guarantees were communist. The real rangers retreated to some covered stands until the storm subsided. They did not stop our female candidates from showering.

"You ladies will never have to do this again once you graduate," they'd grin as they excused our tendencies to put personal hygiene ahead of simulated tactical maneuvers or combat intelligence requirements.

I don't recall a single female officer who was insulted or who felt second class as a future lieutenant because we were subject to the combat exclusion policies. The rangers harbored no hostility against us. Their humor made us feel more accepted despite our physical limitations. Let's face it, if you don't think menstruating for five days in 104 degree weather while lugging a 55-pound pack, carrying 14 pounds of web gear and wearing combat boots and BDUs during round-the-clock field training is not unhealthy and undesirable, you haven't tried it. If you don't think menstruating during exercises replete with night live fire and forced road marches, and without benefit of running water or even regular access to porta-potties should not be a disqualifying limitation for real ground combat service — you never experienced the reality of menstruating while simulating ground combat. And for sure, you never experienced the real thing — real ground combat. I never heard a female trainee complain when the real rangers prefaced their training guidance with the proviso, "Ladies, you will never have to do this again once you are commissioned. Women are excluded from ground combat service. This is just a training exposure. Emphasis on exposure!" Their grins were quite reassuring.

Ranger Orientation week ended with a 12-mile road march from the field back to the company barracks. Despite our exhaustion, the giddiness of our accomplishments in the field actually made the road march a pleasant culmination. We knew when we got back to the barracks, we were one final inspection away from Senior Status. We would, unless we totally screwed up with a DUI or a psychotic break with reality, be commissioned before the month was out. All the guys in the platoon monitored their classmates with the concern of mother hens. They were strong men. They didn't mind spending their energy rushing to the front to slow down the march or shuffling to the rear to encourage the stragglers to catch up. Sergeants often say women are good road marchers because our center of gravity favors this kind of endurance sport. I liked to road march because the silence afforded long opportunities to meditate on the beautiful things of life. The hush of the troops made the sound of the butterflies ring out. The cows would moo their approval as we walked past their fields. Tall corn stalks towered over us when we walked aside some private fields. The blackberries beckoned, but road marching was no time to stop and pick berries. Georgia's red clay trails were painful to trudge through, but very pretty to look at. My peers were silent for most of the march, as I was. We basked in the warmth that would heal our painful joints, comforted with the knowledge that the worst hurdles were almost behind us. Any minute now, our gear would be scrubbed and put away with all of our anxieties. We would be dubbed worthy of all the privileges ladies and gentlemen in the officer corps aspired to.

Strangely, a mental paralysis set in just as we were within reach of our goal. The last quarter mile trek towards our company area felt as remote as home must have felt to Dorothy when she was blown away in a tornado. Our aches and pains seemed to intensify as we got closer to our final destination. When we marched into our assigned platoon area, we halted and upon command, we set our gear in front for inspection and weigh-in (to make sure no one cheated by under-packing their bags). Then we were given a moment to breathe with relief. The whole company hollered and hooted their joy. Then, the student company commander called the company to attention.

"The following individuals will remain in this formation after the platoons are released to their platoon areas: Abdullah, Hampton, deYoung, Alvira, etc. etc. etc."

What was this all about? Certainly, it was too soon to give out achievement medals to the company. We had one month before graduation.

Second Platoon hoisted their gear on their shoulders and hustled up the stairs. The student company commander repeated his roll call. Immediately afterward, one of the TAC officers announced that we had failed our Land Navigation retest. We had 24 hours to justify to the company commander our request to be "Retreads," that is, to be re-cycled for a second complete run through OCS.

All of us were stunned. We thought we minimally passed the test. I had already received a letter from the Adjutant General Corps advising me of my school date and my follow-on assignment to California. Although I was in shock, I had to muster my belongings and get back to the platoon area. As I climbed the steps, Lieutenant Van Delft was yelling and screaming at the top of her lungs all kinds of shrewish insults to the platoon I loved. I was a flight of steps away from our landing when I heard her yell.

"Where's deYoung? Where's Officer CANDIDATE DEYOUNGGGG??"
"I'M RIGHT HERE! I'M RIGHT HERE," I yelled back as I alighted from the staircase. Lieutenant Van Delft stared at me in disbelief. I had committed the ultimate act of disrespect, but she knew exactly what strain I was suffering. The other sure-to-graduate STRAK candidates chuckled and beamed rays of pleasure that I had the guts to fight back. They didn't realize I obviously had nothing to lose. I apologized, got down and did push ups. My classmates did push-up repentance right along side me. Van Delft continued to shriek and yell that Second Platoon would not go out for the weekend unless her standards were met. And obnoxious candidates like me were grounded for the weekend. She had no power over me. The TACs already informed all of the Land Nav flunkies we were grounded until the company commander made his decision about whom to recycle.

Meanwhile, Van Delft was inciting a rebellion in her platoon. One of the cadets who was most likely to end up the honors graduate was so angry at her insults, he was ready to punch her out. I called him into my room.

"It's not worth it. We're done. Let's just clean up this mess and ignore her."

That man calmed down and thanked me for my cool headedness. What goes round comes round, of course. He later rallied the platoon to support me as I tried to defend my right to re-cycle through the OCS program.

After the platoon was inspected and the senior candidates released for the weekend, Van Delft left me alone to begin writing my letter to Captain Miller. After dinner, she called me into her office.

"DeYoung," she started. "I know what you are going through right now, and I know that what you did was completely out of character. But you need to think about this. I can't ignore it, but I understand why you lost your cool. What are you going to do when you have to work for a really stupid colonel? You have to learn how to hide your intelligence. You can never afford to lose your cool, no matter how stupid your colonels are!"

I never expected her to give me this kind of advice.

"Now, I want you to write exactly 1,000 words on the importance of paying attention to detail and put it on my desk by noon tomorrow. And I want to see your letter to Captain Miller before you stand before him to defend your right to be commissioned."

We had no typewriters at OCS. There were no laptops. We had to write by hand, in flawless penmanship and with no errors. That gave a repentant candidate time to select each phrase with exceeding care. Somewhere in my analysis of attention to detail, I noted that officers should not expect to be respected unless they paid the same level of respect to their troops. I stated emphatically that officers who marched around and mooed like cows in front of their troops should expect to be treated like cows. Officers needed to pay attention to all the details: how they dressed, how they performed, how they acted. No doubt, the undisguised reference to the behavior of our infamous TAC would only sink my chances of being recycled. Whether I was committing an act of career suicide or ruthless honesty, I copied the final draft without changing a word.

At the appointed hour, my paper was dropped on Van Delft's desk. I thought for sure she would blast me out of the program. She proved me wrong again. I had guard duty that night. My task for the evening was to redraft a personal letter to the captain, begging his permission to let me retake the OCS course. That night, I sat down in the stairwell as fireguard, staring at my loose-leaf paper for hours. The halls were dead now that the candidates were allowed to come and go for the weekend. The TACs never stopped by to check on senior-status candidates. I sat for hours trying to concoct reasons for my continuation in the program. I couldn't come up with any. I finally wrote a letter of resignation, in which I suggested I was simply not fit to be an officer.

On Monday morning, Lieutenant Van Delft sat with the other TACs at the breakfast trap where they grilled candidates who were exiting the dining facility. She was giggling and playing with the other TACs. They were as happy as the students that our course was drawing to a close.

"DeYoung," she hollered as I tried to sneak out. "Where's your letter to Captain Miller?"

"Ma'am, I didn't write one."

"What do you mean you didn't write one? Why not?"

"Because, Ma'am, I don't deserve to be an officer candidate. I'm not going to be able to pass that test. I don't deserve a commission."

Van Delft stared at the other TACs in curious disbelief. "DeYoung," she whispered. You go back upstairs and you write that letter. Be in my office in one hour."

Who would have thought it? Lieutenant Van Delft had a heart. She took my letter when I reported to her office, suggested I include some of my accomplishments, including the two music programs I led, and told me to report to Captain Miller. She vowed to advocate for my retention, which she did. When I met with Captain Miller, he could barely contain his pleasure that I was willing to go through the program a whole second time. He approved my recycle papers.

Although I moved out of the company into a private room for recycles on the same day, as required, I stayed with my company to prepare them for graduation by playing the bass drum at their rehearsals. Lynda would wander over to visit me whenever there were breaks in the practice.

"DeYoung," she would say over and over. "I just can't believe you. You are grace under pressure. I think it is ungodly that they expect you to help with these practices. Even Catlett says you should be one of us. You are grace under pressure the way you are handling this!"

Actually, I loved all the folks in Second Platoon. I didn't know when I would ever see them again after graduation. I took every opportunity I could to spend time with them while the visiting was easy.

You could say I had bonded with my first OCS class, even if I wasn't going to graduate with them. The two women who made this happen, Lieutenant Van Delft and Lynda, were polar opposites in every way. I doubt I would have gotten through OCS to that point, or through my second trial by fire without their wisdom. Because even though we were not together as a platoon, even though Van Delft and Lynda were both lieutenants when I struggled to win the butter bars for the second time around, they still kept that female-bond. They made it their business to see me through.

Even though my first trial ended in failure, I did not believe OCS was a bad experience for me at all. OCS was a metaphorical purgatory, but the real experience bore no comparison to the movie depiction. I was prepared for harsh physical training, a cadre of inhumanly distant instructors and a program that would make me emotionally and physically tough. Physical training was just as Sergeant Metcalf promised: "nothing the average person can't do!" The cadre was excruciatingly strict when imparting the model of leadership and discipline they expected of OCS graduates. None of us, however, expected to see the human side of the cadre. We anticipated the steely black armor of Darth Vader. We didn't expect the cadre to be understanding or compassionate. But, as ugly as the cadre could be, their altruism was conveyed right at the moment when their discipline overwhelmed. I learned tremendously from the TACs as I learned from my friends.

CHAPTER 3

Redemption Is a Second Chance

Obviously, there was no possibility that I could redeem myself with a second chance in my marriage. How could I redeem the military experience? Even the privates who worked in the OCS supply room knew I would make a lousy enlisted soldier if I were to fail OCS altogether. Not much choice for me but to resolve to excel the second time through.

There was a break between classes, so the TACs encouraged me to take a week or two to get completely away. Rest. Sleep late. Recharge my batteries. Their only advice: "Make sure you keep up with your runs, deYoung. Keep up with the runs!"

My sister, Elizabeth, gave birth to her beautiful daughter, Alice, in San Francisco, California on the 17th of August. She was anticipating a move to Italy sometime after my permanent assignment to the Oakland Army Base. I eagerly flew to California to see Alice and Beeshie. We indulged in our early morning cappuccino orgies down at the local North Beach cafes that have all closed since. These big sunny rooms would fill with artists and writers who sat and sipped single cappuccinos for hours on end. Newspapers from around the country and from Italy were passed around. Classical symphonies and arias wafted from overhead speakers creating such a sense of peace.

Those morning klatches, when Beeshie and I would sit and vehemently disagree about every political subject under the sun were crucial to my revival. That, and Beeshie's instructions to me as a self-appointed housebound running coach to start every five mile run from her apartment on Chestnut by running straight up the steepest hills in the neighborhood. I did this until I could wake up in the morning and think of Heartbreak Hill as a mere pimple rather than the gaping open chest that erupted with the spasms of failed careers and broken hearts. God knows San Francisco's baby slopes far surpassed Benning's Heartbreaker in both grade and height. I never gained lightening speed when I ran the hills of San Francisco. Just the sure knowledge that endurance was a matter of attitude, not innate ability.

In addition to Beeshie's sage advice, my sister, Lucille, cheered me on with the motivational slogans she learned as an Army chopper pilot's wife. Lucille is highly competitive in the business world. She was relentless in her advice that I compete with the other officer candidates based on merit.

When I returned to the class of 5-83, many rules changed. There was now a 300 Club for candidates who maxed their physical training tests. All those who earned 300 points would be permitted to talk during meals. The "300 Club" would not be harassed by TACS as they exited the dining facility. This was enough to motivate me to max the tests from the very beginning.

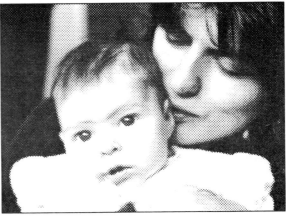

Two Of My Biggest Fans
Beeshie and her daughter, Alice. The photo reminded me of Beeshie's coaching advice.

I needed to talk about classes and world events during meals. Much was happening that year. The Iron Lady took over the Falklands Islands. We invaded Grenada. The Marine Barracks were bombed in Lebanon, inducing fear of mortality to the point of chronic constipation among many of the male candidates. Our chats weren't as fun as a feisty cafe debate with my oppositional sister, Beeshie. There wasn't a single memorable exchange that would illustrate the wit or philosophical depth of thinking among our leaders. In fact, the only exchange I will ever recall was with a Southerner with a thick accent who insisted I stop eating my fried chicken with a fork and knife.

"You are giving yourself away as a northerner," he boomed. "Pick up that chicken leg and chaw on it!"

At least, we enjoyed the stress relief that even casual conversation guarantees.

I suppose the TACs wanted to give all the retreads the best opportunity to succeed the second time around. We were sent to different platoons so that we could be supervised by new TAC officers. I was sent with Gwendolyn Hampton to the 4th Platoon. Our new TAC was an ROTC graduate, Lieutenant Dwight Bruce. In no time, we realized that our previous OCS TACs had brainwashed us into thinking that ROTC officers were ninnies. The "turn-backs" assigned to Bruce feared we were being set up for second failure. We had nothing to fear. First Lieutenant Dwight Bruce was no ninny. Dwight Bruce set no one up for failure, but he sure had fun scaring his candidates into success.

The platoon nicknamed Bruce "Cool Breeze," because he never lost his cool or his smile. He was not tall. He was not macho. He was not elitist in any way. But with his lacy eye lashes, he would mock smilingly to warn the platoon of the incoming rounds he was about to calmly lob into our routines to tighten up discipline or improve the cooperation among the candidates. If we just spent hours preparing our uniforms for inspection, it was his prerogative to conduct uniform drills. We stood by our doors and at his command, switched into dress uniforms in less than two minutes, or full BDU outfit in four. He would walk up and down the hallway, grinning at the devastation we wreaked on our flawlessly arranged rooms just to meet his fleeting standard of success: speed.

"Let's go, you don't have all day, the war will be over by the time you get those boots back on!"

His bark was superficial. We usually met the standard, only to have to spend the rest of the afternoon re-polishing boots, rank, and helmets to put them back into Bruce's less fleeting criteria for success: flawlessly arranged rooms.

Lieutenant Bruce made me a squad leader during orientation week. My success would be directly correlated to the number of squad members I saved from dismissal. My squad was filled with some pretty dinky guys who didn't seem to learn anything in basic training. Worse, they had no sense of urgency. Bruce gave us an hour or two for the men to have their uniforms squared away. If the men had their uniforms completely prepared with the correct patches and rank affixed, they could stay. If Bruce walked in their room and found improper uniforms, the men would be axed instantaneously. A hopeless prospect for men who didn't think it important to have their BDUs standing dress-right-dress in their closets.

Fortunately, one of our squad members, soft brown-eyed, Airborne Sam, was a patient STRAK 82nd Airborne sergeant who had the compassion of Jesus. I sneaked into his room and asked him to help me get the men squared away.

"What do you need?" he asked.

"Lieutenant Bruce expects their uniforms to be squared away in one hour. They say their uniforms are at the dry cleaners. They're pokey. Can you please double-time these guys up to the cleaners and make sure their uniforms are right?"

This extremely religious Southern Baptist who sat reading his Bible when he wasn't shining his boots or doing one-armed push-ups saluted me and quietly ran our guys through the paces. Nobody washed out while I was squad leader. Lieutenant Bruce grinned at me and complimented my leadership style. I always had Airborne Sam to thank when things went right. Over the months, I accumulated many images of Airborne Sam as he quietly took an ill-equipped classmate aside to help them improve their appearance or their outdoorsman skills. Many times in my career, I could recall Sam's example when I was tempted to avoid troublesome soldiers, or to cut my losses with undisciplined junior soldiers. Images of Sam countered any thought that time spent disciplining or retraining the newbies was time wasted.

My roommate was a very young woman named Diane Kisabeth. We never were close. Kisabeth ran like the wind, which made her an excellent candidate for platoon leader. She was very tiny and girlish. Although she was very smart, girlishness was her strategy for winning the men's support. We spent the Thanksgiving weekend together in a nice hotel in Atlanta, but I can't say there was anything but the convenience of being a roommate to that kind of socializing.

Father O'Keefe was not our chaplain anymore. We had a female chaplain named Donna Weddle. Donna was a Presbyterian, very easy to talk to about complex psychological issues. She came out to the field during our road marches to serve Kool Aid and cookies to our company. Father O'Keefe did not visit us once during my first venture at OCS. No one held it against him, though, because he broke his leg while learning how to jump out of airplanes shortly after our class started. Donna, on the other hand, drove to our sites in a truck, and displayed her gear as if she was marching with us. The guys in Fourth Platoon made a point of dragging our women over to Chaplain Weddle's rucksack which appeared to be plump with field gear. When we lifted it, the fact that it was stuffed with paper was obvious. I was embarrassed for Donna, but said nothing to the guys because she had already given me some good survival counseling that was working for me. I had already seen her do some fantastic counseling with our women. But, the lesson from our infantry classmates for all of us who were going to be real officers was unavoidable: If you are going to do it, be real and do it right. Otherwise, just let your weaknesses be known and avoid putting yourself in a situation where you will be ridiculed for your hypocrisy.

I was pretty mad at God during the early phases of class 5-83. I still didn't want my divorce to happen. Although I later realized I would be much happier as a single woman, at the time, it seemed like my world was not going to straighten out for a long time. Chaplains at OCS and throughout the military are always on the lookout for lost souls. Donna Weddle, the new 51st Company pastoral shepherd, asked me to play music for her Protestant service. Sadly, I couldn't bring myself to play for Protestant services because of my upbringing. I was taught to think ecumenically, but I wasn't ready to be ecumenical, fulfilling the common understanding that there is no such thing as a former Catholic — only a lapsed one. Father O'Keefe asked me to buy some guitars for his Catholic soldiers, which I gladly did. While shopping in the local music stores, I stumbled upon a beautiful Martin classical guitar. With no place to spend my money besides the beauty parlor and the Bombay Bicycle Club, I decided to plunk down half a pay check to get this lovely guitar.

Next thing you know, I was playing at Father O'Keefe's Catholic Masses on Sunday morning. Then, Captain Miller called me down to his office. He was going to hand his command over to Captain Michael Wagers. Before the transition, there were a number of community celebrations at which he wanted to showcase my musical talents. Would I volunteer? Lieutenant Van Delft made it very clear to me before I parted from her supervision that I had to learn how not to volunteer for activities that would impede my professional success.

"DeYoung, you have to learn how to set limits. When your work is squared away, then you can go off and do these other things. When your work is behind, you CAN'T volunteer!"

I asked Captain Miller, whom I had really come to love and respect, "Sir, are you asking me to volunteer, or is this a rhetorical question for which the only answer I am supposed to give is, Yes?"

"I'm asking. This is strictly a voluntary tasking." I stared him down until he turned his gaze sideways. He had his commission. I couldn't afford to be left behind in the ranks of the PFCs.

"Sir, you know as well as I do that music had something to do with my flunking Land Nav!"

"Officer Candidate deYoung, Land Navigation is the only thing you have to pass to graduate! You are excelling everywhere else!"

"Right! But if I flunk Land Nav, will I graduate?'

"No."

"Sir, the test is just a few weeks away. Let me pass that Land Nav test. Then, I'll sing in a concert every night, whenever you want. Please. I have to pass Land Nav."

"Deal. Whatever equipment you need. Whatever rehearsal time. Just work it out with the sergeant major..." Captain Miller had a pragmatic spirit of compromise that I've seen again and again in my favorite supervisors. Good teachers will tell you they learn as much from their students as they teach. If I taught Captain Jeffrey Miller anything, it was simply that there was no correlation between human intelligence and land navigation ability. He promised and proceeded to coach me whenever we went out for training, because by God, this time, I was going to pass Land Navigation. He never complained about my obtuseness when it came to distinguishing terrain features on the map. I could name the things I saw on land, but I couldn't correlate the sunny side up egg hills on the map with the terrain feature we call a saddle or the eight or ten v-shaped lines with a valley.

No offense to the many teachers and classmates who outdid themselves to help me to see the light. On this test, it was only with the help of God that I passed, Yes, I passed, but barely. The fact that our first test was late in the fall when the leaves had fallen sufficiently for us to look left and right was certainly an advantage. We didn't have to dead reckon, even at night. We could see our marked sticks sometimes as much as 150 meters away from a clearly defined terrain feature. During the previous two tests, bushy leaves beat us in the face as we tried to push our way down non-existent trails to touch our markers before we could actually see them in the distance. Al Catlett, was right. You had to be extremely competent to pass a Fort Benning Land Nav test in June or July because the brush was so thick. In October or November, luck and logic played a greater part in our success or failure. Al promised me I'd pass the second time around if OCS was just smart enough to schedule the graded test when nature would cooperate and give us the advantages of dry terrain and far-reaching visibility.

I passed, but Kisabeth failed her first test, but not for lack of ability. Diane Kisabeth was completely unaccustomed to failure. She missed by only a few points, and most likely, because she heeded some ignorant advice from classmates rather than her own level-headed calculations. She was in tears when she saw her score. Lieutenant Bruce reassured her that she would surely pass the makeup test.

As soon as our grades were posted, I ran to Captain Miller's office to thank him and to finalize our concert plans. My singing partner, Julius Abdullah and a couple of other musicians were excused from afternoon details to practice a whole repertoire of folk and country tunes. We had a number of talented musicians eager to skip the mindless and futile grass cutting. We signed on as many as we could.

No sooner than our grades were made public than our company started large indoor classroom instruction in nuclear, biological and chemical warfare. Major Rankin, a handsome, wiry Vietnam veteran was the instructor. This man had the pacing energy of a caged lion. He could not teach unless the class was electrified. In his first class, he asked all the women officer candidates who flunked land navigation to raise their hands. About eleven women raised their hands. "Guys," Rankin teased.

"Guys, you know why these women flunked Land Navigation? Because you guys failed to teach these women just how far ten inches is!"

The men were at first embarrassed, but then hooted with laughter when Rankin urged their response. He told a few more jokes of that ilk.

The women to the left and to the right of me were in tears. The more they cried, the more sexist Rankin's routine became. I was incensed. Rankin's jokes violated every principle Captain Miller and the EO officers instilled about sensitivity and respect for all the people who wear the uniform. We were not allowed to talk in the hallways during this phase of training. All the women stormed into the bathroom. The flunkeys were still weeping. I insisted that we should speak out, demand that Major Rankin retract his jokes. My classmates cowered in fear.

"No, deYoung, he'll just make it worse! We can't afford to flunk out..."

Another class hour went by. More rank jokes. More tears and displays of cowardice by the women. Another dispute in the bathroom.

"We've got to say something! He'll never stop if we let him keep this up!"

"DeYoung, just shut up," the women retorted.

My commission was guaranteed. I knew how they felt. I resolved not to instigate any action unless the women spoke up for themselves.

Major Rankin called on me shortly after the class resumed, but only after he told another crude joke at the expense of women. I had no choice but to follow Captain Miller's training guidance, which was to disrupt every public or private display of intolerance by American soldiers. I stood up.

"Sir, I cannot participate in this class so long as you continue to tell jokes that degrade women. As soldiers in the Army we are responsible for upholding the dignity of every man and woman who wears the uniform. Your jokes are not only degrading to the officer candidates in this room, they are degrading to all female soldiers and women in our society!"

The men roared with ridicule that I would dare to confront Major Rankin so publicly.

Our TAC officers, as usual, were behind a glass panel, observing every interaction, every potential display of leadership or cowardice in the room. I don't know if they cued Major Rankin to curtail his rabid humor, but he did tuck in his tail just a tad. His rejoinder went something like this: "Well, Officer Candidate deYoung, if you're so committed, get down and do push ups. Twenty. Oh no! We know women can't do push ups! Give me five!" The men cackled at Rankin's frank disdain for the average Army woman's performance. Women at OCS were different, however. We were not allowed to play the minimum game. I got down and gave him 20 Marine push-ups, by Rankin's own assessment.

Rankin wasn't done with me. He called me to the front of the classroom. Allegedly, he had me demonstrate the non-masked way to keep poison gas out of the eyes, nose, etc. I stood there looking ridiculous, but blind to the obscene gestures he performed to the class in front of both of us. On this point, I am not sure he would have done anything differently if his demonstrator was a male candidate. Most hardcore soldiers will tell you ridiculous demonstrations and obscene humor is often a good motivator of men — seldom impacting their self-esteem or sense of belongingness.

Whatever Rankin did while I was not able to watch, he incensed about eight fundamentalist Christian soldiers — four men and four women. They filed sexual harassment complaints against the major on my behalf and on behalf of the eleven other women who were repeatedly ridiculed in classes.

The women whose careers were in jeopardy were not pleased at all by the chivalrous actions of our Christian classmates. The women blamed me for filing formal charges, which I never did. I did, however, after much prayer and pacing back and forth, put a note in the commander's suggestion box, alerting him to the fact that his model Army company, where men and women would treat each other with the utmost respect was being completely savaged by Major Rankin's insults. I pointed out that the captain's total commitment to equal opportunity was completely undermined by the really racist and sexist jokes Rankin encouraged another male candidate to tell.

Captain Miller never read the note, because he turned his company over to the new commander shortly after I stuffed it in the red suggestion box. But when Captain Michael Wagers read it, he called a special company formation in our large courtyard. He recounted stories of horrible discrimination in the Army. He, too, was a Vietnam Veteran. He recounted the heroism of black, Hispanic and Asian soldiers, as well as the heroism of WACS who served in 'Nam. He insisted there was absolutely no place for sexual harassment in the United States Army. Wagers, like Captain Miller before him, emphatically stated he simply would not tolerate any officer candidate who harassed, ridiculed, or insulted other human beings because of their race, ethnicity, religion, or gender.

What followed was a generic lesson in group dynamics and leadership that really had nothing to do with sexual harassment per se. Most of the men in 51st company except the men in my platoon, and all of the women, to include my roommate Diane Kisabeth, shunned me for speaking out about the sexual harassment. No question then or now that the women failed to stand for their own dignity because they were afraid. They blamed me for the charges that were being brought against Major Rankin. Frankly, I've learned from many disparate military and civilian situations, if the problem was stolen nuclear material, or gun running for the IRA, the enmeshed group reaction would most likely have been the same. Soldiers just don't like to have their mischief and misdeeds brought to light. And, when they act in groups, they tolerate more mischief and more misconduct because they fear mob retaliation. That's why the Army and other military institutions will always have to monitor the sensitivity, the attitudes and behaviors of soldiers — to be certain that gang-like or Aryanist initiation rites don't take on a life of their own.

Major Rankin was no Aryanist. He was not sexist. He bluntly stated time and again that he expected all of the men and women from his class to be thoroughly skilled to survive the hell of guerrilla and NBC warfare. I never took his ribbing personally, because at some deep level, I knew his message was not about gender hostility but about battlefield survival. Even so, in a highly diverse modern Army, one can never leave the problem of racial and gender balkanization out of the communication process.

The shunning lasted right up to graduation day. The TAC officers, especially Lieutenants Bruce and Van Delft reassured me that my outspokenness was a sign of a leader, not a sign of a squealer or a whistleblower. All of the women who were called to give written statements consistently asked the investigating officer not to consider greater sanctions against Major Rankin than a formal demand that he cease and desist his sexist jokes. I put in my statement that in every other respect, Major Rankin was a fine officer who just needed to conform to the new equal opportunity policies. Since Rankin was a combat survivor, I couldn't imagine why the Army would possibly consider anything more than a slap on the wrist to make this war hero comply with new equal opportunity standards.

By this time, my friend Lynda was off to her officer basic course. She heard about the episode from our classmates who were now in the Infantry Officer Basic Course. Incredibly, those guys would stop by during free time to cheer me on, and encourage me to stick to my convictions. Lynda sent me reassuring notes, mostly in German. She herself was the victim of a vicious rumor which she managed to squelch, but the story hurt her tremendously.

The shunning hurt some, but I was very preoccupied with shows and concerts to invest too much of myself in my classmates' response. Captain Miller thought it would be terrific if our band marched out to the field with our platoons, then came back all grimy and sweaty to take the stage for a community farewell dinner. We did. I sang John Denver's, "Annie's Song," which was great so long as you were sitting at least twenty feet from our stench. Julius and I sang "Rocky Top" and "Lay Me Down." At some point, we brought the show to a close with "Country Roads." Our commanders loved us. The Battalion XO sneaked outside to give us some forbidden treats — canned sodas. These glory moments took away most of the sting of peer rejection for speaking up about Major Rankin. Right before Christmas, Gwen Hampton, Julius Abdullah and I were asked to stand on an Army float while singing Christmas carols with my guitar. That tasking put us in the freezing cold for about six or seven hours, but it got us out of the barracks long enough to stop at Shoney's for huge ice cream desserts.

Sometime in the fall, my divorce decree came through. I took it down to the First Sergeant of the company, because the judge required review by a military attorney before he would finalize it. The first sergeant, who often quizzed me on leadership issues and my grasp of day-to-day military problems worried out loud that my decree was economically unfair. When I visited with the JAG attorney, he read the decree. He expressed the same concern. He told me I was entitled to much more than I would get: debt relief, an almost dead VW station wagon, raggedy furniture and the grand piano I bought with cold cash. And why was I paying my soon-to-be ex a monthly BAQ payment? Well, Al helped out significantly with my education once I moved to Kansas City. In fact, I would never have accomplished my music conducting programs without his tremendous emotional and financial support. The airlines were constantly laying off executives. He was on hard times, from which he was only beginning to recover, and I would do quite well, if I earned my commission. I was really glad to have the divorce behind me as I could see a bright future in the Army officer corps. But, I did shed a few farewell tears as I negotiated that last piece of paper that would mark an end to husband-support payments and our marriage. The first sergeant and my TAC officer just let me alone whenever I needed to go off for a good cry.

Ranger Week proved to be the biggest test of my leadership and of the real character of the men in class 5-83. At one point, I was tasked by the ranger sergeants to lead a platoon of more than 40 men through a moonless, heavily canopied forest. Night movements were to be conducted in absolute silence with light and noise discipline from beginning to end. I asked Doug Nicolay, who could dead reckon if he was blindfolded, to be the point man for our night march. This gentleman and I spent another night digging a foxhole together. I didn't have the winter gear the rest of the guys had, since I started OCS in June. Nicolay pulled out one of his extra jackets to make sure I was warm enough when it was his turn to shovel and mine to stand guard. I knew Nicolay would carefully guide us to our retrograde destination.

Robert Manos was a tall, lanky prior service engineer who had a fetish for the RTO. He grinned when I asked him to lug that heavy radio box. By his twinkling smile, you would have thought managing "the commo" for my only platoon leadership exercise was the same as getting into heaven.

The ranger instructors pulled their usual stunts, eventually breaking up our platoon. I sat my group down in place. Since he was our most experienced outdoorsman I asked Airborne Sam to back-trace our steps. For this exercise, our platoon was expanded to include some of the guys who were shunning me, but you would never have known they were upset with me. They followed my instructions, and responded to my team leaders, as well. When Sam sent forward the hand signals to let me know our platoon was completely reunited, I did a front-to-back walk around, then moved us forward to our designated rallying point. When we stopped, the ranger instructors said I was hit by a simulated mine. It was now time for AJ to assume leadership. I could finally relax.

AJ settled the platoon for a couple of hours sleep on the frozen ground. Retreads weren't sent back to the central supply for winter gear so I was never issued "snivel gear." I was the only retread who lacked prior service, so it never occurred to me to run out and buy things like wool sweaters or thermal underwear. That night, I shivered beyond control. After AJ got everybody else bedded down on the frozen leaves and protruding rocks, he broke all the OCS rules about mixed-gender touching. AJ lay down on top of me and wrapped himself around me. My previous memory of AJ's courage occurred on a day when the sick-call physician gave him a complete day of bed-rest. A TAC officer, Lieutenant DeMarco asked AJ what he thought he was doing, lying on his bed mid-day.

"Sir," AJ responded with a cavalier stare, "common sense would tell you, I am sick!"

All hell broke out on our platoon floor until Cool Breeze stepped in to discreetly assert his ultimate authority over the commonsensical Fourth Platoon.

As I remember, AJ was already a married man, a fine Southern gentleman. I had nothing to worry about as far as sexual abuse was concerned when he volunteered to be my human blanket. Besides, I was so exhausted, I fell asleep as soon as I was warm enough to stop shivering. In my opinion, AJ saved my life that night. Thirteen years later, if the same thing happened, some well-intentioned but ignorant non-military gender cop would have pressured the female candidate to accuse her helpmate of sexual assault. Today I can easily imagine a candidate bringing someone like AJ up on charges, because ignorant public figures are blurring the intelligent lines of distinction between harassment and necessary contact for the sake of teamwork or survival.

That night the only assault I feared was the creep of hypothermia. When we awoke, dawn was just about to make her appearance. The ranger trainers called off the exercise. We sat around on the side of a hill, boasting of our exploits, trading food. I traded all my C-ration cans that had meat or tuna for peanut butter or canned fruit salad. Once I had my peanut butter crackers and cocoa all set up, I was happy. An older ranger instructor sauntered over to me. He took off his cap and said in a slow Southern drawl, "Ma'am, you are the most stable person I have ever met!" He never explained himself. He never let on that the platoon breakup was intended, or that it was perfectly okay for AJ to treat me like one of the guys by tucking me in his arms to keep my body temperature above hypothermia levels. For the life of me, I couldn't figure out how this ranger could tell one candidate from the other in such pitch dark training conditions. But rangers can always tell. So, I accepted his compliment and offered him a precious peanut butter cracker.

Late in the fall, we took a physical training test that both Kisabeth and I easily maxed. Woe to us, one of the men challenged the TAC who had the timer. He insisted the TAC's clock was wrong during the run. It was. No problem, the TACs decided. All of us would retest immediately after lunch. Now, in the real Army, it is against regulations to retest a soldier on the same day. But who ever said Officer Candidate School had anything to do with the real Army? All of us moaned about the punishment, but we smartly selected very light lunches. Kisabeth and I both ate rice with brown gravy. Amazingly, we maxed the text for the second time in one day. Kisabeth passed her makeup Land Navigation test, which put our relationship back on track. We resumed a casual friendship. She had nothing to fear now that her graduation was virtually assured. She had no reason to continue to freeze me out. I just didn't have any reason to welcome her back in. Elegantly casual seemed to be the best course to follow.

One friend whom I will always treasure, Gary McKenna, became a turn-back. He had the same doubts about his worthiness that I had when I flunked Land Nav for the second time. It was my turn to encourage a classmate to just put his trust in God and give OCS a second try. I encouraged him to trust Captain Miller to support his request for a recycle. Once Gary was recycled, he lived across the courtyard for part of our class, waiting for the next 50th Company class to start. When Gary toured Korea, he sent me a photo of the really handsome officers in his company. I bumped into him more than once when we were assigned to the same remote posts and to Korea. He never lost his integrity.

OCS Class 5-83 cruised to senior phase, thinking we would be entitled to all kinds of lax and special treatment. Not with our new commander, Captain Wagers. Michael Wagers was a Vietnam veteran. As long as he was in command, soldiers were going to run, march, practice Land Nav, and don their chemical warfare suits. In his estimation, Senior Phase was just a period when we earned a modicum of our civil rights back. Otherwise, we would train, train, train.

The candidates' anger at the progress of Rankin's Article 32 hearings increased, too. They continued to vent their ridicule and hostility towards me, but usually in very superficial, impersonal ways. If the gender war is vicious now, back then it was a mere conflict, the product of confusion about gender roles. Many of the men who shunned me when they were in a group came to me privately with sincere questions.

"DeYoung, if you are against sexual harassment, how can you sing a song like "Lay me down," at a show?"

To me, the difference between sexual harassment and singing a love song was clear. I realized later the men were having problems with the fact that my singing partner was a black man.

Whether or not Class 5-83's shunning of me was partly due to an unexpressed anger that I sang love songs with a black male candidate, I won't know. But, to the end, and only until the end of our class, most of the men and women shunned me expressly for speaking up to Major Rankin about his gender harassment. The guys in my platoon never took sides in the issue, but they were clearly embarrassed at times that fourth platoon got so much attention due to Officer Candidate deYoung's big mouth! The TAC officers continued to pull me aside on occasion to remind me that the whole experience was one big case of artificially induced stress. I knew the game was over when Captain Pesko, a tall meticulous TAC, stared down a couple of guys who started some half-hearted razzing during graduation rehearsal. As we waited on the stairs for the Army Band to march into its performance area, Pesko looked over at me, and quietly said, "Officer Candidate deYoung, this will be all over and forgotten in a few days. It will all be over..."

The men beside me were too inexperienced to understand the import of his remark, but Pesko had a way of encouraging candidates to be ethical by reminding them the price they would pay for doing the right thing would usually never be that great. The investigating officer called me in to sign typed versions of the statements I originally gave to him. I never asked him the outcome and he never provided information about Major Rankin's status.

"On behalf of the United States Army," he soberly closed his folder. "I would like to apologize for all soldiers who wear the uniform. What you experienced was an aberration. I can assure you most of the men in the Army will not behave the way Major Rankin did. Please accept the apologies of the United States Army and know that we will do everything in our power to avoid a repetition of this kind of behavior."

As far as I was concerned, the Rankin case was closed. I already knew the episode was an aberration, because most of my instructors and classmates were perfectly professional in their demeanor and treatment of other soldiers.

January 14, 1984. Our class marched into the Infantry School auditorium to the stride of Rocky's Fanfare, compliments of the Fort Benning Army Band. We were the first generation of military officers, as our commencement speaker, General Cavazos reminded us, who would go to war without the benefit of senior combat veteran leadership. Upon graduation our group, swelled with the cocky pride inspired by Hollywood pugilist fantasies, would soon face international threats to democracy and world peace with the arrogance of schoolyard bullies who never had to fight with blokes our own size. We, as book smart lieutenants would embark on global rescue missions, Cavazos prophesied, with the confident belief that our bombs and stealth planes would protect us from physical harm with the same invincible dependability as the Batmobile or Superman's impenetrable suit of armor.

As a veteran of several brutal wars, General Cavazos firmly disabused us of our exuberant fantasies of superhuman power in his commencement speech. He drummed in the message, "War is Hell" with stories of the brutality, the tears that fighting men shed when they live in the midst of the horror of combat. More than a few of our candidates wept when Cavazos spoke in solemn low tones about our sacred duty to be morally righteous, ever vigilant and always, always prepared, fit, and highly trained, to take our men into battle at the beck and call of our civilian leaders.

After his address, individual officer candidates came forward to swear before God and country to uphold their oaths of office. I was one of six female candidates who asked Chaplain Donna Weddle to witness our sworn oaths. Other candidates had their parents, friends or past Army bosses welcome them to the officer corps. We sat through so many rehearsals, so many advisory sessions with senior leaders to prepare us for the sobriety of this moment. Voila! After repeating a 30-second pledge, we were ready to assume the mantle of leadership.

Our graduation moment of glory was too brief, it seemed. OCS had its own tradition to accommodate that feeling. With our pockets full of silver dollars, we tossed our hats into the air with shouts of "hallelujah!" and then went out of our way to encounter officer candidates from the new class who were just finishing their orientation week. Their crisp salutes were rewarded with our shiny coins and irrepressible grins of hope and encouragement. These candidates were 15 weeks away from victory. We were their living testimony they would make it through.

We Graduated!
The Fourth Platoon Poses for Graduation. (First row: Marie deYoung, Diane Kisabeth, Airborne Sam Murray and Gwen Hampton.)

CHAPTER 4

Uncle Ben's Rest Home

Our new class was quite a motley group. We had reserve officers from Guam, the Bronx, New York and Puerto Rico. At the same time, we had at least a dozen OCS graduates. The National Guard lieutenants acted as if their units were completely independent of external authority of any sort. If you believed some of these guys, Uncle Bubba, the state commander, was the only person to whom they were accountable for personal conduct, appearance and performance. They owed no allegiance to the active duty army, or to the federal constitution. A decade later, when I attended the Fort Monmouth chaplain basic course, chaplains from the National Guard had the same attitude. Some things are hard to change!

We had two professional football players in our class. Stump Mitchell, a Citadel graduate was playing for the St. Louis Cardinals. And Sid Abramowitz, who played for the Baltimore Colts that same year. Sid was interviewed by television reporters in class because his team moved from Baltimore to Indianapolis while we were in school.

Some of our classmates had law degrees and Ivy League degrees. Some could barely read and write. The Army, to defend itself against far fetched claims of unfairness required all lieutenants to take a course in basic English. The self-teaching text had little frames describing the basic elements of the language, with pages and pages of exercises built around the simple construction, "Birds fly." This simple idea was used to teach the meaning of subject, verb, subject verb agreement, tense, the KISS writing principle, the use of modifiers, and even the types of clauses one could construct in English.

Needless to say, our class was not happy with this portion of our training. Imagine having a law degree or a BA from Yale, and being required to sit and parse the sentence, "birds fly" for days on end. Despite complaints to the class instructor, no one was exempted from this remedial training that was designed to ensure a literate officer corps or at the least, to protect the English instructors' jobs in perpetuity. Our only recourse was to develop a class motto, which we could sing in protest of all the themes that were inculcated during that idyllic period. The cheering of class mottoes was an innocuous way to build class spirit. Our OCS motto was, "Lean, mean, fit to fight! Fifty-first is dynamite!" Uncle Ben's Rest Home did not retire from that tradition although so much else about the school was distinctively un-military. Whenever an instructor walked into class, we were required to sing a class motto. Our class protest was choreographed. One half of the room got up to recite the first line, the second half jumped up to recite the second. We sang and waved our arms:

Birds fly!

Eagles soar!

Managers of Violence

2-84!

(And much, much more!)

Uncle Ben's Rest Home was the most apt nickname. Most of our classes were useless and utterly boring. Thank God, the Army's personnel and administrative management program was streamlined and automated. Not soon enough, however. For the three months we attended Uncle Ben's Rest Home, we snoozed through long blocks of instruction designed to help us distinguish between the hundreds, if not thousands of formats required for military correspondence. In those days, the manuals required different correspondence formats for such similar tasks as requesting additional personnel or requesting new computer equipment. You could count on a bureaucrat to reject the most urgent of requests if the incorrect format was used to petition for supplies or emergency leave for a soldier. So, technically, the information covered was very, very important to our success. But, Lord, those formats were stultifying to read and positively discouraging of any commitment to the Adjutant General Corps.

Fortunately, our class boredom was broken up with 40-hour blocks of instruction in matters that were more interesting to thinking young adults. We spent 40 hours studying military ethics, focusing on the moral weaknesses of the military leadership that contributed to failure in Vietnam. Another 40 hours on military tactics. Of course, we went to the field for a week to practice infantry tactics. And no Army training course would be complete without a daily regimen of physical training.

We had one field exercise, during which we saw replicas of Viet Cong tunnels. Springtime in Indiana is perfect for marksmanship. The combat arms cadre took us out to shoot off some machine gun rounds, and act out infantry maneuvers in perfectly sculpted clearly defined terrain features. The men who taught us the combined arms classes supervised our tested field experience. One senior officer prefaced all of his instructions with the comment, "generally, usually, normally, but not always..." Another man constantly railed against the Army's plans to computerize the battle field.

"When that electro-magnetic pulse (EMP) destroys your computer, just listen, lieutenants, in real combat, we are going to be the stubby pencil army! You have to know how to do things by hand... You aren't going to have any computers on the battlefield... at least, they aren't going to be working..."

How prescient! In 1999, the Army still fields computerized tanks and operation centers that tend to become dysfunctional in the heat of merely simulated battles!

We completed officer basic in an era when the Army treated soldiers and faculty like they were all grown up. Imagine! Our faculty, including the men who taught combined arms were allowed to socialize with us at the club. One evening as I sat with the senior instructor for combined arms, I talked over my experiences of Major Rankin, the man who harassed female officer candidates during OCS 5-83. I pointed out that all of the persons required to testify against him believed that Major Rankin was not malicious in his behavior. He was crudely and rudely making the point that war is hell, and that you had no place going there if you weren't fully prepared to beat great odds against death. I felt that his chauvinism, however perversely, was rooted in a desire to protect women from the horrors of the real battlefield. There were not many women in the Army besides the few OCS and West Point graduates who were willing to train as rigorously to maintain a combat ready state. Why should we go into situations where we were physically unprepared to stand to the test?

The senior ranking combat arms officer stared into his drink before he responded to my reflections. This man never said an ungentlemanly thing in class or in the club, so I did not know what to expect.

"You know, when I was in Vietnam," he began quietly. "We saw all kinds of unspeakable things. In one village, I saw a woman who was attacked by the Viet Cong for being a U.S. sympathizer. They shoved a tank round up her vagina. As horrible as this is, I took a photograph of that dead woman's mangled body. I still have that photograph, and I will never lose it. Because no one could ever believe such a thing could happen unless you had seen it..."

He stared back into his drink and nodded again as I repeated my assertions that my experience of men who were hostile about taking American women onto the battlefield was a mixed one.

So far as I had experienced to that point, the men deeply respected the women whom they razzed and even befriended, but they seemed to be anguished to the core about exposing women to the horrendous trauma of battle. In their minds, "creating a hostile work environment," which is now an illegal form of sexual harassment could easily be construed as an act of kindness — moving women away from the bizarre hell that infantrymen face. You could understand how a combat vet might think that if the women couldn't even stomach peer harassment, then how in God's name could women handle themselves in the face of fighting hostilities?

We didn't have to worry about sexual harassment as an impediment to graduation from the AG basic course. It was almost impossible to fail any class at Uncle Ben's Rest Home. One young lady was having some kind of emotional problem, which she never seemed to overcome. She was afraid she would not be accepted onto active duty. She overdosed on aspirin. Of course, she was not rewarded with an active duty assignment for her performance, but she did graduate with her butter bars in tact.

Another young man failed to do physical training, even though he had a leadership position. He managed to track down some steroids, thinking he could pass the running test if he only took a few magic pills. Of course, he passed out. After he recovered and trained for a few weeks, he passed just by running his slowest pace.

The AG basic course was a picnic compared to OCS or the Infantry Basic course my OCS buddies were attending. Unless we were in the field, we put in eight hour days. Late in the afternoon, we changed into running clothes, and leisurely ambled about in physical training to stave off obesity, or at least to ward off the complete disrespect of junior soldiers. Most of the reservists who were in our group were quite unfit, leaving the OCS grads to wonder in amazement that the Army could throw out perfectly fine officer candidates for walking up a steep hill at Fort Benning. At Uncle Ben's Rest Home, reserve officers often couldn't do a straight push up or run two miles without stopping. Of course, it never occurred to us that OCS was too strict. We rather arrogantly concluded that the ROTC commissioning program and the AG officer basic course were both one big joke.

But the issue of physical fitness was complex at the Army's training center for staff weenies. Many professional athletes were assigned to the AG Corps. Surprisingly, they couldn't do Army PT either. One woman, Bambi, was an Olympic Triathlon winner. She could ski, shoot, sling arrows and dance from sunset until early dawn, but she was on a perpetual profile that exempted her from running and daily training. So, on the one hand, you could criticize her for not being a team player in our class, but you could not accuse her of being unfit. Same with the two professional football players in our class. I never saw Sid Abramowitz run two miles. The man was a perfect gentleman, but with his tall 250 pound body, I wouldn't want to get in a tangle with him. Stump Mitchell ran with me for several miles one day, making me feel exceedingly important to be able to keep pace with a professional football player. As usual, I ran much slower than most of the men, but I was plenty fast for Stump Mitchell, because professional football players don't run long distances very well. As we ran, Stump asked me to touch his neck, which felt like a 15-inch-thick band of steel. Stump stressed that his lifelong training habits were the source of his strength. I admired his professionalism, especially the metallic grit he acquired at the Citadel, but I was extremely grateful that as a woman, I would never bulk up the way he did — no matter how many pushups I could do.

Shortly after our physical training test, when another lieutenant fainted from the excess steroids he consumed, Stump Mitchell left the school. More than once he complained about our lack of discipline, about what a joke our class was compared to the Citadel, where he earned his commission. Of course, OCS graduates had similar complaints, but we couldn't look forward to million dollar football contracts, so, we just stayed with Uncle Ben until our forced rest and relaxation period was over. Stump somehow realized he was wasting his time. He stood in front of the formation, boasted once again of the standards the Citadel instilled in him, and encouraged us to be more serious. It was just as hard for serious lieutenants from OCS 5-83 to take the AG Corps seriously as it was for Stump. The best strategy, actually, was to not be so serious. There was plenty of time to party and plenty of classy restaurants around town where you could dance to the light pop recordings spun by local DJs. Since Uncle Sam paid lieutenants about $33 per day to eat at Uncle Ben's Rest Home, we had plenty of money to go out on the weekends. And we did.

Leslie Rich was one of my OCS classmates who had gone through two cycles, just as I did. He failed Land Nav just as I did, but he was a marathon cross-country runner. I still don't understand how he failed, because Leslie was exceedingly fond of nature. He was a fast runner. We never really talked, but he would smile sweetly during class discussions. He was fun to be around. When class 5-83 started to shun me, Leslie would invite me to join him for local running races. One race was a midnight barbecue run, where we ran for three miles through Columbus, Georgia to the final reward: tables full of rib racks and kegs of beer. I think he got our company involved in the Infantry Museum Run, which was a delightful Saturday morning run around the gardens on post. At Indianapolis, running conditions were absolutely perfect. The days were usually cool, not too sunny. No pollen or mold to impede breathing. The trails were almost flat. Perfect for cross-country runs. Leslie invited me to a couple of runs. One benefited the Heart Association. I can still recall the run by neighborhood creeks and through boulevards and gardens that had dirt running trails paved alongside. Leslie was a gem of a human being. His running was a path to beauty, that he knew how to share with friends who needed that kind of uplift once in awhile.

Most of the single officers paired off for the duration of the course. To my surprise, many of the married officers also paired off. One woman, a daughter of a colonel and spouse of another lieutenant explained the phenomenon of TDY "secondary" relationships.

"We can't expect our spouses to be faithful with so much travel and separation. We have agreements with our spouses. So long as we are discreet, and we practice safe sex, we don't want to know what the other is doing. Out of respect for your spouse, you are discreet, and you just don't rub it in their faces. You never talk about it. But you always, always have to make it clear to your spouse that they are your primary partner..."

I was newly divorced. I began a brief relationship with another divorced older lieutenant who was a great conversationalist, a terrific man. When he was with me, he was very devoted. Another woman, a reservist spent much time advocating for a perverse form of feminism. To her, it was very important that women wear the exact amount of brass as the men. She was quite right to advocate for the right of women to wear the exact same brass configuration as men. She railed against men's right to wear two branch insignia, two U.S. insignia, where women could only wear one each. I had no problem with this. I could not understand, however, her push to earn women's entitlement to be just as promiscuous as men were.

Lieutenant R often boasted the egalitarian modern nature of her reserve battalion. She claimed she smoked pot with the battalion commander, slept with all the officers although she was enlisted until her arrival at Uncle Ben's. She railed against men who had scoring contests and insisted women should hold the same scoring contests to prove their equality. She vowed to sleep with at least ten men while she was at Uncle Ben's. Perhaps on Easter Sunday, or some other April Sunday morning, we held a very elegant brunch to celebrate our success as a class. The morning culminated in a celebrity roast of our peers. We had several in the class. At one point, one of the professional football players asked for Lieutenant R's "Perfect 10" to please stand up. After many uncomfortable stares, ten men stood up, to include the man whom I thought of as my companion.

I was too inexperienced to be anything but embarrassed that I had participated in a relationship with a man who was really only in it for the casual fun. He was extremely apologetic to me for the rest of our course, but I really couldn't get too enthusiastic about him or the temporary duty (TDY) mode of relationships. Nowadays, women, even officers, will file charges against a lover (male or female) when they realize they were two-timed. In their rage at being humiliated or deceived, they will march into a commander's office and allege sexual harassment or assault, or just plain adultery to make their pain and humiliation felt.

You may recall the young female naval officer who foolishly made love with her officer boyfriend on a ship. When the boyfriend started showing their secret video tapes to his friends, she turned herself in, and forced the command to prosecute both of them for sexual misconduct.

I don't think adultery or promiscuity, or even non-marital casual sex is wise, but I do believe the advice given by our basic training female drill sergeants should still hold. We would have saved the American taxpayer hundreds of millions of dollars of sexual misconduct investigations in the 1990s, if we just followed the drill sergeants basic formula: If you are woman enough to soldier and you are woman enough to participate in an act of adultery or fraternization, then you'd better be woman enough to keep it to yourself. Real women don't tell. Or if they do, they insist that they should be held equally responsible for the irresponsible acts committed.

Right before we graduated, Colonel Myrna Williamson, who was our brigade commander, gathered all the female students together for a mentoring session. When she finished command, she would pin on her first star. She made it her responsibility to call in the women assigned to her Brigade for an occasional mentoring session.

Colonel Williamson was a gray-haired, tall gracious officer. She was such a perfect lady it was hard to imagine she had spent 20 years in the Active Duty Army. Her voice cackled with age, but her eyes softly lanced the egos of any junior officer who dared to smirk at her wisdom or diminish her authority with militant feminist barbs of any sort. As she sat before us, taking our questions about military careers for women, she shared some of her own frustrations and lessons learned over her 20-plus years. She acknowledged that women who wanted to make rank would most likely be divorced, as she was now divorced, because men had a difficult time accepting their wives and the complex demands of being married to Army officers. Divorce was not a given, she insisted. But we would each have to make our choices as time passed on.

If we were to make it in a man's world, especially in the new Army which catered to military spouses as much as to the men in uniform, Colonel Williamson felt we had to heed several pieces of advice. She summarized,

"Ladies, there are four things you have to do if you intend to succeed in the military. The first: buy a dress! You don't have to out-man the man and wear pants all the time to prove anything. When you come to social functions, wear dresses! Secondly, bake your fair share of cookies for the wives' group. Yes, I know you are officers. Believe me, you will earn the respect of every wife when you show up at a wives' group with your fair share of cookies for the Christmas fund raiser! And thirdly, pay your dues! Don't come to a social or a meeting and eat your way as if you won't eat for another month! You're not in college anymore. When you go to a function, you pay for the privilege of socializing with important people! Don't try to eat up the price of your admission ticket! And finally, stop your bitching, and moaning and complaining! I don't know why women are different, but civilian women can bitch and moan and complain and feel better. In the Army, you have to learn how to keep your complaints to yourself and just do your job! You'll be recognized. You'll be promoted. But you have to stop your bitching and moaning and complaining at every little thing that isn't right!"

Great advice. We never saw Colonel Williamson again to thank her for it. I was not ladylike enough to send her a thank you note, but I'll bet my classmates did. We finished the course with a few more socials, at which we stared each

More Talented Than You Think

The Officer Basic class included two professional football players, a marathon runner, a lawyer, a Yale graduate and several highly unemployable liberal arts majors like the author.

other into abstention, which saved our waistlines if not our reputations. Most of us went on to commands where there were no senior ranking women to mentor us. In fact, I never worked with a female colonel until 1995, when I worked in South Korea at the 19th TAACOM. So the future General Williamson's nuggets of truth were all I had to steer me clear of professional embarrassment or the negative pillow talk of a commander's wife — the most powerful career stopper for any indiscreet lieutenant — male or female!

Since we really had no trials by fire during our AG basic course, there was no need to subject our class to the never-ending parades and ceremonies to mark our class closure. We didn't need to strut to the strains of Rocky II or Chariots of Fire. We ended as we began. We lined up, walked into a small auditorium, listened to the quiet reflections of the 82nd Airborne commander. We were at peace as a nation. The 82nd was nesting in North Carolina. I don't recall a word of the general's speech, or even his name, but I do recall that he provided a lovely conclusion to our very genteel officers' basic course. He shook the women officers' hands as if we were ladies at a ball, not iron pumping lieutenants. Who minded? It was time for us to wake from our sleepy sabbatical, get down to the brass butter bars and start acting like lieutenants.

It was time, at last, to say goodbye to Uncle Ben. After we cleared our guestrooms, we went out for one last drink, one last early morning dance, one last embrace of our close friends and companions. And then we took off for the real Army. Our first permanent duty stations. I was the envy of my classmates. For my first duty station, I would go to San Francisco. San Francisco! I must have known friends in high places, my friends exclaimed! Remember the adage, "Be careful what you ask for. You just might get it!" Well, I asked for the San Francisco Bay Area. I got Oakland Army Base. These two cities are not just a bridge away from each other. They are a whole universe apart.

CHAPTER 5

My Star Was Rising

The soul, at its hidden core has a dislike for novelty, no matter how much the future promises compared to one's last dreary or dreadful experience. I was prepared to experience the fear and loneliness of moving to an unknown community. On this move, however oddly, I did not touch the raw nerve of fear or loneliness. For better or worse, I anticipated no such feeling of dislocation or desolation as I journeyed west to my very first assignment as a second lieutenant. Perhaps I was still on the adrenaline high that lingers long after training schools. I found myself getting more euphoric as I drew close to Oakland, California. I was a free, single woman. I had three years to experiment and shape a whole new way of being for myself as a single officer.

Driving my sleek Maxima, and traveling alone through the mountains from Indiana to California I marveled at the luxury I now enjoyed as a single, independent woman. I knew I had advantages most women would not experience for generations to come. I traveled with no weapons, but I felt perfectly safe. In remote mountain passages, state troopers would follow me for a while to reassure me that my adventure was safe. I stopped in Colorado Springs to visit my friends PJ Crowley and Paula Kougeas. I had sung at their wedding in Newton, Massachusetts back in the early 1970s. Paula and I were friends. During my last year of high school, we volunteered together to help with Catholic social justice projects. Paula wrote one of my recommendation letters for the Army. PJ was the PAO (Public Affaris Officer) for the Air Force Academy at that time. He took me on a tour of the Air Force Academy. He is now a PAO for the National Security Council. Whenever Sandy Berger briefs the nation before C-Span cameras, PJ Crowley is on hand to provide the details. Paula was the PAO for Peterson Air Force Base. She had many stories to share about the impact of family life — divorce, personal problems, childcare shortages — on military effectiveness. Paula tried to reassure me that the crazy things I wrote about in my letters — digging foxholes, road marching, and going on five-day foot patrols — these things were never going to happen in war.

"In the next war, Marie, there won't be any foxholes! Our bombers will fly out, drop their payload, and be home for dinner. And the war will be over! Marie, the Army is obsolete! There's no place for the Army in the next war. Our bombs will end the war by supper time!"

I have often wondered how the two of us had drifted so far from the values that brought us into our relationship in the first place. We were both devotees of Patrick Hughes, a Catholic priest who organized walks to end world hunger and fasts to end the bombing in Vietnam. At that moment, the deeper myth taught by Air Force instructors was that, in fact, there would be no future war. I knew deep down that Paula believed these officers as much as I did. At OCS, one colonel flipped up images of one half-billion dollar plane after another.

"See these babies? One-half billion dollars to make one copy!! We're not ever going to go to war again. We can't afford to go to war! We can't afford to waste these billion dollar babies!"

God, I hoped he was right. I'm sure that Paula had the same faith that technology would actually deter war. I doubt she ever really believed that war could be so risk-free to American ground soldiers. Anyway, I was a wholehearted grunt by then. I believed that ground soldiers were the most honest, ethical participants in international conflicts. They put their bodies at risk, and they had the best chance of keeping American military participation on an honest, defensive plane.

My visit with Paula and PJ was definitely celebratory. They had the most experience moving from post to post. Their home was filled with knick-knacks from their military expeditions around the world. They had upbeat assessments of the military's commitment to diversity, to women, but especially, to the Army family. Since I knew I was to become the Army family services officer at Oakland Army Base, this knowledge comforted.

The Army's commitment to women was embarrassingly obvious to me. The military strove to accommodate the whimsical desires of every female officer who contributed to the military's sincere goal of gender quotas. I had been told by many sergeants and officers who mentored me I could reach for the stars. I would make general some day, if I just pushed myself to maintain the OCS standards. Well, I did my part to meet the Army's EO goals for the officer corps. I sweated, groveled in poison oak, pumped and pushed on the athletic field, marched, stood watch and suffered every humiliation and abuse required for OCS graduation. The Army rightfully claimed affirmative action a success without providing OCS women preferential treatment. I claimed my prize: permanent duty on the West Coast near my sister's residence in North Beach, San Francisco.

Not first prize, however. I asked for an adjutant's job at the Presidio, the post that majestically commands the Golden Gate Bridge and San Francisco's access to the Pacific Ocean. The first hint that I wasn't that important to the Army's scheme for gender integration: I was assigned to Oakland Army Base. I was to be the Chief of Services Branch. That title was a catchall for managing a child care center for 63 children, a guest house with 84 rooms, and all the family support programs the Army could conjure up to project the kindest image of Uncle Sam that liberal welfare programs promise. Because I had to repeat OCS, I arrived in the Bay Area four months late. By the time of my appearance, my sister, Beeshie had moved to Italy. So, I would have to shape my new life completely from scratch.

Oakland Army Base is an oasis just east of the Bay Bridge. On first approach, the base does not lend an impression of livability. Nor on the second or third approach. My gentle passage to Oakland was pleasantly delayed with all those drives through country club neighborhoods in Illinois and Kansas City and Colorado. My last military experience was to jog along Air Force cultivated gardens with backdrops of spectacular settings such as Pike's Peak. I literally reveled in the civility my friends Paula and PJ experienced in their Air Force life. I was shocked to pull up to Oakland Army Base, an installation wrapped in barbed wire, with contract police who scrutinized every visitor as well as every resident who passed through the entrance gate. For the first time in my life, I was about to work and live in a gated community. Not the suburban kind that suggested exclusivity and safety. No, I was about to crawl through the penal kind, where one's only reaction can be an ever-present feeling of imprisonment.

I fully expected to drive into a trim sprawl of grassy lawns and soccer fields with long boulevards graced with the palatial homes of senior officers and sergeants major, as I had seen at Fort Dix or Fort Benning or Uncle Ben's Rest Home. From the first quill of the barbed wire fence to the entrance of Jacobs Guest House, however, there was not an iota of charm or neighborliness.

There were no stone monuments, no bronze statues or brass cannons, no tender leaves of grass to grace the quarters of the living or to memorialize the remains of the dead. There were no football fields or baseball fields. No parade fields. No parade fields? How could this possibly be an Army base?

After the gate guards scrutinized my spanking new lieutenant's identification card, I was waved onto the base. I drove past long brick buildings, warehouses, and a few loading docks. About two blocks later, there stood a couple of blocks of apartments. Flats, really. About 50 enlisted families and 50 junior officer families were stacked together, thus destroying any semblance of commitment to fraternization regulations, and immediately shattering my full confidence in the effectiveness of such regulations. The rest of the base was paved with concrete and macadam. Warehouses and stockpiled pallets were everywhere.

Just before signing into Oakland Army Base, I stopped at a car wash to wipe the bugs and desert dust off my pretty Datsun Maxima. First impressions always counted, of course. Wasted effort. When I drove into the Jacobs Guest House parking lot, I wondered if I had drifted off base, as can easily happen when driving around sprawling, open southern bases. Then, I remembered that

Oakland was enclosed, guarded. The Jacobs Guest House "Welcome" sign clearly indicated I was not lost.

The Jacobs parking lot and guest house lobby was strewn with trash. Very ghettoish. Very un-Army. Cigarette burns pegged the lobby carpet. A mouse dashed along the sideboards, in search, I suppose, of a few cracker crumbs and popcorn kernels that were stowed in the tossed wrappers and snack bags that boldly mocked any semblance of military discipline.

The guest house was not full. I had to check-in, but the filthy ambience was the most dramatic incentive for me to set out first thing in the morning to scour the bay area for a livable apartment. My orders stated I was required to stay at Jacobs Guest House if a room was available until I could find a permanent apartment. If the sprinting mice in Jacobs Guest House were indicative of the quality of Oakland's family housing stock, I selfishly reveled that I was a single officer. Oakland had no housing for single officers. I would have to live off base in a private apartment. God grants small favors — even to self-proclaimed agnostics.

I was not surprised to see young soldiers cruising into the guest house with their girlfriends at this semblance of an Army hotel. I was shocked though, that prostitutes boldly stationed themselves in the lobby. A young, disheveled man seemed to be peddling pot and cocaine, but I was too new to pass judgement. My suspicions were confirmed shortly after, however.

That night, I disregarded all the troubling signs of activities I could not control just yet. I simply concentrated on preparing my class-A uniform and paperwork so that I could sign in, visit with my new boss, and confirm all prior information I received about my first job.

There were no surprises. Before my first duty day ended, I became the Chief of the Services Branch. Jacobs Guest House was to become my ward, along with an even greater motley mixture of family services programs ranging from the childcare center, to the domestic violence counseling and prevention program, Army Community Services, Army Emergency Relief, Survivors Assistance and finally, the identification card section that issued cards for all soldiers, retirees and disabled vets within a 40-mile radius of Oakland.

Colonel Greenfield, a never-married workaholic who headed the Personnel Services Division suggested my kind face would be the asset most needed to succeed as Chief. What was the Chief of Services, after all, but the chief mama, social worker, community lender, records keeper and hostler — if you could call a rat-infested whorehouse a hotel. Colonel Greenfield brushed away my protests that my face might give deceptive signals — I was not really kind at all! Worst yet, I was not professionally trained to run those family support programs. The fact that I was not trained in social work, childcare or the housekeeping side of hotel management was irrelevant to Colonel Greenfield. His philosophy mirrored the Army's leadership then as now: as an OCS butter bar, I could excel at anything I set my mind to, whether or not I was credentialed. Thus, I became the Chief of Services Branch. Hail to the Chief!

There was no way to slither out of this job. When my protest failed, I sighed and voiced my plans to compensate for the depressing stress of this new job by taking an apartment far far away — in San Francisco. Colonel Greenfield's eyes sparkled. His smile was handsome. Most of Oakland's senior officers lived on Fort Mason, which is set atop a wooded hill that divides the San Francisco Bay running path from the Golden Gate Bridge to the Embarcadero into almost equal parts. My social life would flourish if I lived in San Francisco, he assured me, because the command held regular functions at the Oak Club, which sat majestically on the San Francisco Bay, positioned to peer into the rooms of Alcatraz with high powered binoculars. From this club you could watch spinnaker sails glide by and pretend you were as powerful as the young men who maneuvered those splendid boats.

Anxious to flee Jacobs Guest House before my suitcases became rodent infested, I patiently inched through the rush hour traffic and gradually made my way over to San Francisco to scour the city for an affordable apartment. I knew it would be hopeless to search in North Beach unless I wanted my car impounded for parking violations. Because my sister and I spent so many afternoons walking through the city and by the bay, I knew where to look. I migrated to the safe bayside neighborhoods until I found a delightful studio apartment in the Marina. With half my take-home pay, I was able to secure a studio on Fillmore Street. Yes, I was paying too much rent. However, I knew I would do better at my job if I kept some kind of connection to the world I thought I was moving to. Although my sister had already moved to Italy, I felt connected to her as long as I was within walking distance of the cafes and Italian pasta shops that dot the neighborhoods.

My studio faced the bay. The living room/bedroom would double as my piano studio. There was no room to move around. The kitchen provided the only space for pacing or other activities that required movement. I could only afford a few square feet of paradise, after all. At least I was starting to believe there was such a place, and that I deserved a few square feet just like everybody else.

Once my apartment was secured, I focused entirely on my job. The Army Family Action Plan was born about the start of my tenure as an officer. We were indoctrinated at OCS that the United States would probably never go to war again, since the cost of high-tech planes and tanks were too prohibitive to expend in battle. If we weren't going to war, then what did we need an Army for? The Army was ever in search of a mission to keep end strength as high as possible, in the event the political tides turned. You can't grow an officer or sergeant overnight. We still had enough senior leaders who believed the worst thing our country could do was to draw down the Army to such a point that we could only react to world crises. Better to keep the soldiers on duty, highly trained and almost offensively postured to respond to threats to our security. However, you can't keep soldiers on active duty without a larger than life mission. The Army Family Action Plan became our peacetime mission, our raison d'étre.

Other political realities contributed to the birth of the Army Family Action Plan. Female military spouses long since shed their stereotyped roles as self-effacing homemakers and cookie-baking volunteers to become independent, working and often professionally educated spouses. They evolved from passive followers of their husbands to activist community organizers. These spouses lobbied for gold plate childcare centers, family services, Department of Defense employment preference for spouses and special on-base accommodations for the "exceptional," the Army's euphemism for disabled family members.

Although never trained to assume this monumental task, my primary responsibility as Chief of the Services Branch was to take care of the Army Family. I was trained, of course, to take care of soldiers, both on the battlefield, and in a staff office. Once the Army Family Action Plan was implemented, that focus shifted forever. If a soldier happened to be part of the family that sought help from the Services Branch, so be it. Most often, support to families was paramount, somehow construed as the same thing as support to the soldier. It never was. In retrospect, a butter bar should never have held the job I had. The Chief of Services Branch was a captain's slot, but on this post where three AG officers would be assigned, only one was a captain.

Colonel Greenfield was a transporter by profession. He hardly had the professional background to implement these new social mandates, and more and more mandates were issued with unreasonable regularity. Whenever a personal problem of a single solder received media attention, the Department of the Army responded by effecting a new policy mandate for the entire force. The Department of the Army lobbed off new social mandates every year with the speed and accuracy of SCUD missiles. It was Colonel Greenfield's job to see that these new programs were observably in place. Colonel Greenfield probably knew the programs were as futile as they were expensive. In his professional judgement, a woman with a warm smile and a friendly face met the standard of competence to be Chief. My intelligence and sociable manner would end domestic violence, suicide, spousal depression, lack of childcare, alcoholism, poor financial planning, rape or whatever concern surfaced that the Army compulsively wished to eradicate.

That's not to say that I did not come to love my work. Women have their own super hero fantasies. The end goal was not achievable, but certainly not for lack of effort on my part, or the part of my staff, the military police, or the many workers in the community support division.

The most enjoyable department in my branch was the childcare center for 63 children. To get this program running, civil engineers renovated an unused dog kennel into a brightly colored preschool. The children waddled about in yellow and orange rooms that were accented with garish purple and orange beanbags. Every room was stacked with shelves stuffed with old-fashioned alphabet building blocks and hundreds of raggy dog-eared children's books. The naptime, reading circle and play areas were all permanently delineated in the pre-school rooms with bright yellow adhesive tape. Only a military childcare center would attempt to institutionalize this level of order, as if the children needed to learn marching patterns and standing formations before they graduated to kindergarten — or risk lifetime failure!

We had six babies, from the ages of six weeks to 18 months and dozens of toddlers who required special care. I remember a black woman named Delores who cuddled those babies. She was fierce in her struggle to run the baby room "the way she was trained" and not too eager to share the infants with others, although California law required a second helper when the load exceeded four.

The director of the center was a highbrow Jewish woman who drove in from Marin to our treeless ghetto in her classic Volvo. She worked with the Civil Engineers to design an exquisite state-of-the art new childcare center for the children. Her original plans were designed during my predecessor, Captain L's tenure. Unfortunately, L did not oversee the project sufficiently to guarantee its success. Captain L spent about 120 percent of her day obsessing and commiserating with soldiers and family members who confessed, after lengthy interrogations by Captain L to some experience of domestic violence or sexual abuse. I do not have any direct information from her or from my staff that she invested herself in any of the other half-dozen projects for which she was responsible.

Before moving to her new assignment, Captain L was to brief me on the workings of all the Morale, Welfare and Support Activities for which she was the Chief. Her entire briefing concerned her eccentric program to stem domestic violence on the base. She never alluded to the critical issues that needed resolution before our new childcare center could be built. Nor did she apprise me of the obstacles that, if left untended, would result in cancellation of the building project.

Only when Captain L departed did I discover that several of the building specifications did not meet the minimum, albeit gold-plated federal regulations. In the interim, while Captain L was not available to the CCC director for emotional and supervisory counsel, the director spent many hours of the day confiding her anxieties to the Presidio's CCC director. After my installment as Chief, our CCC director confided in me that she was getting most of her advice from the Presidio CCC director. The real threat to our new building project was immediately clear to me.

The Presidio, which is now closed, had grandiose plans to build a three million dollar childcare center. They were short about $600,000 in funding. Our center would cost $750,000. The Presidio director had dreams of becoming a high-paid regional Army director for childcare. He was already a GS-11. I met this Presidio director when I attended a three-week course for management of Army Community Services, the certification program that would declare to the world my expertise. I had the dubious privilege of seeing the Presidio director in action during our short course. Many of the women in my class were completely offended by his unseemly poolside foreplay with a woman who was obviously not emotionally stable. In retrospect, I wonder if any of the higher-ranking women questioned whether this emotionally unstable woman should be working with children, as much as they questioned the sexually exploitative antics of the male supervisor.

Regardless, alarm bells rang wildly in my head when our CCC director admitted she had almost persuaded the OAB chain of command to merge our center into a regional childcare center, directed by this man. First, because I didn't want any sexually immature person to supervise my employees, or to take responsibility for the children who were ultimately under my purview. Second, because I knew that it was impossible for government workers to serve two generals from competing commands in the Army. Oakland could never compete with the Presidio for resources if our whole program reported to the Sixth Army in San Francisco. We would fare better as a stand alone child care program. We could always scrap for our fair share when we reported to the Military Traffic Management Command.

In seminary, social justice advocates often parse texts and situations with a hermeneutic of suspicion. My mother's politically astute family genetically passed down to me a nose for suspicious alliances. In no time, I was able to prove to my commanders that the reason our Child Care Center building project was about to be scrapped was not because of fatal design flaws. Because of the back door alliance with the Presidio director, we had inadvertently ceded our share of the building budget to the Presidio. By communicating to the Department of the Army that we relied on the Presidio director's professional judgement, we gave that guy carte blanche to strongly advocate for the diversion of our building funds to his $3 million project. Who could blame him for persuading the Department of the Army that our $750 thousand dollars allocated for a new Childcare Center should be diverted to his account, because of serious design flaws in our building plans?

My immediate boss was Lieutenant Colonel Al Siegling, the Chief of the Community Services Division. Siegling, a former chopper pilot, was a mensch. He did not need to be persuaded that our project needed emergency resuscitation.

I arranged for a woman, whom I think was named Mary Jo to visit Oakland Army Base to see for herself why it was imperative to build our very own child care center on the base. She needed to see just how remote our base was. How inaccessible to public transportation. How unaffordable it would be for our junior enlisted to pay huge fees to have their kids bussed to the Presidio each day. How unpractical for the Army's mission to set up a childcare package that would require a three hour absence every time the child care center called a parent to have an infected child sent home.

Mary Jo was one of the Department of the Army childcare program developers who designed all the gold-plated regulations and policies that were controlling plans with nothing but the welfare of children at the heart of her concern. Like many army spouses, Mary Jo had a Master's in Early Childhood Education. All I had was a music degree and a soft heart for the kiddies who attended our center. Mary Jo toured our dog kennel-turned-day-school with me. She had pages and pages of checklists that she could have used to shut down our center for lack of compliance with federal guidelines. Most of these problems should have been corrected by the acting CCC director. By the time Mary Jo came for the inspection, however, our CCC director resigned. I was the acting manager until I could upgrade the job description to hire someone with the expertise to run the child care center properly.

Mary Jo had a heart. I took her out to Charlie Brown's, the junior officers' favorite upscale watering hole that sat atop the East Bay. Over a glass of white wine, I begged Mary Jo for a chance to turn our center around. She gave me a long list of violations that needed immediate correction if we were to keep it center open. Things like building blocks that were age appropriate, varying in size so that the tiny tots could actually grip and manipulate them. Another that I can recall: implementation of a hot lunch program. Our kids brought their own lunches, which were microwaved as required. Some real safety hazards included lack of permanently affixed gates to block children from wandering from room to room. And of course, our playground equipment was made of old weather-beaten beams of wood. The children could get splinters. We needed to install those nice big brightly colored plastic swings and slides that make the hard work of being children look like lots of fun.

I promised to get every one of her deficiencies fixed, if only she would please, please help OAB get its new childcare center built. Mary Jo believed I would make the corrections she required just to keep the old dog kennel open. She really did care enough about our kids to lay the golden egg for OAB children — she listed the deficiencies in the new building design that would cause DA to reject our project.

"If you want this project approved, then..."

I can't remember a single deficiency, but I do recall being extremely grateful that our draftsmen and engineers revised the drawings to correct every mistake that Mary Jo meticulously noted.

Oakland Army Base built a new childcare center, but it did not open until a new and polished manager took over. Tragically, within a few years, a nationally reported child sex-abuse scandal was uncovered at the three-million-dollar Presidio Childcare Center. As far as I can remember, the director whom I met in training was not accused of abuse, but my own intuitions about his lack of regard for the wellbeing of children, his lack of oversight, was confirmed. The parents of 50 children pursued claims of abuse perpetrated by Presidio childcare workers. Over the years, my bosses were grateful that I shared my concerns about the safety of our children when I obstinately refused to merge my CCC into the Presidio's.

Ironically, the Oakland Childcare Center could have been caught up in that Presidio scandal, largely due to the neglect of Captain L, the one officer who seems to have dedicated her life to the eradication of abuse. L had the same oversight responsibilities as I, with much more clout since she was the ranking officer. Until her departure as Chief of Services Branch, her only involvement in the center was to document and terminate an untrained African-American male childcare worker. Captain L secretively met with CCC staff for days to document this untrained man for "criminally abusive" behaviors such as putting misbehaved children in corners, or yelling at his squally toddlers to "shut up."

The Department of the Army implemented a 608 series of regulations to ensure quality family programs, especially quality childcare. The biggest problem with the 608-10 regulation was its class bias. The policy stipulated all manner of lower-class behavioral norms and teaching practices as either illegal or abusive. I'm not saying the behaviors were ever acceptable in a government child care center. I would have used a different strategy to change the culture.

The same regulatory advocates who put the child care regulations in place also established a federal registry where every person accused of neglect or abuse would be logged, whether or not the accusations against them were founded. Whenever these regulations were introduced concomitantly with appropriate training for the minimum wage childcare workers who held child care jobs, the effect was indeed to raise the level of care from warehousing to quality pre-school learning centers. The case of C, the toddler teacher, however, exemplifies the admixture of well-intentioned social policy goals without regard to the rights of the individuals who would be affected by the new guidelines. At the Oakland Childcare Center, teachers were paid about three dollars per hour, in an "isolated geographic location" where a one-bedroom apartment could be rented for about $500.00. Governmental standards for quality childcare drastically leap-frogged ahead, without any effort to retrain or update the skills of the military's childcare force. Mr. C, as someone who was hired under one set of rules, but fired and listed under another, needed job re-training, not a criminal record. He was hired, after all, to teach toddlers although he was an uneducated man. The belief, of course, was that when Mr. C was fired, he would instantly be replaced by a college-educated teacher. But then, as now, the shortage of professionally trained childcare workers is acute. You just cannot expect a subsistence wage earner to pursue a college education, and you certainly cannot expect a college-educated teacher to work for less than the income to which a welfare recipient would be entitled. Then, as now, welfare recipients earn more than most childcare workers. This catch-22 left Oakland's childcare center vulnerable to the same abuse that was reported at the Presidio. What saved us was our vigilant oversight, our open door policy for parents, managers, inspectors to come and go to keep the center free of allegations of abuse or neglect.

Although desirable, beautiful buildings are not the most important ingredient to a child's healthy education. Someday, as a nation, we will recognize that decently paid, well-trained child care teachers are far more important to the well-being of kids. Not that we should ever have to choose. Funds for child care programs were limited in 1984, however. The DA had to make choices. They chose in favor of expensive buildings. They wrote strict policies about training and performance standards for child care teachers. Pay scales for teachers never matched the training standards cited in the child care regulations. Of course, the problem still looms. We are the richest nation on earth. We can build an overnight consensus to drop six billion dollars worth of bombs on a third world nation, but do not agree that our own children deserve to be cared for by decently paid well-trained teachers.

Captain L did not seem to have the analytical skills or the desire to address the perpetual problem of unqualified pre-school teachers at the Oakland Army Base CCC. I soon realized that for all her bluster, she was just as untrained as I was in the family social programs we managed. I began to seriously question her judgement when she debriefed me on her unique strategies for intervention.

Until she was evicted from my office, Captain L continued to hone in on a few cases of perceived abuse. All other management and training issues went unnoticed. Her definition of abuse expanded to include supervisory verbal or psychological abuse. Daily, she held court with three or four soldiers who relied on her for protection against whatever supervisory or relationship abuse they believed they were experiencing.

Captain L was a cute dimple-cheeked, fair-skinned, Puerto-Rican African American. She always wore her hair so that it ballooned out beyond regulatory guidelines just enough to be irritatingly noticeable. She would stab the air with her fingered accusations of command-wide domestic abuse, all the while her dimples and twinkly eyes expressing joyful satisfaction that her suspicions were so beyond question. She firmly believed military spousal abuse was endemic, and by God, she was the messiah who would root it out.

Before her farewell, Captain L called me in to train me on domestic violence in-take. In my first training session a young woman came for support after she argued with her husband. The woman tearfully began to describe a fight with her spouse. L cupped her hands and started to bite her fingers. Her face crinkled up in empathic grief.

"Did he hit you?"

L asked this question more than once with a solid expectation of an affirmative reply, only to hear, "No."

"Did he bruise you?"

"No!"

"You know it's against the law to hit your spouse in the state of California... We are here to protect you..."

The woman emphatically negated Captain L's assumptions time and again. L's hysterical response as an officer must have unnerved the young wife, for she quickly regained her composure and left the office, never to return.

Afterwards, L fulminated about the conspiracy among men to keep their abusive behaviors secret. In L's eyes, the young woman denied her assumptions of violence because she feared her husband's retaliation. It was not acceptable to take the woman's statements at face value, despite the fact that feminist doctrine was strongly advocating primary emphasis on the need to do just that — take women at their word.

I am not suggesting that there is not a problem of domestic violence in the military or in society at large. To the contrary. At this writing, I have worked to prevent and heal domestic violence for more than 13 years, both in the Army and in civilian communities where I lived. Even at the beginning of my work, I found that domestic violence victims and advocates tend to globalize their experiences. My concern: if 10 percent of the men in society are abusers, that means that 90 percent are not, usually fell on deaf ears. When I raised the point that it is important for us to recognize that domestic violence is not normal or perpetrated by all men, I was greeted with glazed stares.

Once Captain L was gone, I had the opportunity to form a more pragmatic program. Of all the paradoxes I've experienced in life, Ronald Reagan's new era of downsizing federal government actually made it possible for me to put in place a very effective counseling and prevention program for Oakland Army Base families. Ronald Reagan announced his government policy to contract out all services that could be provided by local providers. Under the old system, my program would never have seen the light of day. The budgeting cycle would have prevented the program's inception for about four or five years. By then, the government's priorities would change and the program would be cancelled. With the principle of local contracting, and my belief that Army officers were not qualified to run these programs directly, we were able to do something constructive to reduce domestic violence on Oakland Army Base.

I researched all of the counseling services in the bay area, made on-site visits, attended lectures provided by local experts and persuaded my command to contract with the best domestic violence counseling center for a full range of confidential professional services for our families. Services that no ordinary army officer could ever competently provide. These included absolutely confidential counseling for victims and abusers, as well as classes to teach prevention to all parents, teachers and soldiers in the command. To get an abuser into preventive counseling, you had to get past his fear of career loss.

Captain L's tenure at Oakland was consumed with the pursuit of the omnipresent phantom, domestic violence — she truly believed this ghost crept into every marital bed, every parental relationship. I would argue that the base owed her a debt of gratitude, because the inappropriateness of her interventions compelled me to search outside the Army for professionally qualified social workers to win the Army's war against domestic violence.

However, with her absorption in the issue of domestic violence, Captain L had no energy to tend to her other oversight responsibilities. Her xenophopbic attention to personal violence meant the other big programs were completely unsupervised. No wonder, then, that the Jacobs Guest House was skipping with mice and rats on the night of my arrival. No wonder the childcare center architectural plans were nearly scuttled by DA. No wonder that the four or five families of the 100 that lived on Oakland Army Base who really needed intervention feared a visit to Captain L's office as nothing shy of a career-stopper. One visit with Captain L and the scarlet "A" for Abuser would never be extinguished from a man's professional record, if she had her way.

Before she left, I naively voiced these concerns about scaring away clients after just a few sessions with Captain L. I questioned some of the assumptions that under-girded her interventions. Though the overlapping period for sharing responsibility would be brief, the captain soon asserted her rank to lend absolute authority toward her agenda to bring down every male whom she suspected of abuse. When I voiced these concerns, Captain L not so subtly intimated my career would be on the line. She was my rater, after all. That would not stop me, because my OCS training prepared me never to cow to such intimidation. But, I knew I was in need of my own intervention.

Lieutenant Colonel Al Siegling, the Chief of the Community Services Division came to my rescue, much as he used to swoop down with his chopper to pick up wounded soldiers in Vietnam. Siegling was the first of many chopper pilots who debunked in my mind the flyboy mythology that is so overstated in the media culture. Once he took on staff jobs, Lieutenant Colonel Siegling did not spend much time analyzing weather charts or sky patterns. But, either my new staff apprised him of the strong shift in approach to domestic violence, or his aviator's ability to see blue skies beyond Captain L's omnipresent dark storm clouds was as razor sharp as a new Gillette blade.

Al Siegling could see that Captain L wanted to hang on to her dark illusion about the omnipresence of men's evil, even if it required an attack on my career. Siegling would not let that happen. He assured me he would be my primary rater, so I had no reason to adopt L's counseling or advocacy techniques. Nevertheless, he advised me just to hold my thoughts until Captain L moved on. And he was ready to make that happen.

After all, Captain L was now excess, merely wasting time at the Services Branch to avoid taking a short-timer's project up in the Headquarters. When she realized she had no power over me, and no reason to stay in community services, she cleared her office and started packing for her advanced class.

Once I took over the branch for good, Lieutenant Colonel Siegling's first practical advice to me was never to be alone with a certain enlisted female who spent hours in Captain L's office behind papered-over office windows. When this female visited Captain L, the window blinds were shut to afford the captain and her junior enlisted "counselee" absolute privacy. This peculiar practice continued for countless hours over the course of a year or so. Although the colonel advised Captain L to discontinue the practice of lengthy exclusive meetings with the enlisted person, his advice went ignored.

It is strange, given male officers' perpetual fear of sexual harassment or sexual abuse allegations that Captain L was so unabashed in her disregard of Siegling's warnings. She had overwhelming "position power," that left her invulnerable to attack. As a mandated child abuse reporter, Captain L's power was derived from her ability to accuse anyone in the command of abuse, on terms that were absolutely confidential for her and the alleged victim, but publicly humiliating and potentially career destroying for the accused. Her justification for holding dozens of top-secret meetings with Specialist R was merely: "I am counseling her." This, despite a woeful lack of any training or counseling credentials. She had no expertise as a domestic violence social worker, child abuse counselor or psychiatric therapist, either. But L was not afraid to use this ruse to spend vast quantities of time alone with her young counselee.

Lieutenant Colonel Siegling was warned that the captain and young specialist were indulging in lesbian activities, both in her shuttered office and in government living quarters. Though pressured to take legal action against both soldiers, Siegling focused instead on creating a work environment that avoided even a perception, not only of inappropriate lesbian sexual activity in the workplace, but any improper or illegal activity. He was not able to teach Captain L to exercise common sense in her business practices. He made it his business to protect me from trouble.

When Siegling sat me down to advise me never to be alone with Specialist R, especially in an environment where we could not be observed, I thought at first he was paranoid. Persistently over time, however, the colonel proffered so much other advice that would keep me out of jail and safely on the path to colonel, that I could not ignore his fears about the history of Captain L's lesbian activity in the workplace.

I was clearly homophobic in those days, but I soon learned from Siegling's compassionate treatment of many gay soldiers in the command, even Captain L, that he was not. Despite his pleadings with L to cease and desist from her unseemly behavior, and allegations by others who wanted her prosecuted, the colonel would not act to harm her.

Siegling was a gentleman. I doubt he ever fit the wild and loose flyboy stereotype. He was not selfish, self-centered, demeaning of women, or cruel to either his soldiers or his family. He never engaged in ego contests with other colonels, though such contests filled the pre-retirement days of so many who served in the Bay Area military "retirement farms." He had a beautiful wife and three sons. While I knew him, Lieutenant Colonel Siegling was focused on his priorities: enjoying his family, especially his boys' scouting and sailing activities. By day, his energies were zoned to provide recreation centers and service programs for families on the base, which he deemed an isolated remote location. Legally, this was not true, but environmentally it was. Plucking down 100 families and another 50 single soldiers into the middle of a shipyard that was geographically in the midst of the nation's worst drug cartels was an idiotic housing plan. The Army's decision to house military families at OAB undermined their goal to eradicate the social diseases that afflicted families.

Siegling's approach to the isolation of our soldiers was to go after every federal dollar he could get to renovate community centers, expand the gym or just put in nice gardens. I railed against that approach as much as I lauded his efforts.

"We'll never solve the social diseases unless we move these families out of this ghetto. Use all those government dollars to let the families buy homes in the safer neighborhoods. After all, we do that for military families when they are overseas."

Siegling never took my complaints personally. He knew the Army would never be smart enough to privatize the housing and social support programs for his soldiers. He just continued to fight to get what he could for his soldiers.

OAB was a retirement farm, a command top heavy with colonels who had no hope of making general, but who could bide their time before starting their next career. Nine-to-fiver's every one, but very useful to the Army as master logisticians. Siegling was no exception. Al Siegling left the office everyday at 4:00 P.M. with a group of near-retirement colonels who all bought their permanent homes inland from the coast where the neighborhoods were quite stable and the prices much more affordable. They belligerently adhered to their scheduled departure to beat the tunnel traffic that could stretch the rush hour commute into hours. He came in before seven in the morning so that he could be home with his family in the evenings.

Al Siegling was very typical of Army officers of the 80s. He resisted supervising the private lives of his soldiers. He demanded adult behavior and he treated all his soldiers like adults whose civil rights were to be respected. He refused to spy into bedrooms or assume parental responsibilities for his soldiers and officers. So long as we avoided even the perception of wrongdoing, we were free to do as we pleased.

Siegling's suspicions about L's indiscretions were not rooted in any desire to harm the captain, or to control her private sexual life. He had to respond to the work-based complaints that Captain L kept disappearing with the young female specialist. Both the captain and the young female MP not only spent inordinate amounts of time sequestered during the duty day. They also invested a significant part of their off-duty hours spying on MPs and other men whom they suspected of having adulterous affairs.

The Oakland Army Base MPs returned the favor with the vengeance of Medea. Some male soldiers brought copies of various intelligence reports that were given to community services for adjudication. The MPs staked out cars with binoculars to spy on Specialist R's apartment to accumulate evidence of her lesbian activity. Siegling and other officers declined to act on the information provided by MPs. When the reports were brought to me for action, I called the MP officer, an OCS classmate who supervised these police investigators. I chided the MPs,

"You obviously don't have a real mission if you can afford to let these men sit in squad cars and spy into the bedrooms of our soldiers. It's time to call off the dogs!"

After Captain L departed, and Specialist R continued to spy on her bosses and co-workers whose sexual infidelities she intended to expose to the world, I brought her into my office for a final warning. I gave Specialist R special instructions, in the presence of two male soldiers to cease her spying activities on philandering MPs. Ultimately, the chastisement had no effect. They were spying on her to gather evidence that she was practicing homosexuality in government quarters. R continued to spy compulsively on her male peers, despite my direct orders to stop her inappropriate monitoring of the extramarital affairs of her male co-workers and supervisors. And, I might add, I repeated admonitions to the MPs to call off their dogs and focus on the real crimes that desperately needed intervention — crimes like drug peddling, gun use, prostitution, and petty theft.

Eighteen months later, Specialist R's warped feminist agenda (liberating women from adulterous husbands while simultaneously asserting her own right to be just as promiscuous) culminated in a travesty. R brought the wife of her immediate supervisor down to the MP station to prove he was engaged in extramarital activity.

This sergeant was to leave the Army within a few weeks to attend the Oakland Police Academy. As an African-American he had an opportunity to tip the balance of the Oakland force to make it more racially inclusive.

Specialist R and the sergeant's wife crept up to her boss's military police car, only to find him in an embrace with another woman. Not only did the sergeant's wife become hysterical. The sergeant proceeded to beat Specialist R in front of his other soldiers.

The Deputy Installation Commander at that time, Lieutenant Colonel James Seaton quickly processed this sergeant out of the Army, with a reduction in rank, but an honorable discharge so that he could attend the Police Academy. Specialist R insisted she was a victim of a more serious crime. She continued to spy on other soldiers; wore a neck collar to prove her beating was very severe. I was so exasperated with R's compulsive spying, and fearful for her life, that I asked Lieutenant Colonel Siegling to throw R out of the Army. My request was based on her uncontrollable urge to snoop and the more than ample documentation of her own sexual activity. The post also had a strong case of child neglect against her. She walked around with this neck brace after her supervisor beat her, which made her even more conspicuous when she spied on her peers. Surely she would be killed if she wasn't removed. Both Siegling and Seaton refused to discharge Specialist R. Instead, they allowed her quick departure from the command. She transferred to the reserves in her southern hometown, where they hoped, "She could sort out her problems and get back on her feet."

In other cases, whenever the MPs brought logs that allegedly proved a married man's affair or a single person's gay activities, I would call the sergeant or lieutenant in charge of the spying activities. Indignantly, like a broken record, I would challenge the appropriateness of their bedroom spying: "Your people must not have a real mission. If I caught my staff indulging in this kind of unprofessional behavior, I'd put them on details that lasted until 9:00 P.M. every night!"

Lack of mission and as the cliché goes, lack of leadership is always at the root of fratricidal spy missions. The two viral conditions that unleash social pandemonium in any and every military unit.

Sadly, the rumor-spy jousts continue to this day. During the Aberdeen sexual misconduct scandal, several media producers asked me if lesbians were being targeted by men, forced to have sex, or brought up on charges for their own gay behaviors.

The first fact that reporters or sexual rights activists refuse to accept is that there are no innocent parties in these competitions. Some lesbian women spy and intimidate each other into relationships; they intimidate straight men into tolerating their lesbian liaisons by spying on the men's adultery. And yes, men play the same leverage games against women. The second fact that should not be ignored is that a tremendous amount of disciplinary and supervisory time in support units is spent untangling these allegations. In other words, in mixed gender units where women and men are working side-by-side, an astronomical amount of time is spent untangling sexual misconduct allegations. At least in the 80s officers could presume that sexual conduct was a matter to be handled between consenting private adults. You could challenge soldiers to act like adults and handle their affairs privately. Now, everything must be investigated, documented, and wherever politically advantageous to the military, prosecuted.

As long as the military has been gender-integrated and prohibitive of lesbian relationships, this mutual spying has occurred. I believe it will continue until the military is either gender separated again, or the laws are changed to tolerate private, consensual gay behaviors, and to tolerate private, consensual heterosexual behaviors as well. I'm not saying that any form of sexual misconduct should be tolerated. And I am not saying that I approve of sexual misconduct, to include adultery. These things happen accidentally and at other times, quite intentionally. They will never be stopped with the imposition of criminal sanctions or lengthy KGB-style inquisitions.

While Captain L, the military police and even Criminal Investigation Division agents spied on each other's bedroom activities, the drug peddlers, prostitutes and rifle-toting dealers and pimps reigned with impunity on the base. The thugs operated in the same places of business that were managed by Captain L. They thrived in the places that were policed by the same MPs who staked out bedroom windows. There is a parallel dysfunctional approach to crime in our civilian society. For the past ten or 15 years, the moral majority and the liberal left have fought bitterly over the need to establish either rigid societal sexual norms or societal sexual anarchy. Meanwhile, our communities are decimated by violent, and often well-organized criminal activities. Teens have been shooting each other. Their ventures into serious crime is simply ignored as if these trends were either harmless or too overwhelming to face directly.

After I got my bearings, I confirmed my earliest suspicions of criminal activity at Jacobs. Again, I had to wait until Captain L departed before I could deal with the problems at the guest house. Until she left and I had supervisory control, I could do nothing to fumigate the place of rodents or thugs. The rats, roaches, pimps and pushers would have to stay until my superior officer relinquished her authority over the place.

Captain L delegated total management of the guest house to a staff sergeant, whose GT score was in the low 90s. An uneducated, insecure man of low stature, Sergeant D was already in serious legal trouble by the time I arrived. But if you know anything about the Army, you surely know that when a staff sergeant has delegated authority to handle a project, a brand new lieutenant without positional authority has no way to take charge of a bad situation. In other words, until you have that positional authority, a sergeant outranks a second lieutenant on matters related to job performance. Some would say a staff sergeant outranks a second lieutenant, period.

After Captain L left, I could see she did Sergeant D no favors by delegating the entire responsibility of the guest house to him. Sergeant D, contrary to every training guideline and property procedure taught in Army leadership classes, signed a bogus hand receipt when Captain L bestowed him the honor of managing her guest house. He assumed control and responsibility for every rusted stainless steel lamp, every vintage WWII metal desk, every hole-filled bed sheet, towel and washcloth.

In his eagerness to demonstrate his dedication and to earn the comradeship of his peers, Sergeant D signed this long list of property for a building with 82 guestrooms. He did so without ever inspecting a single piece of furniture or comparing a single stock number from his hand receipt to the property that was in his building. Quite a few grade school desks, cheap metal folding chairs, and pieces of lawn furniture were passed on to him as government-issue property. Now, more than a year after he signed, the Property Book Office was demanding full accountability for the real furnishings that were placed in Jacobs, possibly decades before Sergeant D ever set foot in the place. Sergeant D was accused of mismanaging tens of thousands of dollars of property. In the strict sense, because he irresponsibly signed for property he never verified, he did mismanage the property. Honestly, however, what the Property Book Office accused Sergeant D of mishandling was long gone.

Two kind soldiers who worked for Sergeant D provided me bits of history that explained the huge property losses for which Sergeant D was being held accountable. Apparently, a number of officers who proceeded me left the management of the guest house to their sergeants. Always the men were untrained and usually not serious about accountability. The men would take government desks, wooden beds, sitting chairs, and God knows what else, and sell them or furnish their houses with them. They maintained their furniture count with cheap or broken down substitutions.

The property management division finally demanded accountability, but sadly for Sergeant D, he signed for all the schlock that substituted for real oak desks and beds. By law, whether or not he ever counted, inspected, or verified the property was irrelevant. To complicate matters, Sergeant D's wife was pregnant. Here was a man without an education, with ten years of Army service, about to be socked with a $40,000 property loss. I was no fool. No butter bar wants to be on difficult terms with the first sergeant she supervises.

The man who would dictate the terms of settlement of Jacob's mangled property records was Colonel S, the head of OAB's Logistics Division. For lack of other mission priorities, Colonel S declared war on the Community Services Division, because, in his opinion, property management was pervasively non-existent. His declared battlefield was Jacobs Guest House, which in his view, was the most irresponsibly managed property in the Army. Colonel S was going to destroy the person responsible for property loss at Jacobs. Worse yet, he wasn't going to let the guest house operate with proper supplies like toilet paper or floor detergent until the darned hand receipt was settled. His method to prevent further property loss: at least one career would end, to set the example of intolerance for theft or stupidity, as the case might be.

No question the officers like me who were responsible for management of the guest house should have been held accountable years before my arrival. This never happened. The pattern was to delegate the authority and responsibility to a few, low-level non-commissioned officers. No question, a junior sergeant would suffer the inevitable back blast when the accountability bomb finally detonated.

I had a meeting with Colonel S to beg his support for a non-punitive resolution to the furniture hand receipt debacle. I wanted him to recognize the property loss as an accumulation of bad practices by a series of irresponsible leaders, and not to hold the last, rather dim-witted sergeant as the scapegoat for this entire debacle. Colonel S, a slender, tall, balding, former aviator epitomized the retirement farm senior officer at Oakland. His final assignment did not afford him the dignity or the responsibility commensurate to his rank. He should have commanded a brigade of soldiers. Instead, his reach was limited to warehouses filled with hand soaps, corroded furniture, and overpriced basketballs. All soldiers go through an identity crisis as they face their transition to civilian society, but of course, those who retire have to make, at times, the most painful transitions.

Most Army posts have amenities that can distract the departing soul from the anxiety of separation. Golf courses, running tracks, water activities, whatever. There was no golf course on OAB, however, to allay the onset of depression when the awareness looms that the soldier's identity would soon vanish, whether by choice or by decree. Colonel S was in a limbo where his usefulness as a soldier was long past, but he had to linger on in uniform until his retirement. What could Colonel S do to disguise the indignity of his situation but inflate the importance of property shortages, and take personal control of inventories and transfers that should have been resolved at much lower levels of command? Colonel S had no diversionary activities, and so, he micromanaged inspections that were run by his office.

Colonel S personally supervised the documentation of property loss at the Jacobs Guest House. The junior officer assigned to do the Report of Survey, another new lieutenant like myself, was incredibly narrow and legalistic in his interpretation of Sergeant D's culpability. His interpretations were obviously governed by Colonel S. The young lieutenant was married and expecting his first child. Nevertheless, he had no sympathy for Sergeant D, who was also expecting his first child. The surveying officer was unequivocally convinced that a sergeant with ten years in the service should have mastered property accountability procedures. LT C was going to crucify my sergeant come hell or high water. And it seemed obvious to me that Colonel S was going to give him a medal for accomplishing the fratricide.

I was desperate when I called Colonel S to ask for a different strategy to get Jacobs under control. When I reported to the colonel's office, he graciously poured fresh coffee, and invited me to sit at his long conference table to discuss the minutiae that bristled him. I calmly presented the scenario that led to major property losses at Jacobs Guest House. He listened intently as I pieced together the stories from civilians and other enlisted personnel who had sympathy for Sergeant D's plight.

I reported my findings. By this time, I had personally inspected every plastic chair, every bedpost, every sheet and towel that was in the Jacobs. Not only did I do this upon assuming management of the guest house, but I also accompanied the surveying officer as he tried to make sense of Jacob's huge losses. Colonel S commended me for taking the trouble to even look into, let alone handle the Jacobs property loss, because heretofore, no officer from the department ever took on that responsibility.

I was lulled into thinking Colonel S would accept some of the arguments I was about to make. Most of the furniture at Jacobs was completely depreciated in value, too old and mutilated to be of value to the Army. This was due to the perpetually crowded conditions, overuse by poor families, and of course, to the lack of a systemic furniture maintenance and replacement plan. Some of the missing property was purchased so long ago it didn't even have a book value. Colonel S could not deny that all of this property was completely depreciated in value, for he was an honest, decent, if overly strict man.

I did not feel disloyal when I agreed with Colonel S that my guest house had been mismanaged for years. He was certainly right that the abysmal situation I was inheriting was not the fault of one sergeant, but the fault of many officers and sergeants who simply ran the operation into the ground for lack of expertise and for lack of interest in guest house management.

Colonel S tacked into a wind that I did not even realize was the energy that drove the storm of his property accountability measures. He ranted about his fundamental belief that the junior officers were not the most responsible for the failure of leadership, but the division chiefs were.

"Before I retire, I fully intend to have your two colonels put into jail. Both Siegling and Greenfield are responsible for this, and I intend to put them in jail."

Not exactly the kind of news that made me confident of my own survival as a new lieutenant. The colonel's paternalism surfaced.

"Look, I have a daughter who is an officer, and she is about your age. And I care about what kind of leadership she is getting. I care about the leadership that Sergeant D is getting. Before I retire, those two colonels are going to jail."

Momentarily frozen by Colonel S's attack on my bosses, whom I really liked, I heard an opening to resolve the entire situation non-punitively.

"Listen, sir, all I know is that this guest house is the only place where families and soldiers can stay when they are coming back from Korea, or when they are headed overseas. We have to keep this operation going. If I can prove to you that we are putting in the property controls that will prevent this situation from recurring, can't we just turn in all this junk that's being called furniture and start over? Let's face it, none of it is worth anything. We really need to clean up the guest house, and get a whole new shipload of furniture."

The colonel was attracted to the idea of completing a refurbishing project before his retirement, but he couldn't quite smile at the idea.

"As long as you have Sergeant D in charge, it's hopeless. That man has the GT score of about 90. He is not capable of managing more than a fast food stand. He just doesn't have the ability to do this kind of complex logistics management."

I knew if I could keep Colonel S in an advisory mode, he would soften and accept my plan.

"Sir, you know I am just a butter bar. There's no way I can get Sergeant D out of the Army, but I agree with you. He has no potential for leadership. Besides, none of these sergeants are trained in hotel management. It's not fair to hold them accountable. I worked in hotel supervision, so I have some of the basic skills, but even I don't have the all the necessary skills to make Jacob's successful. I want to civilianize the management position, get in a professional hotel manager."

The colonel nodded and smiled in agreement.

"But what do I do about Sergeant D? If I slam him, not only will he go down, my career will be over. You know these NCOs are going to sabotage everything I do if I hurt one of their own."

The Colonel melted a bit.

"You don't have to destroy Sergeant D. Just don't let him get promoted. When he gets out of the army, he will get a job that is more in line with his training. He was promoted past his potential, and he can't keep up with the demands of his field. Don't do anything to hurt him. But when you evaluate him, just find out what the rating scores are, and give him the average grade. An average score for an NCO will kill his chances of promotion. That's all you have to do."

When Colonel S heard the rest of my plan to renovate the guest house, he smirked as I told him my mentor and boss, Lieutenant Colonel Siegling was fully supportive. His disrespect for my boss was transparent. I had to let him know that I would only be loyal to Lieutenant Colonel Siegling, because Al Siegling really cared about the families and the soldiers on base. His heart was in the right place. Sometimes he got the details wrong. But, as a helicopter pilot and transporter, he was not properly trained to run these personnel and family support programs anymore than the rest of us. We were all managing by our wits and common sense.

Colonel S refrained from further criticism of both Siegling and Greenfield. "When is this property going to be transferred?" He asked solemnly.

I gave him a time line, which he accepted. My turn to beg.

"Sir, to fix Jacobs, I have to start turning a profit. I can't turn a profit if we aren't providing our customers with the basics like sheets and toilet paper. Can't you just give us a trial period, and I will prove to you that I have strict accountability for these supplies?"

"Just get with Sydney..." Colonel S smiled finally, acknowledging the absurdity of the situation we both found ourselves in. He stood up, signaling that our meeting was now formally over. His vitriolic frustration vanished. He warmly congratulated me for my professionalism, and gave me further career advice to get me promoted at least to his rank.

My encounter with Colonel S played out over and over again at Oakland Army Base. Same dynamic. Different situations. Different cast of players. Bitter senior officers or sergeants turned their fratricidal anger on their peers. This was a downsizing army, and it was a nasty place to be. As one chaplain commented, "When soldiers don't have an external enemy to fight, they turn inward and fight each other."

I had to work between directorates, and so, I could not avoid the venom. My colonels encouraged me to brief our opponents with the charm and innocence that would arouse their paternal instincts. The anger among bitter rivals would melt. Their obfuscation would cease, and Community Services would build another new complex or inaugurate another expensive family support program.

This approach to collegiality doesn't sound very feminist, but I don't think I had any alternative in an environment where departments were one deep — every full bird colonel had a senior sergeant reporting to him. Every lieutenant colonel had a junior sergeant. Every major had a corporal. Every lieutenant except me had one or two privates to boss around. I had a staff of 26 reporting to me, which was an unusually large staff for Military Traffic Management Command. Lynda E's guidance to "smooth my message" was my salvation, the reason I was able to get anything at all accomplished. We could not afford to continue the nasty rivalries. Oakland Army Base was such a dump that we did not have a choice but to cajole some of our less friendly colleagues into a spirit of cooperation.

Besides, there were so many shady management practices that you couldn't point the finger at one person to make any signficant changes to our way of doing business. The only way we were going to turn things around was to call a truce, set aside blame, and focus strictly on the tasks that would clean up this or that building, or this or that operation. But back to feminist ways of being. If I had learned one thing from my OCS roommate Lynda, it was that feminine modes of reasoning could inspire the Hatfields and McCoys to lay down their sawed off shotguns at least long enough to get another crop harvested. Lieutenant Colonel Siegling's version of the same theory of mediation was, "Marie, honey works much better than vinegar..." Oakland Army Base was no place to engage one's adversary in the "contestations of power" that are so requisite to modern feminist struggles for equality.

Getting Sergeant D's property debt canceled, and Jacobs Guest House spruced up with new furniture was the least of my struggles at the base, though. Once we got the beds, bedding and creepy critters under control, it was time to focus on the criminal elements that would always prevent Jacobs from achieving respectability as an Army hotel. My first attempt to rout the pimps and peddlers from my guest house, however, was caught in the same dynamic of inter-directory fratricide. In tackling the dope and pimp problem, I wondered mostly about my chances for career survival, but also whether I, Marie deYoung, the human being would survive. "Look, listen, then lead." That OCS aphorism guided my first successful attempt to fumigate Jacobs of all its rodents, animal or otherwise. It didn't hurt that as a city girl, I already lived in two cities that had turned into crime-ridden ghettos. I knew the underclass when I saw it. When I first asked Sergeant D to inventory his property in my presence, I was able to glimpse daily at the underworld culture on Oakland Army Base. To appease Colonel S, we had to quickly resolve the property dispute. We had to do one last property count. We eyeballed the linens early in the morning. We counted bedroom furniture at checkout time. We lumbered through storage closets and unused guest house rooms. Finally, we inventoried the rooms of all the senior non-commissioned officers who were illegally living in the guest house as a substitute for permanent senior non-commissioned officers quarters.

That the nooks and crannies in the guest house were laden with open boxes of perishable food did not surprise me. The rats and mice were obviously accustomed to a daily free buffet in Jacobs. Sergeant D was mortally embarrassed by the scrambling critters who scattered when we pushed aside bed frames or dressers to count hidden property. I could not understand why a sergeant with ten years in the army was clueless about the logical first step to rodent extinction: depriving them of the delicacies that so aroused their appetites. On this score, I had to agree with my peer, the surveying officer. Sergeant D should have known better! When I ordered the housekeeping staff to thoroughly clean out the closets, to vacuum under the beds, and all of the office nooks and crannies, the exterminators took delight that their lethal traps and sprays might finally have an effect.

Sergeant D, obviously a chairborne sergeant his entire career, paled whenever the peddlars and prostitutes operated in his plain view. I did not fault him for his "see no evil, hear no evil" response, a classic inner city survival tactic where I was raised. He tried to get rid of the thugs, but he was too ashamed at his own failure to tell me why he was so powerless in driving them out of our guest house. Sergeant P, his loyal but frustrated assistant, revealed the truth, one morsel at a time.

The Jacobs Guest House was the Oakland Army Base brothel by covert design. The NCO Club and the guest house were intertwined in a cartel saga that went back several years. The post sergeant major was traditionally one of the primary customers of the services that were provided in the club and guest house. He, and his predecessors had created a drinking culture that began with a Sergeant Major's call at the close of the work day and ended with sexual escapades at Jacobs Guest House.

Captain L also alluded to this history, but she would not admit that this culture prevailed during her tenure as guest house manager.

Sergeant P eventually disclosed the ongoing criminal trials that were hush-hush but in progress during my new tenure. A senior sergeant and a female captain were entangled in an embezzlement and drug dealing operation that dominated the NCO Club.

The Department of the Army would have shut down all of the Morale Support activities at Oakland Army Base, but the command fought desperately to keep the only recreational outlets available to inhabitants of this isolated base. While my immediate boss, Lieutenant Colonel Siegling and the MWR manager, Jesse Mangrum struggled desperately to prove that the club and other MWR activities were now free of these criminal activities, they also knew that the criminal trials were not about the past, but about an intractable present problem.

They were secretly attempting to sweep dealers and pimps out of the club and the guest house without drawing the notice of DA.

When I finally realized my bosses were fully cognizant that peddlers and pimps flourished in my guest house, I asked Lieutenant Colonel Siegling why this mess was even being tolerated. To be sure, Siegling had done his duty. He brought Criminal Investigation Division (CID) in to investigate. As unfathomable as this may seem, CID had already been watching peddlers sell pot, lines of cocaine and God knows what else under the very noses of desk clerks and the general public for two years. They had not made a single arrest, but Siegling's hands were tied. Once CID was involved, CID called the shots. Guest house staff and soldiers could only stand by until CID finally made their moves to arrest the transgressors.

Oakland had two fine young men, both Mormons from rural areas assigned as CID agents. They were both under 30 years of age. They each had about five children. They were repeat ACS clients, in search of emergency funds, because their low pay grades would never sustain the large families they had created.

These agents were decent, kind men. However, they were extremely inexperienced, and left to their own devices for more than two years. Since I had gotten to know them, I called them to my office to determine what their end strategy was. When were they going to arrest the pimps and prostitutes who brazenly strutted in my guest house lobby? I didn't concern myself with the club because it was not in my area of operation.

The men insisted they did not have enough evidence to arrest anybody. Forgetting everything I learned from Lynda, I very unsmoothly exploded.

"Are you kidding me? These guys are peddling under our nose! What do you mean you don't have enough evidence?"

They were studying one peddler, an unkempt lethargic man who was illegally living in my guest house with a single female Marine sergeant who billeted there.

"Why don't you arrest him for trespassing?"

"We don't have enough evidence. We haven't caught them in the act. How do we know that he is staying all night?"

"But you see him passing out marijuana cigarettes. I get reports that soldiers are coming in from San Francisco, from the 7th Division at all hours of the night, for Christ's sake, from Fort Ord. This is the cheapest easiest drug den in the state of California! Maybe in the Army!"

"Ma'am, you don't understand," the kindly CID sergeant instructed me. "We have to pass certain evidentiary tests, or we'll never get a conviction."

At such moments, I never could recall Lynda's advice, to be smooth.

"If you don't get these damned dealers out of my guest house, I'm getting them out myself!"

"Ma'am, you can't do that. We have orders to continue this investigation until we can get a conviction."

I went back to Lieutenant Colonel Siegling, all vinegar, not a drop of honey.

"Sir, this is outrageous. Why can't we just throw these b— off post? They have no legal right to be here. Why can't I just ban them?"

"Because CID has mandated that we leave their men alone until we can put them behind bars once and for all."

The city girl in me knew that was never going to happen. And why, if I was responsible for the welfare of all those who stayed in my guest house, would I want to abet them in jeopardizing their careers with illegal drug use?

"Sir, please, let me work the chain to get these guys bounced off post. Let's just bar them. To hell with this investigation. If they can't convict with what we see with our own eyes, they will never convict!"

Lieutenant Colonel Siegling blessed my decision to call the Provost Marshall. We started work at Oakland on the same day. I felt comfortable calling him because he was a soft-spoken, rational gentleman. He was sympathetic to my complaints, but at first, he insisted we had to abide by CID's mandates. CID did not report to him. They operated out of the Presidio. The point I made about keeping the Presidio out of our child care program was proven once again. The Presidio would never handle Oakland's problems as effectively as if they were the Presidio's problems.

"Sir, do you mean that these guys can take a lifetime to arrest these thugs? Can't we give them a deadline? After two years, if they can't make an arrest by now, they'll never make an arrest! These creeps aren't even military! Let's just kick them off post."

The major gently suggested we needed to give the CID agents more time, but he agreed that we could and should set a terminal date for the drug investigation. We niggled over dates.

"Why not this summer? Why not just ban them from post?"

The major coordinated an ultimate deadline which I recall was close to July 22, 1984.

That date didn't come soon enough. By July 22, I was on Oakland Army base for approximately 90 days. The roaches were gone from Jacobs. The rats and mice traipsed out of our guest house back to waterside warehouses in search of their customary gourmet fare. But the pimps and prostitutes still reigned supreme at Jacobs Guest House.

I did not wait until close of business to make my rounds through the chain of command with a letter requesting that the resident pimp be barred, not just from Jacobs, but from post. Lieutenant Colonel Siegling approved the letter as I wrote it for the Deputy Installation Commander's signature. It needed to have prior approval by officers from a number of directorates, right up to the general's office, to make sure our efforts would not be sabotaged.

Before the big day, we had already notified all of the senior enlisted personnel who illegally resided in Jacobs that they would have to move out. Although these enlisted lived in the guest house by decree of the sergeant major,

our new sergeant major concurred with the written policy changes that would effect these evictions.

As a courtesy, I went to the local MEPPS station to apprise the Marine commander that we were evicting her young female sergeant. This female commander was as quiet and understated as I was emotionally forceful. She listened intently as I expressed my concern not only that the enlisted female marine was not taking action to move out, but that this same marine moved a pimp and peddler into my guest house to transact business.

The female major hardly said a word to me, even after I pointed out to her that we shared a common problem. The very peddler whom I described as a pest at my guest house during the evening hours was working the lobby area of her military recruiting station during the day. The ragtag dealer was amicably moving about from recruit to recruit with his supplies discreetly portioned for palm size exchanges of drugs for cash.

Without a blush or a burst of rage that typified my responses to this kind of insanity, the commander called in her junior sergeant. She asked me to comment on the circumstances I reported. When I finished recounting the marine's situation in the guest house, the major asked, "Is Lieutenant deYoung's report true?"

The young woman burst into tears.

"I love him." She was very petite, and fragile looking.

"Look," I said softly. "We have counseling services if you need help in sorting this out. I am not here to ask for your prosecution. I'm concerned because I don't want him dealing to my soldiers, and I don't want you to lose your career because of your love life with a common criminal!"

The young lady continued to cry and dab her eyes with a tissue.

The commander gazed at her sergeant with frosty disapproval. Quietly, she closed the meeting,

"Sergeant, you have one week to move out of Jacobs Guest House. I will speak to you afterwards about your personal obligations as a sergeant."

"Ma'am, I just want to reiterate," I interjected. " I did not come here to ask for the sergeant's punishment. Only to bring this situation to a close."

"I will take care of this matter. Thank you for bringing this to my attention."

I departed from the commander's office, and walked straight past the straggly dope dealer who was obviously a misfit in this military recruiting center. I marveled that I had just witnessed for the first time, a female commander in action. She was as cool as I was passionate. She was as temperate as I was boldly ready to act. I wondered if I would ever make it to her level. Would I ever "smooth out" the way Lynda encouraged me to?

I handled the next dimension of our pimp and prostitute problem with more finesse but not without personal suffering. The greatest advice every lieutenant is given by OCS trainers: don't lock horns with your sergeant major. Any fool who thinks a second lieutenant can ever control a senior non-commissioned officer will inevitably walk around with cream pie smeared all over her face.

Evicting pimps and peddlers from my guest house on that first go round was a lot easier than evicting the stray sergeants, who enjoyed their accommodations as if by fiat of the command sergeant major. I knew this task had to be directed by my senior officers, not by me. So, I went up my chain, to get Colonel Greenfield's approval, then went over to the Deputy Commander's Office to get my senior rater's approval.

Finally, the sergeant major was informed that Jacobs Guest House would no longer be used as the hangout or crash pad for our senior enlisted personnel. The sergeant major's first reaction was natural. He argued that guest house regulations could, indeed, be violated in favor of soldier welfare. His second reaction was also to be expected. He encouraged and nurtured Sergeant D's complaint that my tepid evaluation of his work at Jacobs Guest House was an act of sexual discrimination, or you might say, an act of reverse discrimination, since Sergeant D was a white male and I was his female supervisor.

After I wined and dined with all of the surveying and property officers who wanted desperately to sock Sergeant D with a huge property loss, he was exonerated from paying a huge debt. I could not let him entirely off the hook, however. After proving to myself that Sergeant D was not irresponsible, merely incompetent and incapable of handling such a huge guest house operation, I knew I had to take some action to avoid the Peter Principle. The advice Colonel S gave me was echoed by a retired sergeant major who managed our morale welfare activities.

"You don't want to hurt him real bad," Jesse Mangrum said to me repeatedly, with his thick down home Southern drawl. "You just want to send the promotion board a subtle signal. See these promotion scores? See how the second decimal place is the breaking point for promotions to E-7? Just take him down one notch. Just one one-hundredth!"

Jesse Mangrum had the girth and height of our post sergeant major. I was beginning to think that all Vietnam era sergeant majors had this imperial presence. He was as different from the active-duty sergeant major as a potato is from an apple. Jesse charmed the women, but he also took them seriously as soldiers and business managers. He taught us every management trick, every business strategy to improve our bottom lines. A heavy man, he had huge beautiful green eyes with sharp bushy grey and black eyebrows. When he slipped back into the sergeant major role to give me "report card" advice on Sergeant D, Jesse scrunched his one eye and held his two fingers together as he repeated, "You don't have to hurt him real bad. Just an eeensy teeny bit! This is a mean Army. You don't need to shoot him with a cannon when one tiny little bullet will do!"

As we drew the Jacobs property saga to a close, Sergeant D was moved to another assignment that would be more suitable to his temperament. My final evaluation was approved by Jesse, the director of MWR activities, Lieutenant Colonel Siegling, and Colonel Greenfield, the head of our directorate. I even visited the Command Sergeant Major of the base. In that visit, the sergeant major sucked on his pipe and almost suffocated me with the smoke as he studied Sergeant D's evaluation.

The sergeant major affirmed the accuracy of this evaluation based on his own extensive counseling of Sergeant D, and commented about the unfairness of assigning a new staff sergeant to such a difficult assignment without training. He verbally approved Sergeant D's report card as written by me and Lieutenant Colonel Siegling.

When the sergeant major gave his approval, and we believed we had his support, I sat down with Sergeant D to go over the final evaluation. Sergeant D paled with anger. Although he did not seem to have the wit to manage a property hand receipt, he could immediately see that his career would end in about three years, because he closely monitored the number of points required for promotion. He knew that the one-hundredth of a point that I shaved off his score would eliminate his chance for promotion, and thereby, retention on active duty.

Sergeant D marched through the chain of command to register his complaints. All my bosses maintained the position that my evaluation was fair. Sergeant D stormed up to the sergeant major's office.

The sergeant major's response taught me the unforgettable lesson of how the Army's enlisted corps really works. It was payback time for me. The sergeant major came down to Jacobs Guest House to discuss "my treatment of senior non-commissioned officers." His message was clear. He was linking my evaluation of Sergeant D to the much broader issue of housing accommodations for senior enlisted soldiers. The sergeant major was representing not only Sergeant D in the bid to have his report card overturned, he was representing all the angry senior non-commissioned officers who were losing their playground, Jacobs Guest House.

I took the sergeant major on a brief tour of the guest house. He could see the dramatic, but terribly inadequate improvements that had already taken place. I reminded the sergeant major how I put my own career on the line by vouching for Sergeant D's honesty, and for asserting that Sergeant D's mismanagement of the guest house was due to lack of training as well as his own limitations. Then I reviewed all of the conversations that were held with Jesse, Lieutenant Colonel Siegling, Colonel Greenfield, Colonel S, and even with the sergeant major himself concerning the fear that Sergeant D would continue to screw up if he were advanced to assignments that he was simply not capable of handling.

The sergeant major continued to suck on his pipe and smother me with the fumes as I stared him down, refusing to yield on Sergeant D's evaluation or on my decision to evict both the sergeants and their resident prostitutes and pimps from my guest house. He knew from my boldness that if he pressed the issue, his entire senior non-commissioned officer corps would be complicit in formal charges that would be wrought in my battle to make Jacobs fit for family habitation. At that moment, the sergeant major's wife appeared at the front desk of Jacobs. She looked frantically down the corridor where the enlisted lived. She peered down the guest house halls. Finally, she came back to the front desk and gazed intently through the glass window into the manager's office where I sat with her husband, the sergeant major. Without ever alluding to my knowledge of his participation in the sexual escapades, I closed the meeting,

"Now Sergeant Major, why don't you go on out there and tell your wife that she has absolutely nothing to worry about."

He left without a word, but not without a plan. The sergeant major ferried Sergeant D through the process of writing a letter alleging discrimination to Ron Dellums, Oakland's U.S. congressman. By that time, we changed commanders. A new general, John Stanford was installed as commander of Oakland Army Base. The general stood aside, avoiding accusations of a cover-up of gender discrimination. He invited a full bird colonel to fly in from Washington D.C. to investigate Sergeant D's charges that I had discriminated against him because he was a white male. Sergeant D was now working for another female captain and a very protective senior sergeant. They both handled Sergeant D with kid gloves. In fact, the senior sergeant would have preferred for me to lose the case. By the time all the evidence was gathered and he had the opportunity to work closely with Sergeant D for an extended period of time, he had to corroborate the problem of incompetence. So did the female captain who was our new adjutant. She was completely unaware of the history at Jacobs. She took Sergeant D to give him the opportunity to work with "a real, competent" officer. She apparently concluded Sergeant D was over his head.

The colonel spent one week interviewing every supervisor, every senior sergeant who worked with Sergeant D before my arrival and after I transferred him to the Personnel Actions department where he desperately wanted to work. After one week of meetings, interviews and statements from people all over the Army Base, the colonel issued his final report. In his estimation, there was no discrimination against Sergeant D. I had done my duty as the new responsible officer for the guest house, and as a supervisor.

The colonel apologized to me on behalf of the United States Army, and on behalf of the Oakland Army Base Command. He looked out over his bifocals, and said very intently, "You must remember that the Army is the finest organization you will ever work for. What happened here is not what the real Army is about. It is extremely unlikely you will experience this again. Don't let this discourage you from your career aspirations!"

I thanked the colonel with relief, and commented that I felt the process was entirely fair.

"I would want the same opportunity to have my case heard if I were in his position. The system works."

CHAPTER 6

Reaching the Gemini

I was beginning to loathe my first assignment. No wonder my sister balked when told I would probably live and work not in San Francisco, but rather, in Oakland. Oakland Army Base's underbelly was bloated with the lawless self-destruction so common in inner cities. The base where I worked reflected the underclass of its surrounding city. I began to place the blame for the seedy encroachments of peddlers and pimps onto the city of Oakland, which was poor, predominantly underclass, and similarly infested with drugs, violence and sexploitation.

I wasn't the first and I won't be the last to hypothesize that the Army's underworld was caused by its civilian surroundings, a direct consequence of the proximity of the bases to centers of gangs and cartels. The tendency to blame organized criminal activity of soldiers on the larger culture persists to this day.

By the fall of 1984, I was still a naive second lieutenant, basking in the glow of my first triumph — the formal eviction of the resident prostitutes and peddlers from Jacobs Guest House. After this fete, I welcomed the invitation of senior officers to surface from Oakland's underbelly. It was time to pay less attention to the low life, and more attention to my private life.

Who would decline the overtures to mingle with Oakland's debonair senior officers, the men who represented the valor and dignity of a long gone Army? These men served in Vietnam and in Korea. Their reticence about past combat ventures was as overarching as their refusal to drown in the cesspool of the modern military underclass. There was much to learn from them (there were no senior female officers at Oakland), but it would have to be learned on their terms. With almost no exceptions, the senior married officer corps resided on Fort Mason, a village community set on a hill that banked over the San Francisco Bay. On the very crest of this hill, the Officer's Club commanded a spectacular view of the bay waters. This O Club was the social center of the OAB community. Most of the functions were "all ranks" or dining-out affairs to garner crowds large enough to keep this albatross financially in the clear.

There was no larger-than-life mission at the Military Traffic Command to forge loyal, affectionate collegiality among the officers. We were all bureaucrats, green suitors who feared no greater danger than loss of a container filled with commissary beef or antique tentage of Korean War vintage. We did no combat training. We never threw grenades or even zeroed rifles to qualify for marksmanship. There weren't any grenades or rifles at Oakland to conjure even a pretense of the warrior spirit. We didn't even sweat together on the running course.

The Military Traffic Management Command to which I belonged was as genteel by day as the post was seedy by night. The professional honor code included personal responsibility to stay in shape, so there were no formal opportunities to build friendships or slap fannies on the PT fields because the senior officers were trusted to train at their own pace. The junior officers worked a hard-charging nine-hour day, then went home to our posh neighborhood singles' gyms and bayside running trails in search of excellent physique and perhaps, a date that could lead to the love of a lifetime.

Command socials were the only ambit by which the Oakland Officer Corps could achieve esprit de corps. Colonel Greenfield was right about my decision to live in the Marina. The proximity of my new home to the Fort Mason Officer housing would enhance my career, if not my private life.

By 1984, alcohol was deglamorized Army-wide. Junior officers would never go to the O Club just to drink. It was too risky to sit under the noses of the colonels and general who could be the ruination of your career, but who could themselves walk only a few hundred feet to their homes if they sipped one too many. One DUI would be the end of a junior officer's career. If we were going to take such a risk at all, we did not want our bosses to have the opportunity to testify against us.

The junior officer preference was to slip into a bayside table at Charlie Browns, just a few minutes away from the flagpole on the Oakland side of the Bay. On Friday afternoons, we could take off about 4:00 P.M. or so, munch on the mountains of fried mushrooms, celery sticks and spinach dip for the price of one Heinegger's in a bottle or a goblet of Chardonnay. Our paychecks did not afford regular wining and dining at the club or "on the economy." Between paychecks, junior officers gathered at each other's apartments for potluck or a nice dinner.

Because we were an organization without a unifying mission, there was a never-ending need to blend the OAB civilians, junior and senior officers into one community. Every MTMC commander took up this gauntlet. The social solution for the commanding generals at Oakland was always the same: Jesse's theme nights. Theme nights were used to muster the insecure and sometimes cynical junior officers into the same room with their intended mentors, their bosses.

At the Hawaiian Luau, for example, each junior officer paired up with their boss or with one of the junior married couples. Needless to say, the huge roasted oinker, with an apple stuffed in its mouth was not the only creature on display. Junior single officers were just as much entertainment for the command group as the roasted pig on the luau table or the music coming from the disc jockey's booming amplifiers. The ratio of single male junior officers to single female officers was about eight to one. As a newly divorced woman, I was not experienced in the dating scene. At first, I played it safe, and chose to handle the officer calls strictly as business ventures.

To this day, I cannot recall a single episode of sexual exploitation or drinking buddy syndrome fostered by the senior officers at Oakland Army Base functions. Not by the Air Force, Army, or even the Navy. These parties were like political clambakes or charity fundraising balls. The older folks were quite paternalistic, pleasant and respectful, even of the young female officers who were still novelties. Not only were the senior officers mannerly, they expected us to be just as cultured as they were. The senior men could not help but play matchmaker, though. Or if not matchmaker, watchful observers of the romantic officer liaisons within the command.

At all these parties, my own boss, Lieutenant Colonel Siegling would sit with a group of civilians and two or three officers from his division around a single table. He had a warm laugh, a big toothy smile. He was quiet, but he loved a good party. Siegling would sip a glass of white wine, shake hands with the men, and then stand back to laugh at the crowd.

Because Siegling did not want to police the private lives of his soldiers, he never made observations, asked questions or even suggested whom his officers should date, or whom we should not sleep with. He always, always offered a gentleman's greeting to the companions of his officers. I noticed he stood a foot taller, though, when his junior officers could sustain the repartee at a party with grace and sensitive humor.

Every personality test I have ever taken has revealed I am an introvert, probably just as much as my boss, Al Siegling was. Work and intellectual passions have usually required high visibility and a lot of socializing, so I learned to compensate with a lot of gregarious chatter. I had to be careful as a female junior officer, though. My work at Oakland primarily focused on family support programs. I was extremely self-conscious of the jealousies and suspicions that could surface among the wives of my fellow soldiers. Mostly, though, I was conservative in my social behaviors because I wanted to be judged the best. I wanted to be known as THE junior officer who walked on water. In a command that had about a ratio of one private, one sergeant and one junior officer for every field grade officer, the competition was keen, much more so than if we were assigned to traditional combat units.

Somehow in my first year, I felt that Fort Mason was not the place for a single female junior officer to dance, if she were to compete successfully with the dozen or so lieutenants who were also reporting directly to other colonels. Repartee? Always. Befriending the wives of junior officers and visiting with the spouses of our superiors? Of course. But, the traditional distinctions and separations between junior and senior officers were so blurred at this intimate flagpole command, I could only anticipate negative consequences if I danced, or let my hair down.

My instincts were largely right. The O Club was very much the old boys' club where an awful lot of business was transacted. Professional perceptions were too often finalized under the glazed veneer of sparkling repasts. My struggle, shared still by women today was to project my femininity, but in such a manner that my superiors and peers never lost sight of the fact that I was an officer and a soldier first, just as every man thought of himself. Today, a recurring fret of soldiers who are also officer's wives is whether or not to attend their spouses' functions dressed as an officer or as a civilian wife. There is just as much worry today that one's professional identity would be compromised by showing up as a mere woman as when I was a lieutenant.

Also, personal relationships could compromise the integrity of one's professional judgement. One episode can illustrate this point. While dating Patrick, commander of the HQ, the conflict between one's social and professional obligations became very obvious. He organized a wonderful bowling match between junior and senior officers. About 25 senior officers were pitted against another 25 lieutenants and captains.

There we stood in our shorty short-shorts, sipping sodas and beers as we junior officers pretended to challenge our bosses on the lanes. I had just successfully fumigated the Jacobs Guest House of pimps and peddlers. The command recently agreed to uphold the housing regulations, to evict all of the soldiers who resided there as a matter of convenience — never as a command necessity, in the hope that this would discourage the low life.

Just before the bowling match started, Patrick asked me to create an apartment for a young specialist, Jerry M, because his headquarters failed to prepare a barracks room for the new soldier. In anticipation of this, I huddled with my own boss, Al Siegling. He strongly agreed to back me up in my decision to refuse this unnecessary exception to regulations.

Lieutenant Colonel Siegling left the game promptly at 4:00 p.m. with his commuting pool, to beat the horrendous tunnel traffic. I held my ground with Patrick, refusing to take in a soldier who should have been moved immediately into the barracks. Patrick pouted because of my intransigence. Friends we were, but I knew that his request was not born of necessity. He stormed away to discuss the matter with his rater.

Colonel Jankowski, the MOTBA (Military Organization for Transportation in the Bay Area) commander, approached me. He was Patrick's boss. The MOTBA command was parallel to our own Community Services Division. My bosses were not at all accountable to Colonel Jankowski. Neither was I.

"Can't we just make this one exception?" The colonel asked pleasantly.

My bosses and I anticipated Patrick's strategy of going up his chain of command to force another bad housing decision on Jacobs Guest House. This would be a much less cumbersome strategy for a lieutenant headquarter's commander than forcefully instructing senior sergeants to stay late to reorganize the barracks to provide a home for their new soldier. Senior sergeants at a flagpole command are treated with kid gloves just as senior officers are. Working after hours at a retirement farm was simply out of the question for senior sergeants, as it was for senior officers.

In that moment of frustration with my friend Pat, who just pulled rank on me, I forgot the fundamental rule of military communications: listen to a senior officer's tone to determine if his rhetorical question was an implied command. I did not listen beneath the surface of Colonel Jankowski's question. I heard him repeat his question sweetly and quietly:

"Can't we just make this one exception and house just one specialist at the guest house?"

"No, sir," was my repetitive, or you might say, blockhead response.

"Sir, the housing regulations state clearly that you cannot use guest houses as a barracks for single soldiers. We just spent three months moving all those geographical bachelors and single sergeants onto the economy. Sir, the detachment commander has room in his barracks. They just need to clean the room and put sheets on the bed. He needs to have a barracks room prepared for this new soldier."

I thought my response was smart and sharp. I knew I would be backed up by my chain of command, which could not be overruled by Colonel Jankowski. Only the general could overturn our decision.

There we stood as a threesome: my wordless beet-red friend, the detachment commander, tall and handsome Colonel Jankowski, and myself, the rock-steady, straight-backed OCS lieutenant who was taught to rely on regulations, position authority, and chain of command to stand up for what was right, no matter what the cost. And it was there, in our shorty short-shorts, with beers and sodas in hand, amidst a friendly game at the lanes, I almost lost my career. At a command social — not a work setting. I almost lost my rank for standing up for correct procedure and for persisting in this sincere, but in retrospect, absolutely hopeless effort to keep my guest house free of live-in drug peddlers and prostitutes.

I won the battle with my friend Pat, but almost lost the war. Colonel Jankowski, without ever raising his voice or losing his gentlemanly demeanor quietly instructed my blustering friend to go back to his barracks to prepare a room for Specialist Jerry M. Patrick sulked as he walked off to his office to do the inevitable — take care of his soldier.

The next morning, Lieutenant Colonel Siegling came to my office and closed the door. I knew I must have done something wrong, because Siegling only closed the doors to counsel me about my mistakes and errors.

"Last night," he began quietly with a sigh, "I spent hours on the phone with Colonel Jankowski. He insisted that you should be court-marshaled."

"For what?" I was flabbergasted.

"Welllll, Marie." He sighed again. "Jankowski felt he was humiliated by you. All those other colonels standing there, and he asked you to do something and you refused."

"But he knew he was asking me to break the regulations. How can he court-martial me for that?"

"He's not going to court-martial you. I talked to him and let him just blow off a lot of steam. The other colonels told him he should have you court-martialed for insubordination and refusing orders." He laughed and shook his head.

Lieutenant Colonel Siegling was describing the precise moral dilemma for which OCS cadre prepared new lieutenants. How to clarify orders that are illegal, immoral or unethical. Jankowski's request or implied command to move a soldier into my guest house was clearly illegal. How could I have blown it?

"Listen, Marie, I keep saying that honey works better than vinegar. Jankowski didn't want to hear about the regulations. I know I just told you, we just talked about Specialist M — that he could not move into the guest house, no matter what the circumstances were. For years, these commanders have been breaking the regulations and using Jacobs as a crash pad for their divorced sergeants. What's one more time, one more little emergency..."

Lieutenant Colonel Siegling repeated the rest of Colonel Jankowski's comments. He assured me that Colonel Jankowski would not court-martial me, because, at the very least, he had no jurisdiction. The colonel did not write my report card, and he didn't write my boss's either. Siegling assured me he smoothed Jankowski's ruffled feathers, then offered me this advice.

"Marie, next time, just make sure nobody hears you when you are standing up for what is right. Step outside, then close the door. Whatever. Just don't let anybody hear you contradict a colonel in public. Even if it will keep them out of jail, just don't do it in public."

I was crestfallen, but at the same time relieved. Colonel Jankowski would never be my boss, but I certainly did not want to be on his enemy list. At the same time, I had worked so hard to get the slime out of Jacobs Guest House. Lieutenant Colonel Siegling's strong affirmation that our tactics were correct and his defense of me to Jankowski vindicated my efforts. When Siegling opened my office door to take his leave, he smiled broadly again and quietly chuckled.

"Just remember, Marie, honey works better than vinegar..."

My friendship with Pat did not end over this episode. As Lieutenant Colonel Siegling reminded me, the commander was a young, inexperienced man. My age and background made him look weaker than he really was.

By this time, Jesse Mangrum was managing not only Fort Mason's Officer Club, he had fiscal responsibilities for all the morale and welfare activities. Jacobs fit that category, which made him my financial overseer, as well as a friend. Jesse was tickled that I held my own against a colonel, but he couldn't say too much in the weekly staff meeting when our civilians made hay with the story. Privately, he reiterated Lieutenant Colonel Siegling's words to me.

"You know, as an ol' Sergeant Major in Vietnam, I had responsibility for all the clubs. You were right," he twinkled with approval. "But just remember, you don't ever want to embarrass a senior officer. You just tell them to 'step aside... or Sir, can we go outside, or into this room, here?' Then, you let them have it when nobody's listening. Nobody but you and maybe God. Nobody's proved to me that there is a God, but he might be listening. So, maybe be careful then, too!"

That close brush with career fatality scared me more than any drug pusher did at Oakland. I thought I had a strong, unwavering integrity burned into my leadership style by OCS cadre. Lynda's words came back to remind me that being right is just not enough to survive in the ethics-conscious, post-Vietnam army.

"You have to learn to be smooth, Marie. You're right, but you have to find a smooth way to say it!"

Colonel Jankowski never warmed up to me after my first and only conversation with him. He was always the gentleman, but the wall built with my tactlessness and his bruised ego was as thick as twelve inches of concrete. I had nothing to fear administratively, though. He was a transporter. I was a paper pusher. There was no chance that he would ever write my report card, but I still minded the fractured relationship. Now, I regret I did not have the maturity as a new lieutenant to make an appointment to visit with the colonel privately to put the situation behind us. The stoicism between us prevailed.

Every year, the Army has a theme that guides leadership initiatives. I was fortunate to start my career during the Year of the Mentor. Lieutenant Colonel Siegling was my mentor, supervisor, and friend. I was lucky to have him as a boss. He was comfortable with my priorities and leadership style. I can't recall ever bumping up against his ego. I knew Colonel Jankowski was a good mentor to his junior officers as well. At our junior officer parties, both at Charlie Brown's and in our private apartments, I had come to know many of the transporters. Jankowski was just as much an affectionate papa bear to his logistics officers as Siegling was to his paper pushers and club managers.

Among the junior officers, though, I discovered I wasn't the only strong willed officer at Oakland. Mike Scott was one captain who refused to smoothly accommodate anyone's ego needs. Mike never talked about his job when he was away from it, so I never learned anything about his work as a transporter. He would bring his banjo to our apartments, sing silly songs, and then sit quietly as the ladies screamed with laughter at the absurdities that military life brought to our existence.

Mike dispensed philosophical wisdom as freely as the local druggist dispensed cough drops for the common cold. Mike only proffered two bits of advice to me. Early on, when I was managing three operations that really needed separate managers, he stated quietly that no one should make a career of working more than 50 hours a week.

"Document every task, every meeting, every report you have to write. If, after three months, you are still working more than 50 hours a week, it's time to get another staff person in your shop."

Within 90 days of my arrival, it was clear that three managers were needed to run the shops for which I was responsible. We needed one manager for the 84-room guest house, one for the childcare center for 63 little rug rats, and one for the full array of family support programs such as domestic violence, suicide prevention, survivor assistance, Army Emergency Relief and the Exceptional Family Member Program. Mike's encouragement gave me the confidence to write up those job descriptions and to agitate until the three slots were filled by professionals.

More than a year later, Mike announced his resignation from the officer corps. The Deglamorization of Alcohol Program was now in full force. We were forbidden to drink alcohol while on duty, and strongly counseled to avoid intoxication or even the perception of excessive drinking in any public place. Mike was from Milwaukee.

"I was raised to drink beer with my lunch and with my dinner since I was a small child. Milwaukee is beer country. If I can't be adult enough to manage my alcohol consumption and to know what the limit should be... The Army is making children out of the soldiers and the officers... Nobody is going to take that much control over my life... And we shouldn't be babying soldiers either!"

Mike went on to law school. He eventually became an environmental lawyer.

I never saw Mike inebriated. I do not believe, as counselors would immediately suspect today, that Mike's motivation was due to a "classic case of denial about his alcoholism." Truly, he was prescient about the Army's new addiction to social engineering. Although I think the alcohol deglamorization program was, for the most part, good for soldiers, it also was the beginning of a two-decade trend to change the culture by imposing harsh sanctions on soldiers who did not conform to whatever new social policy was in force. Each new policy would further erode the locus of responsibility for careless or immoral behavior from the individual to the big brother enforcer. Soldiers, even officers, have been infantalized, over protected, and under-trusted as each new edict is put in place to protect us from ourselves.

One of my OCS classmates lost his commission due to the alcohol deglamorization policies. I didn't like this man, because he was very cruel to my friend Gary McKenna. After Gary was turned back for a second cycle at OCS, Officer Candidate W would drop McKenna for push-ups whenever he saw him. OC W and I graduated from OCS together, and we showed up at Oakland Army Base within days of each other. He was married to a gorgeous woman with long red hair. He had financial and other problems, as most junior ranking soldiers and officers who had dependents did. For some reason, Lieutenant W was very jealous of the success and attention I received at Oakland. Once, when I was briefing the command about our plans to completely renovate Jacobs, this MP interrupted the briefing to inform me that there was a child molestation case I had to respond to. When I came to the phone, he told me an African American sergeant had attacked a blond, six-year old girl in the housing area. I asked him for details. What hospital was the girl taken to? Whether or not the man was apprehended. He didn't have any of this information, so I asked him to get all the facts while I finished my briefing. When we met later on, the fact was that the six-year-old male child of the African-American sergeant threw a stone at the six-year-old blond child because she called him a racial epithet and rebuffed his kiss.

Months later, when General John Stanford insisted on a command Dining-In, where officers indulge themselves in silly repartee, there was a toss as to who would be Mr. Vice — the MP or myself. I was chosen. The Undersecretary of Defense who was at this event said he had never seen such witty repartee or such esprit de corps among officers as he did that night. My OCS classmate allowed himself to get drunk, despite the provision of a non-alcohol grog bowl. He allowed the sergeant major to take him back to the bar instead of going home on the bus our general provided to ensure that no junior officer would lose their career because of a DUI. Lieutenant W foolishly went home with the sergeant major at two in the morning, had a fight with his wife, then got in his hot rod and started driving around our deserted post. The MPs on Oakland Army Base arrested him for drunken driving. Despite his legal appeal as high as Cap Weinberger's office, the lieutenant was out of the Army for good. He was not offered the chance to complete alcohol rehabilitation counseling, or to plea for a second chance since he hurt no one, damaged no property. He set a bad example for his troops, and the Army saw fit to have him removed from the officer corps post haste.

Too many fine officers were dealt bad hands by the Army during this reduction in force (RIF) era. My best female friend at Oakland was Kathy

Burrus. Kathy was a Ukrainian transporter from Philadelphia. She was vibrant, with beautiful frosted blond hair. She and her husband, Carl, lived on Oakland Army base, in a pretty apartment with oak hardwood floors and large sunny windows. Kathy was an immaculate housekeeper. She was an accomplished floral arranger. Best of all, she was a tough officer.

Kathy chose not to attend many of the command socials. I never missed a command function. The day after we would do lunch, or a happy-hour Margarita, and I would tell her the gossip. She would filter each unbelievable story through her city-girl sensibility and point out the real social undercurrents.

We often trekked to the Oakland A's Stadium on Tuesdays. Ladies Night. With no men around to criticize our appetites, we ate cheesy nacho chips, fat ballpark hotdogs, and sipped on large plastic mugs of beer. You couldn't beat the $2.00 entrance fee. The Oakland A's were terrific morale boosters for anyone who suffered underdog syndrome, especially female soldiers. The A's played their hearts out, kept the crowds stomping and jumping with support. They had a knack for losing in the bottom of the ninth every time, but their persistent hopefulness was truly inspiring. I don't usually like live baseball games, but the A's had all the drama of a great romantic symphony and all the spiritual uplift of a trek through the Holy Land.

To be sure, Kathy and I had a feeling of kinship that was not rooted in persistent underdog syndrome, but in our East Coast heritage as Philadelphians. The fact that we grew up with so many sisters also drew us together. I was kind of an older sister to Kathy, but she had such great common sense. She was my mentor as a worldly officer.

When Kathy walked into a room, her eyes sparkled. Her smile was at once bubbly and blithe. I could never fathom how she could be disliked, but she soon told me her story. Kathy worked for a colonel whose basic mentoring guidance was an expletive version of "kick tail and take names." She did. She thought she followed this guidance carefully, and it seemed her boss completely backed her up.

As a lieutenant, Kathy mostly supervised civilians who had permanent status. They were often unmanageable. They were fireproof. Supervisor-proof. Often, you could count yourself lucky if your workers stayed at their desks for a full eight hours. The best way for a lieutenant to earn a union complaint or equal employment complaint was to monitor productivity.

My civilian staff was eccentric, but they did their jobs. They loved their jobs. Kathy had no such luck. She followed her colonel's mentoring advice. She earned dozens of equal opportunity complaints in no time at all. The down side of the equal opportunity system is that, even in the early stages, it was often used by disgruntled employees to get back at fair, but demanding supervisors. The supervisor always loses in the equal opportunity system, even when they are right, because every complaint is a blemish on the supervisor's record, not the complainant's.

When Kathy received her last evaluation and her promotion, she had the aura of a Greek Goddess. She was confident her commander fully supported her hardcore approach to supervision. She was informed she would be promoted to captain, then assigned to Germany. This beautiful, first generation American whose parents had emigrated from the Soviet Union, whose mother survived a concentration camp had exceeded all expectations of success. Philadelphia girls were supposed to get married, and buy a house three or four blocks from their mothers.

During an officer development day, when the transportation branch career management officer was sent to Oakland to give advice to all the transporters, Kathy's joy ended with a blunt whack. The discreet career management officer asked Kathy if she had called Branch lately. Kathy already received preliminary orders for Germany. What did she need to call Branch for? While the rest of us sipped wine and beer at the officers' call that afternoon, Kathy called her branch. Only then did she find out she was going to be released from active duty. RIFFED. The Army had already begun a very depressing RIF. Within days of pinning on her railroad tracks, her captain's bars, Kathy was advised she wasn't going to Germany. She was going home.

If Kathy ever shed a tear of regret, it wasn't in the company of other soldiers. She continued to smile graciously, but her radiance was gone. The same colonel who told her to be tough and get results rewarded timid officers who took no chances with "Promote Now" evaluations. In the end, the officers who tolerated the routine disappearance and perpetual nonperformance of their civilian subordinates were rewarded not only with promotions but also with continued active duty status.

This is the perennial paradox of military leadership in the modern Army: the mission is to be accomplished, and high standards of conduct are to be maintained. But let there be no accountability if such would result in the glare of career-killing investigations, racial or sexual discrimination, sexual harassment, loss of property or whatever media-sensitive issue that would send a red flag to higher headquarters. Civilians and soldiers alike have learned to avoid accountability for their own misdeeds by filing that equal opportunity complaint.

One situation has always left distaste in my mouth concerning the fairness of the government's equal opportunity complaint system. A stunning woman lieutenant who had the creamy complexion of a film star went to work in the command suite. She wore expensive makeup, with nails sculpted to perfection. Lieutenant S never looked or acted like a working soldier. She was gentle, and before her baby was born, a good personnel administrator.

General Stanford did not miss the opportunity to move this woman to his office to work with his executive staff because his command would receive media attention, and there was much work to be done to cultivate relationships with the community. Lieutenant S was married and pregnant when I arrived at Oakland, which would never impact her work as a headquarters paper pusher. After her baby was born, she moved to General Stanford's staff, which was when her problems spiraled out of control.

At first, the reports of conflict between Stanford's staff members filtered down to me indirectly. Two male assistants from my office were hired consecutively to be the general's driver. Both men, especially Specialist Borja thrived on the serious sense of purpose in the General's office. He couldn't stand the softness and laid back style that made our family support and Community Services office friendly, but in his eyes, lacking in tough military discipline.

Somehow the junior soldiers who had become the general's drivers were drawn into the conflict between Lieutenant S and Captain M, a single officer. Captain M demanded equal sweat equity from all the enlisted and officers who worked for him, whether they were married, single, in school, pregnant, or caring for elderly parents. The single enlisted soldiers who worked for him in the command suite responded enthusiastically, tied as they were to the Oakland Army Base center of power.

Lieutenant S, on the other hand, had only one priority as a new mother: her baby. As all working mothers do, she needed to leave her job by a certain time each day to pick up her child from the day care center. Her husband was also an officer, but he refused to participate in the childcare responsibilities. Lieutenant S's priorities were no doubt in the right place: the well-being of her child.

The question raised in her situation and every situation thereafter, is whether or not it is fair to give an officer so much time off because she is pregnant, or nursing, or the primary caregiver for her child. The related question is whether or not the mothering soldier's absence or non-performance due to her healthy priorities ought to be measured fairly against the performance of others, especially when those others work tremendously long hours to cover for the soldiers who are juggling with parental responsibilities. Shouldn't we reward those who do what it takes to get the job done right with the better performance evaluations? Is it fair to pretend there is no performance differential?

The Army prides itself that promotion is a meritocratic system. No other organization promises to reward stellar performance with promotions, good evaluations — even guaranteeing a 20-year hitch. No other organization can punish even administrative wrongdoing with prison, discharge or career destroying rebukes. Soldiers who have primary parenting responsibilities have always been the sole exception to the emphasis on performance. Lieutenant S, Oakland's pregnant conflicted Madonna, surfaced the first female case where the meritocratic system is abandoned for political expediency: pregnancy. Somewhere along the line, external advocacy groups persuaded Department of Defense equal opportunity managers that any reference to absences or non-performance of one's duties due to pregnancy or child rearing is a form of de facto sexual harassment and discrimination.

That information was never filtered down to the men who supervised the first wave of female career officers in the mixed-gender Army. The command staff section's conflict boiled to a roiling conclusion when the section chief, Captain M evaluated Lieutenant S as honestly as he was able to do, without condemning her absences, early departures, or her routine requests for exemption to duties requiring night or weekend duty. Perhaps Captain M felt he could afford to be honest, because Lieutenant S had let it be known that she was leaving active duty to care for her family. The army's favorite aphorism, "Never assume, it only makes and ASS out of U and ME," came to mind when Lieutenant S's true feelings about her career were made known.

Lieutenant S first complained to her senior rater, a man who was my first senior rater, a Navy commander. The senior rater stood by Captain D's summation of her performance. Perhaps Lieutenant S would have left well enough alone. She told me her husband coached her to file complaint after complaint to get the evaluation changed.

When that did not happen, Lieutenant S finally retaliated by filing a formal sexual harassment and Inspector General complaint. As the only woman in the command suite office, she claimed she was being held to a higher standard. That could easily be proven untrue. Shorter workdays and exemption from duty rosters and exemption from physical training tests are only three examples of where she was, in fact, given preferential treatment.

Her pride wounded by the documentation of poor performance, she also alleged many violations of Army regulations by the officers in the command suite. The most significant one she cited to me. She alleged that the Navy 0-6 (Captain) used the command sedan to send out for Burger King or Popeye's fast food whenever the staff worked through lunch. Officially, it was against regulation to use a military vehicle for private transportation. One could rationalize the use of the sedan as a labor saving device. (Seven or eight people sit at their desks and work while one driver takes the mint white sedan on a five-mile round trip to scoop up the fast-food bags, drop them off to each employee at their desk. The eight workers munch as they work, never missing a beat.) The regulations clearly stated, however, that military vehicles were to be used exclusively for government business.

Just as I underwent the hyper-inflated weeklong investigation of Sergeant D's accusation of sexual discrimination for giving him a well-deserved average evaluation, so did Captain M and our mutual senior rater, Captain J. I was completely exonerated, however, and when my investigation was over, I received a complete apology from the investigating officer. Captain M, whose evaluation was also deemed fair, did not experience negative repercussions. The Navy O-6, on the other hand, who was a Vietnam combat veteran, was formally reprimanded for allowing his sedan to be used as a fast-food delivery cart.

So we had this peculiar situation that you see time and again on active duty. The female soldier, in this case, Lieutenant S, who was unable to cope with the cumbersome tasks of toddler childcare and high pressure staff work in a command suite, was nevertheless, overjoyed that her counterattack had some effect. The Navy Captain, an over-achieving, hard-working man was forced into early retirement. I was never close to him, but he treated me with the utmost respect and dignity. His early retirement smelled foul to me, and played a role in my own decision to consider return to civilian life. I didn't want to give my heart and soul to the Army, only to have someone jealously tear down everything I worked to achieve. As one officer was fond of saying at that time in the Army's history, "there are no external enemies, so the Army is engaged in mutual annihilation."

Two people whom I admired were brought low by unfair allegations of harassment or discrimination. I was luckier than Kathy and the Navy captain, but the institutional practices made me just as vulnerable to downfall as my friends.

Most of my subordinates were also civilians, but most did not have the security of a government service (GS) job. The childcare and guest house workers were mostly non-appropriated fund (NAF) employees. Real accountability and productivity yardsticks were built into the NAF system. The GS system, on the other hand, was a towering giant dinosaur. Not pretty to look at, and basically useless to the conduct of business or military missions.

Even the GS employees who worked for me, however, were cut from a different cloth than the average warehouse worker. I was blessed not only with my boss, Lieutenant Colonel Siegling, who carefully mentored me through the maze of supervisory procedures and practices for civilians, I also had two eccentric but wonderful civilian women who taught me the ropes.

Marge, our Army Emergency Relief officer was a single mother, a self-made counselor who stood about five feet tall. She had worked at Oakland since the Vietnam War. Marge was as sensible and compassionate as she was scornful of pretentious, well-educated people.

Shortly after my arrival, when I thought I was her supervisor, I questioned a second grant to a large family. Marge stood tall, lowered her bifocals over the tip of her nose and squinted her eyes and nose with indignity.

"Looky here, Lieutenant. I've been here almost 20 years. I see lieutenants come and go. Come and go every year. And I'm still here. I know who needs money and who don't! I know who can repay and who can't! Now you just listen to me, and you'll do all right. You'll stay!"

So much for my supervisory authority. Thereafter, Marge dictated to me and to the colonels who would receive AER grants and who would receive loans.

In Marge's case, I did not need to monitor her work closely. She kept meticulous accounting files. She had the kindness and softness of the perfect mother nobody ever had. So when young GIs would buy beer instead of diapers, even when their paychecks were short, she had this tender, tough way of telling them off. Then she would sit them down and teach them how to do a monthly budget. Only when she had a keen sense that the soldiers would return for follow-up counseling would she cut a check to their landlord, or to the electric company. Before turning over the check, she issued a very stern speech about their responsibilities as soldiers and fathers, and a speech about her confidence that these men, indeed, would use the tricks she taught them to stay out of trouble. Why? Because, of course, if they knew the tricks in the first place, they would have done the right thing because it's right!

She never ceased to complain about her low pay. More than once, I had her desk audited by the Personnel Department to upgrade her pay by at least one grade. Despite repeated rehearsals, it was impossible to get Marge to explain her work in non-secretarial language. She made loan decisions, she counseled soldiers, she taught them how to budget, and she managed her financial records. To Marge, her work amounted to filling out forms, just being a good mama to the lonely soldiers, teaching them the common sense household management their mothers should have taught them, and typing and filing records according to Army regulations.

OPM, the Office of Personnel Management rejected my request for Marge's upgrade, citing in classic bureaurcratese that Marge's self-description did not suggest any responsibilities that could not be handled by a junior secretary. The fact that Marge had the same job for more than 20 years made no difference to OPM. Her grade level had a salary cap that she had achieved a decade before. Unless we could prove Marge's responsibilities were greater than her self-reports, her pay grade and her salary would not change.

When I made first lieutenant, I decided to try a new strategy. I scheduled Marge for some career development classes that would, hopefully expand her understanding of her work. I was soon to learn something about women in the workforce that the feminist movement has failed to come to terms with. Marge thought of herself first and foremost as a mother of five, and a grandmother. One of her kids was about to deliver a baby at the same time as the job training. As we got closer to her professional development training, she asked me to cancel her space. I insisted she had to attend, since she was always complaining about her low pay. This training, I was sure, would give her a second opportunity for promotion.

When Marge laid the ground rules for our good working relationship upon my arrival, I never challenged her. She wasn't a senior non-commissioned officer, who was to be obeyed by a new lieutenant. She was more powerful than a non-com, more powerful than God, in some respects. She was a government-civilian, with more than 20 years of experience. Most important, she was fire-proof. Marge was even more lieutenant-proof than any sergeant in the Army.

For the first time since my arrival, I asserted my right to be Marge's boss. I told her she had to go to this training. Marge bolted down to Lieutenant Colonel Siegling's office. Fifteen minutes later, she came back, tear streaked but squinting with determined confidence that she had won her first and last battle with me.

A few minutes later, Lieutenant Colonel Siegling drifted down to my office. He tried to be delicate about Marge's victory. He came into my office and closed the door. I knew I lost right there.

"Well, you know, Marge is a mother, and ya' just have to understand, Marie, that when it comes to new babies... She's gotta have time off when that baby comes."

I reminded the colonel that I had allowed for the possibility that Marge might not make the training, due to her family situation, but that I did not want to cancel her slot, just in case the new baby came sooner or later than planned.

"You just have to understand, Marie, that when it comes to babies..."

That was my first, but not last experience of preferential treatment that is given to women who are pregnant or already parents in the military. Until that day, I was always angered when employers would begin an interview, "I know I can't ask you this because of Equal Employment Opportunity, but are you married?"

To get the job, you had to ignore equal opportunity policies. Employers were frank about their worries, but you have to be a supervisor or have fiscal responsibility to see the real problem.

"Well, my concern is that we will train you and your husband will move or you will get pregnant. We can't afford to..."

Now I could see why employers were wary to hire women. No matter what you did to accommodate their concerns, you could get yourself in trouble. If you let them stay on a mommy-track, and not encourage them to compete for promotions, you could be vulnerable to attacks that you created a glass ceiling for women. If you insisted they compete by putting in the same hours, the same effort into professional development as men, you could be accused of insensitivity to women's family responsibilities.

My experience with Marge did not convince me that women were actually using birthing issues for preferential treatment. It took several experiences with dozens of female soldiers to see that women were being treated preferentially whenever birthing and childcare issues surfaced on the job.

I soon realized Marge never wanted to be promoted. She wanted to be paid a decent, living wage for all the family miracles she worked as our Army Emergency Relief coordinator. That is a whole separate issue, which Lieutenant Colonel Siegling and I worked together to correct for Marge and the other civilian working moms in our Services Branch.

I will always think of Helen Fleck as the grand dame of Army Community Services. Helen owned an elegant Cadillac that she drove to every funeral for retired military families who sought her support as Survivor Assistance Officer.

Helen was just as eager to mentor the female officers who ran the ACS department as any male officer in the chain of command. In fact, since there were no senior female officers to mentor the women, Helen made it her business to coach women in the art of military politics. She knew that the Army was crude in its organizational psychology, but she also knew that women could not afford to lower their standards to the ways of Army men if they were to survive long term. Helen mentored every female soldier who crossed her path. Those who were smart enough to listen to this retired Air Force colonel's wife, who never did a pushup or a road march, are still thankful for her shrewd coaching. Helen taught me many gracious secrets about officer protocol and she protected me from many bloopers I could have made. She was masterful in the arts of hospitality, command and ceremony.

Until the Army began formalizing most of its counseling programs, Helen thought of herself as the mom that every soldier needed in moments of despair. Her primary response to every depressed soldier who came to her for counseling was "let's go back to the kitchen, and I'll make you a sandwich!"

When the Army assigned domestic violence to the Army Community Services program, Helen was the first counselor at Oakland. She applied the lessons of her own married life to most counseling situations, "Now tell me," she would ask. "What was it that brought you together in the first place? What was the magic that attracted you to each other?" Over the years, American family life had become more and more unstable. Army families became, despite the investment in family programs, more and more dysfunctional and more violent. By the time I arrived, we had bizarre guest house cases where drunk, drugged angry men would cut their wives' fingers off by jamming their hands in the door hinges. By then, Helen and I both knew that as uncertified professionals, neither of us could use normal family counseling approaches on rampaging soldiers. When the Army mandates for prevention of domestic violence were inaugurated she graciously yielded to theories about battering and learned helplessness syndrome. She let me replace us both with civilian social workers.

The pace of our family support programs, even the domestic violence program increased so rapidly, however. There was no indication of let up. Helen

The Winning Team
*Jerry Montana (bottom right) and other soldiers
win The Lunchtime Sports Tournament for
the commander.*

eventually retired in grand style, with the same panache that characterized her tenure at Oakland, but she never lost touch with any of her military family. She still sends out the annual Christmas letter, updating all of us on the whereabouts of the civilians and the military who served together. In 1995, I let her know that our male enlisted soldier, Jerry Montana, was stationed in Korea with me. Sergeant Jerry Montana had worked for us through most of my tour at Oakland. When I apprised Helen of Jerry's great work with the 44th Combat Engineer Battalion in Korea, she wrote back, "Tell Jerry he was a hell of a guy!"

He was. Jerry Montana was erroneously assigned to Oakland Army Base in 1984. Jerry was a mechanic, accustomed to heavy field duties with field artillery and tanker units. Only the United States Army would assign such a technical specialist to a base that had absolutely no jobs for mechanics, and then tell the soldier, "Tough. You have to stay there at least one year before we can move you."

Jerry was a storyteller and a philosopher. He would sit at Helen's kitchen counseling table next to my office and regale the women with stories about the real Army. None of the women in the Family Support Programs could imagine that his stories were remotely true. They had never seen a ditch, a tank, or a battle training site, let alone a battlefield. They had to take his word when he reiterated his embarrassment that Oakland Army Base was a country club with no mission or circumstances remotely consistent with what soldiers were supposed to do.

Yet, Jerry was never bitter about the detour to Oakland. He used the time to be an advocate for soldiers. He didn't hesitate to advocate for changes that would benefit soldiers, whether they were active duty, retirees or combat veterans. All the handicapped renovations in buildings I managed were because Jerry insisted the ramps had to be installed. Together with Sergeant Penalosa, he insisted all our renovation plans include handicapped access ramps and railings. One day he dramatized the humiliation a Vietnam veteran must feel whenever he had to be carried into and out of a building that had no ramps or elevators.

"They're soldiers, Ma'am! They served their country! They deserve to use our services just like anybody else!"

Jerry injected his commentary into every situation where he believed the Army was letting the troops down. Once, a soldier with a large family was discharged through the Oakland Transfer Point. This sergeant was in serious debt, with no funds to move his family back home. He was being discharged because of his financial problems and because he had several nervous breakdowns. Marge Brown actually sent the man to me, because she had no legal avenues to give the man any financial support. He was leaving the Army within three days. She could not give him a loan. Technically, she was not supposed to give him a grant.

This man had no extended family to help him. Because he was a Jehovah Witness, his family shunned him because he violated the pacifist principles of their faith. All the while I talked to the sergeant, Jerry Montana paced back and forth outside my office, telegraphing signals to me that we had to find some way to help this guy. At first, I said there was no legal way we could help him. He quietly left the office, with sunken shoulders. Jerry came into my office and paced back and forth.

"Ma'am, that's what's wrong with the Army. The Army just uses you, and then throws you away. That man made a sacrifice. He lost everything. He gave five years of his life. And what does the Army say? That's what's wrong, Ma'am. The Army don't take care of soldiers. They don't care about soldiers. That's what's wrong..."

I heard that speech dozens of times from Jerry Montana, and every time, it pushed me to take a risk.

"Jerry, go out and get that guy. We'll figure something out."

I can't remember what we did for the soldier. Whether we gave him a grant, or got some help from Red Cross. The situation resolved, and Jerry was satisfied enough to go back down the hall and resume his work in the I.D. card section.

In Korea, ten years later. Sergeant Jerry Montana was still giving the same speech, and he was still right, every time. Only as a sergeant, he had more power to take matters into his own hands. He treated soldiers the way he always thought they should be treated. Helen's assessment of Jerry is still right. Jerry Montana is a hell of a guy.

General John Stanford had the most profound influence on my life at Oakland Army base. My other supervisors, staff and friends have given me much, but I think Stanford was sent as an act of Providence to help the racially-mixed base come to terms with many historical resentments and divisions that resulted not only in polarization, but disintegration of the command.

Although the Army could pride itself in its extraordinary efforts to overcome racial discrimination, the racial divide in our country still expressed itself in an unsettling social separation, even in contexts governed strictly by government regulations. This color divide was nowhere so delineated in the United States Army than in the greater San Francisco Bay area.

The Presidio was the Army's pride and Oakland Army Base her embarrassment. They were not only a bridge and a bay apart, they were as pure in color separation as the layers of an Oreo cookie. The Presidio was a white, middle class installation. Oakland Army Base was predominantly black, and perpetually prey to the forces that are destroying inner city African-American neighborhoods throughout our nation.

The statistical hegemony of African-Americans was so irrefutable, that Hispanics filed and won a lawsuit against the base. Sometime before 1984, the base hired blacks in disproportionate numbers, thereby excluding Hispanics from their rightful share of the Affirmative Action pie, their rightful share of the economic security provided by GS jobs. The California courts ruled OAB should have a quota system to increase the representation of Hispanics in the GS workforce. Once the ruling was made, OAB zealously recruited Hispanics for strategic permanent jobs to overcome at least the perception of discrimination against Mexican-Americans.

As in other sectors of American life, however, statistical hegemony did not translate into a social victory for the vast majority of blacks who worked at the base or lived in the surrounding community. Oakland Army Base was the dregs of military transport. Doomed to eventual closure, the base, by virtue of its location in a ghettoized urban community had its purposes: to ship that which could not be handled in more prestigiously zoned communities.

In its glory days, Oakland Army Base served as the transfer point for hundreds of thousands of soldiers right until the Vietnam War ended. Since then, small numbers of soldiers dribbled through the base as they traveled to and from Pacific Rim assignments and the continental U.S. (CONUS). Until it closed, OAB was a shipping port. Ostensibly, the Military Traffic Management Command shipped commissary and post-exchange materiel to troops in the Pacific. In a last minute effort to save the base from premature extinction, Team Spirit exercises were added to the pretense of routine mission. The true value of OAB, however, was its usefulness as transport center for nuclear, biological and chemical weapons. This mission was denied for more than a decade after personages such as Martin Sheen protested the presence of nuclear weapons on the base.

The City of Oakland passed Nuclear Free Zone legislation, requiring the removal of hazardous weapons, just as other East Bay cities had. Anti-nuclear activists stood on street corners of most cities, including San Francisco, demanding the removal of weapons and closure of military installations that were designed to handle NBC weapons. The U.S. government, however, never conceded during those protest years while I was stationed at Oakland that NBC weapons were shipped through Oakland.

Contrary to the theories of many environmental activists, who coined the phrase, environmental racism, I did not believe that the U.S. intentionally stockpiled nukes at OAB because the city was predominantly black. More likely OAB was selected because the base was an oasis, set apart from the city population at the edge of the bay. There is no community life outside the gate — only a confusing maze of railroad tracks and trucking terminals and highway overpasses. Community activists persisted in their conspiracy theories. Further research proved many of their theories had legitimacy.

Robert Allen, Alice Walker's companion, published a book on the Port Chicago Mutiny trials from WWII. There were 50 black men who where selected to work in outrageously unnecessary danger. They committed a spontaneous act of civil disobedience.

Most of the blacks assigned to Port Chicago were actually trained for other military occupations, not at all associated with munitions. Yet, throughout WWII, these same blacks, though never trained for munitions handling were sent to Concord. As Robert Allen reports the story, white officers directed the stacking and placing of munitions without regard to the safety of handlers. Gunpowder was stacked dangerously high and in close rows that all but guaranteed an explosion.

Allen documented the story of white officers who placed bets on the likelihood and the timing of injuries to the black soldier population. One day, when the piers were deemed exceedingly dangerous, the black soldiers who were told to march down to the pier spontaneously refused to do so. Someone at the head of the column of 50 or so men sat down. The rest sat down and refused to work on a pier that was stacked with ignitable ammo power. Shortly after, the ammunition on the pier exploded, shattering the barracks windows and everything in its path.

When the Port Chicago pier finally blew, the Army should have prosecuted the officers assigned for reckless endangerment and criminal negligence of safety standards. Instead, the brass tried the 50 African-Americans for mutiny, specifically, for refusing to march down to the pier shortly before the walls of dynamite blasted the pier and several barracks buildings into oblivion. That story, published in the mid-80s, was in the folklore of activists who believed that arms shipments from any port in California was part of a racist militarist agenda.

I could not fathom that such an agenda existed, because men and women who worked at Oakland Army Base were considerably more well-off than other African-Americans who lived in the bay area. Relationships between blacks and whites were friendlier. Moreover, African-American men and women held many positions of power on the base.

There was not a real sense of transcendent or multi-cultural harmony at the base, however. For all of the EO Martin Luther King breakfasts, the Humanity Day Festivals, and the bi-annual EEO training sessions, the racial divisions were most apparent when the duty day was over. Where there was freedom to associate, the base tended to fall out, for the most part, on color lines. Integration has been forced on American schools, in federal institutions, and even, in businesses that depend on government grants. No one could argue that this is bad for America, for the economy, or even for local communities. True, the military strives to maintain social cohesion by providing command social events that almost require racial integration. Command socials are always ethnically diverse. Nevertheless, as soon as the commanders declare that the formal functions are concluded, sub groups tend to fall out according to color and ethnicity.

Whether to create a new, abiding sense of oneness in the OAB workforce, or to dispel the civilian protestor's accusations that OAB was a racist imposition on the liberal black city of Oakland, someone at higher headquarters decided that racial unity must be achieved in the MTMC command. The persistent racial divide both on the base and between the base and its neighbors in the San Francisco Bay Area were brilliantly, if only temporarily, overcome with the assignment of Brigadier General John Stanford, who became the new commander of the Military Traffic Management Command, Western Area.

When General John Stanford arrived at Oakland Army Base, he created a transcendent unified spirit that is rarely found, even in government institutions today. Before his Oakland tour, he was a diplomatic general who served for five years as an assistant to Cap Weinberger. His wife, Pat, often teased that John never saw combat, although he did serve in Vietnam. He was, she would say, a pilot, who flew out on missions, then returned to a safe barracks each night.

Regardless, General Stanford's charisma was matched with technical competence and an extraordinary capacity to inspire confidence and hope in the old timers, the civilians, the young soldiers and the civilian community alike. He embodied the walk-around management style to a maddening extreme.

John Stanford began walking around the moment he arrived at Oakland. His change of command ceremonies provided many glimpses of what we could expect from our future commander. He was like a magnet, drawing dozens of acolytes to his side for bits of wisdom sprinkled in with his wry commentary on military life.

No soldier was too insignificant to escape his notice. No soldier or family member was beyond his reach of support. Yet, he exuded a personal standard of perfection that could at times, be overwhelming. I do not know if other junior officers were intimidated by his standards, but I was. Even though I felt great affection for him, I could not ever imagine living up to his expectations. At command socials, we could joke about our foibles with all the self-deprecating humor that makes having lieutenants in your organization at least a tolerable experience. But in the workplace, I never knew if it was possible to meet the goal post.

John would walk into your area and hand his service cap to his aide. When asked, "How are you doing today, General," he'd smile and wryly respond, "Perfect, but you knew that!"

General Stanford took his first walk through my guest house when I wasn't there to escort him. That was his style. The housekeepers called me, in a panic. Shirley, the mother of one of my OBC classmates, worried for me.

"The general wants to know why there are carpet burns in the lobby carpet, and why the bathrooms smell of Pine Sol."

We could always change the tile soap and the fragrance at the snap of a General's fingertips, but there was nothing we could do to change the lobby carpet. The cigarette burns were going to be around for a long time. The carpet was less than five years old, and Colonel S from the Property Directorate refused to fund its replacement before it was capitalized.

Not that I hadn't tried. An elderly engineer, I think his name was Al had already begun to work with me to replace some of the rusty vents and mildewed tiles in our guestrooms. But like the rest of us, Al had budgetary constraints and five-year timetables that guided his schedule of big repairs. I was very self-conscious when General Stanford touched upon our rawest nerve. He was noticing a situation about which we could do nothing. I called the senior engineer at the base, Steve Leite. My language was not ladylike, definitely colorful, and vividly descriptive of my anger that this new General could dare to walk into my shop without any courtesy notice. Steve stopped the conversation.

"Let me close my office door, Lieutenant, before someone takes those bars away from you."

Steve Leite invited me up to his office to assess the rehabilitation needs of the guest house, then accompanied me on a tour of all the buildings for which I was responsible. I don't think he had ever visited Jacobs before, but Steve's pay grade was oodles above mine. He had already discerned the general's priorities even before I called him. Steve asked me to work with him on a complete renovation of the guest house. Knowing that I had such an ally, my embarrassment about the decade-long debilitation of Jacobs melted.

What unsettled me at first, was the drastic change of protocol. By this time, I knew enough about soldiering to know that it was not appropriate for a lieutenant to seek out the direct support of a general. I assumed that General

John Stanford would abide by the same protocol. General Stanford did not rate me for the first year of his Oakland command. I had no legitimate reason to speak to him unless he approached me.

I avoided his contact in the workplace, but knew that I would visit with him inevitably at the command socials and weekend officer calls. At the next social, I had my chance. I looked the new General in the eye, completely avoided the subject of Jacobs, and made my impression instead by mentioning the classical performing groups that would make his family's time in San Francisco most enjoyable. I wanted General Stanford to think of me as a worldly, sophisticated officer — not as a ghetto girl who couldn't tell that her hotel rooms were permanently stained with rust and mildew.

General Stanford's first officers' call was at the Fort Mason Officer's Club. Just a few doors away from the General's bayside mansion and a few blocks from my apartment. It was not difficult to turn our cocktail banter to the cultural smorgasbord that was just a short walk away from those who resided at Fort Mason. He wanted to know how I had gotten to know San Francisco's cultural scene so well in such a short time. He was impressed when I told him about visits with my sister, Beeshie.

By the time John Stanford arrived at Oakland, Beeshie had moved to Italy, and I had no one with whom to enjoy the symphony. I was sorely in need of cultural renewal. The Oakland underbelly almost asphyxiated me. Between the petty drug peddlers, the domestic violence situations, and the repeated bedroom spy sagas, I felt I was being snuffed to the ground by the huge belly of a Sumo wrestler.

Intuitively, I knew that stultification was one of the dangerous side effects of a military career. This was confirmed by researchers at least once in my career. A study was conducted to determine which American profession placed the highest value on personal and professional integrity. General officers of the Army scored highest, except for one area: their lack of cultural exposure left them lacking in the soulful, creative, life-giving appreciation of art and culture. I did not want this to happen to me.

General Stanford created an aura of transcendence that made it possible to think about the many other important things in life besides soldiering: love, friendship, adventure, culture, even faith. I was almost burned out, so I was grateful that John Stanford encouraged his officers to expand their interests beyond their jobs. But who to venture out with? My first peer group at Oakland disintegrated for all the right reasons. Kathy and Carl moved to Washington, D.C. to make their careers as civilian transporters. Mike Scott went to law school. Some of the others went to advanced schools to pave the way for their captain bars. I sought relief in companions who had cultural interests that were similar to mine. Pat certainly enjoyed music, but he was reclusive and uninterested in live concert performances. It was time for me to find a new male companion.

A wonderful man, David sought my attentions at one of General Stanford's command socials. He was married, but legally separated from his wife. By all accounts, his wife left him, not the reverse. I informed him I would not go out with a married man. David showed me the UCMJ regulations that stipulated that legally separated men were permitted to date in the Army — unlike 1997, when General Ralston, the Air Force general lost his opportunity to be Commander in Chief due to his affairs while legally separated. (Ralston's tormentors attempted to leverage his promotion to Chair of the Joint Chiefs in exchange for the exoneration of Lieutenant Kelly Flynn, a female Air Force pilot who committed adultery with more than one enlisted person or spouse, and who repeatedly lied about her affairs.) The Army regulations stipulated that during legal separation officers would be free to date, so long as family financial obligations were satisfied.

General Stanford seemed to relish the spontaneity of his junior officers. He inspired us to break out of the bureaucratic mold to show ourselves to our staff and our customers as caring human beings. Once he sent a letter of congratulations to a captain, Bob Kant, on the decision to serve a customer at the Class Six store by carrying her case of spirits to the car without his service cap. Those were the days when privates were trained to call their officers to account for such breaches of the regulatory code. I recall his pleasure at the officers who had enough spunk to run the annual Bay to Breakers in San Francisco. I was one of them. It was at a barbecue after this run that John Stanford first remarked that he would take me to the stars. He probably encouraged all of his officers with this theme, but during the Bay to Breakers barbecue, it was my turn to hear the awe-inspiring invitation,

"You know, I am always going to encourage talented young officers. You have a special magic. If you stay with me, you'll get your first star."

The general pulled all the record briefs for his junior officers soon after he arrived, to determine how his new staff should be structured, who would be his aide-de-camp, and who would be his headquarters detachment commander. I was not committed to an Army career, so I did not even attempt to compete for one of the plum jobs. The general didn't rate me, and I didn't want him to rate me. I did not aspire to be a career chairborne ranger, either. I just wanted to serve my tour without ever taking on the Adjutant's job. All I wanted at the time was for the general to think I walked on water as a social services lieutenant. I did not pay too much attention to the fact that generals influence the structure of the future leadership by rating the men and women whom they think should make it to the top of the pyramid. I was flattered to know that I was being considered for his three lieutenant slots, however, because he made it known that good leaders surround themselves with positive, successful people. The constellation you create can either tarnish your command or create a burst of fire and energy strong enough to ignite a storm of creativity. General John Stanford was definitely hoping to form a constellation as creative in spirit as the zodiac Gemini purports to be.

Lieutenant Colonel Siegling encouraged me to compete for the headquarters detachment command job. I have a strong, perhaps exceedingly strong personality. This flaw, I knew, would not make me happy as a commander, especially in a command where all the senior officers pulled the strings of the detachment commander as if he were a wooden puppet. The job I had, Chief of the Services Branch, gave me much freedom, thanks to my supervisors. After all the whining I had done about the need for the Army officer corps to divest itself of the family support programs, I expressed my preference to remain the chief.

On the first go around, in the fall of 1994, Siegling respected my wishes. We had plenty to do in the Community Services Division. The guest house renovation was still a dream. The childcare center plans were approved but not yet a reality. I seemed better able to handle the family situations than the average lieutenant — particularly the domestic violence situations. Until Stanford made his final staffing decisions, he continued to poke his nose into my area of operations. Fortunately, a cocky young lieutenant from Korea intended to become general someday. The aide-de-camp position was the first rung up that latter, so he won that prize. Patrick was the senior-ranking transporter in line for the command job, so he earned the headquarters command slot.

If, as the saying goes, the Army is your wife, and your life is your mistress, I started having an affair with life soon after Stanford settled in. The army was an isolated world that was starting to choke my soul. Although I loved spending time with John and Pat Stanford and my friends at command functions, I needed to stretch, to get in touch with all the political and artistic scenes. I was itching to get out of the Army, but I still had no marketable skills that would permit me to stay in the Bay area. No one was going to hire Marie deYoung to conduct the San Francisco Symphony, to be sure.

I started taking classes in accounting and computers. One class I had to take twice, but that was okay, because I bumped into my childhood neighbor and friend, Ira Katuran. We became study buddies for that class, and extended kin for the rest of my stay in the Bay Area. I began to date men outside the Army, and moved in with a group of left wing Berkeley radicals to test my loyalty to the military and mainstream capitalism. It was a safe way for me to test my ability to live with my radical sister, assuming she would finally return to San Francisco.

After John Stanford's first year, the fizzle from all our sassy efforts to turn Oakland Army Base into a cutting edge enterprise started to dissipate. A lot of the officers started to go off in their own direction. General Stanford, always the diplomatic general, an officer who was accustomed to using extravagant efforts to lubricate the social relationships, called his brood of officers together. Jesse's socials did not really bond the officers together anymore, which was probably why John Stanford began a series of officer development meetings, where senior and junior officers talked about serious leadership issues.

These conferences would begin in the late afternoon. We sat around a highly polished mahogany command conference table, green suited and officious, as if we were discussing strategic policy at the Pentagon. In one roundtable, General Stanford asked the question, "Is it permissible for an officer or a soldier to cry?" Lieutenants and colonels alike were tentative in their first responses. Junior officers, all post-Vietnam vintage were rather harsh in their judgement of those who emoted while in uniform. Senior officers hesitated, but later disclosed situations in combat where they and their men cried. I couldn't help but advocate that crying could indeed be a sign of strength, a way for men to express their deep bonds, not only because I was the designated nice person, the command's family and domestic violence counselor, but also because of family memories of big burly men who cried at family gatherings.

Although I was defending the right of male soldiers to cry when they are grief or terror stricken, I was just as unlikely to tolerate such weakness in myself as the men were unlikely to tolerate it by any soldier. John Stanford had already put this question to me late one night after a command social. He, Jesse and I sat at the bar for a nightcap. Stanford expressed concern about a personality trait of mine: terminal seriousness and a tendency towards depression when I am not running five miles or playing the piano daily. He asked each of the women at the bar but zeroed in on me.

"Do you ever cry, just cry? Isn't it natural for women to cry? I have a woman friend who would just sit and cry and cry and cry."

When John elaborated on his question, inviting his entire cadre of officers to grapple with this feminine response to tragedy or sadness, I felt free to add my two cents worth, probably to defend my own reluctance to just "cry and cry and cry" when I was sad.

"I don't think it's a masculine or a feminine thing to cry," I said forcefully. "I have five cousins who are burly truck drivers and factory workers. When their baby sister was married, these guys cried like babies, and so did my uncle. They cried in church, they cried at the reception in between dances. Not too long ago, one of these male cousins died. His surviving brothers cried for weeks and weeks, at the funeral, at home, and in their sleep. These men are about as strong as men can get... I don't think crying is such a feminine thing..."

Lieutenant Colonel Siegling sat in silence, but he twinkled with delight at my response. The other lieutenants asserted their masculinity by denying the appropriateness of tears in any situation. Stanford was pleased with the exchange and with my comments. The next day, Al Siegling stopped by my office to congratulate me for levelheaded participation in the officers' dialogue. Then his smile evaporated.

"Marie, these young men, don't let them fool you. When you are in combat, you cry. When I was a chopper pilot I cried in Vietnam. Every time I had to put a body bag of a young boy in the back of my chopper, I cried. We all did."

He smiled again and laughed, but it was the saddest laugh, one that tenderly revealed this kind man was still hurting from Vietnam.

"If you were a commander on the DMZ, and one of your young officers came to you and pleaded for help," Stanford began the scenario for his next Officer's Call. "She is married and terribly depressed. For the past few weeks, you've noticed that she has suddenly become vibrant, alive. You couldn't understand the change until she came to your hooch and confided that she was in the middle of an affair with another soldier. What would you do?"

Senior officers refrained from commentary on this indelicate subject, which we would all have to confront at one time or another in our careers. Most of the junior officers recommended harsh judicial punishment, especially since the Army was emphasizing family values and strict adherence to the ethical code. Perhaps my morality is skewed or perhaps my role as Oakland Army Base's designated nice-person-counselor gave me different insights. I found myself giving the sole contrary answer as a junior officer.

"The command policy regulations do not require judicial punishment when an affair is uncovered. Affairs are usually the result of some other problem that must be faced."

I responded as if the experiences with which I dealt as services chief were the equivalent of a Ph.D. in psychology.

"I'd tell the officer she had to cease and desist with the affair, and go to confidential counseling to determine what other problems needed to be resolved. If her marriage was doomed, then she needed to take action to ensure she was legally separated before she started to date another man..."

I was, as my non-commissioned officer in charge (NCOIC) reminded me, an older woman. Most of the lieutenants were fresh out of college, never married or newlyweds. The act of infidelity or forgiveness for such a grave offense was simply inconceivable to the younger officers. Once again, the older officers were mute, perhaps because their experience of soldiers who had indulged in adulterous relationships was so vast, they knew that harsh judicial responses would surely create a hollow army. Again, Lieutenant Colonel Siegling beamed with pride, though he said not a word in the meeting.

One of my proudest days in the Army was in July of 1985, eighteen months after I pinned on my butter bars. Lieutenant Colonel Siegling and Lieutenant Colonel James Seaton, the new Deputy Installation Commander pinned on my silver bars to promote me to first lieutenant.

The women on my staff held a big party, and ordered a fancy cake to celebrate. My cousin, who was a research assistant at Lawrence Livermore Laboratories was present. He was dating my senior rater's daughter, which infuriated me. But, he was a handsome pre-med student, so I knew that my rater, a strong Evangelical Christian Navy Captain was not unpleased by his daughter's attraction to my cousin Paul. The party that Siegling, Marge and the others threw was probably the kindest and tenderest gift I have ever received from my co-workers. I still feel the warmth of their support when I think of that celebration.

I did not realize that my bosses, Lieutenant Colonel Siegling and Lieutenant Colonel Seaton, were lobbying for my placement as the next Headquarters Detachment Commander even before my promotion. While still the detachment commander, Patrick asked me to cover for him during his first vacation, which I did. The week passed unremarkably. That stint persuaded me unequivocally that I would never be happy with command, as the HQ had no mission, and the unit was too small to invest any energy or creativity in it.

My bosses were determined to give me the best career chances so they continued to lobby to have me named as commander. That evaluation from the general would go far ten years down the pike. General Stanford did not limit his career influence to the three lieutenants he rated, I would discover years later. This walk-around general who would snap his fingers, then move mountains to rebuild, reshape or remodel any broken down building or situation, did not make himself scarce from the rest of the command group. Most of us were not experienced enough to know that General Stanford typified the new army boss with his endless generosity as a mentor.

In all the staff sections, at one point or another, Stanford would call his young officers in, ask them to discuss their vision. He wanted to know their strategies for taking the broken operations, the crumbled infrastructure at Oakland to new, unimaginable levels of service and, as far as a military base could, to aesthetic beauty. He would suggest changes, ask you to come up with rational plans for renovations or team reorganizations. Then, he would set you to work. In reality, General Stanford sprinkled the fairy dust of command priorities after your meeting with him, and the entire intransigent Oakland and Sixth Army workforce responded to your lowly lieutenant's bidding to realize the General's dreams.

I never understood the extent to which Stanford was responsible for my success or effectiveness as a program manager. I truly believed my hard work and diplomacy accomplished the renovation of the guest house and childcare

Doubling My Good Fortune
LTC James Seaton and LTC Al Siegling pin on the author's first lieutenant bars eighteen months after she was commissioned.

center. The drug dealers and pimps appeared to be permanently banished from my guest house. Only months after my arrival, one of the Pentagon's directors for the Child Care Program acceded to our strategy to build a new childcare center, and to hire our own GS-9 manager, rather than put our operation in the hands of the Presidio. I handled many domestic violence emergencies, and put many prevention programs in place. In time, I facilitated a contract for a civilian counseling program that gave soldiers the opportunity for confidential treatment. John Stanford obviously gave the command to release $60,000 per year to effect the contract, but he always made it look like I was the miracle worker who got this thing going.

Both Stanford and Siegling made me feel that these successes were mine to claim. At one point, General Stanford even took me to Washington D.C. with his wife Patricia to showcase Oakland's model domestic violence and family support programs. Numerous other days, Siegling and Seaton, our new Deputy Installation Commander would sit quietly and pour coffee as I briefed generals about our model family support programs to such men as General Vuono, who passed through Oakland enroute to the Pacific Rim.

Perhaps more humility about my own role in these projects would have prevented the onset of ennui. Humble lieutenant is one of those oxymorons that I did not embody. So, one building refurbishing and renovation, one childcare center project and many family support programs later, boredom set in. There were no job challenges left. My bosses recognized they would lose me if they did not drop another challenge onto my horizon.

During my friend Pat's second vacation, I was again named acting commander of the headquarters detachment. On the first day, I was alerted to a possible date rape committed by a chaplain's assistant against his subordinate.

The chaplain's assistant, Sergeant H plied his private first class with alcohol while they were on duty at the Presidio chapel on a Saturday afternoon. The two drove to a beach in South San Francisco, where other men joined their party. The woman, who was Caucasian, performed numerous acts of oral sex on the men. The men who engaged in this consensual gang bang were all black. PFC R, the junior chaplain assistant who performed sex for her boss and friends was dating an Asian military policeman when this happened. After she sobered up on Sunday evening, she confessed to her boyfriend that she participated in this sexual escapade.

The humiliated MP proceeded to beat Private First Class R up in her barracks room when she refused to characterize the sex with her black boss as rape. In any remote command, it is almost impossible to police the police, that is to hold policemen to the same standards of accountability as other soldiers. The MPs on duty that night covered up for their co-worker by writing up a blotter report alleging that Private First Class R was not beaten up by her Asian boyfriend, but rather, raped and sodomized by her African-American supervisor and other males. They did not take her to the emergency room for checkup, or gathering of evidence, which left their rendition of the facts almost impossible to substantiate.

As soon as the blotter hit the Deputy Installation Commander's desk, Private First Class R was sent to me for crisis counseling. It was the Monday after her boyfriend beat her up. She was presented to me as a rape victim. The young woman, very timid and soft-spoken yet deliberate in manner insisted to me that she was never raped by Sergeant H, her supervisor. She did not want to get her supervisor in any trouble because she really liked him. She was an alcoholic in treatment in the Army's unforgiving Drug and Alcohol Rehab program. Private First Class R insisted she was fully aware of her decision to drink, even though she was supposed to be taking Antabuse, a drug that nauseates alcoholics when they take even a sip of alcohol. For the sake of her adventure, she threw all caution to the wind, chose to drink, and then, as her own written MP statements attest, had a wild time with several men from the Headquarters Detachment and some civilians, to boot.

PFC R wrote statements at the MP station detailing her sexual activities in the back of a van while parked aside a beach in South San Francisco. The other Army specialists and civilians who participated, all black males, also detailed their activities in written statements to the police. All of these statements were official documents before I ever had a chance to question the way this case was being handled. The MPs expected the case to be handled as a rape, because new California legislation was arguing that women could not give legal consent to sex while drunk.

Because I was only an acting commander, Lieutenant Colonel Seaton, the Deputy Installation Commander chose to handle the disciplinary hearings. I stood by in his office to learn how these things are handled. After each participant was interviewed and questioned about their police statements, Lieutenant Colonel Seaton asked my opinion.

Seaton, commanding in an era where open marriage and recreational promiscuity had been normalized, was pragmatic but deliberate. He recognized, as I did, that consensual activity between two adults, even in a supervisory relationship should never be construed as rape. With that, we had no disagreement. We both agreed that all parties, including the female, needed to be held responsible for the misconduct, albeit to varying degrees. The female, who was relieved of her chaplain duties and sent to work with me in the Army community services section so that our women could keep her focused on rehabilitation, was a menace to herself so long as she chose to drink to excuse her dangerous sexual practices. Seaton relied upon fraternization, adultery, sodomy (defined in the UCMJ as oral sex), drinking on duty and pandering statutes to hold all of the soldiers accountable for their misconduct while on duty at the Presidio and on the San Francisco beaches.

By the end of these proceedings, and without further episodes of soldier misconduct during my watch, I was happy to return to my real job. One week of command made me thankful at last for the boredom that was becoming routine in my regular job. Siegling and Seaton knew for sure, though, that my contentment would not last. They both wanted me to stay in the Army. They must have sensed that my desire to leave at the end of my tour was strong, especially since some of my good friends were gone. Siegling began to lobby behind the scenes once more to have me named Detachment Commander.

One day, in the fall of 1985, this position was mysteriously offered to me. Disgruntled and disillusioned as most of my peers at the cruelty the on-going reduction in force had inflicted on my friends, I reminded Lieutenant Colonel Siegling I was not interested, and probably not the best choice, either.

"Marie, the General is not asking you this time, he is telling you. You will be the next Headquarters Detachment Commander!"

All that stood between me and the change of command ceremony was a face-to-face interview with the big guy.

At the appropriate time, I put on my dress jacket and marched up to the General's office for a formal interview. I thought the purpose was to screen me and two other candidates for final selection, just as he set up three candidates for his first selection. General Stanford began briefing me about his expectations. I was to get on his calendar, at least once per quarter. I was to challenge the troops to do their absolute best, no matter what job they were tasked to complete, no matter what their age or career plans. I was to lead by the highest example. I was to call him anytime day or night if I ever needed to discuss anything. Then, he pulled out his standard traveling speech, "Love Em and Lead Em," and instructed me to memorize and take the text to heart, for it was the essence of his command philosophy. I went into this meeting a bit cynical towards the Army, but I left mesmerized, because General Stanford was like Jesus to me. All-powerful, yet all kind. All commanding, yet all compassionate. A teacher and taskmaster, yet he extended the hand of collegiality and friendship to the climbers and the stragglers alike.

After accepting General Stanford's offer of command, I went back to Lieutenant Colonel Siegling's office, completely forgetful of my earlier decision to reject General Stanford's charm, as well as the golden egg he wanted to share with me. When I approached Siegling's office, he almost bit his fingernail with anxiety. He knew I was quite capable of declining opportunities, even if they were in my best interest. My swagger across the threshold told the bragging tale. I was going to be the new Headquarters Detachment Commander.

Lieutenant Colonel Siegling jumped up from his desk and almost hit the ceiling as he yelped for joy. Then, he hugged me. A perfectly joyful, proud, non-sexual hug of shared victory. Then he stood back and apologized, for even then, such an activity could have been misconstrued by a fool as sexual harassment.

"No apology necessary, Sir!"

I thanked him profusely for his confidence in me, and his everlasting support of my work.

We both knew it was time for me to move on. The Services Branch was well on its way to self-sufficiency by the time I took command. I hired my own replacement for the guest house manager slot, a retired air force officer, Mr. Louis Greene. I hired my own replacement for Army Community Services, Diane Newcomb, and finally, I hired an extraordinary man to run the childcare center, whose name I can't remember, but whose kind gray eyes and indefatigable energy to get the best childcare teachers for our children I will never forget. The childcare center manager did not start until a few months after I assumed command. But all in all, there was nothing for me to do but watch these folks do all the work.

The only question that remained was whether or not I could ever come to appreciate the work of commanding, especially if I chose to stay in the Army and reach for the constellation of stars with whom General John Stanford said I belonged.

CHAPTER 7

It Must Have Been Comet Dust!

I lost Lieutenant Colonel Al Siegling as my primary rater when I assumed command. My new bosses were Lieutenant Colonel James Seaton and General John Stanford. Stanford already briefed me on his expectations. My relationship with Lieutenant Colonel Seaton would most likely change. I just didn't know how. I was moving from the role of Oakland's official nice person, the Community Services earth mother who provided for the wellness of Army families, to that of a real soldier. Before Seaton was my senior rater. Now he would be my primary rater. We needed to talk.

I reported to Lieutenant Colonel Seaton's office for his guidance. Our session was just as friendly and mentoring as the day before. In fact, we pleasantly haggled for a few minutes as if I still had the sweeping power my old job afforded me. A wonderful captain, Bob Kant would assume my job as the Chief of Services Branch, but Bob still had club responsibilities.

"Would you," James Seaton asked me, "for the time being, continue to manage the Child Care Center, since none of the male club managers have that kind of experience, at least until our new Child Care Center Manager formally starts his job?"

The little tots who played at the Child Care Center brought me joy and calm no matter what else was happening on post or in my private life. Under the guise of inspecting or monitoring of teacher activities, I loved to go over and watch the kids glow with pride as they colored or built block houses. They paid no mind to rank or military protocol, except to grab your hat, toss it on their own little crowns, parade around, all the while demanding a few minutes of adulation from you and whoever you brought with you. How could I refuse?

After the usual discussion of policies and lines of communication between the colonel and I, he expressed total confidence in my ability to command.

"Lieutenant, now that you are at the helm, what is the first thing you are going to do?"

I answered without pause, "Sir, I am going to put Sergeant H out of the Army."

Seaton's jaw dropped as he smiled with profound approval.

"Why are you going to do that, Lieutenant?"

"Sir, Sergeant H is a menace to junior soldiers. I don't think he committed rape, but I think he is dangerous. If he exploited one subordinate, he'll exploit another. I want him out of my Army."

"You have my support. Every document has to be run through JAG, but you are the authority who must make this decision, then follow through. Let me know what JAG says we can do."

No one asked or hinted that I should start proceedings to discharge the chaplain's non-commissioned officer because of his sexual misconduct. I just had a gut feeling that this had to be done. I called David, my companion who was still the claims attorney for JAG, and asked him to meet me for lunch. He was more conservative than I. Surely, he would provide the legal language to explain my decision to a captain named Steve, the command's prosecuting attorney, who would have to guide me through the process.

David was fully supportive, and even arranged for another meeting with Steve, so that I could be sure I had a legal case before garnering the Headquarters staff to drudge through the paperwork to effect a discharge. Captain Steve laughed at the prospect of discharging Sergeant H from the Army. In every conversation I had with him for days afterwards, he would say, "We'll be the laughing stock of San Francisco. These people were engaged in consensual behaviors on a San Francisco Beach! The media will laugh and call us fanatical puritans! We can't be snooping in people's bedrooms!"

Frankly, if the behaviors had occurred in someone's private bedroom, and I could be sure that the young female soldier was not being exploited, but fully consensual in her participation. I would have agreed with Steve that the behaviors might be considered immoral, but nobody else's business. As it was, Sergeant H plied his alcoholic subordinate with vodka while on duty. He then took her to the park to participate in group sex. I wouldn't want this man taking my daughter or sister into a chapel alone knowing his propensity to exploit the vulnerabilities of his first assistant. I sure as heck would not want this man taking female soldiers or other male soldiers off on a gang-bang expedition while in a combat situation. Today, we would call Sergeant H's behavior rape proneness. Back then, his actions were simply considered the prerogative of sexually consenting adults by the JAG attorney who would prepare our discharge paperwork. Steve was not persuaded by my argument.

"Their behaviors were consensual, and he was already punished with a summary court-martial. You can't separate him from the Army — that would be double jeopardy!"

The fact was, however, that Army command policy does allow for double jeopardy. When a soldier is convicted of a crime, it is perfectly legal and desirable to separate him from the Army if one can show a pattern in the soldier's behavior that is detrimental to the Army, and beyond rehabilitation.

Why the disconnect between my attitude and JAG's? Captain Steve was definitely a civilian defense attorney who just wore the uniform to complete his service obligation. You couldn't reason with him about the personal conduct standards that applied to soldiers. In exasperation, I drew the line.

"Look, Steve, I know you are the command JAG."

He was pleased that I affirmed his authority.

"But I am the commander. Now, I'm telling you, this man is not staying in my Army. If you don't prepare the administrative discharge papers, I will! He's out!"

When I hung up, I belatedly remembered that Captain Steve still outranked me, for I was only a first lieutenant. Although our command treated all junior officers as if we were one rank, on a first name basis, a disgruntled senior officer could always allege disrespect or insubordination if the situation got out of hand. I rushed immediately to Lieutenant Colonel Seaton's office to apprise him of my faux pas. He was not in, but his secretary made an appointment for me after the duty day was over.

I returned about 5:30 P.M. and briefed the colonel on the status of Sergeant H's discharge. I expected Seaton to lecture me about courtesy and protocol when I recounted my last conversation with Captain Steve. Instead, he grinned with reassurance and said emphatically, "Gee, you really ARE a commander!"

The next impediment to be overcome was Sergeant H's supervisor, the chaplain. My working agreement with this chaplain was simple. The day he arrived he made it clear that as an evangelical chaplain he was not interested in social work. He would conduct bible studies and worship services. I, as the official nice person, the Chief of Services, would handle all social crises ranging from domestic violence to suicidal or alcoholic episodes. This new chaplain was actually a breath of fresh air, for in his own evangelical way, he was a feminist. He did not take his wife for granted, and insisted that the Army hired him, not his wife to work as a chaplain. He zealously guarded her right to refrain from participation in command or officer's wives socials.

I was bewildered however, because our new chaplain positively opposed the removal of Sergeant H from the Army for two reasons. First, it would take the chaplain six or seven months to find a qualified funds clerk to replace Sergeant H, which meant that the Chaplain would have to handle his own funds. Second, the chaplain's Christian capacity for forgiveness made the double punishment of Sergeant H intolerable.

On the chaplain's request, I occasionally attended the Protestant services. My visits to the Protestant services never tempted me to reconvert, but they did let me in on another Army secret, however. Protestant chapel services are, for the most part, sparsely attended. Oakland Army Base was no exception. On any given Sunday, 15 were considered a crowd. That was the wedge that helped me to break down our new Chaplain's first objection to Sergeant H's expulsion. If, as we had already agreed, this chaplain were relieved from all social counseling responsibilities on the base, and only 15 people attended church on Sundays, surely, the responsibility for counting the collection would not overwhelm. What would it possibly amount to? Fifteen or 30 dollars? How long would that take each Sunday? Three minutes?

I was almost willing to concede the Chaplain's second reason, that Christian forgiveness required our confidence in Sergeant H's potential for rehabilitation, if not redemption. Lord knows, I was in need of forgiveness. And I had the same initial reaction to Sergeant H's overall character that our good and decent chaplain had.

Sergeant H was an extremely likeable fellow. His family looked picture-perfect. His wife was immaculately dressed. The children came to church in suits or pretty little dresses with shiny patent shoes. The sergeant's uniforms were crisp. On the surface, Sergeant H presented as a totally STRAK soldier. He was hard-running during physical training, even after his summary court-martial. His standards for church maintenance and altar layouts were such that the average chaplain only hopes to see in the life beyond. His financial records were meticulously kept. The Oakland chaplain was not unrealistic to believe the man was quite capable of redemption.

For a brief time, my gallop towards H's administrative discharge was slowed down to a trot. Ironic, because as a flaming agnostic, I was particularly immune to the logic of Christian faith, and very vulnerable to the reasoning of law. I tossed off Steve's pragmatic but discouraging legal advice as inane, but I was stumped by the chaplain's appeal to give Sergeant H a chance to redeem himself.

Then, out of nowhere, I began to receive complaints that Sergeant H was still relating inappropriately with the single young women in the unit, and that he was trouble for the male soldiers, too.

Various sergeants and residents from the housing neighborhood tried to alert me to the fact that Sergeant H was a pimp and a drug dealer. I thought I had single-handedly removed the last drug-dealing rodent from my guest house a year before. Now that I was commander, and I was responsible for all the crimes and indiscretions my soldiers committed, even when they were off duty, I was learning differently.

Drugs never left Oakland Army Base. Nor did the dealers. Like a pack of mice, they simply burrowed underground and found a new warm, dark location to call home. Two homes, in fact. The NCO Club and the housing area.

Sergeant H was the perfect foil for much of the drug activity. He was amiable. A compliant soldier. He was beyond reproach in appearance and job performance. Invaluable to his boss. He appeared to be a family man. And he had God on his side. His drug involvement was protected by his ostensible work as a chaplain's assistant.

More than one sergeant came forward to remind me of my duty to protect the soldiers from drugs and prostitution, and by inference, Sergeant H, so far as I was able. Soon, it could not be overlooked that Sergeant H continued to mingle with single females, even in his family's apartment when his wife was out of town. The women were provocatively attired, and there were always many men in the apartment.

With only confidential reports and gut feelings to go on, I asked the post chaplain to reconsider his commitment to Sergeant H's rehabilitation. First, did he want the reputation of the chaplain's department to be smeared by this self-serving immoral adulterer? And second, did we really want to take the chance of confronting another situation where Sergeant H had corrupted his subordinates, while indulging his own sexual fantasies?

The chaplain aired his own suspicions. Why was Sergeant H driving a Mercedes Benz on the salary of a junior sergeant? The Bay Area was beyond the financial means of many senior sergeants. How could the sergeant support a family and afford such a flashy car on his meager pay? Secondly, the people Sergeant H surrounded himself with had nothing to do with the official chapel program, of which the chaplain was very protective.

The chaplain finally agreed to support my administrative actions to discharge Sergeant H.

Sergeant H was assigned an attorney from Fort Ord, a handsome and clever young captain. In two or three calls, I made it clear to H's defense attorney that I would not drop the action, so he asked to meet with me. We met. The captain proffered no legal wisdom that would negate the appropriateness of my plan to discharge Sergeant H. His next strategy was to use the continuances and delays that very often discourage the average American from achieving justice in our legal system.

My determination was not undermined, however. We forged ahead with the administrative hearings. I received a confidential call from Lieutenant Colonel Siegling, which disturbed me deeply.

"Marie, I'm just telling you, you have to be careful with Sergeant H. He is an identified drug dealer and pimp. CID has been watching him for years. He's considered dangerous. You have to be careful!"

Great. Now he tells me Sergeant H was always part of the low-life at Oakland. How come the colonel didn't push the previous detachment commander to get H out of the Army? Of course. Just as before, when I wanted to toss the drug dealer out of my guest house, CID would not allow the command to touch Sergeant H, because they were observing him, hoping they could catch the big fish in the Oakland Army Base drug ring.

I had no hard feelings against Siegling, who offered this advice to protect me. Though he was no longer my boss, for a long while the revelation of Sergeant H's membership in the drug ring offended my beliefs as an officer. What kind of Army was this, anyway? Either we were drug-free or we weren't. Tolerating an uniformed drug dealer for more than two years didn't seem right. Either we were a moral Army, or we weren't. Allowing an identified pimp to hide behind the respectability of the Chaplain's Corps for more than two years on the delusion that you would nail him someday seemed to deny any possibility that the Army could ever be a moral institution.

No matter. My job right then was to get Sergeant H out, post haste. We proceeded to hold administrative discharge hearings. On the first round, Sergeant H lost. His attorney immediately filed appeals.

All we could do was wait. Wait and tolerate any behaviors suspected by Sergeant H that the MPs and CID were futilely observing. I had no authority to follow Sergeant H into the housing area to do my own citizen's arrest if I caught him pandering the sexual services of female soldiers. The Provost Marshall had that authority, which he abdicated to the Central Investigating Command, because they controlled the overarching drug investigation.

Christmas came and went. The new chaplain held a lovely candlelight service on Christmas Eve, attended by about 15 people. He invited me to join his service as a representative of the command. I'm glad I did, because I saw a side to his evangelical faith that he didn't reveal when he walked around on base. I was impressed at his tender devotion to those present who would be so far away from their families. I realized I never celebrated Christmas in California before. The candle-lighting rituals were a little different — in keeping with the breezy spring-like weather.

One Friday afternoon, a new MP reported for duty. He stepped into my office to inform me he planned to arrest several of my barracks soldiers that evening. No one had ever been arrested in my barracks, because our policies gave the soldiers freedom to come and go, almost as free as the BOSS barracks policies of the '90s. Besides, there were only 50 soldiers in the barracks. Why did this man expect a rumble on Friday night?

He recounted some of his experiences at Fort Campbell, from where he had just transferred. My only visit to Fort Campbell was a brief one to the enlisted barracks while traveling with my OCS classmates. The barracks resembled a prison, with thug-like soldiers running in and out in intimidating postures. The soldiers had no sense of home. They were subject to strict policing and inspections carried out by CQ guards.

I reminded the sergeant that our command was high-class, a flag pole assignment, not a prison. Surely our soldiers could be expected to live to a higher standard of conduct? The man rigidly clung to his aspirations to jail at least one soldier that evening. Anticipating trouble, I remained in my office, which was about ten feet from the CQ desk. Sure enough, at 6:00 p.m., the CQ obnoxiously halted a senior non-commissioned officer, treating him with total disdain, as if he were some street thug. The sergeant first class who came to visit his friends reminded our CQ that he deserved to be treated with professional respect. Our CQ continued to verbally abuse this senior-ranking sergeant. As I approached the door to my office to interrupt this scene, the two almost came to fisticuffs.

In my panic, I called the sergeant on duty at the MP station and asked him to send help. I yelled at the two men to separate, or face immediate arrest. When they calmed down, I called the MP station and asked them to cancel my request for MP support.

"Are you sure you are safe, Ma'am?"

"Yes, I'm sure. There's a new sergeant here. He's an MP. I don't think he understands how things are handled here!"

"Yes, Ma'am, I know!"

"Let me just debrief both these men, and if I need help, I'll call you."

"Ma'am, let me know what happens, regardless, okay?"

The sergeant first class who was attacked by our new MP was not assigned to our headquarters, but he worked on base at the graves registration department. He belonged to a medical unit based at the Presidio, as did the CID agents.

I had no reason to suspect this man's decision to visit one of the geographical bachelors upstairs, and according to our own standing operating procedures, no reason to stop him from this visit. I chose not to inquire about his intentions. As a woman who was senior in rank, but quite junior in age and military experience I did feel it my duty to sit with him quietly, to review military regulations concerning mutual affrays. If I had not overheard the transaction leading to his mutual affray with our new MP, I could easily have interpreted the conflict as his fault. After all, senior non-commissioned officers are supposed to keep their cool, no matter what, right?

The graves registration sergeant left my office soberly. After sending him on his way, I asked the new MP to visit with me. Once again, I reviewed our barracks policies, and the command tone I wanted to set at OAB. On the one hand, I truly appreciated his intentions to keep our barracks crime-free, but I didn't want the single soldiers' only home to turn into a prison.

When it became evident that our new MP was truly hoping to make a terrific impression on me, I realized the only way I could get through to him was to change the subject altogether. I sat and listened to his history until he was comfortable enough to go back out to the desk and resume his watch, not as a policeman, but as part of the command family, so to speak.

Before turning my office light out, I called Sergeant M at the MP station. "Ma'am, is everything all right over there?"

"Please, don't make any report about my call. This was all a mistake."

"Ma'am, you called back before I could send my car over. There's no need to report unless you want us to follow-up."

"I need your help. This young sergeant is really, REALLY Gung-ho!"

"Right."

"Sergeant, you know this command can't work like that... This is a country club. Can you please talk to him, smooth him out?"

"Ma'am, on Monday we start his formal orientation. We'll get him up to speed. Don't worry."

Sergeant M did not expect me to reveal my plans for the weekend, but I felt a need to reassure him that I was not going to hang around, paranoid that a blotter report would blossom upon my departure.

"Don't worry, Ma'am, I'm on tonight. I'll stop by and start breaking him in tonight!"

A few weeks later, the senior sergeant, the graves registrar came to my office. He saluted me, then took his seat at my suggestion. The sergeant was about to pin on his master sergeant stripes. He asked me if I would act as his commander, since his own commander was not readily available. Would I pin on his stripes at the promotion ceremony?

No other senior sergeant had accorded me that kind of respect before. The other senior sergeants from within MTMC tolerated me as a token female officer. That's what I was, so they couldn't be blamed for their cynical assessment of my status.

"Doesn't your wife want to pin on your stripes?" I asked in disbelief.

"Oh, Ma'am, yeah, yeah. She goin' to pin on the other collar. But if you would do me the honor..."

I thanked him, and tried not to act surprised.

The sergeant continued to sit quietly. We had never talked in depth. I never served this man's family while I was the Services Chief, although he had lived on the base since before I arrived. His family was obviously self-contained. What could possibly be on his mind?

"Ma'am, that chaplain assistant. Sergeant H. He's in your headquarters, right?"

"Yes, that's right."

"Ma'am, he ain't nothin' but trouble."

I was taken aback for the second time. I did not expect a senior African-American sergeant to confide his fears about another young African-American man to me, since I embodied the stereotypical white middle-class, take-charge female who would probably have no interest in the African-American community.

"Ma'am, he's nothin' but trouble."

"Go, on."

"Ma'am, he lives in my building. It's not safe. He brings in all kind of people that don't have no business on this post. Ma'am, he's bringing in women. And guns. My family's not safe."

This sergeant was the first man to confront me face-to-face about the secret life of Sergeant H, the secret life of Oakland Army Base residents. Lieutenant Colonel Siegling's warning sprang to mind, "Be careful, Marie. He's dangerous. Be careful how you handle him..."

I collected my thoughts. Looking the Master Sergeant in the eye, I finally admitted the real reasons why I was going to discharge Sergeant H from the Army.

"Sergeant, I know he has been investigated, and I know that I am not allowed to touch that issue at this time. But please, please be patient. I'm putting him out of the Army."

"Ma'am, he's trouble. I've got a family. It's not safe over there."

"Can you call the police when you see something suspicious?"

"I'm tellin' you, it's not safe!"

"Believe me, I have been warned. I can't do anything about housing. But I can put him out for some things he's done. We already have the documentation. Please, give me time. I can't pay attention to the housing situation, but I am going to get him out..."

I had to speak with a forked tongue now, or lose all my credibility as a white officer.

"Look, Sergeant, I'm chaptering him out of the Army. It's in appeal right now, but we know he's going. It might take three months, but he will be out of here one way or another. Just keep your family out of his way for now."

The sergeant relaxed his furrowed brow.

"Okay, Ma'am. See you tomorrow, at ten o'clock."

I looked perplexed.

"For the ceremony, ma'am. For the pin-on!"

The next morning, I pinned on the master sergeant's stripes, and gave him a hug, as a female officer is allowed to do, in lieu of the pounding ritual, where the new rank is ground into the chest of newly promoted soldiers. His beaming wife kissed him and stood by his side as he gave his promotion speech.

Not long after, Sergeant H's appeal was denied. He was issued orders to move out of the community housing, out of the Army. Once Sergeant H's legal status was clear, his wife filed a domestic violence complaint. I often assisted the Services Branch captain in assessment and intervention of domestic violence situations. This branch chief let me know he helped Sergeant H's wife move out of the housing area, but she took everything the couple owned. He observed that Sergeant H was such a meek fellow. He felt the wife was exploiting the Army's domestic violence program to get a free move away from our troubled sergeant — that she made a false accusation to give herself a strategic advantage. She was able to take the family possessions without the interference of a divorce court judge, who would probably have divided the furniture and cars between the couple.

It was hard to know the truth of that situation. Mrs. H drove the couple's Mercedes just as much as her pimping and dealing husband did. For all we knew, she was complicit in his trade, because she never questioned the legitimacy of their lifestyle while their military peers lived on the verge of poverty. On the other hand, the military mafia seemed to operate much like the mythical mafias of the movies. Men conducted their business in tightly controlled circles of insiders. The women, by and large, were ornamental, not privy to the inner workings of the men in underbelly activities.

I hoped we could take our headquarters in a really positive, mission focused direction when our new first sergeant signed into the unit shortly after Christmas. First Sergeant Bolduc wanted passionately to turn our unit into a real headquarters, with high standards of soldiering. He had immense pride in the Army. He made it his mission to instill that pride in the rest of our troops.

I commanded in the good old days, when NCOs prided themselves in running the day-to-day business of the Army, and the officer corps trained commanders to let NCOs run the company. Today, we have generals and colonels running companies, pulling strings from their command suites, ratcheting up the stress levels of both the young junior officers and the non-coms.

My new first sergeant immediately put me out of work, taking all the standing operating procedures home for a complete rewrite.

"Mama, you just sit back, and let me get this straightened out. This is NCO business!"

He followed the more genteel tradition of calling male commanders, to include our superiors, "Dad." Tougher sergeants called their commanders, "the old man." I was the first female commander Bolduc ever worked with, hence I was Mama.

He would pace back and forth, wired tightly as he discovered each new deviation from strict military policy.

"When I was in Italy, boy, we were really STRAK!"

Our new first sergeant expressed his stress as all great soldiers do. He constantly compared his disappointment in the present moment to great experiences he had at his last unit, which was of course, what the Real Army was supposed to be like. The best trained soldiers are most guilty of this, because once you are sent to a rag-tag outfit, the sloth, lack of ambition and hopelessness that things could get better induces transition shock. The first sergeant obviously worried that I would cheat him out of a good rating, since I was such a green lieutenant, and he was already warned by the sergeant major that I had standards, too. He had nothing to worry about. Lieutenant Colonel Seaton arranged to rate him, with the sergeant major serving as his primary NCO rater. It did not occur to me to be offended, because I was losing my appetite for military life, dwelling on the other life options I had. I wanted to stay in Berkeley near some of my cousins after my tour was over.

Lieutenant Colonel Seaton tried to compensate for his subtle undermining of my authority over my staff by challenging me to organize another building renovation. Team Spirit was about to gear up for the first time in 1986. Oakland Army Base would participate in this Pacific Rim exercise by shipping out a bunch of reserve units who were going to Korea to support the 19th TAACOM. We had not run this kind of exercise, or expected reservists to stay in Oakland Barracks in at least a decade.

Since the end of the Vietnam War the kitchens and barracks designated for visiting reserve units were not only in need of repair, they were not only rat-infested, they were literally replicas of bombed out war zones. Ceilings had fallen in clumps onto the floor. Equipment was broken and in disarray. The colonel obviously expected me to use my feminine charm to set aside the scruples of the Civil Engineers who would have to scrap their five-year plans once again to work another timely, but strategically unplanned renovation.

Old Al came down from the Civil Engineer department to inspect these reserve kitchens. He chuckled as he reminisced about Vietnam. Many stories later, and with serious shakes of his head each time another rodent scurried by, he joked that he couldn't wait until the day when I wouldn't be the one to show up at his door pleading in desperation for another miracle.

"I'll see what I can do, Lieutenant. I can't promise you anything, but I'll see what I can do!"

Unbelievably, reserve units met at this kitchen site every month, but they did not use the facilities. Without making any effort to have the structure repaired, their commanders declared the barracks and kitchen uninhabitable, thereby making it possible for the troops to stay in local hotels and eat in fancy restaurants. This was about as realistic as Reserve field training ever got back then, which used to make me scream that the Reserves needed to be disbanded altogether. Although I had no intentions of ever marrying again, this new renovation project gave me the high housewives experience when they are encouraged to completely redecorate their homes. I really needed the boost, because each new encounter with the drug dealing low life just got me more and more depressed.

General John Stanford, seemingly oblivious to the Oakland underbelly, proceeded to host a series of socials and commanders' conferences to lift our wintry spirits. Stanford's son was now a Stanford University student, so the general managed to bring the Stanford Cheerleaders to the Fort Mason Officers Club for the Super Bowl, which of course, included the San Francisco '49ers. We needed to sit around in casual winter attire as if we were kin, so we did.

Soon after, General Stanford brought all his commanders from Western Area posts to Oakland Army Base for a four-day conference. As his Detachment Commander, I attended all the formal daytime meetings. None of the conference subjects were relevant to my command, because I was not a transporter, and I commanded a unit that did not have an organic mission. I learned a lot about organizational planning, however, and about the missions my detachment soldiers completed down in the transport sections.

Each afternoon, the conference meetings ended with a reception at the club. I might have been the only female officer in the entire gathering. The gender ratio definitely felt like it was fifty-to-one during the first two days, when staff officers were not included. By now, I was accustomed to being the super-minority at any leadership meeting. I was not uncomfortable. The men were quite accepting, so I had no reason to feel out of place.

When the general finally hosted a reception to introduce MTMC commanders to all the other officers in his headquarters, I was finally flanked by one or two female junior officers. They drifted in and out, since they had families to go home to.

Suddenly, a strange male officer boisterously intruded on a chatty exchange between me and a few silver-haired colonels, who were describing their sailing expeditions off the Japanese and Thai coastlands. His eyes darted and twinkled as he boldly challenged our superior officers with sailing and flying exploits of his own. The senior commanders were gentlemanly and self-deprecating. DJC interjected a few more boasts of his wealth, and his toys — his private airplane, his horses, and his beachfront property. Our senior officers drifted away nonchalantly when they realized this contest would not end until DJC won.

"What's an intelligent, attractive young officer like you doing with these clowns? Shouldn't you be at a concert or a ballet?"

He asked as if he was a concerned friend. Who was this man? I had never met him. DJC stood with another elderly warrant officer, a man known as KookKook who claimed to have served as a boy in the Dutch Resistance during World World II.

DJC had the capacity to inspire rebelliousness in the most loyal and dedicated of soldiers. I wasn't the most loyal or the most dedicated, so, my rebelliousness bubbled up almost immediately. I suddenly was questioning the value of my association not just with the commanders who assembled from ports around the Pacific Rim and the West Coast, I questioned my association with the Army itself. I still didn't know who this man was, though. He identified himself as a security inspector, on loan to the Provost Marshal's department. His purpose was to inspect security procedures at all of the transport facilities to determine which could be breached by terrorists.

DJC's story was plausible. More than once, the Provost Marshal had briefed our command that there were more than 90 anti-military terrorist groups based in the Bay area. Not only were our bases accessible targets. All who wore the uniform were moving targets. We were discouraged from wearing the battle dress uniform at all when traveling off base. At one briefing, the Provost encouraged us to take different routes to and from work, and to be careful about our social contacts in the city.

DJC's story held up to my own experience while assigned to Oakland. Anti-military protests were held daily in San Francisco and outside of bases and ports that were transfer points for nuclear arms. Peaceful protestors waged daily demonstrations against our bases and the shipment of arms. Demonstrators provoked their own arrests. No one on base cared a whit when these self-appointed messiahs were sent to jail. Peace activists generally treated military personnel as if they were the antichrist, but they were basically harmless to the soldiers in uniform and to the base infrastructure.

On the other hand, terrorists were anonymous, necessarily stealthy in their plans to disrupt the U.S. military. Since my arrival at Oakland in April of 1984, one Air Force officer was injured in a UC Berkeley laboratory when a pipe bomb was exploded at his workstation. The ROTC Building at UC Berkeley was burned to the ground by protesters. Once, I went to an accounting class on the UC campus to take my final exam. I was wearing my class B uniform — a safe bet, since it makes women look like junior girl scouts. As I climbed the hill from my parked car to the classroom, a large crowd of anti-military demonstrators came running down the hill. I did not think they would attack me, but I took no chances. I turned around, ran to my car, and locked myself in.

The instructor honored my decision to leave the campus when this demonstration erupted. He gave me a no-penalty makeup.

So, DJC's claims about working as a counter-terrorist inspector made sense to me. Even outside Oakland Army Base, demonstrations were conducted. One series of protests culminated with a march along the post access road, led by Martin Sheen, the actor turned peace activist. He was peaceable. He walked somberly down the access road with a large crucifix. Every now and then his group knelt down to pray for our repentance. If all the protestors were like Martin Sheen, the Army would not have to worry about sabotage. But few of the Bay Area anti-military activists practiced his pure, disciplined form of civil protest and disobedience.

At the last MTMC commander's reception, DJC tossed a few more ironic jokes that were like night flares. They managed to illuminate every absurdity about military life. As his routine wound down, I couldn't wait to get out of the club. Mercifully, the general left, at which time, we were free to start our weekends. When mine started, I went back to Treasure Island. The next weekend, I slipped out of the BOQ to indulge in my usual five- or six-mile jog around the perimeter of the island. That quiet dusky ritual was the only faithful religious practice I maintained while I commanded troops. When I stepped off the elevator to run, I noticed DJC was dressed to run, bouncing his leg in urgent expectancy, as if he were waiting for a date. He climbed out of his chair and moved to my side as I crossed the lobby.

"Need a running partner?"

DJC was kind of pudgy. I wasn't eager to run with him because I did not want to be held back.

"It's not really safe at this time of day," he said determinedly. "You know, the Navy Brig is right next to this running trail."

"I know. Worse, the Navy Brig is right next to the Navy's child care center! The MPs have discouraged me from running alone at this hour. I feel safe. It's too beautiful to stay inside."

DJC was wearing headphones, with a cassette radio strapped to his waist. I thought he would probably be absorbed in his own music soon enough, so I consented to run with him. His looks deceived. The man was a strong runner. He was better than song for killing the pain, the boredom of running. The six miles flew by, to my delight.

"Run tomorrow?"

"Sure," I replied. "Same time. We have the whole bay to ourselves at dinner time. There's a method to my madness, isn't there..."

I didn't expect to see this man before our next run, but he and KookKook showed up at my office on Monday morning, ostensibly to introduce themselves to the Detachment Command staff. They had been attached to the MPs since November, about the same time I assumed command. Now, suddenly, it was important for them to bond to the unit that temporarily owned them.

My first sergeant said nothing. He was preoccupied with the disturbing signs of corruption soldiers were displaying in our base housing area.

"Ma'am, Specialist R," he was telling me before my new counter-terrorist running partner walked in. "She was over at Sergeant H's house last night. Her dress was absolutely see through to the skin...."

There were a few hints that this female specialist was using marijuana, and neglecting her son. Because my first sergeant observed some of the abnormalities as her neighbor, we had more latitude to make sure she would be alright. We called her into my office. This woman was absolutely defiant when she found out she was reported for child neglect. Specialist R had large Lamb Chop eyes, which she could fire up as good as any F-14 plane could light up the night sky.

"I was raped, and I was counseled, and it did me absolutely no good! No good, do you hear? I just want to forget everything! You can't make me go to counseling! You can't make me. I won't go into my past ever again. I AM A SURVIVOR!"

Specialist R's exhibitionism, her apparent promiscuity, and her unwillingness to see anything wrong with her behavior were all signs that I have seen in too many female soldiers who were previously victimized by rape or child sexual abuse. As a commander I could not force her into counseling just because she was victimized in the past, and I would not. I had to remind her, however, that she had legal obligations as a mother and as a soldier. If she failed to live up to her parenting responsibilities to the point that CPS required an intervention, or if she broke the law, I would have to be more directive.

Specialist R seemed to think that all the men who benefited from her sexual indiscretions would protect her from prosecution or career derailment. Another diatribe confidently rooted in the belief that she would be protected from prosecution spewed from Specialist R.

"Look," I responded. "I wouldn't care if this hadn't been brought to my attention by our first sergeant. Your behavior has drawn the attention of people who CAN affect your career. Do as you wish. If CPS deems your behavior as neglect, I won't cover up for you. Your career will be jeopardized. If you are brought up on sexual misconduct, I won't cover. Don't get counseling. But just remember, we can't protect you if you don't take steps to protect yourself. If you do get counseling, I think you can put a lot of your suffering behind you. You could feel much much better."

Specialist R left my office defiantly. The first sergeant was absolutely stumped that I would allow this junior soldier to vent as much as she did. More to the point, he was shocked that she was as open about her sexual past and her present activities to both a commander and a first sergeant. We both knew that she was being sexually used by other men on post and Sergeant H, as well as men from the civilian community. She was a rape survivor. She also was participating in the escapades as a consenting adult, who did not want to report the men with whom she slept, or the nature of their activities. Why go after her, and let these men off?

These impossible situations drained me. My heart was broken when our best, finest, most selfless junior enlisted came up "hot" on a drug test. By all accounts, this man made the error of his life. He started bragging to his friends that he saved $13,000 to get out of the Army and go to college. They fed him lines of cocaine for free until he was hooked, then cleaned out his bank account in less than one month. We put this man into rehab, a decision I have never regretted. I saw him years later. He stayed in the Army. He spent much of his time mentoring junior soldiers, helping them sort out their problems.

Once I realized that no soldier at Oakland was safe from the scourge of drugs or human rodents who would steal away with our soldiers' dreams, my world began to bifurcate. During the day, I was confronted with Oakland's underbelly, the dealers and pimps who invaded government housing and the lives of my soldiers. At night, since I lived on Treasure Island, tucked out of harm's way, I would succumb to the temptation of pretending I was no longer in the Army. I stopped working long hours, dropping in on my barracks during the soldiers' private time. I wasn't making a difference, anyway. I started imaging a different way of life. What would life be like if I could go back to a middle-class existence, where my biggest frustration would be keeping the weeds and bulb-eating moles out of my garden?

During my daily jog at dusk my mind would split away from Army life. DJC continued to join me each day. When he joined me, it was impossible to forget the morasses I found myself in. As he gently pushed me to improve my pace, he confided many of his exploits as a CID and MP investigator. He talked about his life as a civilian lawyer. His stories were not implausible. He had documents that traced his employment, his work. After some days, DJC said that he was investigating bigger problems on Oakland Army base. The problems there were much bigger than the two bit terrorists who dreamed of shutting the base down with their pin prick raids on military installations.

This pudgy, gray-haired captain carried around several government IDs. I was mystified that he could know so much as a mere captain. He claimed he sat in the National Security Council, just three seats behind George P. Schultz. The Provost Marshal, nor the commanders ever contradicted the public claims he made. When we appeared at social functions together, he was identified as "Mr. C from the State Department." The restraint, if not the respect accorded by senior officers to this overweight elderly captain, who were as baffled as I was by the incongruence of his rank with his responsibilities, had something to do with his stature at the State Department.

I kept meeting him for daily runs. DJC broached the subject of faith as the sun was setting one night. The purple sky was streaked with veils of orange and soft pink. I foolishly commented that running was the best spiritual high a person could hope to experience. DJC was Catholic. A rabbit-foot Catholic.

"I've been truly lucky. I put five dollars in the plate every Sunday. The close calls I've had... That five dollars saves me every time..."

Two or three runs later, he commented that he believed I was still Catholic at heart. DJC made it his personal mission to "bring me back to God."

I was still allergic to God at that point in my life. Only when duty beckoned would I set foot inside a chapel. Command memorial services. Command holiday services. To avoid latrine duty during basic training. DJC persisted in his mission to bring me back to the faith. I was tacking toward a more palatable spirituality: the Arts, symphonic music, the opera scores of Puccini or Verdi. Even the canvasses of Van Gogh or Ansel Adams provided a higher spiritual awakening as far as I was concerned.

"You don't belong in the Army," DJC finally concluded. He wasn't the first to assert his opinion on my military career, and he wouldn't be the last, he knew.

"What makes you think you have the right to..." I huffed.

"I'm telling you, you don't belong in the Army. Where are you going to find people to go to the symphony with? Where are the officers who even know who Van Gogh was?"

"I go to the symphony regularly with officers from Oakland."

"Oakland Army Base is not the real Army. You know as well as I do, it's a retirement farm..."

Once we ran past the housing and the Navy Childcare Center on Treasure Island, the running trails were solitary. Squawking gulls. Rattling sailboats. Creaky piers. The crunching of sandy, rocky soil as we padded our way along the edge of the island. I could hear my breathing, even hear myself think on these trails. I lapsed into a quiet mindful meditation to avoid DJC's stinging reminder that I was a cultural misfit in the military.

"So tell me about your work in the CIA," I countered. "Why are you serving in the Army if you are in the CIA?"

"My expertise is counter-terrorism. That's what these security inspections are all about. Our biggest threat isn't the Soviet Union. It's the two bit terrorists... Our ports in Korea... Jesus, Oakland is wide open..."

He recounted more stories of trips to Washington for special CIA assignments while he was a corporate attorney.

"I would just jump into my plane, fly to D.C. and write the whole thing off. You have to learn how to do your hobbies as part of your business..."

DJC's CIA stories seemed credible. I asked him to look up a professional writer that I knew, who identified himself as a former CIA agent. The man, now a reporter for a major newspaper, claimed back in the '70's that he quit the CIA to embark on his career as a writer. DJC returned to the subject a few days later. He confirmed R's status. He asked me how I knew R. More than a decade before, we served together on a church steering committee that ultimately voted to retain a married Catholic priest, a decision for which our community was excommunicated. After that brush with democratic Catholicism where the Church suddenly reneged on its promise to let us select our own priests, I had no desire to become an un-lapsed Catholic.

Although my runs ceased to be escapes from military life, running with DJC seemed to be a perfect antidote to the sloth, the ignorance, and the persistent intrusion of underworld criminality at Oakland Army Base. He gave me a perverse hope that someone in the Army somewhere was really trying to excise that element — even as my hands were tied to solve any problems at my level.

One episode shattered any hope that individuals could turn the situation around. A reservist, assigned to our detachment to support the Team Spirit exercise, was arrested at the club one weekend. I was not notified of the arrest until Monday morning. Lieutenant Colonel Seaton called me to his office to review the MP blotter reports, the statements prepared by our soldier and by several men with whom he had gotten into an altercation. The men were in the back storage room of the club when the reservist began to wildly thrash his way out. Four or five men together could not subdue him. Subsequent professional experience as an emergency room chaplain confirmed what I could only intuit by reading the blotter reports.

"What do you think is going on there?" Seaton asked me. I didn't hesitate to bluntly give my opinion. The statements implicitly described a cocaine deal gone awry. What were these men doing in the back storage room? How come four burley men could not subdue one short, skinny, physically untrained man? He obviously had already consumed more than one line of cocaine. He was either craving more than he could afford, or he failed to pay up as promised and the club bouncers, all army soldiers, creamed him.

My low-grade depression and submerged anger about the persistent drug culture at Oakland almost exploded, but I quietly stated the case. Seaton did not react to my analysis.

"What do you think we should do about it?"

"Court-martial him. Send him to jail."

"No, that's a waste of taxpayer dollars. This man's a reservist. If you want to hurt him, give him an Article 15 and send him home. No job, no income. If you want to send a message to the other reservists, send him home."

Seaton handled the petty disciplinary hearing for this sergeant. Disturbingly, the same cast of characters who were disciplined as participants in the chaplain assistant's consensual gang-bang were called in as witnesseses for this reservist's defense. Off-duty, these men worked at the club. What a perfect marriage for illicit activities: otherwise model soldiers work nights and weekends at the club or the Chapel. Transactions right under the nose of the commanders, investigators, chaplain, and military police. Very difficult, apparently, to interdict. You couldn't just pull the Oakland soldiers from their part-time club jobs to minimize their participation in the drug scene, either. The suggestion to curtail their privilege to work after hours at the club was seen as counterproductive: all California bases were high-cost living areas. Men had to work two jobs to support their families. Especially after a young Irish teenager killed himself to lift the financial burden on his bankrupted soldier-parents. Whether the teen's parents were fiscally irresponsible, or involved in drugs was irrelevant to the media-sensitive leadership. The fact that the parents were bankrupt was deemed the military's fault. The child's suicide was an event the army believed it could absolutely have avoided.

When Lieutenant Colonel Seaton finished with the Article 15 proceedings, I ordered the man be sent back to his civilian home. In a sober moment, the young sergeant came to my office and begged for a second chance. He had no job, no opportunity back there. This was his one chance to catch up on his bills. Such pleas are very convincing, especially when the Army mandates its top priority is to take care of the Army family. If I gave him a second chance, however, I risked infecting the rest of my barracks with his blatant drug use.

I sent the sergeant back to civilian life.

However convenient, this punishment was not satisfactory to me, as it did not solve the exacerbating problem at the base. Sending this soldier home was like lighting citronella candles to mask the smell of an offending skunk. The drug infestation at OAB was organized and entrenched. Oakland's leadership seemed to be powerless to stop it. I finally had to admit the limitation of our personal power, our charismatic and moral authority as Army leaders. At Oakland Army Base, drugs were unavoidable, because the base was located in the middle of a shipping area where drug cartels flourished.

What I hated was that the command was not doing anything structurally to get rid of drugs at the source. The drug dealers were in housing. They were back in the clubs. Unless the command eradicated the drug dealers and fiercely guarded against their return, my job as a commander would be miserable. I would have to punish one good soldier after another who succumbed to the temptations that were wafted daily under their noses in government funded buildings and at government subsidized recreational sites.

Lieutenant Colonel Seaton never refuted my exegesis of the MP statements which described the reservist as a man high on cocaine who was in the back room of our NCO club with several men who were identified pimps and dealers. Seaton, who was the deputy installation commander did nothing structurally to stop the flow of drugs into the club, even though this business was part of his command. I couldn't blame him. His hands were tied by the Criminal Investigation Command, too. But the unwillingness of the senior officers at Oakland to take these drug dealers by the scrotum and drag them off post was at the same time infuriating and debilitating to me.

After the reservist's Article 15 hearing, I broached DJC with my concerns. "Since I've been here, there's always been a drug problem at Oakland. There's been a trial in the last year of officers and sergeants who were allegedly involved in a drug operation before I got here..."

DJC was wholly attentive. I recounted my own feeble efforts to expel the two-bit peddler from my guest house. The man whom I just expelled was benign compared to the stories that were bubbling about Sergeant H. I noted that some of the same men who were involved in Sergeant H's consensual orgy were also in the backroom of the NCO club when the reservist's drug transaction turned into a bust.

"Stay out of it, Marie."

Gone, for the first time, was DJC's generous brotherly encouragement of my brash command style. He usually encouraged me when I made bold moves to solve command problems.

"Stay out of it."

"I'm sick of it. These CID agents are supposedly investigating. The senior officers know what is happening. They don't go after the dealers, they go after the soldiers who are petty recreational users."

"Marie, stay out of it." DJC was starting to echo Lieutenant Colonel Siegling, who begged me to be careful, because of Sergeant H's involvement with outside drug lords.

"Marie, there are guns in there. The CID agents have cited Uzis and AK-47s. There are all kinds of guns in that club. These aren't petty dope dealers. These are well organized..." Understatement of the decade.

My mood blackened, even as we were achieving our running high.

"That's what I'm being told about housing, too. That Sergeant H is bringing outsiders with guns and connections into his apartment. Why can't the MPs just arrest these bastards and get them off post? What the hell do we hire guards for anyway?"

"That's the biggest joke!" DJC laughed. These guards are part of the organization. They aren't really guards. They don't have weapons. They let anybody in. Stay out of it. I'm telling you. This is not something you can take care of..."

DJC reverted back to his overarching mission to reconvert me to Catholicism.

"Why don't you come to church with me on Sunday? Just one Mass?"

DJC's unsinkable sense of humor almost made me jealous. He would quickly shift from an intense conversation to biting satire or ironic commentary that brought gales of laughter. If my mood was dark, the storm clouds had to dissipate before I could rattle off a few jokes. He would fit in well with my Irish Catholic relatives who would stand at a wake and pun through very sad evenings with dry, witty, irrefutable observations. Although I would not admit it, I could feel myself sinking into depression, the kind that draws you down like quicksand. Strangely, I began to associate DJC's indomitable buoyancy with his Catholic faith. I consented to attend Mass with him.

Sunday arrived. We went to church. The Treasure Island chapel was adjacent to our BOQ. The only hazard of attending this chapel even once, was the unavoidable attention that would be paid to a single officer who actually climbed out of bed before noon on a Sunday morning. I was a bit leery of being trapped into a commitment on my first visit.

The priest who said Mass had large Bing Crosby ears, and a very unmilitary spiritual presence. It never occurred to me that the priest was a naval officer, because I never saw him wearing anything but priestly collars or liturgical robes. DJC was almost euphoric as we slipped into the pews. Proud that he accomplished the humanly impossible: he got a renegade Catholic back in the pews. The Mass was modern enough, but the music was awful. Post-Vatican II Catholics are notoriously feeble singers.

I sang with the gusto of a folksinger. During the Kiss of Peace, those around us suggested I should become the cantor, that is, lead the congregational singing. After Mass, DJC introduced me to the priest. He insisted that I should be considered for the cantor position. The priest invited me to take on that task, for lack of any dependable alternatives.

Treasure Island's chapel was much smaller than the inner city pseudo-Cathedral of my childhood years, but just as bright and homey as my mother's hometown village church. You couldn't help but feel God's presence there. Men of all ranks sat in the pews, but somehow, the Catholic community abandoned rank consciousness in the vicinity of the chapel.

When we next jogged, DJC persisted in a raw theological confrontation.

"If I accomplish anything, I am going to bring you back to God. I'm going to bring you back to the Catholic Church!"

Any city girl would have enough sophistication to reject the sincerity of that challenge. I came from a religious family that repeatedly expressed its disdain for my choice to leave The Faith. Now, I could feel myself tempting fate. If I was really meant to reclaim the faith, my experiences over the next few months should reveal that fact. If I wasn't, time would tell. We continued to attend Mass. I stood up front and led the congregational singing.

Preparations for Team Spirit, the consummate military mobilization exercise, helped me to avoid the kind of burnout the soup kitchen manager or the street social worker inevitably experiences when they find the same kids doped up week after week. Negotiating for cooks, food rations, maintenance and supplies gave me a sense that I was accomplishing a real military mission, that the Army could be worthwhile after all. Still, too much time and effort was required to get the reserve support battalion to work cooperatively with the active duty MTMC personnel and the Presidio Food Service departments. But time spent working out dining facility operations was infinitely preferable to time spent in the legal machinations required to finally get Sergeant H and some of the other troublemakers out of the Army. Even the reserve battalion that drilled on the other half of the Army Community Services building showed signs of underbelly creep. When I attended the first reserve drill to solicit command support for the Team Spirit project, there were cooks and other soldiers laying around on pool tables, on the floor, wherever they could sleep off their drunk or whatever. The civilian administrator for this battalion shared many stories of intimidation he experienced. Reservists would come to his office during the week and lay their weapons on the table to demand payment for drills they did not serve. Pay up, or pay the price. He was alone in a long building, but he did not seem to buckle to their demands. After I left Oakland the problems got far worse before they ever got better.

Off duty, my daily bayside runs, song leading at Mass, and DJC's constant companionship provided the boost that propelled me back to my dreaded command job each day.

Some of the care-taking responsibilities of command did not bother me. One of my female soldiers, a single woman was about to give birth. She asked for support when her fiancé, a navy enlisted person said he could not return from his ship to help her through her birthing process. Several women in the barracks created a family-style community, an extended kinship network. They tended to the pregnant soldier's every whim before she delivered. Although I was very caught up with DJC, usually disappearing from the base after unit physical training was over, I rushed over to the hospital to make sure she had support. Her sister was supposed to come to help her deliver, but her labor was early.

Specialist B was alone at Letterman Army Hospital, in an environment that was not even conducive to a civilian woman's birthing experience. I was surprised to see the male doctor treat Specialist B callously, giving her soldier commands. Was the harshness due to her rank, her unmarried status, or her color? As many first sergeants or commanders have done in similar circumstances over the years, I decided to stay as her birth companion until her family or friends showed up.

That was the first time I went through the birthing experience with a woman. Hospital and military chaplains get called to dozens of births, but when you are a lieutenant and a commander, the last challenge you ever think about coping with is comforting a soldier who is suffering, not the injury and pain of battle, but the pangs of birth. For hours, all I did was give B bits of ice when she asked, wipe her forehead with a damp cloth, and let her squeeze the dickens out of my hand while she push, push, pushed. Before too long, she was wheeled into the delivery room, and her baby was wailing with dissatisfaction at being so rudely brought into this life.

I never wanted to have my own children before that moment, but I have to admit that Specialist B's miraculous delivery made me crave the experience. That evening, DJC nudged me to think about getting married again, and having my own child. The experience seemed to promise only joy and satisfaction. I allowed myself to dream for a time about how I would experience motherhood. Then, my mind reverted to the demands of my career, which in reality, had been the only thing that had ever really given me a sense of accomplishment. I knew that I could be satisfied with my work accomplishments eventually. I wasn't sure I would ever enjoy giving birth to my own children.

I must have gone daft because in no time at all, I began dating DJC seriously. We spent long evenings in Italian trattorias in Berkeley and ristorantes in San Francisco. We headed out for the opera and the symphony whenever I could break away from command. We took trips up the coast to hike in Muir Woods and along the Point Reyes Trails. It was wonderful to walk through the galleries together, or just sit on the bay waters to drink in the salty sea air and mellow in the sound of steel drum bands and the patter of Italian and Chinese and Russian and Japanese tourists who wandered along the water's edge. Every day spent away from the Army with DJC was a day when I could feel myself stirring from a deep sleep. Every day that I spent in the office dueling with the intransigently non-productive reservists or the rumors of guns and drugs put me in the darkest of moods.

General Stanford must have seen the mushroom cloud that was settling over my head, because he laid down a challenge that made Army life palatable again for a short while longer. He never lost his eagerness to contrive situations that would inflate our confidence. He asked me to coordinate the first command run at Oakland Army Base.

The regular Army was not only taking control of the soldier's private life by monitoring relationships, finances, and drinking habits, but the Department of the Army was also insisting on daily physical training schedules at command posts, with weekly company or battalion four-mile runs. Stanford probably considered my voluntary private commitment to that intensity of physical training when he selected me for command. Very few officers maintained regular training schedules. I never slacked off from the OCS standards for fear my credibility as a female officer would take a nose dive.

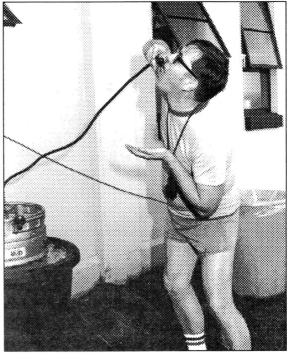

Navy Doesn't Run
This Naval officer who declined to run two miles in the St. Patrick's Day Run beat the Army to the Keg.

Some of the sweet old colonels were not only unaccustomed to the new training standards, they were positively allergic to them. But the Army was no longer tolerating fatness or lack of physical conditioning. To give the officers every opportunity to protect their career status, group training was now required. No more trust in the officer's ability to manage their time or to live up to their commitments. Soldiers who served in line units were already doing group physical training.

So now, we were to organize the first ever Oakland Army Base Command Run. First Sergeant Bolduc relished the opportunity to mold his enlisted troops into a tighter, high-speed group. He mandated attendance at our daily training sessions. That brought flack from the sergeant major and the officers. Every private at Oakland had three godfathers to protect them: a captain, a junior field grade officer and a senior field grade. No sooner was the announcement made than we were inundated with calls from senior ranking officers who were very interested in protecting their soldiers from the foolishness of group physical training.

We anticipated these kinds of complaints. General Stanford assured me that he would stand by our efforts to introduce the Command Run. He signed a letter stating there would be no exceptions, including for himself. Officers were

The Command Run and Barbecue
Command photographers recorded this historic, if disheveled, headquarters gesture of esprirt de corps.

Top Of The Morning To You!
General John Stanford accepts his St. Patrick's Day hat at the barbecue following our first run.

expected to train on their own, but all enlisted would report to the detachment for daily training runs.

I was anxious that if push came to shove, and we firmly required our soldiers to participate in training, all the colonels would register their complaints to the general, and that would be the end of it. The status quo would prevail, and the colonels would spend hours complaining to my boss that I should be court-martialed for insubordination.

I had nothing to fear. I diplomatically held my ground. General Stanford stood behind us. First Sergeant Bolduc would refer each of the majors and colonels to me for clarification and consideration of exceptional circumstances that might qualify for a soldier's exemption from the run. There weren't any. Not by our standard. Not by the general's.

MTMC was a joint command, which complicated our job. The Army, Navy and Air Force do not have the same physical training standards. Fortunately, all the Navy and Air Force personnel were officers. Surely, they could be held to the Army's minimum fitness standards for enlisted. A Navy lieutenant called me to complain that our memorandum of instruction was completely out of line.

"Lieutenant," he complained, "Navy doesn't run."

"Sir, we clarified this with the general. Everyone is to participate in this event."

"Lieutenant, you don't understand. Navy doesn't run!"

"Sir, we're only running two miles at an airborne shuffle. Some of the colonels haven't run in years. You could probably walk faster than we'll be running."

"Lieutenant, I'm telling you. Navy doesn't run. We don't have to run two blocks to pass our PT test!"

"Sir, just come on out, and run two blocks then. Just see how far you can go!"

"Two blocks. That's as far as Navy runs!"

Not all naval officers had this attitude. My first rater ran long distances, and he ran fast. But he was now gone. The junior naval officers now thought they were free to make up their own standards. After several more calls like this one, though, our diplomatic persistence prevailed. The entire command broke out of its denial. We were going to run, and we were going to have fun. The Department of the Army said so. The general said so. So we were going to run to have fun.

To ease the pain, or to seduce our fellow soldiers into thinking a command run really could be fun, we selected St. Patrick's Day as the inauguration of this new tradition. The first sergeant coordinated a home-style picnic, with barbecue grill and kegs of beer waiting at the finish line. Everyone showed up for the run, from the newest private to the oldest colonel. Ironically, the only soldier who did not run was General John Stanford. He was injured. He was also a regular runner, and a weightlifter, so there was no hypocrisy on his part. John came down to the picnic afterwards.

Kids from the base neighborhood cheered us as we jogged past their apartments. Our St. Paddy's Day hats probably encouraged a few of the taunts the more brazen kids tossed our way. The Navy lieutenant who called to educate me about navy standards was true to his word. Navy wouldn't run. We didn't get more than two blocks away from the headquarters parking lot when he made a beeline straight back to our picnic tables. The first sergeant and I had a good laugh, because this man was also the first to make a beeline straight to the keg of beer. I still have the official photo of this gentleman with the beer spout up to his lips and the caption, "Navy doesn't Run!"

The general visited our victory party briefly. Although attired in his class B uniform, General Stanford graciously ignored uniform regulations and took his St. Paddy's bowler to pose for the camera. He wasn't thumbing his nose at regulations, of course, but cared more about spirit than legalistic perfection. He didn't mind having a scandalous photo taken for the command newspaper. Several choice photos that depicted our elderly stout colonels and just as many skinny sergeants were taken. DJC took great pleasure that he appeared in several of the official shots. He was especially thrilled that he was in the background of a photo depicting the general and me.

By this time, I had fallen in love with DJC. I disregarded every promise I made to myself when I got divorced to avoid getting involved or committed to any man before my first tour of duty was over. About two days before the St. Paddy's Day Command Run, DJC proposed to me. I threw all caution and common sense to the wind and said, "Yes!" DJC took great pride that he was able to distract me from total preoccupation with military life at a time in my life when wealth, music, not even God could get in the way of my love affair with the Army. I did not mention the engagement to my peers or my bosses until after the command run. DJC selected a huge diamond for an engagement ring. I had never worn an engagement ring before. DJC insisted that I wear this ring as a symbol of all that was precious to us.

For the first couple of weeks, I was absolutely elated, caught up in the whirlwind fantasies of romance turned prenuptial bliss. DJC moved with the speed of a Concorde jet to secure a private apartment in San Francisco's Marina neighborhood, just a few blocks from my old apartment.

We moved out of the BOQ. Junior officer peers and my many bosses met our engagement announcement with reserved looks of surprise. I was completely oblivious to their nonchalance, however, because I was caught up in the fantasy of escape from the Army to a world of art and music — not to mention middle-class marital bliss.

We began looking at art galleries. Several meetings with DJC's old acquaintance, Ron H from Austin Art Galleries and many planning sessions later, we agreed to open an art gallery as a three-way partnership.

Within weeks of our move to San Francisco, DJC's mood darkened. Our roles suddenly reversed. For a few nights, he would cry, then sit in a stupor. Then he would rage. Then dance. Then cry again. He finally told me that he had to go on several missions down to Tegucigalpa. He was being paid several thousands of dollars for each flight, during which he took arms down to Nicaragua, through Tegucigalpa, Honduras. For several weeks he publicly alluded to his role at the State Department both on base and in the art world. His loyalty to Ronald Reagan was absolute. Now that he indulged his whims by proposing to a woman who was as unconcerned about world security as he was unconcerned about inner-city drug dealers, he was trapped. DJC was issued orders to leave Oakland.

DJC wept as he said he was being called back for missions that were directed by "The Colonel" in the White House. I was not politically astute, so I did not draw any moral or legal inferences from his repeated mantra,

"It's a deal that we can't get out of. We got our hostages from Iran. We sell them arms. We take those profits and we fly arms down to Nicaragua."

This was March 1986, and I had not an inkling that DJC was describing illegal "arms for hostages" swaps in defiance of American public laws. All I knew was that he was running guns down to Nicaragua in dangerous circumstances under the auspices of our government to pay off serious debts. How could such a high powered attorney, with all the connections that officers from the military and other dignitaries in the city seemed to honor be stuck in this situation?

DJC wept as he explained that the government made a deal with him to act as an agent for the CIA to run these various counter-terrorist missions in exchange for clemency. He admitted he lost his license to practice law when he embezzled or co-mingled huge sums of money. His connections to the CIA gave him the authority to do all kinds of legal and investigative work as part of his counter-terrorist assignment. Thus, he was able to function as an attorney without having his real license to practice.

"Why don't you just quit?" I pleaded with him. "If you don't want to do these runs, why don't you just quit?"

Naiveté has always been my failing. DJC insisted that he couldn't quit. He stayed up all night, weeping in despair that he could not get out of the gun running. For days he described the ways in which he would suicide if his plane was downed. He often talked about his role as a very young pilot in Vietnam. He claimed to have a Silver Cross, and to have been downed during a bombing mission. He swore if he was ever shot down again in enemy territory, he would suicide.

I did not understand the sheer illegality of DJC's gun running mission, because I tuned out of national politics while in California to avoid any personal discomfort with the morality of the military missions Ronald Reagan might send us on. As a young Vietnam War protester, I could pick or choose the morality of any war. Now, as a soldier, I thought I no longer had that right. Ours was not to question why, ours was just to do or die.

I was suddenly consumed with rage, however. Rage at the Army. Rage at the Federal Government. I had no proof, but I felt there was a connection between DJC's insistence that I stay out of the way of the Oakland Army Base drug dealers and his entrapment, if that's what it was, as a gun runner to Nicaragua. I did know from friends in Boston and California, that the Mafia and other gangs extorted criminals to carry out their organized crime under threat of death. How could the Army put so many of our young men in the path of drugs and guns at isolated bases like Oakland Army Base, and then destroy the soldiers if they were dumb enough to succumb to the temptation? How could the government exploit men who were trapped in some non-military crime, by coercing them to participate in a never-ending underworld drama as informers, gun runners, or whatever?

The federal government was fully aware that gangster drug dealers were operating at Oakland Army Base. They did nothing about it. In the late '60s and early '70s, civil rights activists argued that the federal government allowed drugs to be poured into black neighborhoods in Washington D.C. and other East Coast cities when black power started to coalesce. This seemed to be no different to me. This African-American community, the African-American soldiers who were caught up in Oakland's drug transactions were all basically expendable, and not worthy of vigilant intervention as far as Uncle Sam was concerned.

I just couldn't believe that DJC was trapped into gun running by the government. I refused to believe that he had no choice whatsoever to stop. My cynicism about the American justice system, and the lawlessness of the government itself was as volcanic as my anger that DJC felt he had no choice but to fly to Tegucigalpa.

After several days of DJC's manic highs during the duty day and his weepy depression at night, I reached my wits end. I was absolutely exhausted. We both made a pact to get out of the Army. I imposed a condition: that he come with me to a confidential counselor to deal with his depression, and I now had to admit, my own depression.

Meantime, I filed my resignation papers.

Both of the men who pinned on my first lieutenant bars, Lieutenant Colonel Siegling and Lieutenant Colonel Seaton implored me to reconsider not only my decision to leave the Army, but my decision to marry DJC. Did I know everything about him that I needed to know? Their questions only infuriated me. How could they have known about his gun running missions and never inform me? If Siegling could tell me of impending danger from a petty drug dealer, why couldn't he apprise me of DJC's background before I fell madly in love with the guy?

Every plea from Seaton, Siegling and even from my new co-workers just caused me to bridle with anger. The command group thought they could persuade me to change my mind after my passions cooled, so they just set my resignation aside for awhile. I pressured the new adjutant to call Department of the Army to determine if I could be discharged as quickly as all my good friends who had recently been riffed on a moment's notice.

"You are not within the window of consideration for this RIF," I was informed.

I got cynical. How come all my friends who loved the Army, who planned long careers were being booted out, yet I was being told, despite my perpetual ambivalence about the military I was "not within the window of consideration" for a RIF?

I made an appointment to see the general. But first, I made a few splashy appearances with DJC at command functions. After a string of holiday parties, General Stanford graciously invited me to sit with him to review my seemingly sudden decision to leave the Army. I apprised him for the first time that I had contemplated leaving the Army for more than a year, and that was why I had not wanted to take the headquarters detachment command. I could not imagine myself ever being satisfied with military culture.

General Stanford picked up a photo album from his coffee table. He slowly leafed through the photos of him in command, him at Department of the Army, and finally, him posing with Cap Weinberger, the Secretary of Defense.

"I spent five years as his personal assistant. Marie, you have that potential. You will have that opportunity."

I was not impressed.

"Marie, if you stay with me, you will reach the stars. You will wear a star! Do you know, you are the only woman officer I ever met who not only earned the respect of every officer in this command — you earned the respect of every spouse! You were born to be an officer!"

Despite my feelings about the Army, I still worshiped John Stanford, as did many of my peers and civilian co-workers. However, in that moment, the anger that roiled inside me absolutely blinded me to my awe and love for this man.

"Sir," I began officiously. "I have had to work hard for everything in my life. It took me ten years to earn my college degree to make something of my life. Oakland Army Base is nothing but a ghetto. The Army, with the drugs and the violence, has become a ghetto. I didn't work so hard to get this far in my life only to wind up back in the ghetto! I love spending time with you. When we sit at the club, or in your meetings, it's inspirational. But let's face it, most of the time, we're dealing with things that we shouldn't have to deal with. Spending time with you, one evening per quarter is not enough to make up for all the lowlife that has crept into the Army!"

John Stanford pursed his lip. He asked me if I loved DJC. Of course I did.

"Enough to sacrifice your career? Marie, I know your personality. You can't give up your career. You are not the marrying type. You will never be happy as a housewife in some suburban ranch house!"

That infuriated me. Who was John Stanford to tell me I would be a failure in my second marriage? Of course, he was not implying that I would be a failure, just that I might be walking into a disaster.

"Sir, I have to make these decisions for myself. You said that you have lifelong friendships with your commanders. I hope after I leave, that I will still be your friend. I have to do what I have to do, but I'm grateful for your friendship and all the support you've given me and my programs. I just don't think I have what it takes to stay in the Army."

John graciously concluded the meeting by promising to approve my request for release from active duty. He never once mentioned any misgivings about DJC or about my decision to return to the world of art and music. He made it clear that if I stayed with him, the Army would be different, a much better experience. In my mind, why should I be treated differently from my other friends? They were much better officers than I, and much better logisticians, too. Why should I get special treatment to stay in, when I didn't care as much as they did?

I left knowing that General Stanford cared about me and that he respected me enough to honor my request for a discharge. But my mind was irrevocably made up. I was leaving. My paperwork sailed through to the Department of the Army. My orders for discharge arrived after repeated calls to the Adjutant's office. Determined to celebrate my leave taking, I reserved places for both DJC and myself at the next command Hail and Farewell.

Meantime, the man who sold DJC my engagement ring came pounding at the door. DJC's check for $5,000 bounced. I never wore an engagement ring before, and it was not important for me to wear one then. DJC was humiliated. He insisted his Certificates of Deposit were supposed to be available for cash any day. He asked me to write a check for $500 for a Cubic Zirconium substitute until his CDs were released in May, 1996.

Shortly before I left Kansas City, Missouri in 1983, a middle-class woman was robbed. When the thief couldn't get her expensive diamond off her finger, he literally sawed her finger off to get the ring. I was so uncomfortable and fearful about wearing the real five thousand-dollar diamond, which I had never done in my life, that I gladly substituted the CZ.

So, I wrote the check.

The business relationship with DJC and Ron H was getting very complicated, but it was time to say goodbye to the Oakland community. We walked into the MTMC Hail and Farewell at the Fort Mason Officer's Club dressed like stars in a Hollywood movie. I wore a flashy red suit with red heels. General Stanford made a few light remarks about the woman in red, and introduced DJC to other guests as "Mr. C from the State Department." CID agents took DJC, who had left active duty status to work fulltime in the art gallery, to the side. Since he worked for CID and the MPs, I didn't think anything of his disappearance.

My friends and co-workers sat in total silence when my name was announced as a Farewell. The accomplishments rattled off didn't seem to resemble who I had become in that moment: music major, folk singer, OCS grad, community services manager, guest house manager, and now art gallery owner and a Mrs. To Be. A moment of regret overwhelmed me. Did I really want to leave these friends who took pride in everything I did from singing at humanities fairs to scrubbing down moldy barracks buildings?

Then the rock and roll music began. DJC and I began dancing to the '80s rock bands. His energy was infectious. There was no time to reflect with old friends in this hideaway club. We didn't stay for drinks, as I usually did before I met DJC. The general, Jesse and Jennie and a few others sat around the bar overlooking the glassy onyx bay waters. I would have sat with them for hours on end. Now that I was engaged to be married, it didn't seem appropriate anymore. DJC and I slipped out. I was free from that moment to concentrate on gallery ownership.

DJC's financial troubles mounted as we approached the gallery contract closing. His depression didn't seem to lift, even after weeks of counseling. He confessed that he lied to me. Not only was he divorced, he was a divorced man with three children. His finances were tied up in legal proceedings with his ex-wife.

Ron, our gallery partner, was an old acquaintance of DJC. When I consulted with Ron about the wisdom of proceeding with the gallery contracts. Ron just shrugged the whole financial situation off: "He's always been like this. He's a high stakes player. You have to roll with the highs and the lows. He always comes through. Listen, I've known him for a long time..."

The end of April, DJC started to hint that he would disappear again. He went to D.C., then called me to discuss his ambivalence about living.

He wanted to commit suicide. I went back to D.C., where we worked out a survival plan for the next six months. We went to visit my family in Philadelphia.

My sister threw an engagement party for us, which was actually the only party my extended family ever attended before or since on my behalf. DJC's personality reverted to his manic, super-confident self, which sure brought out the best in others — at least before they got to know him. He felt and acted like a good luck charm. They especially approved of his Catholic faith, his law, military and police background. My mother joked with him,

"DJC, we have a doctor, a pharmacist, a priest, and with you, a lawyer.

Now all we need is an undertaker to make this family a complete enterprise!"

DJC and I drove back to California in his station wagon. We moved our business into the gallery, and prepared for the grand opening on June 27th. All the legal paperwork prepared by DJC and filed with the state of California was approved. Before the first reception, we had to scrap for walk-in business, clients and partners. Artists, dealers and clients were all enamored of DJC. He inspired lawyers, wealthy families and established artists alike to abandon all caution. He would walk into a studio, chat with the artist for a half-hour, and walk out with a $20,000 oil painting. Or a whole gallery full of oils with which to start our first advertised show.

Our only problem was cash flow. DJC took me to several banks to arrange for a small loan until his CDs could be redeemed. Any American woman can tell you that a divorced woman with no savings, no house and a lieutenant's paycheck will not successfully walk out of a bank with a loan in her hand unless there's some collateral or co-signer. DJC assured the lender in a public and private conversation that he was officially planning to handle all of the financial obligations, but his hands were tied until his CDs matured.

The bank gave us the cash to start operations. Only I was the only signatory on the loan. DJC's contribution to repayment was, I discovered in due time, to form a legal corporation that would free him and Ron Hunter of all financial liability for the operation of art gallery partnership. I did not have time to worry about the loan structure, however. We had a few weeks to prepare for the gallery opening, upon which our financial survival would depend.

The grand opening was really a smashing social success. A glamorous group of San Francisco natives attended our grand opening to give their good wishes to their friend, the artist whose work was being shown. No one was tempted by the imitations of Cézanne and other popular French artists, or fond enough of the artist to actually buy her works. The guests were most impressed by the watercolor of Nureyev by Andrew Wyeth and the original Maxfield Parrish oils. Not enough to take out their American Express cards, though.

A few of the colonels from Oakland Army Base attended our gala opening. The new director of the Personnel and Administration Division charmingly sipped his way across the gallery and warmly endorsed our choice of location, the gallery lighting, and the chic crowd that appeared for the opening. General John Stanford did not attend that evening, but shortly after, he did come to the gallery. DJC and I had dinner with Pat and John down in the Marina, in a small Italian restaurant that had become our office, where our deals were made and broken. If John and Pat had any misgivings about the gallery or my engagement to DJC, they discreetly refrained from expressing their concerns, probably fearful that I would be even more unrealistic and rebellious about my decision to choose DJC over the Army. I think they and all my friends were praying their nonchalance would give me the graceful opportunity to just change my mind without feeling totally humiliated by the mistake I was obviously making.

On another occasion, the priest from Treasure Island whose Masses I sometimes cantored joined us for dinner. We discussed our wedding plans, then took him down to the gallery to show him what our future life would be like. By this time, we were showing a lot of Picasso, Miro and Chagall lithographs in the gallery. The priest's eyebrows crinkled with his ironic observation,

"You know, Picasso was on many a cruise ship in his later years. I had a wonderful time as a chaplain on those things. But he would just laugh and say his later works were just scribblings. They were a joke to him. To him, it was hilarious that star-struck ignorant buyers would pay any price just to have the Picasso signature at the bottom..."

None of our artwork sold in those first few weeks. DJC and Ron worked out an arrangement with our dealers to hang Renoir etchings on the wall. More worldly gentlemen began to drift into the gallery. DJC had long chats with one man who worked for the Foreign Service. DJC mentioned his own work at the State Department, our plans to marry, and his plans to take me to an overseas assignment some day. The silver-haired man listened, nodded his head, and glanced at me in disbelief. They continued to talk.

Ron was supposed to work for us full time, but he claimed Don Austin, from Austin Galleries was placing great demands on him. To cement the personal confidence in our relationship with him, he invited us to his condominium at the edge of the Marina district.

His place was filled with expensive collectibles. Vases. Candlesticks. Sculptures. Things you couldn't buy in the San Francisco tourist gallery row if you could afford to pay any price. I was stunned by his collection of original oils. When I asked him how he acquired his large Niemann oil, he said he was a friend of Leroy Niemann. Their friendship was decades long, and borderless. There were small impressionist oils on his living room walls. Canvasses that should be hanging in public galleries.

Ron worked on commission for the Austin Galleries. He could barely afford a cup of coffee, or so he claimed as he taught us the day-to-day strategies of gallery survival. His secret lifestyle was at once impressive and disconcerting. As gallery owners would we eventually come to own and treasure works by some of the greater artists? Would we always be one step away from bankruptcy, with our wealth accumulated in treasured but economically useless non-collateribles? What was going on here, anyway?

Our next visit was an evening with the dealers who provided all of our lithographs. Their home was tucked away in the quiet neighborhood of Danville. Once again, I was taken back by the opulence, the lavish accumulation of oil paintings and expensive sculptures.

The integrity of the art world was proving to be as ephemeral as the integrity of the CID command that was supposed to keep Oakland Army Base crime free, all the while protecting the drug dealers from any serious threat. Now that we had visited the homes of two art connoisseurs and earned their confidence, (or shall I say, they earned our confidence), we were invited to take our gallery dealings to a new plane, to the sphere where the real money is made. Allen and Ron asked DJC to help them deal original works to clientele who demanded absolute confidentiality concerning their holdings and transactions.

The desire for confidentiality did not alarm me. Many times in my life, I have been in the homes of wealthy collectors or simply lucky individuals who inherited this or that piece of art, music manuscripts, or music instruments. No one wants his or her valuables to be displayed anymore than the streetwise city girl would flash her cash. These men were not motivated by the security concerns of their clientele, however. DJC, Allen and Ron mapped out a strategy to sell original works belonging to a man from out of state. The wholesalers paid DJC's way to fly to Montana to scout the man's estate for works that could be marketed publicly or through confidential channels. DJC returned from his trip with photos of an original Modigliani, other oils, and many sculptures the man was making available for confidential sale. DJC persuaded the man to loan him drawings by C.M. Russell.

The more Allen collaborated with DJC, the more the look of the gallery changed. Allen brought in Remington bronzes. The C.M. Russell was hung in our gallery window. Professional businessmen were attracted to the new displays. Several attorneys purchased Renoir etchings, Picasso lithographs and a few other trifles, trusting that DJC's word was as irrefutable as the certificates of authenticity accompanying each print.

The purchases these attorneys made were not enough to cover "the nut," the cash flow needed to keep the gallery in business. Up to this point, I was paying all of our living expenses for an expensive San Francisco apartment. I paid daily operating and entertainment expenses to push the business forward. Economic security was paramount for me. I began to panic and slumped into another depression. I was obviously a failure as a gallery owner and salesperson. I began to nag DJC to change strategies. Perhaps I should move back to the world of music, teach piano to earn income, and DJC could run the gallery with the guys, since they left me out of the loop on every decision anyway.

Once when I threatened to walk out forever, DJC took me upstairs to discuss this threat in our back office. He locked the office, and did something that was threatening. I started to scream, at which point, he went for my throat, then tried to cover my mouth and pull me away from the window. I bit his hand, grabbed one of the wine bottles left over from our grand opening, and threw it out the upstairs window. As the glass shattered, I started to scream again. I ran for the door, and went downstairs. The police came at someone else's bidding. DJC went over to the officers, told him he was both a lawyer and a former cop. He went outside, joked with them, gave them money and sent them on their way.

I can't say I was so afraid that I couldn't just leave that minute. I just didn't know what I was dealing with, or how to get out in a way that I would feel safe and free forever. I knew that he would use whatever resources he had to maintain the status quo he preferred at the moment. If he tired of me, it would be as the song goes, "Please be gone, I'm tired of you." If he "couldn't live without me." as he was telling me in these days, I knew just from running the Domestic Violence Program all these years I would have to make a very careful, getaway — best accomplished when I outlived my usefulness to him.

DJC left for a couple of hours, came back with a gift and some beautiful flowers. He taped a conversation where he tried to prove that I was emotionally very unbalanced, and the cause of all of our communications difficulties. He was right about one thing. I was quite capable of pointing out all of his weaknesses, and didn't hesitate to do so. He promised to be a different person, to take more responsibility for the business and our relationship.

He drafted a resume for himself, visited a headhunter, and acquired a job as a temporary attorney, to handle Ginny Mae and Fanny Mae transactions for the United Savings Bank. Within days, our financial situation seemed to turn around. He insisted we move to a larger apartment, where we could entertain clients, and I could have a piano with which to begin work as a piano teacher.

DJC, on his good days, wrote the most convincing love letters, persuading me to just take one more risk, to let myself move into this world of high finance, art and culture and let him do the rest. I completely withdrew from the gallery business, which made life as his fiancé much more bearable. We bought a hugely expensive piano, which once again, could never have been bought with my financial collateral — my Datsun Maxima. The woman who sold the piano to us took my signature alone. She was the first business person to check DJC's financial credibility before she had me sign the contract. She never told me that none of his financial holdings were as he stated. She simply had me sign the contract as if DJC were truly going to be the financial guarantor on the loan for the piano, which would pay for itself as I gave piano lessons to Italian children in the Marina where we lived. Later, my own piano teacher from the same store told me the saleswoman was completely aware that DJC's was lying to me about his financial situation. I was able to return the piano and cancel the contract because of her cognizance that DJC's report was fraudulent.

Several customers who were persuaded by DJC to buy Renoir etchings and other lithographs began calling the gallery and threatening to sue us if they didn't get a full and immediate refund on all of their purchases. They had the

John Stanford Weaves Magic

The General sparked creativity and initiative by acknowledging the training and management efforts of his leaders.

works appraised and were told all of the etchings and lithographs were phony, as were the appraisals by Allen. We were back in an economic slump, but I started to fight back in restaurant meetings when the men would make light of the returned purchases. I finally blew a gasket when both Allen and his lover asked me if I would like a great vacation down on the Cayman Islands. They wanted DJC to run large sums of cash down to the banks to avoid taxation, or whatever. My fury essentially put an end to the dinner and our business relationship.

"D, you promised me you would never go back to this kind of dealing," I raged. "We did this to get out of the Army, to get away from these kinds of deals..."

He tried to quiet me, and at the same time, to appease his friends. He made it clear to them he was going to run the money whether or not I helped him. I told them both I wanted out. I think they knew the stakes were too high for them to dicker with me. I wasn't contributing anything to their bottom line, and I could easily muck up one of their Cayman transactions if I didn't stand aside and let them do as they pleased. They all accepted my decision with equanimity, but left me holding the financial bag for all parts of the business. Don Austin, the owner of Austin Galleries and Ron's boss, was convicted of nationwide art fraud. I hope, but I will never know, that Ron, Allen and his lover were also nabbed in that sting.

Fortunately, I was completely out of the Army when the art world's seamy side began to show itself. I found out afterwards that the CID was fully aware of DJC's slide into the art scene's underbelly. If there was a connection between his running money and paintings to the Caymans and his running guns for the Iran-Contra covert program, I will never know. The priest from Treasure Island called me towards the end of the summer. "I am really concerned about you," he said softly. He did not divulge details, but he said he knew I was having great difficulties.

"I'll be okay. In a few months this will be all behind me. I have to bide my time. This will be over soon..."

"I'm really concerned about you," the priest whispered again, not volunteering to divulge the kinds of specific concerns that Lieutenant Colonel Siegling provided when he told me my efforts to discharge Sergeant H could prove dangerous to my life.

"I'll be all right. This will be over soon."

"God bless you! I will pray for you." The priest said.

My last days on active duty were actually very healing because my bosses made it clear to me they did not want to lose contact with me. Lieutenant Colonel Seaton left Oakland Army Base before I left. He carefully gave me his final rating. It was stellar, the kind that said I was the only lieutenant to walk on water since Jesus. He made sure General John Stanford wrote similar words in his senior rater box. James Seaton threw the rating down on his desk after I read, signed and returned it to him.

"I only gave this to you because you deserve it. But I didn't want to give you this, because you quit! You quit, and so, you shouldn't have gotten this!"

Seaton was always the moralist, but in this instance, I couldn't disagree with him. I was just as ashamed as he was, but I sure wasn't going to tell him so.

My mentor, Al Siegling was the new Deputy Installation Commander. He begged me to reconsider my decision to marry DJC. I fussed, fumed and stormed out of his office. By this time, I knew in my heart I would probably leave DJC. But he was in such an emotional funk, I felt I would be criminally responsible if DJC went and suicided because of our breakup. I called Lieutenant Colonel Siegling after I cooled off.

"Sir, this will be all over in a few months. I can't change anything right now. But I know, in a few months, this will all be behind us. I really value your support and your friendship. I hope when this is over, we can be friends again."

He sadly accepted my peace offering. In my last days, Al Siegling insisted that I stand in front of the formation to say goodbye to my troops in a proper change of command ceremony. He gently rehearsed the moves with me, and insisted that I say some personal words to the company after relinquishing command. General Stanford came down to the ceremony, as did DJC. DJC wore a very expensive gray suit.

I muddled through my farewell, because I really was very confused and not prepared to say goodbye at all. I don't remember if John Stanford assessed my command to the entire unit. I think he gave his final thoughts to me privately as we stood to the side of the formation.

"Marie, by the sheer force of your personality, you worked miracles in this command. You don't realize how much talent you have, what an influence you have been on the soldiers and their families. By the sheer force of your personality, you can make really good things happen!" He stared into my eyes, pleading for me to somehow come back to my senses, to take back my life again.

I did, in time. I left the Army. And I left DJC.

CHAPTER 8

Back to Planet Earth

Before I could put my Oakland tour behind me, I had to come to terms with the tremendous anger inside me. I had to sort out the legitimate anger from irrational expectations I might have had from the military. The Army is not paradise. Not every expectation that I had could or should have been fulfilled, even in the best of all possible worlds.

My anger at the Army and at our government for allowing men like DJC to be used as pawns in illegal war-making resulted in a personal catastrophe, no doubt. But this anger certainly cleansed my spirits enough to make me aware of my true calling. It somehow brought to light every illusion I held about the purity of the Army's motives in the conduct of military operations or in its conduct of disciplinary actions against soldiers.

If I learned anything, it is that anger is not a sin, and should not be cast as the root of all murderous evil. Anger is not the root cause of murder or violence anymore than joy is at the root of personal or societal peace. Anger and joy are both feelings. As such, they are morally neutral.

Legitimate anger, when it is denied or submerged, can turn on itself or erupt in violence. Good soldiers often kill themselves or others when their anger is not acknowledged and handled appropriately. Pacifists erupt in the same violence. In a 1980s religious study, one Mennonite group estimated their peace-loving, anger-condemning community had extremely high rates of domestic violence. As many as 25 percent of the Mennonite women were identified as battered in this insular, nonviolent faith group. I would maintain the root cause of violence in that community was not anger but denial of the right to express legitimate anger at all. You see this too, when counseling young mothers who abuse their children. Too often, they smother their feelings of hostility. In misguided efforts to be peacemakers, they tolerate all kinds of inappropriate behavior in their children. Neighbors and childcare teachers think such a mother is a living saint. Then all of a sudden, she snaps and half-kills her child over a misbehavior that would hardly be noticed on one of her better days.

The human mind is the true catalyst for evil. Our minds, not our feelings contrive our responses to the full range of human experience. The saddest trait of our culture has been its primacy on feelings as the coin of social interaction; its distrust of intellectual strategies for the resolution of personal conflict or societal moral crises. Too often, we believe that if we can just keep ourselves in a perpetual state of happiness and joy, we will also be better, peace-loving citizens. We do not tolerate legitimate expressions of anger or sadness because we fear the emotions qua emotions will explode in violence or sink into paralyzing depression. Of course, the healthy balance lies somewhere in between.

When the principle of anger management is taken too far — preachers and counselors alike can demonize anger as if it had intrinsically evil properties. This is neither biblically sound, nor therapeutically helpful.

The hurt I felt when my military friends were sent back to civilian life was cauterized to numbness, which in turn permitted me to suddenly blossom with a clear sense of purpose. I decided it was time to return to the world of music and find some way to work with the next generation. What I couldn't accomplish as an officer, I would as a civilian. I only joined the Army to buy time, to give myself a chance to recover from my divorce so that I could return to graduate school and finish my Masters in conducting. Perhaps I should not have lost sight of this goal. Perhaps I could somehow teach young people spiritual truths through music rather than through military service so young men and women would never be tempted to sell their souls to Uncle Sam for the price of inflated self-pride and self-delusion about one's patriotic accomplishments.

Once financial matters related to my gallery debacle were settled in late September of 1986, I put my personal belongings on the pavement of the Marina street on which I lived. My childhood friends, Ira and Mona came by to help me sell all my antiques and furnishings. I sold everything. My mahogany bureaus. My collection of Bartok performing Bartok and Duke Ellington jazzing the Nutcracker Suite and Toscanini screaming during his radio symphony orchestra rehearsals. I did not sell my orchestral scores or my library. These were tools that I would use. The furniture and recordings were status symbols, serving no functional purpose — things I could easily replace if I ever needed to do so.

I took the cash from this pavement sale to Stanford University and rented a single room in a very large house that was managed by the Morris family. My sister Diane and her husband Jack gave me a generous cash gift to make it possible for me to complete one quarter at Stanford without taking any loans. I worked part-time, as most graduate students do. After interviewing with Professor Toth, I signed up for his conducting course for one quarter.

This leap into the world of middle-class higher education was almost idyllic, except that I could not get the Stanford University student services department to process my VEAP benefits. So I was perpetually hungry and broke and madder than ever that I could have so stupidly believed that the Army took care of its own.

I took a work-study job in Stanford's undergraduate library, and signed up for two music classes. One, a course on 18th Century ornamentation, was so esoteric I couldn't imagine ever using the material if I were fortunate enough to teach in American public schools. My conducting class with Professor Andor Toth was very frustrating. He expected me to learn one Haydn symphony and one movement from a Schubert symphony for the entire course period. This was simply no challenge. While an undergraduate, I studied conducting with Doctor Glenn Block. Doc Block required his conducting students to learn one movement of a symphony per week for each of his classes, and one movement of a symphony per week for student rehearsal. I thought Professor Toth's class was a complete waste of time. Later, I realized that Professor Toth was not the problem. My state of mind was. Professor Toth expected us to savor every detail of the scores he assigned, but his pace afforded me much too much time to dwell on DJC. I hoped this would change as I continued weekly therapy sessions to try to put my past behind me. Meantime, I worked and practiced the Haydn symphony.

Two classmates offered me a great deal of companionship. One was a female oboist. She complained incessantly that our professor did not take her seriously because she smiled like a girl. She came to the conclusion that although she was a married woman, she would have to pose with an ultra serious expression to earn the serious consideration of the male faculty at Stanford. Her complaint was legitimate, but not entirely the professor's fault.

Stanford was the first university campus I ever visited where women were obsessed with their appearance, the impression they made on men. They lined up in the bathrooms 50 or 60 deep to stroke their well coifed long hair and to touch up their makeup. The music department area swarmed with women who were more focused on looks than accomplishment, although I am sure that these women were exceedingly accomplished. When our professor's attitude toward the smiling oboist did not change, I wondered if I would be happy if I were a permanent Stanford student. This made me miss the Army, where if nothing else, I didn't have to frown all the time to have my professional status validated. In the Army I was taken very seriously.

My other classmate, Geoff, was a brilliant organist and organ builder, but he was extremely stubborn about some of his theories of music. The music professors at Stanford were a bit old fashioned. As if the academy was a medieval monastery, students were to absorb every bit of precious information their masters imparted, and then regurgitate with much flattery in tests and public lectures. Geoff had a really difficult time since his opinions were considered oppositional rather than the considerations of a thoughtful scholar. I was so opposed to this kind of teaching, that I immediately embarked on a new career path. I paid too much for these classes to just quit, so I finished the quarter before allowing my body to catch up with my mind.

DJC was almost completely out of my life during my respite at Stanford. I still had relationships with many of my friends from the Community Services Division at Oakland Army Base, however. Near Thanksgiving, my friend and mentor, Jesse Mangrum died suddenly. I had a falling out with him during the time I managed the Child Care Center.

I had given Mary Jo from DA my absolute word that I would provide hot lunches for the kids. I contracted with Jesse's club to carry over warming bins of hot kiddy lunch platters. Of course, we went slightly into debt because our sliding scale fees did not support this luxury. I thought the club would charge us on a sliding scale, but that wasn't happening. Just about a year before he died, Jesse threatened to shut down my center if I didn't raise the fees or do something to eliminate the CCC's red ink of about $1,400. I was furious and counter-argued that the childcare regulations stipulated that the CCC could operate with a deficit when necessary. None of the other morale activities were permitted to run deficits. In fact, the profits from booze, cigarettes, and slot machines were supposed to be redeemed with just this sort of community service.

Jesse very uncharacteristically refused to budge on the issue of profits and loss. Until that day, Jesse backed every decision I made. He coached me to win over the hearts of other officers who interfered with our programs. He sparkled whenever my maverick programs won approval of Department of the Army. He encouraged me to take risks with the adage, "It's always easier to beg forgiveness than to get permission."

But here, for the first time, we opposed each other like two bulls in a pit. Neither of us would budge. I would not stop the hot lunch program or charge my parents rates they couldn't afford. He wouldn't share the O Club profits. We had never reached this kind of impasse before.

He threatened to shut down the center or to spank me for being so stubborn. My friend Captain Bob Kant was present, but exasperatingly silent as he mediated by listening to both sides of the argument. Jesse was treating me as if I was his small child, since I was more than young enough to be his daughter. I was livid.

"Fine," I said snootily. "You think I'm doing such a terrible job? I shouldn't even be managing this center because it conflicts with my command responsibilities. If you think you can do better, you run the CCC all by yourself!"

I walked out on Jesse, which absolutely stunned him.

Bob tried to bring us both to the bargaining table again in his quiet way. He came down to my office in the Headquarters Building, told me how he understood my side of the disagreement, but that I was wrong not to see Jesse's side, too.

Bob Kant knew he would have to manage the CCC if I didn't. I told him I would visit with Lieutenant Colonel Seaton. At the end of the duty day, I visited with Jim Seaton and cried with frustration because we had reached an impasse.

On the one hand, Lieutenant Colonel Seaton agreed with me that the club profits should be diverted to provide hot meals for the children of our junior enlisted. On the other hand, he realized it was time for me to get out of the childcare business and to concentrate on soldiering.

He turned the CCC over to Bob Kant, to my relief, but unintentionally, to Jesse's humiliation. I don't know if Jesse ever forgave me for walking away from his authority altogether. Sergeant majors, whether retired or active-duty, are never supposed to be overruled by lieutenants.

A year later, I was out of the Army, and Jesse was dead. General Stanford gave the eulogy for this great man, who was buried in his sergeant major's uniform at the Presidio. I cried all the way home from his funeral. During the Thanksgiving weekend, I visited with his young widow.

After that, whenever I spoke with General Stanford, he would give me an update on Jesse's widow, who was a very vibrant woman with terrific career potential. He offered me her new phone number when he found out I was moving to New England to be a pastor. I found I did not have as much in common with Jesse's widow as I did with John Stanford or with Jesse himself.

I discovered the glue of my relationship with Jesse's widow had dried up. She and I had very different understandings about what marriage relationships should entail, and about the meaning of loyalty between friends and spouse. I had discovered that a number of folks were in adulterous relationships. I didn't want to cover up for them. I didn't want to gloss over my own situation, either. Until my relationship with DJC, I had meticulously screened the backgrounds of the men who asked me for dates. Lieutenant Colonel Siegling would sneak into my ID card section and look at their files. Invariably, Siegling would call me and say, "I'm sorry to say, colonel or major so-and-so is married." He would chuckle, because he knew I would never date a married man. "But, I can't blame him for trying!"

I never checked DJC's marital status or any of his background even when we were deeply entangled as business partners and engaged to be married. Since DJC was treated so deferentially by the command group, even General Stanford, I believed everything this man told me. Even his financial problems were explained away by his friends as nothing to be really concerned about — the strategy of a major league financier. "You've got to be willing to lose big to win big!"

Only when I made a decision to close my art gallery and get away from DJC, did I discover the missing piece of DJC's personal mystery — the reason my commanders asked me if I was sure that I really wanted to marry this guy. I thought they were alluding to his role as a gun runner for the CIA. That wasn't their gravest concern at all. As I gathered documents to close the gallery and our apartment, I found some phone bills that had Michigan phone numbers. I called the number, and spoke to a woman who said she was still DJC's wife. She confirmed all of the career identities that DJC claimed to have. She confirmed the extravagant lifestyle he described. Yes, he did use his own private plane when he flew from Laguna Niguel to Washington, D.C. Mrs. C said she always waited for him to come back when he went on wild jaunts for the CIA, and that in fact, they never divorced.

My decision to gather documentation to close the gallery helped me finally discover that DJC had lied to me about being divorced. The very last time I saw him, to collect a small fraction of the money he owed me, he gave me one last kiss and apologized for the fact that he could neither live with nor without me. Not only could he live without me, but he would be living without me. He had already reconciled with his wife, so it was safe for me to move away forever.

After Jesse's funeral, I found out that my command group, even Jesse's wife seemed to know that DJC was married, but they never let me in on their secret. They played along with DJC's story that he was divorced and perpetually strapped for assets because of the divorce decree his wife bitterly contested. Jesse's wife seemed to think that adulterous relationships were the spice of life. My engagement with DJC was an initiation rite as far as she was concerned, into the sophisticated world of power, money, and fame — without all the trappings, and hassles of marriage. She encouraged me not to be so hard on myself for being deceived. She argued that I should not be so hard on others in our circle of friends who were in adulterous relationships, either. I didn't know what to believe about anything, so I just kept to myself and those whom I knew to be true.

Stanford University was such an oasis of peace and renewal. I was too poor to buy a parking permit, so I parked at the edge of campus every day. To get to classes, I had to walk past the Rodin sculpture garden, then through a lovely courtyard where the Memorial chapel stood. These walks were a constant reminder that I was extremely fortunate as a woman who bumped up against so much failure. I wasn't homeless, jobless, or without friends. Palo Alto was far removed from every care in the world. Before I realized it, my academic quarter at Stanford was over. I wondered if I could stay in the area after my courses finished, not as a pretentious scholar — just a human being.

The university is located in the quaint city of Palo Alto. Palo Alto's terrain is perfect for running. Perfectly flat streets. Beautiful homes, each with unique ornamentation and painting schemes that brought out the subtle background colors of the town's natural surroundings. The trees had mammoth trunks. There were wide boulevards to run on, exotic flowers such as birds of paradise to greet runners along the trail. The cafes in Palo Alto were a student's delight, too. We could sit and read for hours while nursing cappuccino.

My hosts, the Morris family, had a son who was also a Stanford graduate student. Don was in the hospital when I first moved in. He was recovering from a kidney transplant. This extraordinary young man, although completely agnostic, communicated a spiritual wholeness that is rare even among the most devoted of religious leaders. When he was medically stable, he came home. His family invited me to join them for a weekly game of bridge. The Morris family knew I was subsisting on a diet of sweet potatoes and inexpensive vegetables. Every week, they invited me to a barbecue where they cooked fat, juicy filet mignons with fresh vegetables right out of their garden. While recuperating from his surgery, Don seemed to enjoy company. I grew to love these folks, and looked forward to our weekly dinners.

Don Morris had an optimistic thirst for truth and adventure that was not only reflected in his research. It brought him fame. He spent his days doing mathematical modeling to determine if there was such a thing as an altruistic gene. When he was a teenager, Don discovered tons of mathematical errors in the college preparation workbooks sold by the national testing service for SAT test takers. His teenage crusade to correct these textbooks culminated in a segment with Betty Furness on the Today Show.

His conquering spirit was an attitude, a way of life. He always directed his energies toward such life-affirming projects as the protection of wild birds from off-shore drilling. When Don was fully recovered from his kidney transplant, he decided he wanted to run in a formal race. Although his mother taught him to sail, he had never participated in formal sports because he was sick during his teen years. Don's friends were afraid to help him train because they feared he would have a medical setback. His mother worried, too, but Don was adamant. He was going to run in a race. He asked me more than once to help him. Here I was, an old lady, who was never professionally coached, yet I was in the position to train a young man in sports. Well, all that military training counted for something, didn't it? I didn't want to upset Don's mother, so I told him I would help him, but only on the condition that his doctors approved.

Don's mother, Jeanne, used to stop me on my way to my room each day to ask me questions about the Army, especially about DJC. She never expressed disbelief when I unraveled the intriguing story of our troubling relationship. Jeanne was quite an armchair philosopher. Each week she would share thoughts about mothering, gender, mentoring young adults, the military, the environment, the art of sailing, and bridge. Her husband Bill was extremely kind to me and tender to both his wife and son.

When my classes were over, I knew I had to think differently about my career plans. I took all kinds of part-time temporary jobs to bide my time before finding a permanent job and residence in the East Bay. I drove vans, delivered packages, processed data, shelved books, and finally, I was hired as a secretary.

While temping, and continuing to sort out my life's direction, I received a call from Lynda, my OCS buddy. I was ecstatic to hear her voice, and especially to know she was in-country. She came to visit me in Palo Alto. Even before I left Oakland Army Base, she had been serving as a public affairs officer for the Sixth Army Reserve Headquarters in San Francisco, unbeknownst to me. She wanted me to join her unit as a reservist. I bluntly declined.

"No way. The reserves are a joke." I was livid that she would even suggest such a thing.

"DeYoung," she retorted. "I'm in the reserves. I'm not a joke. We need good people. We need to shape up the unit. You'd be terrific. We'd be buddies again!"

"Lynda, last spring, I tried to get the 90th ready for Team Spirit. The cooks were lying all over the floor, sleeping off their drugs and their beer. The unit administrator said the men still come in and physically threaten him with weapons if he doesn't pay them for not showing up for drill. When they do come to drill, they're stoned! The reserves should be disbanded. Biggest waste of taxpayer dollars..."

Lynda looked at me glumly, then down into her coffee cup.

"Marie, it's never going to change if we don't get in there to clean it up." She told me a story wherein she was to brief the Reserves' commanding general at the Sixth Army. A senior officer came into the room and saw her sitting. There weren't enough chairs to go around. He impolitely challenged Lynda to leave the room, to make room for the senior ranking officers. I was appalled. I never experienced that kind of public humiliation by officers at Oakland Army Base.

"Don't you see, Marie. The joke was on him. I smiled and left the room. The general entered. The briefing was supposed to start immediately, but it couldn't because I was outside. That same colonel had to come out and ask me to return to brief the general. The joke was on him!"

"Lynda," I was suddenly revolted with the idea that it was our responsibility to make things better, make the policies and people work properly in the Army. "I'm sorry that man was such a jerk. You should never have been treated that way. I don't think the Army will really change. We can't change it. I don't think you should continue to subject yourself to that kind of humiliation. You make them look good wherever you are assigned, but they treat you like you are just fluff!"

Lynda did not dispute my view. She talked about a marriage proposal she had turned down. A distinguished European wanted to marry her. He never told Lynda until close to the wedding that he presumed she would give up her career, her public life. Even the staunchest feminists in Germany and Austria did not think twice about leaving the professional world while they raised their families. She didn't mind the career sacrifice so much as his lack of spontaneous affection. He wanted her to give up everything, Lynda said, "Yet, he could never say I love you."

How could such a beautiful woman inspire such complacency in men when it came to love and marriage? I couldn't fathom the stupidity of the men who were afraid to let Lynda know how much they truly adored her. I erupted and let a stream of invectives fly.

As we sat there sipping herbal tea, we realized we had both changed so much, yet the world around us was still the same. I let Lynda know I was glad she returned to the United States, and that we lived so close. I begged her to allow me to continue the friendship in a civilian context. She was more stubborn than I about how our future would unfold together.

"Marie, I need you to join me at the Sixth Army," she said, grabbing my arm. "I need — a buddy."

I could not fathom why our relationship had to be contingent upon military service. I was still really depressed about my experiences with DJC and with Oakland Army Base. As I processed out of my assignment at Oakland, some of the senior officers there tried to recruit me for the reserve unit where Lynda was working. Did they send her here? I wasn't going to be seduced this time.

"Lynda, I will always be your friend," I said, putting the breaks on her appeal. "If you ever want to visit, we can get together here, in Danville, in Berkeley. Just not at the Reserve Center. I can't pretend that the Reserves are doing America any good. I'll be your buddy. Just not in the Army."

Lynda's lips tightened. She looked disheartened, but she left without saying a word. I never saw Lynda again after that day. She would soar with the upper crust of society. She could master the inner workings of the military and the government. I wasn't sure I could ever hold my own in the Gemini constellation, the star cluster of generals and heads of state whom Lynda catered to during her work as an attaché. I would probably do best as a down-home teacher or neighborhood social worker. I would find some way to keep a small group of kids out of trouble. I didn't need fame, glory, or star dust to make me feel alive anymore.

In March of 1987, I went to work for a female minister at a Protestant seminary. My cousins and my mother encouraged me to pursue Protestant ministry, since church work seemed to bring out the best in me. I had already made a number of career, faith and lifestyle choices that resulted in family disharmony. Thus, I was really hesitant to be so bold. My mother was a devout Catholic. My family was devoutly Catholic. I had already been ex-communicated for accepting a married priest, Patrick Hughes as my pastor for several years. I asked my mother how she would feel if I went ahead and became a minister.

"Well, your cousin Corky is a priest," she answered dryly. "When he travels on cruises, he takes his mother as his secretary and they both travel for free. When you get ordained, if you just remember to take me as your secretary..."

Before I knew it, I was enrolled in the Starr King School for the Ministry on Berkeley's Holy Hill, where a consortium of ecumenical seminaries combined resources to provide accredited seminary degrees under the banner of the Graduate Theological Union. After that, I returned to Stanford University in the summer of 1990 to do hospital chaplain training, and then, to All Souls Unitarian in Manhattan to do my parish ministry training under the supervision of Forrest Church.

Before the Gulf War, I wrote to Lynda to let her know that as a UU minister, I was in the final stages of ministry training, and that I would be ordained within one year. I told her I had serious moral reservations about the impending Gulf War, but that I would always support her as a soldier. During the Christmas holidays, I received a letter from Lynda's mother telling me that Lynda had died of Leukemia the spring before. Lynda's mom wrote that the addresses of Lynda's Army friends were all written in German. As was much of the correspondence she exchanged with us. She waited for each of us to send Lynda a Christmas card to send us the terrible news about Lynda's death.

Although I will never regret my decision to stay out of the Army Reserves despite Lynda's strong urging, I will always regret that I let my anger at the Army interfere with my gut reaction to her pleas. I should have asked her, "What do you mean, you need a buddy? I am your buddy! Tell me Lynda, what is really going on?"

According to her mom's note, Lynda was first diagnosed with cancer much later than our meeting in Palo Alto. But Lynda was the kind of person who might have known something was seriously wrong with her much before she ever did anything about it.

Although I spoke with him several times, I never saw General Stanford again, except when he was on television promoting the Atlanta Olympics or the Seattle School System. I watched him give the education speech for Mr. Clinton's second nomination as the democratic presidential candidate in 1996. We did speak by phone more than once. He wrote a wonderful letter of recommendation for my ordination to the Unitarian Universalist Ministry, in which he cited the "magic" that I was able to "weave" throughout his command to create programs that cared for people.

While a seminarian and later a parish intern, I worked with a number of parish social justice committees that ran soup kitchens, funded housing programs, mentored kids in Harlem and tutored kids after school. I worked in the Bronx as a community organizer where I witnessed far more lawlessness and violence than I ever experienced in the Army. In the summer of 1991, as I was about to

Ministry — Responding To The Call

Reverend Forrester Church, son of Senator Frank Church, spoke at the author's ordination service after supervising her internship.

be ordained to work with the youth in the inner city, I realized I still wasn't prepared to cope with urban decay. I needed more training. I was accepted in the University of Pennsylvania's clinical pastoral education program. I had all kinds of marvelous, cutting-edge medical experiences, with the best clinical training money can buy.

HUP was located in a dilapidated, gun and drug infested neighborhood in West Philadelphia. All chaplains in the CPE program provided emergency room coverage. This meant that in addition to learning about liver and heart transplants, and resurrecting the bodies of two-pound babies, we had abundant exposure to the urban rod-and-gun culture. The HUP trauma director believed that emergency room chaplains could transform young men and women who were brought into the trauma bays in much the same way that the Army believed chaplains could turn the lives of troubled youth around. The difference was that most of the young men and women we were called to support in the emergency room were dead on arrival, or as the trauma director's own studies confirmed, they were less than eighteen months away from violent death.

It was 1991. Many studies had already documented the epidemic explosion of violence in the American city. There were no cures in sight. The only redemption to a gun-related death was the surviving family's decision to donate the organs of otherwise perfectly healthy victims. It doesn't take more than a few deaths to become cynical about curbing gun deaths, so long as there is a shortage of transplant organs in this country. No other good came of these murders. Our nation does not stop to grieve the deaths of men and women from the urban underclass the way we grieve the massacred children in suburban high schools. In '92, more than 20,000 teens were murdered with handguns — almost half the number of men who were killed in the entire Vietnam War. But our nation paid no attention. There was no agenda to interdict, to end the urban fratricide.

I never thought the military could be of use to American society in the 21st century. I couldn't imagine the Army teaching the underclass anything, especially since I saw first hand how gang members and drug dealers thrive inside the Army. We had no values to teach young soldiers anymore. The Army was as corrupt as the rest of society. But one year in an inner city hospital changed my mind.

The urban underclass had nowhere to go but to die or go to higher class war-making organizations. If the youth stayed in the inner city, the odds were three in four they would wind up with a criminal record, and one in four they would die by the age of 24. If the youth joined the Army, at least they had the chance, the potential to learn the basic living and social skills necessary to leave the gangs that plagued their schools and neighborhoods. I began to think of the Army, like many court judges and Secretary of the Army, Louis Caldera now does, as a civilizing influence on desperately marginalized youth. The Army could be the parent, the teacher, and the probation officer of last resort. Where family, church, school and community probation officers had failed, the Army would miraculously level the playing field for these youth. Perhaps, where society failed, the Army would be used defensively, on the home front, to end the urban drug war by ending the reign of violent urban gangs.

In 1992, I took my first parish on Martha's Vineyard. Although the ministerial responsibilities were full-time, the parish could only afford half-time compensation. As we negotiated my contract, the parish fully recognized the best way for me to earn a living wage was to join the Army Reserves. I did. My time on Martha's Vineyard provided the same idyllic respite after a year of urban gun violence that Palo Alto had provided after three years in Oakland. Full of charming, loving parishioners, the Unitarian Universalist Society of Martha's Vineyard welcomed me to preach as often as I wished, and to be part of every facet of their community life.

All the paperwork for my entrance into the reserves came through in time for me to attend the winter Chaplain Officer Basic Course in January, 1993. On December 1, 1992, Harry Hallman ferried to the island in his Cav hat, and a bomber's leather jacket. Two of my parishioners, Tom Hale and Bob Farwell stood beside me at the water's edge in front of The Black Dog Café. Harry swore me in as a new chaplain. Inside The Dog, we celebrated by lapping up a huge heart-stupid breakfast of fried potatoes, muffins, and eggs saturated in butter.

Chaplain recruiters urged me to consider active duty despite the fact that I would be an extreme minority. Only 38 chaplains out of 1400 were women at the time. This gender ratio in the Chaplain Corps has never changed. The vast majority of chaplains are fundamentalist. I would go active as an almost extinct breed — a Unitarian Universalist. There was only one other Unitarian on active duty. I worried I would not be able to keep up with physical training requirements — I was in my late 30s. But chaplains were not expected to be as gung-ho as real soldiers. Just so long as I did regular PT and maintained my competence in counseling and preaching skills, no one would expect me to run like a ranger anymore.

Two female chaplains in the class, both much younger than me, should never have been considered for active duty. Both of these women experienced sexual trauma prior to their acceptance into the chaplain corps. They were both receiving rape counseling. They were useless in the field and on the athletic field. Their rape experiences were used as excuses to refrain from every kind of emotionally stressing experience or physically challenging training event. By the end of the course, I was disgusted with the Army's double standards for women. I theorized that the Army should exclude women if they were still afflicted with symptoms of sexual trauma.

Ironically, my experience in urban ministry and in trauma hospital chaplaincy made me extremely competitive for an active duty slot. The chaplains needed men and women who could handle war trauma — whether it happened on foreign soil or as a result of American gang warfare. I had proved my grit by completing the high-speed Hospital of University of Pennsylvania chaplain residency. Even though I longed to settle into Martha's Vineyard, I feared that my urban experiences would always make me an outsider on the island. The island was a cocoon, safe from the travails of urban life. I bought a home. I really wanted to stay there. At the same time, I could not forget the young people who were screaming for the chance to get out of the ghetto. Islanders were not concerned with the plagues that were destroying the inner city. I was constantly trying to come to terms with our youth crisis. My preoccupations were irrelevant to vineyarders.

I talked the whole thing over with many key parishioners, some Catholic priest friends, and even some high-ranking chaplains. When I talked to various chaplains about Oakland Army Base — my experiences with the chaplain assistant who doubled as a pimping drug dealer and my relationship with DJC, the men would say, "Don't talk about this. Just don't ever talk about this." I knew that the Army, although an organization of about one-half million people, is very much like a small family. You don't leave behind your past that easily. Before going active, I would have to bring closure to my experience with DJC.

To complete the chaplain board packet, I needed recommendations from some of my former raters. I called General John Stanford. He was very charming, smoothly avoiding any references to our past. He had already written the recommendation letter that resulted in my ordination as a Protestant minister. If I were to go on active duty, I would need the recommendation of some of my previous bosses. What would he say?

"Marie, you hated active duty."

I believe this was the only negative feedback I ever received from John in our entire relationship, besides, "Marie, you'll never be happy as a married woman!"

He sighed, then continued, "You didn't want to have anything to do with the Army. What are you doing? Why don't you stay on Martha's Vineyard?"

"I spent the last few years doing inner city ministry. Working with homeless. Working with gangs. These experiences have prepared me. I think I can contribute something, I think I can handle things better — things that I couldn't before."

"Well, why did you leave? You ran off and got married the last time!"

I didn't know if he was playing devil's advocate or just plain disgusted. It was my turn at bat.

"John, you know what happened last time. I was really furious when DJC told me that he was running guns for the CIA! How could the Army let that happen? That man was ruined!"

There was dead silence.

"We didn't know anything about that," John said, as if he were coaching me. "We didn't know anything about that." He repeated emphatically.

I still loved John Stanford, but I did not believe he was innocent in the guns-for-hostages swap. I believed he knew, or was forced to tolerate it while he commanded Oakland Army Base. At the very least, Army leadership sold out when they tolerated the infiltration of CIA agents who operated the guns-for-hostages program out of military installations.

"Look," I said, trying to catch up on our personal history, in what I sensed might be our last conversation. "I'll be the first to admit I wasn't very mature. I was not ready to handle the gang activity or the gun running. I was angry with the Army. Especially when Colonel Siegling called me and told me I had to handle sergeant H with great care. He warned me again and again that my life was in danger because of the drug dealers on the base. I loved DJC because he tried to protect me in the same way. They both begged me to stay out of the Sergeant H case."

A longer silence.

"I didn't know about that," he said earnestly. "Siegling, Seaton should have told me about that. Why didn't you talk to me about this before?"

"Both Siegling and DJC warned me that I needed to be quiet about the drug problem. They both wanted me to stay away. I thought you knew all this..."

"No, Marie. I give you my word. I should have known about this, but..."

I asked if I would have any security clearance problems after my relationship with DJC. He assured me I wouldn't. Could I count on him to write a recommendation that would make it possible for me to go on active duty?

"My secretary will send it to you. I'll have her prepare my letter," he responded, as if none of our previous conversation had transpired.

John Stanford's charisma always left me in awe, yet frustrated. He acted as if the sheer force of our personalities could set everything wrong in the world aright. I seldom felt I had the abilities he expected me to have. I once wrote a ditty to exorcise his Godlike stature from my soul. Whenever you asked him how he was doing, he would answer with a smile, " I'm perfect, but you knew that!" I could never live up to his standards. That was why I never believed him when he said he would "take me to a star." I loved John and his wife Pat Stanford, but, I finally had to accept that I was different. Although my conversation with John Stanford did not bring us any closer, it certainly helped me to put the past behind, and to realize once and for all that he was not Super-human. He was just a wonderful, simple human being. Like me.

I never saw John Stanford again, although I did talk to him once or twice while he was in Atlanta as the county manager. I asked him to help with a CBS 60 Minutes investigation of gender issues in the military while he was the Superintendent of the Seattle School Board. He did not take my calls then, because he was ostensibly mired in a $20 million budget shortfall. He sent word he simply could not afford to dicker with military matters while he worked so intensely to improve the lives of Seattle school children.

Almost two years later, I learned John Stanford was dying of almost the same leukemia that Lynda endured. I sent him a note, telling him I was writing this book. Although I wanted him to read the manuscript, I could only send him my wishes and prayers for recovery following his bone marrow transplant. Although John expected complete recovery, he died shortly thereafter with his wife Patricia and his two sons at his side.

After I talked with John Stanford about our time together at Oakland Army Base, I wholeheartedly believed I was destined to be an active duty chaplain. I confirmed my decision with my parish board. A kind lieutenant colonel helped me assemble my packet, which he hand-carried to Washington D.C. on the 15th of March, 1993. By April 24, I was notified I would be accessed onto active duty.

CHAPTER 9

Answering the Call

Did you ever watch Bill Cosby threaten his television son with a march to the Army Recruiting Station as a last exasperating effort to instill discipline and values in him? I don't personally know Bill Cosby, but we have a few things in common. We have a common birthplace, Philadelphia. We share a love of education. In 1993, we held the common belief that traditional institutions such as the Army could serve our youth by instilling solid American values, discipline, and strong work habits. We share the same aspirations for America's youth.

The Army Chaplain Corps promised opportunities to recivilize the urban youth. I had great hope we could stem the tide of destruction.

I was wholly impressed that the Army had vigorously confronted the social issues as a command responsibility. This was such a drastic change from the "see no evil" approach to drugs, gangs and sexual misconduct that we faced in the '80s. I could see a whole generation redeemed through the efforts of sergeants and officers who were dedicated to molding the characters of our young into citizen soldiers. I wanted to be part of the winning team. So, I accepted an assignment to be the first female chaplain in the Second Armored Cavalry Regiment.

The Second Armored Cavalry Regiment was one of the elite units to serve in the Gulf War. This unit was the subject of the movie, Courage under Fire. The Second is still the longest continuously serving active duty cavalry regiment in our Army, but it is always under threat of extinction. Until 1993, women were excluded from The Cav. Whether or not women will continue to be assigned, I am grateful for a lifetime of learning that was squeezed into an 18-month girdle that was my first chaplain assignment.

Cavalry units perform a reconnaissance function, mostly a suicide mission, as young lieutenants reminded me during indoctrination sessions. Cavalry scouts roam the battlefield, searching out the enemy's location, strengths and weaknesses. Their whole existence is fraught with danger. Women were excluded from combat or near-combat situations, even when assigned to support operations, until Mr. Les Aspen lifted the ban in 1992-93. So, although by doctrine the Support Squadron for the 2nd ACR was located 25 kilometers ahead of the battlefield, by political decree, all common sense was abandoned. Women were front-loaded into support units in near-combat situations like the Cav. Upon my arrival, women comprised 22 percent of the Support Squadron. There were a few women in the Regimental Headquarters, but the three line squadrons were exclusively male.

I had no plans of serving the Cav when I returned to active duty. I begged for an assignment at Fort Hood, so that I could be near my classmates, perhaps increasing my chance for survival as a token female chaplain. But I received a call from Lieutenant Colonel Joe Donnelly while at my island home, during which Donnelly literally begged me to join his team.

Donnelly knew all the buttons to push to recruit me for the Cav.

"We are 22 percent female, and we never had women before. We have all kinds of problems with alcohol and domestic violence that we never had when the Cav was stationed at Fort Lewis, Washington. Now, at Fort Polk, the soldiers have nothing to do but drink and we need someone who can be a spiritual leader, and help us work with these troopers... Can you help us with domestic violence, maybe with some retreats and some family support programs..."

The colonel wasn't entirely truthful with me. The Cav's social problems were just as great at Fort Lewis as they were on Fort Polk. Fort Lewis had an infestation of gangs just like every other major post. Many of Donnelly's long-standing domestic violence, incest, and alcohol rehab cases were brought down from Fort Lewis. I had prior service and a clear picture of what the problems were. Donnelly's denial of the Army-wide long standing problems was similar to the alcoholic's emphatic statement that his watermelon-sized belly was due to the consumption of a mighty spicy squirrel that he had eaten. Despite Colonel Donnelly's little white lies about this sudden statistical upsurge, I sensed he wanted positive direction for the troops at Fort Polk. He had faith that I could provide that direction. I changed my dream sheet.

On 8 August 1993, I said farewell to my parish, packed up my car, took one final ferry ride back to the mainland, and began my trek towards my first assignment. I arrived at Fort Polk on the 13th of August. Three days ahead of schedule. Colonel Donnelly was so desperate to get his squadron settled down, that he asked me to come in for orientation as soon as I arrived. After unpacking in the Bachelor Officer Quarters, I took a quick shower. In that hot August Louisiana humidity, where the rain would bounce off the pavement in a steely gray cloud of steam, the rejuvenative effect of a shower was short-lived. My new chaplain supervisor, Stanley Copeland, took me to meet my new bosses, Major White and Lieutenant Colonel Donnelly. When Donnelly was assured that my feet were on the ground at Fort Polk, and that I could not finagle an assignment to some comfortable retirement farm, he sighed with relief. His wrinkles evaporated as he released me for the weekend.

The following Monday, I went about completing forms, signing records, reviewing records, and signing bogus track sheets used by social support departments to provide statistics documenting their impact on the Army community. Most of these programs — Army Emergency Relief, Education Center, Army Community Services, the Library, Recreation Center — operate during hours that are not soldier-friendly.

Grumbling, I drove from support program to support program until my first visit with Lieutenant Colonel Donnelly. Briskly, he escorted me to every office and workplace — motor pools, medical clinic, parts warehouse, barracks, and the dining facility. Rapid fire, the Colonel greeted this soldier, then that, asking about their wives, their children, the condition of their bodies, as some of them hobbled about on casts or crutches. He was really tight, nervous, and hyper-alert to any problems, but he seemed to be genuinely caring of his young soldiers and their families. He knew every private, whether Black, Filipino, white, or Hispanic by his or her name. He knew the names of their kids and their wives.

Donnelly impressed me.

When Lieutenant Colonel Donnelly developed total confidence that I wouldn't worm out of this hardcore XVIII Airborne unit, he let me know that he was going to depart and return to Fort Lewis Washington within the next two weeks. I became fretful. Every soldier knows that command priorities change like the wind when new commanders are assigned. Did I make a mistake by responding to Lieutenant Colonel Donnelly's invitation to be his spiritual leader? What if his successor was a technocrat who didn't care about people or their problems? In that case, I'd drown. I care about people and their problems, but not enough about technology or bureaucracy. What a fool I was for not doing a background check before accepting Donnelly's offer!

My fear appeared to be groundless.

Before he left, Lieutenant Colonel gave me a packet of disciplinary cases he had recently handled, involving criminal misconduct and a full range of sexual misconduct allegations. I took the packet thinking, "Great, this man is leaving, and now he wants to dump all his racial, sexual, social problems on the token female chaplain for mending. The packet changed my mind. Lieutenant Colonel Donnelly had worked hard to set high standards for professional and personal conduct. As he reviewed his cases with me, I was impressed with Donnelly's efforts to ensure there was no double standard by any equal opportunity measure: race, religion, ethnicity, or gender.

Donnelly tried to create a better life for young soldiers. Although his tactical mission had been accomplished, Donnelly admitted that he was not successful in promoting the social well being of his soldiers or their families. Citing high rates of single soldier pregnancy, sexual harassment, alcoholism, racial conflicts that were played out in unit rivalries, and the creeping influence of gang culture in the Cav's ranks, Donnelly was the first to say the problems were out of control. He admitted that all of these problems were easier to sweep under the carpet, because aggressive responses, no matter how right, could backfire with negative publicity, and destroy a leader's career. Tailhook had not yet happened, but Lieutenant Colonel Donnelly's perception was dead right.

Although Donnelly's records proved his sincere efforts, the statistics and individual cases revealed serious gender problems and a racial divide within the battalion. Over time, I could see a racial and gender divide throughout the Army, one that was exacerbated by double standards for performance, fitness and personal conduct. Curiously, female soldiers were the beneficiaries of the double standards. Across the board, performance standards, conduct standards, and physical fitness standards were lower for women. Black and other minority senior enlisted soldiers were somehow, after any adverse entanglement with women, doomed to career failure.

I did not have enough personal experience to make a judgement or recommendation about this seeming correlation. I knew that Colonel Donnelly had done his best to avoid even a perception that it was true. I relaxed as Donnelly handed the battalion over to me for spiritual leadership. He was not asking me to put out the fires because I was the token female. He wanted me to help the succeeding commander turn the squadron around.

The Army had already spent countless billions on equal opportunity, affirmative action, alcohol prevention, domestic violence prevention, suicide prevention, anger management classes, rape prevention, sexual harassment prevention, and diversity training. Yet, the more the Army invested, the worse the problems got. Perhaps as a last leap of faith, Donnelly believed that heavy investment in another social program, this time religion, would turn the problems around in his newly gender integrated unit, if not throughout the Army.

As a minister of the liberal social gospel, albeit of the Unitarian Universalist persuasion, I naively agreed with him. I took my own leap of faith. It was time for me to put my money where my liberal mouth had been. All of the problems that plagued our society were reflected in that damned squadron. It was time for me to get to work. Maybe, this time, I could make a difference.

CHAPTER 10

Always Ready!

When the Second Armored Cavalry Regiment returned from Germany to the state of Washington, then to Fort Polk, Louisiana, it underwent a reverse metamorphosis from a configuration as a heavy combat armored unit, to the new experimental light cavalry regiment. When the 2nd migrated back to the Western United States, heavy tanks and armor were left behind with the 2d ACR mascots, the prized Lippizaner Stallions associated with many Cav victories in Europe.

By the time the Cav alighted at Fort Polk, it was designated a Rapid Deployment Force. The 2nd ACR stood up as a force that could deploy to a flash point anywhere in the world on two hours notice, becoming an elite XVIIIth Airborne Corps asset. But because we were hundreds of miles away from Fort Bragg, the Corps Headquarters, in reality we were the Corps' bastard children. The mystique of the XVIIIth Airborne Corps created an illusion that the 2nd ACR was highly selective in its assignment of personnel. Women had been assigned to elite Combat Service Support Units in the past, but they had to meet stringent physical and performance standards to earn that red beret, the Airborne soldier's crowning glory. Even so, the few women assigned believed they would not be in close proximity to battle.

Before Donnelly returned to Fort Lewis, our new commander was installed. Lieutenant Colonel Thomas Ed Tucker rotated between logistics and armored units over the years. He was an expert in Demings' philosophy of Total Quality Management, well suited to the task of building up the support squadron's reputation for mission accomplishment. He also had an unusual method for developing his people — if they were open to his innovations.

Colonel Tucker's management style was the opposite of Colonel Donnelly. Donnelly seemed to micromanage, but Tucker empowered his subordinates, even when they were accustomed to micro-management. Donnelly seemed to consider the appearance of propriety when he made his decisions about disciplinary action. Tucker called each decision as he saw the merits of the case. Donnelly seemed to take care of his enlisted subordinates, but officers noted that Tucker seemed to take strong actions to ensure the future of both his enlisted and his officers. Donnelly played it safe. Tucker took risks. Both were good men, but as the troops will tell you, you don't make general by taking risks when you lead soldiers in peacetime. Donnelly made rank because he was more cautious about his decisions. His caution was the mark of the 90s field grade officer, the ones destined to make general. Tucker didn't care. When problems surfaced, he asked all his enlisted soldiers and officers to help him generate solutions. He did not shy away from problems or politically incorrect situations.

Lieutenant Colonel Ed Tucker was one of those officers who preferred his integrity to the sheen of a star. Tucker coordinated some extraordinary logistical support for the Gulf War. He was renowned for his efforts to provide wholesome morale boosters in combat environments. Although not a lifelong Cav man, he was as eccentric as any Cav officer you will ever meet. Perhaps his empathy for the difficulties of working women and disadvantaged youth made him the man to lead as we trained for a rapid deployment.

Rapid Deployment Forces require the toughest, hardest, most disciplined soldiers. Your go-to-war bags must always be packed to respond to a two hour alert. The all male fighting units are not allowed to shave or shower when an alert is called. If they do, and they are caught, they can be punished with an Article 15. I have known male soldiers who lost rank because they primped before they reported to their orderly rooms. Fighting men are required to report to their unit within twenty minutes with beards and bad breath intact. First the grunts load their gear on their vehicles, perform preventive maintenance and safety checks, obtain their weapons and ammunition, and go through security and safety briefings. Only when they are told to wait for the call to roll out do they perform field hygiene. They are given a few minutes to slack off. They waddle off to the side of their vehicles. Though loaded down with flak jackets, web gear, gasmask and rifle, they take out their canteen cups, pour a cup of water, and tidy up.

In Support Units, the standard is a lot more relaxed. Our Support Squadron, in keeping with Army-wide standards for support units, allowed junior troopers a full two hours to sign into the company. The first time I rolled out after an alert was called, I observed first hand the difference in standards and discipline expected of a line or combat unit, and that of a support unit. The strictness in combat units is necessary and cannot be eradicated to make the military more comfortable for women. That's not to say that my support squadron troops didn't take rapid deployment seriously. Most of the experienced troopers in the Support Squadron were veterans of the Gulf War. They knew how to live stylishly in a field environment.

At 2:30 A.M., when our first alert was called, I rushed to the headquarters to sign in. Mechanics, medics, administrative clerks ambled about with their large camouflaged mugs filled with steaming hot coffee. Men and women were fully showered, shaved, groomed, and perfumed. Knowing they would not get a hot meal for several hours, the old-timers had sacks of fresh fruit, cheese and crackers, and all manner of goodies to comfort them through this disruptive drill. One mechanic revealed why his coffee was prepared on such short notice.

"Easy, ma'am!" He grinned, "Everybody knows when these alerts are coming down the wire. I set my alarm last night. My automatic coffeemaker had the coffee ready just as the alert was called. You must be new here!"

I sure was. I soon made my own intelligence connections in the squadron so that I would have my own coffee the next time the secret code was passed down our phone trees.

Already, being a chaplain was terrific fun compared to my experiences as a garrison personnel manager. The great fun of Army chaplain life is our mobility. Chaplains are not chair borne — as airborne soldiers tease in their running songs. We move around to visit soldiers wherever they were positioned. You see an awful lot when you get out of your truck or tent to visit your soldiers.

Support soldiers are often in close proximity to the whiskered, skunk-smelling grunts. Contrasts are heightened and worthy of notice. The high standards in all the male units I saw while visiting my own troopers was awesome to watch. Down on the rail tracks, for example, where our vehicles were loaded, the all-male squadrons sat with Meals Ready to Eat (MREs, prepackaged, premasticated meals that wouldn't appeal to an unconscious nursing home patient). Support Squadron soldiers, accustomed to all the comforts of home, would organize Humvee rides back to the dining facility for their three hot square meals, and a side of fresh fruit. Or they would call Dominos Pizza for on-site delivery right next to our rail cars.

All-male squads were closely bonded, with obvious loyalty and mutual commitment to work out their problems within their group. Mixed-gender units have lower tolerance for frustrated expectations. In the mixed-gender units, soldiers crossed leadership chains to garner support when they wanted to stray from the group.

Lieutenant Colonel Tucker wanted his soldiers happy, but tactically correct in the field. We set up tents, took them down and reset them until they were properly placed 50 meters apart to minimize the impact of an enemy attack. He believed soldiers should have plenty of ice and a nice mess tent to provide them with a dignified, clean, homey ambiance for their brief 30-minute respite from the elements and the drudgery of field duty. Once again, the contrast between all-male and mixed-gender units was vivid.

Troopers from the line units would sometimes eat at our dining facilities. The mess tent was theirs to sit in during their scheduled meal periods. But the grunts took their food, smiled, moved out next to a tree, sat on the ground, and ate quietly.

Any well-qualified soldier, man or woman, who serves in a rapid deployment force will tell you the assignment is gruesome, but most satisfying. The training must be realistic, focused only on survival and mission. The hours are long. Training exercises go from days to three or four weeks. No weekends off as the mid-90s family-centered Army dictated! With each field exercise the unit goes under deep transformations — psychological growing pains. There's no substitute for time spent training in the woods. Weaknesses that must be rooted out are exposed only when the unit spends a lot of time together in the field. While on a major exercise in Arkansas, Colonel Molino, the regimental commander, planned for a "night passage of lines," the classic-but-dangerous Cavalry movement in the dark. Many a battalion commander will avoid moving their support vehicles in a tactical road march because they fear accidents, the sure career killer in the peacetime Army. Tucker had no fear, because he knew how to define success not only as mission accomplishment, but as safety. Tucker and Major Carter, the Training Officer for our support squadron, taught his company commanders how to move this large, bulky unit in a night passage of lines without accident.

The exercise was beautiful to watch, as the commanders built the confidence of their junior leaders. Sergeants taught their subordinates how to rally, keep pace at 25 meters with night vision goggles, how to divide shooting and driving responsibilities, how to fan out the vehicles for a sudden halt or attack, and how to interpret lights and signals along the way. I never saw so many proud men and women as when these young soldiers completed their first night passage of lines. Later, I realized some of the learning stays with you. Whenever the roads would flood during a sudden Louisiana downpour, which was often, the cars on post would fan left and right as if they were part of a tactical road march, thereby avoiding sudden collisions!

To build esprit, troopers greet each other with a special salute. The XVIII Airborne salute is "Airborne!" Each subordinate unit has its own coded greeting, much like service fraternities such as the Shriners Club. Second Armored Cavalry Regiment is quite a classy regiment, with a distinguished history. The regimental patch is a bright lemon trefoil on a dark green background with the French motto, Toujour Prets – Always Ready! Our salute involved the call and response, "Always ready, Sir (or Ma'am)!" With the senior responding, "Toujour Prets!" The challenge of the Cav trooper is to be always ready. The challenge of getting yourself in condition to live up to this motto is worth all the frustration, setbacks, humiliation, and tests you have to endure to meet the standard. Since the newly designated Light Cavalry Regiment was being tested and certified as a rapid deployment force, many alerts were called in our first year together. Some were called early Monday morning, to test the troopers' ability to respond after a weekend of rousing on Billy Goat Hill. Some were called mid-week.

My fondest training memory was of an emergency drill that was called on a Friday morning. I was surprised the troops did not complain about the possibility that they would miss their weekend free time. When an EDRE was called, troops were locked in — confined to the training area until higher headquarters called the exercise off. This time we were testing our ability to roll out as far as the airport in Alexandria, Louisiana, so we knew we were going to be locked in at least overnight. Our Support Squadron was divided into three support slices. Key staff, including the chaplain, participated in all of the alerts. We supported all our slices. Each slice supported a different line squadron when that squadron was in a green or hot status.

Older, more mature soldiers were accustomed to leaving their families for deployments or training exercises. Family support groups dealt with the separations, especially by helping inexperienced spouses learn how to cope. When this particular alert was called, the soldiers knew through their own intelligence channels that they were not going home anytime soon. They brought their pillows, books, radios, card decks, letter writing materials, college textbooks, domino games, and magazines — whatever they needed to pass the time.

Any trooper in our squadron not fresh out of training had already experienced at least one deployment. Some had been to the Gulf, others to Somalia. Some had been to the Honduras. Some to Panama. Some had watched the leveling of Rwanda. Some of our highly skilled technicians had been to all of these hotspots. They knew the first rule of survival was to bring along stuff to alleviate boredom. Boredom was the bacteria that bred the worst strain of low morale in any support unit. Because the number one thing every soldier does in deployments is hurry up and wait. And wait. And wait. During those waits, soldiers expect their chaplains to give out Bibles, Korans, Crosses, Rosaries, prayer cards, and all kinds of wholesome materials. My first assistant, Andy Wicks, helped me prepare for this part of a deployment. We always had games, books, and bibles packed. I gave out boxes of religious literature during each alert. I stopped being surprised when a Gulf War Veteran would say, "No thank you, Ma'am. I always carry my Gulf War Bible right here. It's what got me through!"

When you do field counseling, soldiers have lots of philosophy to share — reminiscences about their most difficult experiences during real deployments. They are full of wisdom about what their chaplain needs to do to be helpful. During this Friday night lockup some of our sergeants asked if I would let them use the chapel for the soldiers to relax. I thought it was a great idea. They called for pizzas and cokes. They set up card games. They wanted me to set up the chapel movie machine. Since we didn't have any religious movies that would cover the broad religious needs of the soldiers stuck in my chapel, I asked them to provide a good selection. The slice leaders prodded one sergeant into getting a movie that is appropriate for the chapel. He brought back *Free Willie*. I had never seen this film, but during physical training, Sergeant Mac from the motor pool always called the Army's scissors kick exercise the Free Willie. I was curious to see the connection, so I kept my eye on the story line.

Pull Up A Chair, Chaplain!
Visiting the troops at their field site for expedient counseling sessions.

About 60 soldiers sat on this Friday evening watching *Free Willie* like kids at a Saturday matinee. Sixty tough guys and gals, who might otherwise spend their Friday evening in a smoke-filled, beer-smelling dance joint. They were drawn into the innocent world of the child despite their very harsh life circumstances. Other soldiers were out in the lobby passing photos of their kids, talking about their jalopies, or the latest engine they spent their Saturday afternoons tuning up.

The fear of divorce, of breaking up their serious relationships was on the mind of many of the troopers, especially the ones who had been through real deployments.

"Ma'am, you just can't believe what happens," a staff sergeant would say. "You go out to the field, or you go overseas, and before you know it, your next door neighbor is sleeping with your wife in government housing! Can you believe that? He's sleeping with your wife in government housing, and there's nothing you can do!"

Late that Friday night, we were told we had to go to the warehouse to sleep. I asked the soldiers who used the chapel as their home to please help me straighten it up and to leave it as we found it. They bent over reverently to pick up gum wrappers and fuzz balls that most likely preceded our use of the chapel. We left in three or four minutes with the chapel in better shape than when we found it. In the dark, we convoyed down to the warehouses and the maintenance depot area. There were bathrooms and wide open bays in which we could spread out our cots by squad. Men and women slept side by side. In a highly disciplined unit, men and women dress modestly in tents or warehouses, not revealing their undergarments or their private parts. Later, I was to discover that many units lacked the discipline and standards of privacy required for mixed-gender units. But during Tucker's tenure, the RSS troopers were very respectful of each other's privacy, to the extent you can call sleeping in a warehouse or tent with 15 to 125 other people a private experience. In fact, most of the soldiers were so exhausted by the time we were allowed to sleep, they zonked out as soon as their heads touched the cots.

Take That Puddle!

PFC Andy Wicks, the author's assistant, stands by his Humvee after they were pulled from a sink hole.

I sat awake for awhile, just to observe our group dynamics. Young lieutenants sat talking to troubled soldiers who were having problems with their bills or their spouses. Sergeants were scattered here and there, dispensing parental wisdom to their young soldiers, and sometimes, to their lieutenants, who were often the same age as our privates. There were sharp leaders everywhere. These experienced men and women were anxious to prove that our squadron could hold its own in the Cav. Even though our style was different from the line units, we were still real soldiers.

The rest of the weekend EDRE was routine. Vehicle inspection. Vehicle reinspection. Vehicle inspected for the third time, just to be certain there were no class three leaks missed during the first two inspections. Vehicle certified. Driver criticized for not washing his engine out with a hose. Driver criticized for not reporting his class three leak. Driver criticized for not telling the last two inspectors about the class three leaks they failed to find during their inspections of our vehicle. I think my assistant, Andy Wicks, deserved a Purple Heart for the abuse he took from the maintenance technicians, most likely because he was a chaplain assistant. There were briefings. Records were checked. More briefings. Lineups. More lineups. One more safety briefing. Finally, we began to roll out in small groups. In each subsequent alert, we added on one or two more phases of an exercise until we went through the regimen of packing, deploying, arriving at a field site, setting up our field gear, living in the field, and jumping to a new site.

If this kind of repetitive training sounds mindless, I can say with certitude it was the stuff of fighting and winning. If you lived at Fort Polk and served in the Second Armored Cavalry Regiment, that had to be your overarching mantra — Toujour Prets! Always Ready!

CHAPTER 11

Almost Ready!

Almost immediately after my assignment to the RSS, key leaders in the unit began to complain about the social problems that drained the leadership. The Second Armored Cavalry Regiment may have been the showcase RDF for the '90s, but it was not exempt from the Army's intractable social problems that interfered with our mission. Fort Polk Louisiana was just a terrible place for soldiers to be stationed, especially during idle times. Only one slice element was hot, that is, dedicated to intense deployment training during green cycle. The hot slice for a particular green cycle groveled in the mud like happy farm pigs. But the remaining 600 or so in our squadron were left out of the training excitement. The rest were stuck in amber or red cycle. About 175 soldiers out of 700 plus could obliterate their unhappiness by training intensely and fantasizing about their participation in the next Third World brushfire that was beamed into every chow hall and every dayroom via CNN's *Headline News*. While stuck in lukewarm amber or cold red cycles, their military training regimen was limited to just a few hours each Thursday morning — known Army-wide as "Sergeant's Time." When soldiers were red cycle they were fair game for endless petty details to be accomplished all over post.

Regardless of training cycles — red, amber, or green — dedicated troopers, whose raison d'etre was a two-hour mission anywhere in the world, were superb and usually too busy to get into stupid, reckless trouble. Most of our problems, as throughout the Army, occurred with the bored soldiers who remained in garrison – the soldiers stuck in amber or red cycles. At Fort Polk, there just wasn't a whole lot for soldiers to do.

The temptations of the local nightlife were irresistible for most. Consensual relationships between soldiers broke up the monotony. Affairs blossomed between garrison soldiers and the spouses of soldiers who were in the field or on deployment. Women who did not want to take their turn in the deployment training cycle worked very hard to get pregnant. All these occur at army bases throughout the world. They occurred at a troubling pace at Fort Polk.

Some advocates for military readiness recommend that women should be excluded from support units such as the 2nd ACR support squadron. I believe that some women have proven that they can hold their own in elite support units like RSS. You can predict that women who barely meet the minimum requirements under the double standards for physical training are the same women who will find some way to be excused from field training and deployment assignments. On the other hand, women who train up to the standards of men, (and there aren't many who even try!) can accomplish good things. Women like Major Jayne Carson and Sergeant First Class Rachel Foster.

Major Carson managed the RSS training section (S-3) for a time, and Sergeant First Class Rachel Foster was her non-commissioned officer in charge. Major Carson was a branch-qualified field artillery officer who was eventually diverted to the logistics field. It sounds impossible that a woman could have been branched to Field Artillery, but there is a precedent. During the Civil War, there was a female chaplain who served a field artillery unit for nine months until Congress discovered she was a woman and had her removed.

Rachel Foster was a first-rate, non-commissioned officer who later became the first female First Sergeant in the Second Armored Cavalry Regiment. These two women were as different as east and west. Major Carson, a slender, blue-eyed super-jock, worked hard to establish herself in Field Artillery. She was sharp, succinct, and totally mission-focused. Her hands would chop the air as she directed the male captains who commanded the five troops of RSS. Carson pointed her finger and glared right into their faces as she called out tasks to be completed yesterday.

While I was with RSS, I don't think there was ever a tasking from on high that Major Carson declined. Perhaps her upstream journey in the Field Artillery Branch taught her to be overly accommodating, daring never to refuse, for fear of being labeled inadequate because she was female. Carson got the job done, though. Somehow, she had our squadron completing impossible missions for opposing troops on the battlefield, as relayed from higher headquarters.

Sergeant First Class Foster was a non-commissioned officer from the old school. Her heart was divided three ways: love of God, love of her family, and love of her soldiers. She didn't hesitate to yell at the troops, or sit quietly rubbing the shoulder of a trooper as he grieved a family loss. She could patiently teach soldiering skills, or stiffly establish a disciplined atmosphere when the soldiers got too casual. Foster was a woman of God, and as you often see in the Army, she freely expressed her faith to her troops and her leaders.

There were several male sergeants in the S-3 shop who departed shortly after my arrival. Two men, both minorities, retired early after they were disciplined for inviting two junior women to their apartment for several barbecues. The women attended many parties. Eventually, the sergeants made sexual overtures to the women. Both male sergeants were reprimanded, which ended their careers.

The third sergeant in the training section, Sergeant J was previously a drill instructor. His reaction to the reprimand of the two senior sergeants typified the feelings of the entire RSS group of senior male non-commissioned officers.

Sergeant First Class J whipped up and down the hallways, angry, tight, and furious that he was locked in his RSS Cav assignment as part of the BRAC (Base Realignment and Closure) moves from Fort Lewis, Washington.

"Ma'am, I've been a good soldier all my life. I have accepted every deployment, every hardship assignment. I was a drill instructor. But this has got to be the worst assignment you could give a soldier...."

After two or three emotional outbursts while he puffed on his cigarette on the lawn outside our headquarters building, Sergeant J knew he could trust me to handle his complaints.

"Ma'am, the Army just ain't any good anymore. You just can't count on the leaders anymore."

"What are you talking about, Sergeant J?"

"I'm telling you, the Army is a dangerous place to be. Me and my wife, I love my wife. I wouldn't do anything to hurt her. But it is dangerous being assigned to this unit. These women!"

"I'm a woman. Are you telling me I am dangerous?"

"No, Ma'am. But I'm telling you it's not right. Those two women went down to that sergeant's apartment not once, not twice, but several times. How can they go turnin' around and claim those two non-commissioned officers sexually harassed them? Whatever happened to personal responsibility?"

This scenario replayed itself more than once. Same game. Different cast of characters. After being worn down by the inane frequency of consensual relationships gone awry, I soon joined the unceasing chorus chanted by the sergeants to vent the rage that boils when you see lives abruptly destroyed by such petty antics.

Sergeant First Class J explained the consequences of the most expensive barbecue our senior sergeants would ever hold.

"It's not right. Those women were guilty, too. They should be punished too!"

I agreed, and spoke to the commander about the situation. After conversations with Sergeant Major Jones, the colonel, and many officers and sergeants who were furious about the perception that two female soldiers were using sexual harassment policies to avoid discipline, the colonel agreed that the women should receive counseling statements. He wrote each a counseling statement advising them that their participation in such an intimate social relationship with their bosses was improper.

Still, the two senior non-commissioned officers who committed the faux pas of inviting their 20-something assistants to their apartment quietly left the unit in shame and anger. Sergeant J, however, was not appeased by the slap on the wrist given to the women. His taut monotone voice would pierce the hallways as he droned out his objectives each day.

"I'm going to get me a transfer, and get back to an all male unit. I am not staying in this unit."

His fear was rooted in a personal experience, which he recounted.

"You know, ma'am, when I was a drill sergeant, a woman begged me to excuse her from the gas chamber exercise. She started to take her shirt off, saying she would bare her breasts, and give me a blow job. I stopped her and then I reported her. You know what my commander did? He called me on the carpet and told me if I couldn't suck it up and drive on, I just needed to find another job. I got a family Ma'am. I don't need this...I am out of here!"

Steam spewed from J's nostrils every day until he got his transfer.

That kind of blind anger seethed through conversations with the other senior sergeants and the disappointed junior officers while the commander made his determination about the consensual-relationship-turned-sexual-misconduct event. Each day, I would go back to my office after listening to my troopers, disappointed at the problems of gender relations in this otherwise high-speed squadron.

The other chaplains would sit in their offices, playing with their computers, or preparing papers for their next promotion course. They would always cut off my expressed concerns with self-congratulations.

"We don't have that problem in our squadron. When the unit is all men, you just don't have these problems."

Sergeant Major Jones had more faith than our male chaplains in the ability of the Second Armored Cavalry Regiment to integrate women properly into the ranks. He insisted every problem could be overcome with proper leadership and training. He asked me to teach several sexual ethics classes to the non-commissioned officers and the troops.

The effort was remedial, like trying to save the dike with one's pinky. At least, an uneasy truce prevailed between men and women for the duration of Sergeant Major Jones and Lieutenant Colonel Tucker's command.

Despite massive investments in housing upgrades and facility improvement, Fort Polk was the most despised Army installation in the country. For the longest time, I wanted to believe that the men were displacing their endless frustration with the geographical limitations of a Fort Polk assignment onto the women.

I recalled one of my officer candidate classmates back in 1983 who was slated for Polk. He rocked back and forth in a daze when he found out he was assigned to Fort Polk, disbelieving that someone with his God-given looks, leadership, and beautiful new bride could be condemned to the ugliest, swampiest Army post in the world. Polk is so swampy that even in 1993, when the streets were paved, crawfish would crawl out of the street drains after major rain bursts would overload the sewage system. Folks would eat them, too.

Surely, the RSS men were angry because of their resentment that they were doomed to Camp Swampy during the Army's most demoralizing period, the downsizing. Resources and personnel were scarce, to be sure. When new senior sergeants arrived, they saw the terrible working conditions. We inherited trashed, rat-infested barracks from the 2nd Armored Division after the division moved to Fort Hood. Our senior sergeants had earned their chance to lead a smoothly coordinated, high-speed mission at the close of their career. Yet, we had to build up our organization from scratch. We had to reconstitute garrison facilities before we could do anything.

New RSS senior sergeants looked at their equipment, most of which should have been mothballed. They looked at the budget. We ran out of training money the second quarter each year, leaving half a year for soldiers to be stuck in garrison raking leaves or gravel around the motor pool. After one-too-many indignities, they would turn in their retirement papers. Not everybody left. The sergeants who stayed soon began to express their disgust while exchanging salutes with the secret motto, "Almost Ready!"

Soldiers live and are sustained by the glory of the myth that they are part of an elite, lean, mean, fighting machine. Patches, medals, green, red or black berets mean everything to good soldiers. They believe they are specially chosen, and the Army leadership perpetuates that myth. Despite massive investments in housing upgrades and facility improvement, Fort Polk was the most despised Army installation in the country. Soldiers think the XVIIIth Airborne Corps is highly selective in its assignment of personnel. This was probably true when the Army was bloated with dollars and people. Non-commissioned officers tell stories of soldiers who had been excluded from all of the elite units because of their family problems, their struggles with alcohol or indebtedness, or even their mediocre performance in physical training or field duty. When a relentless spate of social problems was manifested at Fort Polk, the old-timers knew their lean, mean fighting machine was going to be different.

At first, I did not believe the analysis of senior sergeants that the Second Armored Cavalry Regiment would never make the mark as a disciplined RDF because of the oversupply of female soldiers. I thought their real complaints about non-existent infrastructure was displaced onto female soldiers. After about ten months, I was forced to admit that the continued disgruntlement of STRAK or high-speed soldiers was not about location. Their seething anger was justifiably about the gender gap and the generation gap.

Two gender issues lay over the squadron like a heavy wet blanket. The problem of improper sexual relations and occasional false allegation against male authorities kept the emotional temperature of many leaders at a fever pitch, even though they were satisfied with the outcome of many cases. The most important gender issue to surface was impossible to resolve. Although we had a good number of women who were superbly qualified to be in a rugged, hard-charging unit, we also had far too many women who were assigned against their wishes. They did not have the personal ability or the desire to serve in the Cav.

In the Gulf, women were assigned to elite Combat Service Support Units, but their units were not intended to be placed in close proximity to battle. These units experienced high rates of pregnancy.

Physician assistants related stories of planned pregnancies to obtain the right to return to the U.S. A soft, pastoral, Southern Baptist chaplain confided his concern about women assigned to his field medical unit. Some of the ladies who came to him for counseling threatened to get pregnant when they learned they were going to be deployed. When the chaplain tried to reason that this would only hurt their chances of success in life, they retorted, "I don't care. When I get out, I'll get an abortion."

Whether or not we could ever agree that abortion is a morally acceptable alternative to an unplanned pregnancy, we surely can agree that women who have abortions contend with some kind of regret. Tragically, regularly deployed soldiers know many women who intentionally got pregnant, only to abort after they were freed of their military obligations. Can you imagine the sadness these women eventually must come to terms with, all because they were pressured to serve in a unit for which they were not emotionally or physically qualified?

Stories of women who provided sexual favors in exchange for financial remuneration were also common. Strangely, I heard peace activists try to dissuade teenage girls form joining the Army back in 1990 because they were receiving reports of prostitution rings at overseas Army assignments. Doctor after doctor and chaplain after chaplain has complained about command tolerance for prostitution in deployment zones. One female captain sold condoms for $40 each. Her sales pitch: you had to try it on in her presence. Another chaplain related the story that his wife could not understand why women were sending such enormous sums of money back to their German bank accounts. "They are doubling their salaries," she said with surprise. The chaplain explained that the soldiers preferred using American women rather than local prostitutes, under the mistaken belief that they would more likely be free of sexually transmitted diseases.

Sadly, when the 2nd Armored Cavalry Regiment opened its doors to women, the Department of the Army did not screen the women sent to the regiment for physical or emotional readiness. Many young women who found out they were being assigned to a unit that could deploy anywhere in the world on two hours notice were not happy. Neither did it please them to know that regular, vigorous field training was required of all RSS soldiers to certify the unit as RDF. There were a lot of men who were similarly unhappy about their new assignment to this remote training post, but there was little the men could do besides retire or volunteer for another deployment to Kuwait, Rwanda, Somalia, or the DMZ. Men had no way to be excused from an RDF once assigned.

Unfortunately, many of the young women believed they would be transferred to a desk job back in some headquarters if they got pregnant. That's what happened before the Gulf War. That's what happened before the downsizing. Pregnancy brought a transfer to a more comfortable assignment, such as a headquarters element where you could be noticed by a colonel or general and be given impact awards for timely report submission. No one wants to admit these propensities. Feminist groups slam-dunk truthful prophets with the accusation that dwelling on such statistics reveals a misogynist bias. I am a woman who wants women to succeed in the military. That won't happen until we begin to address the problems women experience, and the problems they bring, with forthrightness and objective analysis. The Gulf War statistics speak unequivocally: women were four times as non-deployable as men in the Gulf War, usually due to pregnancy. The Army hid this fact by sending other soldiers, usually male, in place of the women who were to deploy. The first revelation of the depth of the problem was recorded by the Presidential Commission to study the role of women in combat.

The Army still glosses over the problem by deploying men for the second or third tour to cover for women who evaded their turn by becoming pregnant. This strategy avoids a confrontation with public advocates and with the women who will allege sexual harassment rather than admit that their pregnancy was planned to avoid deployment.

While the 2nd ACR was standing up with a rigorous worldwide mission, the Army was standing down. The garrison reached its saturation point. We often hear about the ridiculous peacetime tooth-to-tail ratio. Because we keep so many non-deployable soldiers on duty unnecessarily, the tail is exceedingly out of proportion to the tooth. By 1993, there was nowhere to transfer pregnant women. They had to remain with RSS.

On any given day, we had 30 or more female soldiers pregnant in the squadron. Although the overall statistic was five percent, in sections that required heavy field duty or long working hours, the pregnancy rates were much higher. Nine of twelve female cooks assigned got pregnant. Sergeant Pia Dowling, a tough NCO who proudly took care of her troops, was so frustrated at this statistic that she volunteered for overseas hardship — first to Guantanamo, then Korea.

Female leaders are just as frustrated by irresponsible pregnancy as men. A pregnant soldier is exempt from field training, exempt from physical activity that could hurt her pregnancy, exempt from worldwide deployments. It takes two people to do the job of one pregnant soldier. The pregnant soldier gets paid to sit at a desk, watching telephones. The other soldier must do his own work, and that of the pregnant soldier.

The Army used to require first-term soldiers to be single, or without dependents so they could live cheaply in the barracks and concentrate on soldiering during the first enlistment. Feminist groups mistakenly thought they could further the advancement of women by suing the Army to force the government to subsidize the lifestyles of single-parent soldiers. After a few court cases, where the needs of the service and the hardship of military life were ignored in favor of individual rights, the Army gave up.

Jealous, immature, male soldiers started to marry to get out of the barracks, because in the short term, married soldiers are paid more to cover housing expenses. But the men were still required to work long hours, go to the field, and concentrate on the mission. The burden of premature family responsibilities would most likely deprive the men of the ability to concentrate on development of their professional skills, and obtaining the college degree that would provide access to much higher salaries. Officially, they were not discouraged, however, because they still were able to handle some of the field duties, deployment responsibilities, and hard labor required in warehouses and motor pools. Pregnancy afforded women the right to ignore the responsibility for readiness and training for up to a year per newborn child.

By and large, Army leaders have gone overboard to accommodate pregnant soldiers, displacing their work and their field duties onto other soldiers. At Command and Staff Meetings, or Quarterly Training briefings, the problem of high pregnancy rates is usually avoided. When a commander or other leader addresses the statistics forthrightly, they are often greeted with comments that such commentary is a form of sexual harassment.

If you watch television debates such as *Crossfire*, you will often see retired female generals or admirals minimize the problem with the deceptive statistic,

"We know that on any given day, only five percent of the women in the Navy are pregnant."

As I mentioned, units that have heavy field duty, an imminent deployment, or a mission that requires night and weekend work experience an explosion in pregnancy rates. As one woman, a West Point graduate said, "Five percent? It may be five percent Navy wide, but if I have two women assigned to my section, and both are pregnant, my section is 100 percent non-deployable. If the personnel section has four out of four pregnant, it is 100 percent pregnant. If six out of seven are pregnant in a Patriot Missile squad, that's 85 percent!"

The RSS was no more plagued with high rates of pregnancy, accusations of sexual misconduct, or barracks problems than other mixed-gender units in the Army. Since these problems made us increasingly non-deployable, we could not refute the mocking salute, "Almost Ready."

CHAPTER 12
How Are Things In... Gomorrah?

The nine-to-five army, the garrison that pushes paper and waits on repair parts or the arrival of new babies, burgeons exponentially as long as the Army is without a meaningful mission. By meaningful I mean a mission that is psychically linked to the hot spots to which the United States Army will be called as the savior of the free world. Worse, the longer the Army stays in garrison without a mission, the more problems there will be with misconduct allegations. There will be more single-parent pregnancies, more adultery, more domestic violence and all manner of alcohol-related misconduct. Remote Army garrisons like Fort Polk do not provide healthy, stable communities in which military society can flourish. When military families move to installations like Polk they express the feeling they have been sentenced for crimes they did not commit.

Gomorrah, the ancient city in Hebrew Scriptures destroyed because of its unrepentant wickedness, is an apt metaphor for the creep of amorality, and the kinds of locations the Army has chosen in which to settle its post-cold war fighters. The most pitiful consequence of military downsizing in the 1990s and liberal disaffection with military culture, was the banishment of Army fighting troops to remote, backwoods locations. Large army bases are hours away from cosmopolitan centers that offer culture, stimulating social outlets, and exposure to national and world events. Rural Army posts nationwide have all the virtue of Gomorrah to offer young people who join the military for thrills and adventure.

Fort Polk is set in rural Louisiana, a region that depends on the Federal Government to sustain its local economy. Racial bigotry, religious intolerance, and gender discrimination are cultural norms. The Federal Government's presence mandates a pretense of tolerance, but instead, inspires bigotry that is expressed where ever it can be subtly loosed. In the winter of 1993-94, I invited the late Henry Hampton to speak to the Fort Polk community for Martin Luther King's Birthday. I was tasked to coordinate this post-wide event. Hampton, who produced *Eyes on the Prize*, received an honorary doctorate from Starr King School for the Ministry while I was a student there. On the Saturday after this graduation, I spent hours with him discussing American race relations and the value of military service for young, disenfranchised minorities. In our first conversation, we agreed that the military could have an extraordinary impact on African-American youth. When I called him in the winter to extend the invitation to speak, a racist campaign to intimidate a black man to flee his

Vidalia apartment just ended. Throughout our conversation, Henry would laugh cynically at my naíve beliefs that Fort Polk was sincerely upholding Louisiana's decision to honor, for the first time, the national holiday for Dr. Martin Luther King. He declined my invitation and throughout our chat, repeated the refrain, "How far did you say Fort Polk was from Vidalia?"

In isolated communities like Fort Polk, alienated young men cultivate their commitment to hate-based violence of whatever stripe their skinhead or urban gang demands. If the Army needs to invest in an intensive mentoring program for single, troubled young men and women anywhere at all, the greatest need is in remote locations like Fort Polk. With the exception of the 67th colonel of the 2nd Armored Cavalry Regiment, Colonel Tom Molino and his subordinate commanders, at Fort Polk, there was little encouragement to address the problems of single soldiers while I was there. As statistics for misconduct and psychiatric hospitalizations mushroomed, Colonel Molino demanded programs, barracks renovations, and a post-wide command emphasis on quality of life for single soldiers.

Tom Molino was an old-fashioned leader, who placed strong emphasis on the morale and well-being of his troops. But he was not the post commander, and the limitations imposed by his subordinate status provoked him to find unconventional ways to obtain support for his troopers. Colonel Molino adhered to the walk-around management style, the Army ideal recommended by '80s management gurus. This model was taught at every military leadership seminar. Of course, when the Army hired industrial consultants to teach officers to be more effective in the mid-1980s, Reagan had approved phenomenal budgets for the Army. It was possible for commanders to feel and act like God when they walked around. They snapped their fingers, and insisted they should see a new barracks, or a new handicapped ramp the next time they visited an ugly, dilapidated facility. And by God, the next time they walked around, the facility was transformed.

Long after the Army lost interest in its walk-around management philosophy, Molino still walked around. Other colonels and generals curtailed their observations to pre-planned, reassuring inspection routes, or to lengthy inspection reports transmitted via the non-confrontational e-mail system. Molino never slackened his direct involvement. He would personally inspect his barracks and then demand immediate support from the garrison engineers to clean up the dank, dark, and dirty buildings. When he couldn't fix the physical, he tinkered with social policies to humanize the barracks. He loosened sterile policies to let the soldiers create a feeling of home in their barracks space.

"What is this policy that soldiers can't hang family pictures in their rooms? Let them hang their pictures. I believe a soldier who has a picture of his mother hanging in his room is going to take much better care of himself. Give them frames!"

Army programs are usually funded years after they are conceived. Every new program or renovation goes through a rigorous process of prioritizing and budgetary planning. Soldier barracks had not been on anybody's priority list for a decade or more. Building the new youth center for children of career officers and sergeants was important. The golf course, mostly used by retirees and high-ranking officials, was top priority on every post in the world. Providing rust free furniture, mold-free barracks or sitting chairs for soldiers was not on anyone's priority list. This tendency to divert infrastructure funds from the community of single soldiers to the community of families that lived in government houses is not just a Fort Polk problem. The trend is worldwide.

The status quo dictated that the golf course, the social clubs, the new recreation center and family housing were priorities because of their importance to local constituencies and politically enfranchised family members. Soldier barracks were not a priority for Fort Polk planners or commanders, because no soldier who ever lived in one would remain long enough to see the improvements. Furthermore, soldiers were not permitted to organize or lobby for reforms the way military spouses can unite and hold press conferences or meetings with their congressperson to build programs.

After his departure, Colonel Molino was cursed as someone who would not accept the way things were done at Fort Polk. As one sergeant major put it, "There are five local families who control the post. All the civilians who work on post are related. The military has no power over these families. The only agenda that is met is theirs. Do you know those families kept Wal-Mart from building a Super Wal-Mart in Leesville? I'm telling you they own everything, including Fort Polk! The locals did not like Colonel Molino because he would not take no for an answer!"

Another logistics major expressed his philosophical agreement with Colonel Molino's frustration at not being able to execute basic contracts to paint the barracks, fix plumbing, or repair leaky roofs and ventilation systems.

"Everyone here is governed by fear. They are afraid that if they do the wrong thing they will get fired. They do nothing at all, because it is so much safer. We pay for safety. We pay to get nothing done..."

Fort Polk culture was schizophrenic in its concern for the moral and physical well-being of troops. Ethics and disease prevention classes by day. Complicity in the culture of sexploitation by night. To make matters worse, the new BOSS (Better Opportunities of Single Soldiers) administrative policies provided military leadership with an excuse for not creating a healthy social world for single soldiers. New national standards of non-intervention into the lives of junior soldiers were put into effect in 1993, as they were handed down through the BOSS program. The program was raved about in *The Army Times*, but the guidelines were not distributed until March 1994, under the signature of Lieutenant General Shelton, the XVIIIth Airborne commander.

The BOSS program left single soldiers to their own devices to find entertainment, support, or mentoring. At the same time that single soldiers were abandoned, the Army asserted that its locus of concern should be the Army family. Leaders would be evaluated, not by how well they accomplished the mission of training young men and women, but rather, by their commitment to the Army Family. Single soldiers were abandoned once again, when Army leaders were directed to leave their offices and their barracks soldiers at 4:30 P.M. to concentrate on their own families.

The Fort Polk chaplain program had 18 to 22 chaplains assigned to care for 7,000 soldiers. The chaplains had little to offer Fort Polk single soldiers. Chaplains and their assistants were also expected to live by the nine-to-five philosophy just like the rest of the Army. After all, officers and sergeants were held accountable for the degree to which they took care of their families. Night and weekend programs for single soldiers would deprive the chaplains, their assistants and other support workers, proper recognition for taking care of their own families.

Local churches, though abundantly spaced throughout the towns surrounding Polk, were not much of a healthy alternative for soldiers either. Fundamentalist religions dominated the area. Military army chaplains assigned to Polk were mostly fundamentalist, too. This was a mixed blessing, of course. The churches in Leesville and DeRidder and the little hamlets in between had strong family programs because families provide the bedrock of the fundamentalist agenda. And just as in urban and liberal churches, families provide a stable source of membership. Young, single adults do not provide any stability. When they come to church, they come to have their needs met, not to be "living stones" or church builders of any sort.

Terry Hershey, an Evangelical leader in the Young Adult Ministry movement, has been teaching all denominations how to reach out to alienated young adults who have been ignored by their churches. Hershey facilitated a workshop for Unitarian Universalist young adult ministers and leaders that I attended. He argued that young adults dabble with faith issues not for deontological reasons, but rather utilitarian reasons. Perhaps because religious communities ignore them the minute they graduate from Sunday school classes, young adults tend to seek church involvement only when they are in crisis or have urgent needs. Their approach to religion is need-based.

I had one experience at Polk that typified this trend. A beautiful young woman came to church each Sunday to sing solos in the choir. After each service, she would talk to me at length about the problems she had with her boyfriend, another soldier in her unit. Their relationship culminated in a very weepy breakup. Within a few weeks, another handsome GI captured her heart. She stopped coming to church without notice. We were left waiting for her to come and sing her solo. Fortunately, there were other needy soldiers who could step right up to the microphone for their moment of affirmation and comfort.

The length of a young adult's church participation is typically three to six months. I have often conjectured this sub-conscious pattern is rooted in the college academic calendar. By time young adults are in college, they expect to meet people for a semester or two, then move on, never to be with each other again. Young adult separation processes are very often automatic, until they realize they don't have to be that casual in all parts of their lives.

The churches of Leesville and DeRidder were abundant and powerful. The Pentecostals controlled the city of De Ridder. They prevented the building of a movie theatre in their town because modern films were considered corrosive to the Christian ethos. The DeRidder Pentecostals didn't allow their members to watch television, either. Pentecostals told jokes on themselves, of course, about hiding their television sets in their big walk-in bedroom closets. The Baptists dominated Leesville. A theatre, liquor stores, and Billy Goat Hill were the cultural contributions of the predominantly Baptist Leesville. The Baptist message as it was preached in Leesville was that salvation is achieved not by works, but by faith and grace alone. Salvation is freely given to all who sin, so long as they don't turn their backs on their personal Lord and Savior, Jesus Christ. We don't care how you pump your money into our community on Saturday night, just so long as you spend your money in Leesville, and repent on Sunday by sitting in our pews.

In mentioning the cultural contrasts between the fundamentalist faiths that dominated the backwoods, I do not want to suggest these groups have no value. Conservative religious leaders deserve accolades for their emphasis on the family. No one would deny that in American society the family needs all the help it can get. Of course, every denomination, liberal or conservative has learned to accommodate the licentious indulgences of modern culture. Our society has normalized promiscuity, drunkenness, and fatherless families to such a degree that appropriateness of these personal habits cannot be questioned too harshly by preachers without jeopardizing church coffers. In that respect, our fundamentalist ministers learned to peacefully co-exist with our society's decadence as the liberal church had done a long time ago.

Rural teens residing next to any military post are highly sexualized, not just because of the concentration of handsome young GIs who drive around in souped up sports cars. The girls are saturated with television programs that romanticize casual sex, out-of-wedlock pregnancy, boyfriend stealing, welfare, and the sex industry. In 1993, these girls watched their parents work for $3.15 per hour at the local dry cleaners. A computer operator in Leesville could earn the minimum wage. A part-time church secretary might earn $400 per month. But a dancer at any club on Billy Goat Hill could earn $3,000 per month.

Not all the teens want or need to work as hard as exotic dancers do. Girls who were less ambitious dress up, prepare phony I.D. cards, and set their sights on good-looking soldiers who can provide excellent genetic material for their out-of-wedlock babies. Having a GI baby, especially as an unwed mother, could prove a lucrative form of welfare. The military requires dead-beat dads to pay child support or lose their active duty status. The unintended consequence of the military's strong, if insufficient, commitment to enforcing child-support laws through wage garnishment can be told by every first sergeant in the Army. At Polk, there was a real economic trend among teenage welfare girls. They would upgrade their choice of sperm donors from local boys, who could only qualify them for a lousy welfare check, to foolish GIs who provided a much greater financial return — so long as they stayed on active-duty.

Many Fort Polk officers and senior sergeants begged me for advise on how to protect their daughters and sons from the influence of the local teenagers with whom they went to school. One major, an involved but strict father, worried that his efforts might be futile.

"These girls are already pregnant at the age of 13! You should hear them. They have it all figured out. If a GI gets them pregnant, they will automatically collect a BAQ check from the soldier for $300 per month. And they can keep their Medicaid and food stamps. They say the best deal is when the soldier dies in a training accident. Then they collect $200,000 life insurance! Unbelievable!"

The only advice I could give was to compete with the culture. Stay involved with your teens and make it more fun for them to stay in school and to spend time with the family than it would be to hang around with the dead-end crowd.

I could never figure out why, for all the emphasis on traditional family values and promise-keeping by fundamentalist clergy, there was never an attempt to elevate the dreams of the teenage girls who lived outside Army gates. Clergy and chaplains were just as likely to sexually exploit nubile adolescents as ignorant hormone-driven young privates were. Shortly after I arrived at Polk, senior sergeants and officers expressed their anger that a married chaplain had gotten a 16-year-old pregnant. When a military commander attempted to discipline this chaplain, the Chaplain Corps quietly moved him to another assignment.

Sexual contact between soldiers and rural adolescent girls is not only amoral, but a health and welfare crisis that will only get worse before it gets better. The epidemic is devastating to unit morale and readiness, but it is most harmful to the disenfranchised adolescents. In rural America, adolescent girls are free to date, have sex, and raise their illegitimate children at government expense, one way or the other. They plan to survive either on welfare or military child-support checks. Southerners from the Mason-Dixon line to the

Brownsville border will tell you this is not a new trend. Speak to the issue with concern for the young girls' future and you will be greeted with a chorus of "It's always been this way. It will never change..."

Perversely, the only consistent religious effort on Fort Polk to cope with teen sexuality has been on banning abortion, since the local leaders and most military chaplains officially oppose abortion. In their efforts to reduce the number of teen abortions, these ministers often target pregnant white girls to put their babies up for adoption. White babies are worth tens-of-thousands of dollars to private adoption agencies. The religious leaders who pressure adolescent girls to give their babies up for adoption are not disinterested advocates for the girls or their babies. By and large, however, the backwoods girls aren't interested in adoption. They are interested in motherhood as a path to a paycheck. That has not stopped religious leaders from soliciting women to put their babies up for adoption.

Either way, when they get pregnant before they are able to handle family responsibilities, young girls lose. Either way, their unplanned children suffer poverty or the stigma of adoption. As much as I understand the desperate feelings of white childless couples who depend on fundamentalist adoption agencies and ignorant adolescents to fill their family longings, I don't think these people care one whit about those whom they are exploiting — the adolescent birth mothers. If they cared, they would invest substantially in programs that taught young girls to think differently about pregnancy, about their futures.

Adoption may feel like a wonderful gift to the receiving parents, but is usually torture for the birth mothers who must give their children away for life. I sat with many a weepy, depressed female soldier who, as an adolescent, put a child up for adoption only to be obsessed years later with the need to regain custody of her child. At some point, they begin to realize they were subtly coerced to relinquish their child in the first place. When will we develop self-esteem and prevention programs to keep these young girls focused on school and job training and hopefully disinclined to even think about parenthood as their escape from life's problems? Religious and civic leaders could do much to eliminate the bane of teen pregnancy and prostitution, especially around military bases. A campaign to elevate the wages of women in socially respectable jobs would go a long way to lessen the temptation of young girls, and even married women, to provide sexual services to GIs for financial remuneration.

Leesville and De Ridder illustrate the structure of the problem. Both towns, perhaps because of outdated religious beliefs that women should be subordinate to men, cling to the ardent belief that women should earn less pay than men to protect the men's self-esteem. So the wages for women's traditional occupations are inadequate. On the other hand, strippers and prostitutes are condemned socially for their choice to market their bodies to the highest bidder, yet no successful effort is made to raise their sights or to expand the interests. No effort is made to elevate the recreational tastes of the young male soldiers who tend to be hormone driven most of the time. For these reasons, the sex industry is as lucrative in Louisiana as anywhere else in the world.

The super-concentration of fundamentalist chaplains, both on and off military posts, should make it possible to transform the situation. The lack of transformation is irrefutable evidence that religious leaders and chaplains per se are not able to influence the moral climate of the Army at this time. They cannot impact local communities or the nation as far as the culture of sexploitation is concerned. It's not that religious leaders can't change the culture, but rather that they won't. Female soldiers are no less vulnerable to the pregnancy epidemic than the adolescents who lived outside the post gates. At Fort Polk, the birth and delivery room at the hospital was nicknamed the RSS Platoon because so many of our women, fearful of field duty or overseas deployment, impulsively got pregnant. Most of the sergeants and officers who serve today are married with children. Whether male or female, married soldiers provide an enormous amount of nurturing and mentoring to these misguided pregnant women. First sergeants and section leaders invest much time teaching unwed pregnant women how to cope with their lives as single mothers. I have seen men coordinate labor coaching partners for the young soldiers in the event that there was no boyfriend or family member available to help them deliver their babies. First sergeants have borrowed my chapel folding chairs to hold baby showers so a single mom would have all the diapers and bottles she needed. Commanders show up at the maternity ward in the middle of the night with teddy bears for every new born baby in their company.

The Army's gold-plate welfare program for single pregnant women has taught me one extraordinary lesson that arch feminists have never adequately understood. Women who feel safe and capable of providing for their unplanned children will most likely choose life. They will not choose abortion if they have some sense that they can cope with the struggles that parenting inevitably entails. And many fine military men and women have gone to saintly lengths to make it possible for women to bear their unplanned children — even when the single soldier's irresponsible timing adversely impacted the unit's mission. That is not to say that every leader is sensitive to the special needs of pregnant soldiers. I recall a young black woman who was in love with a white soldier at Fort Polk. She miscarried after seven months. While she rested in her barracks room, an unmarried sergeant pounded on her door, demanding that she report to the physical training field a mere five days after her miscarriage. Men, however, often receive similar shoddy treatment when it comes to their wives' miscarriages.

The most prevailing trend, however, is that Army women are perfectly protected by the system. They are assured housing, medical care, child care, and adequate time off to care for their children. Unless they have been traumatized by violence or mental illness, they feel no need to abort unplanned pregnancies. And they don't.

There is always a downside to this kind of welfare system, however. The Army's policies were designed to protect pregnant soldiers who have planned carefully to balance the professional demands of soldiering with the never-ending responsibilities of parenting. It mostly protects women who cannot cope with their professional duties as soldiers. The Army's pregnancy policies encourage women to make very irresponsible choices. A dysfunctional soldier can get pregnant year after year and be completely protected from professional accountability. Her pregnancies don't make her any more functional to the unit, and they are seldom the result of stable family relationships. All of the rewards given to single pregnant soldiers make the lifestyle extremely attractive to less ambitious soldiers.

Colonel Molino and Lieutenant Colonel Tucker asked me to help reduce single soldier pregnancies in their regiment, and thereby improve the statistics on our unit readiness reports. When Colonel Molino first asked me to help reduce the pregnancy rate, I believed all the liberal myths about sexual responsibility. I believed that knowledge would make the difference. Regular family planning education would go a long way to encourage women to delay parenthood until they met their educational and professional goals. I believed if you made birth control readily available, women would use it. I also believed nobody wanted to be a burden on the government.

It was very difficult to get birth control at Fort Polk when I first arrived. Polk was the worst Army post for providing timely birth control and family planning classes. A strange mix of fundamentalist zeal and hostility towards women conspired to create a climate where doctors and nurses felt morally justified in withholding timely birth control.

Colonel Molino asked me what could be done to encourage women to postpone their pregnancies until they could afford children. I recounted several options. When I served in the '80s, women were briefed at every training school about birth control and the prevention of sexually transmitted diseases (STDs). A woman could walk into the medical clinic in the morning, and walk out with the birth control she needed. If she was a hard worker, and she didn't want to take time off from work, she could drop by after duty hours. In the '90s, the medical team at Fort Polk was no help. Women couldn't get birth control until they had a pap smear. They couldn't get a pap smear for three to six months. Every doctor, company commander, and nurse would agree that if a woman had to wait three months before getting birth control, she would probably be pregnant by the time she got her pills. Often, she was. In the civilian economy, the wait for a visit to the gynecologist can also take three months, but doctors prescribe birth control for the interim period. At Fort Polk, Army doctors refused to do this.

Women assigned to the Rapid Deployment Force were required to have their B Bags packed at all times for a six-month deployment. The hospital refused to give six-month supplies of birth control pills for women who were being deployed. Even married Army nurses complained about the problem of unplanned pregnancies when they returned home from the Gulf War and had no timely access to birth control. If you want to reduce irresponsible pregnancies, educate and medicate!

The physician assistants in our regiment and the Ob/Gyn doctors at the Bayne Jones Army Hospital were furious that these recommendations had come from me. One doctor called me to the hospital. Their concern was not about the health of female soldiers and it was not about morality. The doctors simply wanted women out of certain ground troop units.

"If these women signed up for the Army, they should just be given a shot of Depro Provera! That way they won't be able to get out of a deployment because they got pregnant."

With Tucker and Molino's encouragement, I started an RSS support group to educate pregnant soldiers about their dual roles. The intentionality of the women's single-parent lifestyle was made woefully clear to me in these meetings. The young women often thought their pregnancy would protect them from the daily demands of physical training. Because so many pregnant soldiers have difficulty passing the physical training tests — even six months after their babies are born, special physical training programs have been mandated. Although the demands on pregnant women are non-existent compared to regular soldiers, the complaints about training don't stop. Concerns raised in the pregnancy support sessions seldom varied. One woman asked, "Why do we have to do physical training while we're pregnant. Our babies are gonna miscarry." The Army's answer: Pregnancy is not a disease. Army doctrine states it is a physical condition. All of the training programs for pregnant women have been approved by the medical staff, and you must have the medical permission of your doctor to participate. Other complaints revealed the chronic state of dependency these women would be in. "I can't make it on the housing allowance. Why don't I qualify for food stamps? I can't make it on this pay!"

"Why don't some of you share an apartment to cut your expenses?" That turnabout question was not well-received. "You could help each other with babysitting, share a car..." There was open rebellion when I suggested cooperation among the women.

"We didn't get pregnant to share no apartment. We need our own places..."

Another woman complained, "My supervisor is stressing me. I'm going to lose my baby because this stress is killing me!"

"If your doctor says you are medically fit to work, you must work. If your doctor says there is no medical reason for you to leave work, you can still quit the Army - but you will be pregnant without a family care plan!"

"I don't have enough to live on. The government is giving me my apartment. I can't afford a car so how am I supposed to take my baby to daycare?"

"Isn't the father of your child paying some of your expenses? You have the right to ask the father of your child for financial support. If you name the father on the birth certificate, and our DNA tests prove he is the father of your baby, he will be required to send you child support. He has responsibilities, too!"

Another open rebellion from the women.

"I don't want no man in my life! Are you kidding?"

"What about your baby? Doesn't your baby have the right to a mother and a father?"

The women retorted, "I didn't have no father. My grandmother raised me. Children don't need no fathers..."

When you face a soldier who confronts hardship and pain, you want to do everything you can to mitigate the pain. I admit that when I finally left the Army in 1997, I completely agreed with the Fort Polk doctors who felt out-of-wedlock pregnancy was a medical condition that should warrant removal from active duty. Not as a punishment, but as a practical matter. The Peace Corps not only bars single parents from serving, pregnant women are sent home. Feminists do not rail against the Peace Corps for being so mission focused.

Regrettably, the aspirations of young, underprivileged girls in America are just as shortsighted and money grubbing as the adult prostitutes who line up at the barstools outside any Army post in any foreign country around the world. As if we were a third world country, American adolescents and female soldiers are just as likely to prostitute themselves as civilian adult women. The problem is so prevalent, that in January 1997, the Pentagon JAG revised its Bench Book to allow for the possibility that girls as young as twelve may give consent, undermining the legal standard of statutory rape for girls under 16 years of age. According to military law, signed by President William Jefferson Clinton, the soldier's defense can be that, if she presents herself to be 16, she acts like she is 16 and she willingly participates in sex, she is to be treated as if she is 16. Under the law, chronological age is now legal fiction when it comes to protecting America's children.

American society is unnecessarily confused on this issue. When Mr. Clinton acquiesced to the norms of his own backwoods upbringing by lowering the age of consent to twelve years of age, he all but conceded the possibility that young men and adolescent girls are capable of responsible behavior. They are capable. Our cultural, and now our legal standards, should be set to achieve the behavioral goals we want our youth to aspire to, and are capable of achieving. We should not lower the legal bar to accommodate the aberrations that presently exist.

Women's advocates backed themselves into a corner on the issue of adolescent sexual consent in the 1990s. On the one hand, they have refrained from protecting 13-year-old girls from predatory men because to argue that an adolescent is too young to make her own decision about having sex is to also argue that she is too young to practice choice. If a girl can't legally consent to have sex, she certainly can't consent to practice birth control or elect an abortion, can she? It would never do to take away a girl's right to choose, even if the absolutizing of choice encourages the rape and prostitution of adolescent girls.

To add further confusion, at the same time that Mr. Clinton and feminist advocates lowered the sexual age of consent in military law books to twelve years of age, they created a new victim class of soldiers. Grown women who wore the uniform were deemed legally and psychologically incapable of giving consent to have sex if that consent was given to their bosses, or if their consent was given under the influence of alcohol. Throughout the '90s, the Army has been plagued with sexual misconduct cases between consenting adults. Feminists and cowering military officials have strangely argued that a woman of the age of 19, 26, even higher, is incapable of giving consent if she goes to bed with her boss or supervisor. In 1997, at the court-martial of Sergeant Delmar Simpson at Aberdeen, this man was actually sent to prison for 25 years because he had consensual sex with soldiers in his platoon. He was convicted of constructed rape — a legal fiction that presumes adult women are incapable of voluntary participation in illicit sex — while on the military law books, the presumption held that twelve-year-old children were fully capable of giving sexual consent to their GI boyfriends or customers!

To sum it up, we are a morally confused society that literally defends to the death the right of a six-year-old to participate in a highly sexualized beauty pageant or a 14-year old child's right to indulge the sexual fantasies of insecure men. Yet, since the Tailhook scandal, women's advocates have infantalized grown female soldiers by insisting they are incapable of choosing for themselves how they will use their body to make their place in this world. I look forward to the day when we reverse this logic. The day must come when we consider 14-year-olds incapable of giving consent for exploitation of any sort: prostitution, media exploitation, sports, music. Then, when a girl reaches the age of 18, when she becomes a woman, her "yes" means "yes." If she chooses to sleep with the boss to get ahead, it should never be construed as rape. Merely as a business decision, however immoral. That day hasn't arrived, and it was nowhere in sight when I served at Fort Polk or at Fort Hood.

The first time I was called to the Bayne Jones Army Hospital emergency room to help a woman who, it turned out, filed a false allegation of rape, I visited a female soldier whose Navy husband was on extended sea duty. This woman was caught in flagrante with her boyfriend, another Army soldier, when her husband called long distance. The woman's lover answered her household phone.

The female soldier so feared her husband's reaction to her infidelity that she told him she was being raped. She maintained this allegation for two days, despite all evidence to the contrary. When she finally admitted her lie, the woman's commander had the female soldier committed to the psych unit for a few days to avoid the alternative: charging the woman with the crime of lying to criminal investigators and with the crime of adultery. Now I know that many feminists have argued that women are put into Army psychiatric units to cover up the crime of rape in the military. Actually, the only women I have seen in the psychiatric wards are women who lied about consensual experiences and called them rape either to cover their shame, to indulge their fantasies of revenge after having been spurned, or to obtain post-coital birth control. Their psychological disintegration is usually associated with avoidance of punishment for falsely accusing an illicit lover of rape, or fear of violence from the woman's primary sexual partner.

That early morning, when I visited our RSS soldier in the emergency room, I sat with her for hours. Her commander and her first sergeant went home. The social workers didn't show up until about 7:30 in the morning. Criminal investigators had already uncovered her lie. When we were alone, she never stopped saying, "You don't know my husband, Chaplain. You don't know my husband." I could understand how fear of prosecution or spousal abuse would motivate a woman soldier to lie about rape. But I could never figure out how this woman, or any other woman could put the life of a lover/boyfriend/paying sex-partner into such jeopardy when caught in the act of unfaithfulness. But it happens frequently in the military.

Women make false allegations of rape for many reasons. Sometimes the reasons are negative: the fear of being caught in adultery, the anger at being humiliated by a higher ranking person one had an affair with, the dread of unplanned pregnancy, or fear of humiliation by peers or parents when a naïve soldier's naughtiness is exposed. Sometimes the allegation of rape results from a need for attention. Homely girls will link themselves to the hunk or the athletic superstar in a military unit. Once, a woman was assigned to me temporarily because she was being ridiculed by her peers because of her promiscuous string of relationships. While her troop was still at Fort Lewis, she accused three men of raping her. A big court-martial ensued. Men and women from the unit insisted the woman boasted of her sexual encounters with the men. When her lie was finally uncovered, her chaplain had her committed to the psychiatric ward for a week. For some God-forsaken reason, all the individuals involved in this case were transferred to Fort Polk as members of the same company. Within months, she was making fresh accusations. The same cast of characters. Only now, the woman was sleeping with a different guy. She came to see me, desperate because she thought she was pregnant by her new boyfriend. She started to hint that this man raped her. I realized she had serious psychological problems. I tried to arrange for a counseling appointment. She started screaming at me that I betrayed her, she was outraged when I said she needed psychological counseling. Her face turned deep red, then purple. She cried. She refused to go to the emergency room to be treated as a rape victim. She refused to file a criminal report. She just wanted her pregnancy to go away.

About two o'clock in the morning, she called me. She was doubled over with cramps. She had tried to self-abort by taking a handful of birth control pills. We spent hours in the emergency room. A very compassionate male lieutenant honored her request for a pregnancy test, which was all she wanted from the emergency room. After her pregnancy test seemed to come up negative, I told him privately that this woman made a rape allegation, and asked him to help me to be sure she was being cared for properly. He gave her birth control pills and showed her how to create a morning after pill.

Military hospitals are not allowed to perform abortions. Female soldiers are publicly humiliated when they try to get abortions off-post. They must be diagnosed as pregnant. They must receive a permission slip from the post doctor. Then, they must travel across state to get an abortion in a far away big city clinic. Too often, they are subject to the ridicule and hostility of their peers for carelessly getting pregnant (all soldiers are repeatedly taught contraception and safe sex practices) or for choosing to abort their pregnancies. After responding to this woman's pregnancy crisis, I realized women like her were making false allegations of rape to avoid the public humiliation they experienced when they try to obtain a civilian abortion. By signing rape allegations in the military emergency room, they think they earn the confidential right to an abortion. They are given the morning after pill, which makes their pregnancies magically go away. They usually don't realize until its too late that forensic analyses and mandatory criminal prosecution of either a rape allegation against their sexual partner or their own false statements will strip them of their privacy, anyway.

I immediately had this woman transferred back to her company, and I arranged for private, confidential counseling through the hospital's psychology department. Weeks later, her first sergeant confided that the girl was indeed pregnant. She chose to get an abortion on the economy. Her moods swung wildly. When I explained to her commander that this young woman might be too emotionally unstable to remain on active duty, he was fearful at first.

"Look, you can't have her leveling accusations of rape every time she gets pregnant," I argued.

Even though he was afraid this woman would bring his command to a premature end, he did not think that as a male, he could do anything but treat her as a victim.

"She is not taking responsibility for herself. Just be careful with her. Her moods flip mid-sentence and she can go off the handle in an instant."

This soldier's mother called the commander shortly thereafter and revealed that the soldier had been treated for years with medications for bi-polar disorder. Here she was in a unit that could deploy anywhere in the world on two hours notice, strapped with bipolar disorder and a serious case of sexual narcissism that would eventually put her over the edge if she continued to get her needs met in such destructive ways.

Whatever the motivation, after responding to more than a few false allegations of rape, I wasn't the only feminist Army chaplain who noticed the rape crisis response paradigm needed to be doctrinally reworked. It is simply not true, as advocates would have you believe, that women who make rape accusations always tell the truth. FBI statistics suggest that in 15 percent of the cases, women file false charges of rape. Because the young soldiers today lead such amoral lives, but in the context of a disciplinary system that arbitrarily metes out severe penalties for such things as adultery, fraternization, group sex, pandering and prostitution, I can say unequivocally, that in the military, the rates of false allegations are much higher. At the same time, my experience leads me to conclude that false allegations are a symptom, of course, of women's emotional problems that are exacerbated by their ill-suited military occupations.

If how you spend your time, money and psychic energy is the content of the deity that you worship, then Billy Goat Hill was the false god worshipped by off-duty single soldiers, and too often, by married soldiers and their spouses. The Hill was a strand of tin sheds painted in gaudy colors, strung with twinkling lights. The more posh facilities glowed with neon lights and painted billboards of buxom ladies of the night to attract sex-starved, very lonely young soldiers.

Ironically, Billy Goat Hill was the safest place for soldiers to congregate off post, because rural Louisiana was, and probably still is David Duke Country. God-fearing church goers by day turn into Aryan separatists by night. These white gangs are sophisticated enough to leave their hoods at home, but however disguised, the Klans do brisk business — particularly in the vicinity of multi-cultural multi-racial military communities. I will never forget an experience in July 1995 in Tongduchon, Korea, when I heard a black soldier tell his long lost buddies he felt so safe in Korea, compared to Louisiana.

"Man, a brother can't travel around the back roads of Louisiana at night. In Pitkin, if a black man is seen there, they'll try to kill him."

The soldier was disbelieved. His buddies thought he was exaggerating.

"No," I interjected. "He's not exaggerating. One of our black teenagers drove into Pitkin. He was followed back to his home on post. The Pitkin locals flashed their guns on Fort Polk to teach this boy's mother a lesson — if the boy ever returned to Pitkin, the men were going to kill him."

The young black soldiers in Korea were surprised to hear a white lady chaplain confirm another soldier's experience of American backwoods racial bigotry. They were accustomed to hearing denials that any race problem existed in Louisiana, or in the Army for that matter.

At Polk, racial rivalries were sometimes acted out between Army soldiers both on and off post. Of course, racial rivalries are still acted out. While I served the 2nd Armored Cavalry, the occasional crowbar ruckus would erupt in the regimental parking lot. Sergeants would immediately intercede and work behind the scenes to get their men under control. This gave the regiment a false sense of security — that the sergeants were truly in control of their men.

Every couple of months, racial rivalries were carried off post. They flared up in the Billy Goat clubs. There was a string of stabbings on Billy Goat Hill. The fights had become an epidemic. General Magruder, the Installation Commander, finally exerted his authority over his off-duty soldiers by declaring the Billy Goat bars off-limits to Fort Polk soldiers. After two or three days, however, local business leaders were hit so deeply in their pocketbooks, they insisted that the General lift the ban. Regrettably, he did. The local community never saw fit to shape new, healthier forms of recreation for the American tax dollars that flowed into town because of our soldiers.

The potential for teaching our young recruits to relinquish their addiction to handguns and violence cannot be realized fully at our stateside posts, all located in the heart of NRA territory. Not until our soldiers are sent overseas can we teach them to withdraw from their gun obsessions. When our GIs are shipped to places like Korea, they must leave their guns behind. Most often, brawls in Korea are concluded with the far less lethal throw of a punch. Egos may be bruised after a fight, punishment meted out for all parties to the mutual affray, but for the most part, our soldiers survive their fights when they are overseas. Not so on American posts. Soldiers who lack trust and confidence in the world will often stockpile rifles, ammunition, and handguns in their little trailers off-post. Some are so fearful of being attacked that they stow their guns illegally in the barracks.

During my tenure with the 2nd Armored Cavalry Regiment, two single soldiers died of handgun wounds within a two-week period. The second death occurred off-post, a shoot-out that resulted in the death of rival gang members. The state authorities deemed our soldier's death a homicide, because he was killed in a mutual spray of bullets after a rival gangster entered his hotel room. Military criminal investigators were aware that the deceased soldier was a gang member. His Army leaders were already working to break the gang association. The deceased handsome black man was well liked, a hard worker, and father of three children. His downfall in life was associating with a group of men who had gang affiliations.

To quickly close the case, the Louisiana State police suggested that our soldier, M, was killed because of rivalry over a girlfriend. During the shoot-out, however, M's girlfriend rolled over, missed all the shots, and when both men were killed, she called other members of the gang to retrieve her and M's car. Usually, when a girlfriend is two-timing, she gets hurt in the obsessed lover's act of rage. This girl was in control. She was safe before, during, and after the shootout, suggesting her dalliance with our RSS soldier was not an act of infidelity, but an act of collaboration with his rivals.

Since Louisiana law dictates that a man can defend his room, his home with a gun, we were advised our soldier died under honorable conditions. I was required to prepare a memorial service for this young man. As we prepared, the leaders in the unit, to include Lieutenant Colonel Tucker and Colonel Molino, were insistent that I should avoid glamorizing the gun deaths. Believe me, I needed no encouragement. I had already ministered to many family members and survivors of gang violence by the time I completed my clinical pastoral education at the Hospital of University of Pennsylvania. After two or three deaths in one weekend, I wrote my own crude theological manifesto denouncing the use of chaplains and religion to sanctify the carnage created in American gang wars.

Our RSS memorial service was dignified, with the entire chain of command, including General Magruder, attending. For the three days prior to the memorial service, Colonel Tucker and I visited every company to conduct Critical Incident Debriefings with the troops. Colonel Tucker, a Southern, gun-toting, but most respectable Baptist from Alabama invoked reason as he appealed to our soldier's macho need to have guns.

"Now, listen up. I have used shotguns and weapons all my life. I'm not here to tell you to throw away your guns. Responsible people use guns to hunt, to kill scorpions, to protect themselves from grizzly bears. Now I'm serious, now. Sometimes you need a gun to defend yourself — But this goin' around with your nine millimeter pieces and huntin' each other — I'm here to tell you misuse of guns is a career stopper. There's no tolerance for using guns on the streets to settle your disagreements. Using guns to settle your arguments is not the act of a man, it's the act of a coward. I'm tellin' ya. It's a career stopper."

Tucker's strong personal engagement with our soldiers stopped the escalating trend, at least in our squadron.

After Colonel Tucker spoke to each formation, I sat with the survivors of this gun tragedy, and listened as they expressed their grief.

"I knew he was going to come to a bad end.."

"He was just starting to get his life together. He just started paying child support for his kids."

"He was a hard worker. I never knew he had this side."

"He was so funny. He wanted to keep everybody smilin'."

The only people who knew the whole story of this deceased gun-toting young man were the officer who completed the line of inquiry into the soldier's death, the commander, and myself. M's gun case was in the barracks room with his other unsavory paraphernalia. The belongings he left behind screamed louder than words that M was on the fast track to hell.

How do you prepare a memorial service for a young man whose highest aspiration was inflicting nine-millimeter holes in the flesh of his feared opponent? I preached a meditation that brothers have got to stop killing brothers, comparing the story of Cain and Abel to the story of Joseph and the many-colored coat. I recalled how Cain killed Abel in a jealous rage, condemning himself to misery in the process. Joseph's brothers tried to kill him in their jealousy rage at their father's favoritism. Years later, when Joseph was a powerful leader, his brothers came a-begging for food. Joseph had the upper hand. He could have let his brothers die of starvation, but Joseph, the leader, transcended the betrayal of his brothers, and gave them new life. Joseph was the true leader. At the right moment, I asked our soldiers to put their guns down in honor of their deceased friend. Brothers should not kill brothers. Soldiers should follow the example not of Cain but of Joseph, the leader, and turn ugly situations around and away from death and violence.

After the service, General Magruder sent me a handwritten note, thanking me for my message. But some of the gang members who attended the worship service were angry with me. One in particular came to my chapel office several Friday afternoons to vent his anger. How dare I tell these young soldiers to lay down their arms? He also talked about his fear that he would be the next hit. Each week, I begged him to listen to the guidance of his first sergeant, to stay away from the bad gun-toting crowd. The young man would pace back and forth in anger, and deny he was really in danger. His first sergeant warned him that he would pay a big price if he crossed the line and committed a crime. The young man cockily retorted his sergeant major would protect him from trouble. Eventually, this man drew a gun in the barracks against a civilian lady friend. No one was hurt, but he was sentenced to two years in prison.

I visited the soldier in jail, before his court martial, while he was still seething with rage.

"You should never have talked about guns at M's memorial." He said angrily. "How do you think his mama felt?"

This man was from the Philadelphia neighborhood surrounding HUP, where I trained as a chaplain. My primitive save-the-youth manifesto flashed before my eyes. "Look. You are from Philadelphia. I'm from Philadelphia. For nine months, I prayed over young men who were shot up on the streets. The first time I prayed over a dead young man, I didn't say anything. The second

time, I didn't say anything. The third time, I prayed with that boy's mama that the shooting and the killing would stop. His mama thanked me."

The soldier slackened in posture, as if I had just punched him in the gut.

"Look, it doesn't have to be this way. Now, M is dead. Did you see that M's mamma didn't come to the memorial? This crowd you're with is trouble. I have been begging you to get away from these guys. I don't want to pray with your mama at a funeral. You are alive. At least, your mama knows you'll be coming back to Philadelphia when you are done. If you change, you do two years, when you get out, you can start a new life. But you have to start now."

This man sat quietly on his jail seat for the first time ever. I took liberty and gave him a bible.

"I have all that," he sneered.

I asked him if a certain sergeant major had come to visit him now that he was in jail.

"No."

It was my turn to be tough.

"You don't have time to continue playing these games. You know the answers are in here, in this book. I just thank God you are alive. M's dead. But you'll have a life when you get out of Leavenworth. I know people in Philadelphia, and your mother knows people who can help you. Thank God you are alive!"

The young man quieted down.

"My mama's a Pentecostal preacher. My father's a Pentecostal preacher. Everybody in my family's a preacher."

Do you know the only soldiers from my own unit I ever visited in the Louisiana jails were preachers' kids. All three of them.

When this man's court martial was over, his troop commander said he was surprised at the soldier's sudden change — all that arrogance, spewing rage had dissipated. Lots of people tried to get through to him. He survived, but still his friend was dead and he lost his career and his freedom before he would listen. What will it take for us to reach the hearts and minds of these angry young men before they commit to the violent rampaging paths that will ultimately destroy them?

It was not surprising to me that the young men who dallied with gangs were angry that I asked them to give up their guns, their need for revenge. I could not imagine, however, that I would confront the same violent rage for speaking against the use of handguns from my chaplain supervisor. To my everlasting shock, for the next eight months of my assignment to the 2nd Armored Cavalry Regiment, my chaplain supervisor, Brett Travis, expressed his outrage that I encouraged soldiers in my unit to lay down their guns at Specialist M's memorial service. "Get off your feminist NRA agenda," he would command as he stabbed his finger in my face, even after I showed him the handwritten note of gratitude that General Magruder sent me for clearly professing that guns would lead to unnecessary bloodshed and death.

Chaplain Travis' threats were a message that I could not and would not accept. Although I was a junior chaplain, I was more experienced with ministry to gang and survivalist members than he. Travis chose to ignore, to avoid these troubled youth by staying focused on combat training, field tactics, and staff work. I understood his desire to keep the Army pure, but there were too many soldiers caught up in the swamp of violence and retaliation to ignore this situation.

Two things made me believe the right message could make a difference in the lives of our young soldiers. Chaplains are the only trained counselors assigned to soldier units. If soldiers didn't get a strong anti-violence message from us, they weren't going to get it from anybody. And in the absence of a clear, moral vision, our young people will create their own narcissistic, cynical, destructive codes. If chaplains weren't going to try to work with the violent individuals or with the militia culture the Army had become, what was the point of having chaplains at all?

Eventually, for taking a homiletic stand against retaliatory gun violence, and other social issues I will recount later, I had to leave Fort Polk. My commanders and my soldiers were not unhappy with my work. My chaplain supervisors were outraged. Chaplain Travis took this message so personally that he made it his business to drive me not just out of Fort Polk. He tried to put me out of the Chaplain Corps.

CHAPTER 13

The Sisyphus Slope

Meantime, the need for spiritual mentoring of Fort Polk single soldiers was limitless. Colonel Molino demanded initiatives to capture the attention of single soldiers. Colonel Molino understood that young inexperienced soldiers were much like latchkey kids — bound to get in trouble if left too long to their own devices.

Chaplain Stanley Copeland was still my supervisory chaplain at the time. Prior to my assignment at Polk, Copeland declared he could not work with me because my faith, Unitarian Universalism, was not officially Christian. All chaplains are required to work with endorsed chaplains from other faiths. Officially, if you can't work with ministers of other faiths, you are supposed to leave active duty. For the most part, chaplains from the underrepresented faiths — Unitarians, Muslim, Jewish, liberal Protestant, and sometimes even Catholics are simply pushed out by the dominant faiths.

Stanley Copeland served in Vietnam as a medic and in the Gulf War as a chaplain. His heart and mind were forever preoccupied with the exigencies of battle. His office was laid out like a tactical field office without the camouflage netting. He was extremely anxious around female soldiers. On his door, Copeland posted an article about secondary virginity, the notion that promiscuous women could reclaim their virtue by renouncing casual sex before marriage. Copeland proved to be an ill, but very good man. He compulsively repeated his story about a female soldier in the Gulf War who asked him more than once, "Chaplain, do you want to help get me pregnant? I've already slept with eleven guys and I'm still not pregnant! Wanna try?"

He was blunt about his decision to become an Army chaplain because of his horrible experience of chaplains in Vietnam.

"Once, the first time I killed the enemy, I was in a torment. I killed three men with my bare hands. I went back to the chaplains because I just needed to talk. I couldn't find a chaplain anywhere who wasn't drunk..."

Copeland prided himself on being ever combat-ready, ever sober, and ever ready to win a soul over to Christ.

During my first week at Fort Polk, Chaplain Copeland took me to visit with the Regiment's Executive Officer, Lieutenant Colonel Trahan. While alone, Lieutenant Colonel Trahan alerted me to the fact that my Unitarian Universalist faith was an obstacle for some of the other chaplains. He assured me that Colonel

Molino's command would tolerate no religious discrimination, anymore than it would tolerate gender or racial discrimination. If I experienced discrimination, I was to report it immediately. Lieutenant Colonel Trahan asked me questions about my beliefs. I noted that my denomination was predominantly not Christian, but that I reclaimed my Christian faith. I was part of the ten percent of Unitarians who called themselves Unitarian Universalist Christians.

My chaplain supervisor was called into the room to work out some kind of mutual understanding about my place in the Cav. The contrast between these two men put me on notice. Chaplain Copeland was an inarticulate, fear-filled, if well-intentioned fundamentalist. Trahan was a well-educated arrogant Catholic. We discussed Augustine, Vatican II, the Trinity, family support programs and why I would be extremely challenged as the first woman chaplain in the 2nd Armored Cavalry Regiment. Trahan turned to Copeland and abruptly concluded our meeting.

"She talks Christian. She sounds Christian to me. What's the problem?"

"There's no problem, sir." Copeland replied. "We'll work with her!"

Stanley Copeland made up a reason afterwards to exclude me from preaching or even assisting in his chapel services. Furthermore, he would not so much as listen to sermons I preached in other contexts. His denomination, Scottish Presbyterian, not only despised Unitarians, they did not respect the authority of women. His ostensible reason for excluding me from his preaching roster was not that I was a woman or a Unitarian, but rather that he was picking only one chaplain to be his assistant. This strategy to mask over the Chaplain Corps' discrimination against women and liberal or marginal Protestants was devised at higher echelons to avoid the accusation of intentional discrimination. Chaplain Copeland picked another fundamentalist, Haydn Goodwin to be his pastor. The rest of us were supposed to sit and watch these two preach to a congregation of about 50. With my commander's blessing and strong pleadings, I was completely absorbed in family and single-soldier ministries I planned with my squadron.

There was no reason for us to squabble about preaching schedules. So long as Copeland gave me the freedom to do prayer breakfasts and the soldier support programs I was setting up, I would keep myself so busy I wouldn't have time to think about his arbitrary reasons for excluding me from his Sunday pulpit. I formed a little choir for the Catholic community when I realized the Catholics received no support from the Regiment. My regular attendance at the Catholic Mass under the guise of song leading was very therapeutic. Every pastor needs opportunities to be supported religiously. I nurtured my own faith with the Catholic community. As my relationships in the squadron grew strong, however, the pulpit discrimination against me was noticed time and again by my members of my squadron. By the late fall of 1993, my officers and sergeants were asking me why I was the only chaplain excluded from the preaching schedule at the regimental chapel. Was it because I was a female or a Unitarian? Both, undoubtedly. I inquired about Chaplain Copeland's change of plans, his decision to drop the pastor/associate pastor model and let everybody preach and pray in front of the congregation except me. I got all kinds of obfuscation, and some indications from two peer chaplains, Goodwin and Tyree, that they were quite happy to exclude me because I was a Unitarian.

I called the Chief of Chaplains, Matthew Zimmerman and asked him if I was the only chaplain who was required to sign the agreement to honor religious diversity or lose my active duty status. I was later told that five chaplains called within days to register the same concern. Fort Polk's Deputy Installation Chaplain, Kurt Pedder, conducted an investigation during which Chaplains Copeland and Tyree asserted their Presbyterian religious obligation to refuse to work with Unitarians. After exhausting meetings with Chaplain Northrup, the retiring post chaplain, it became clear that the non-cooperation would persist. Despite the Chief of Chaplain's policy to send bigoted chaplains home, I did not think it would be fair to remove Chaplain Copeland from the active duty ranks when he already served two or three combat tours. Regardless, Stanley Copeland had generals in high places to protect his interests. There will never be a win-win solution to this problem of religious diversity. I didn't want to compromise my single-soldier programs with the arrival of a new supervisor, but, I knew we were sending a very bad message to our soldiers if we allowed religious bigotry to become official policy. Copeland was moved to another assignment on post when he refused to incorporate me into his preaching schedule as he included all the other men. There was no consistency in applying the rules, either. Chaplain Tyree documented more than once his refusal to work with me because I was a Unitarian. Yet, he was made the Army's chaplain of the year before his Fort Polk tour was through.

Before Chaplain Copeland made it his business to exclude me from his pulpit, I accompanied him on a visit to see the XVIIIth Airborne Command Chaplain, Chaplain Adams. This visit gave me very high hopes for a different outcome to the problem of religious bigotry in the Chaplain Corps. Chaplain Adams was a respectable Presbyterian minister. I think he felt it important, without naming the problem directly, to let me know that he would brook no discrimination against Unitarians so long as he was the command chaplain for the XVIIIth Airborne Corps. The meeting with him was very warm. To my surprise, his deputy chaplain was Father Joe O'Keefe, the man who got me involved in the OCS chapel program back in 1983. Colonel Adams blessed all the single-soldier programs that I was trying to maintain — even if they might not draw large crowds, they would have their impact. Jesus discipled twelve, Adams reasoned. If you just worked with twelve, but taught them how to ripple outward to the next twelve and the next, your impact, or shall we say, the impact of the Gospel, would indeed be felt.

Chaplain Adams emphasized that 67 percent of soldiers in the Army have no religious preference. The Chaplain Corps still hasn't learned to cope with this trend. Soldiers may have identified themselves as Catholic on their dog tags, but they think of themselves as belonging to no church. These kids are called NRPs (No Religious Preference). Since they don't come to chapel, it is assumed they won't go on retreats. They are written off by the chaplains. Chaplain Adams challenged us to respond, to fill the spiritual void in their young adult lives. If we didn't, then who would respond to their spiritual or emotional emptiness? Who provided outreach to them? If we didn't reach out, then the bartenders, bar maids, prostitutes, drug dealers, gun dealers, gang lieutenants and survivalist nations would capture the young NRPs when they were most vulnerable: far from home, friendless, and with too much disposable time and money on their hands.

In retrospect, I regret my decision to challenge Chaplain Copeland's policy of pulpit exclusion, because as the devil I knew, he gave me wide latitude to initiate soldier support programs. And he cared. He really cared about those programs. He cared about soldiers as much as he believed there was only one way to accept Jesus Christ as your Lord and Savior: the Scottish Presbyterian way. For that, I have to thank him. Copeland would take all kinds of risks to help soldiers in crisis. He worked out a beautiful "theology of flight" to help women understand they should never remain in a violent relationship. He helped many women to flee from abusive spouses and boyfriends. As the devil I knew, Chaplain Copeland was really an angel in disguise.

When Chaplain Travis replaced Copeland as the regimental chaplain, he made all kinds of promises he never intended to keep — from tolerating the Unitarian faith to support of our single-soldier and family support ministry. Chaplain Travis promised to be an angel of mercy, Brett Travis was the devil I would come to know. Travis earned the metaphoric title on the three horns of religious bigotry, racism and his violent intimidation of those who did not bid him satisfactorily by threatening gun violence to those who angered him.

Soon after Travis was installed as the regimental chaplain, he insisted I would go nowhere as a Unitarian in the Army. If I intended to get promoted, I had better change to a Christian denomination. The fact was, I was in the process of reconverting, and I was already exploring a number of Christian denominations. Not because it was good for my career — I was already coming to terms with the fact that I could easily lose the privilege of being a chaplain just because I changed my faith group. I encouraged Chaplain Travis not to put himself in the situation of being branded a religious bigot by demanding my immediate conversion to the faith of his choice. I asked him to give me time, because I was shopping around for the Christian faith community that I could happily belong to for a lifetime.

On the advice of Chaplains Travis and Pedder, I went to the Church of Full Gospel endorser, Jim Ammerman, and attended his gathering of all stateside military chaplains in February of 1994. I was so excited about the possibility of resolving the Christian issue, that I bought myself an electric piano just before I signed into the hotel quarters. Since I wasn't going to preach very often in the Chaplain Corps, perhaps I could start playing church music again, as I had during my teenage years!

I discovered the Church of the Full Gospel is a one-man denomination. Mr. Ammerman collected all the independent white Pentecostal churches together to give them an umbrella power structure that would make it possible for them to win chaplain slots. Only denominational endorsers can approve a chaplain's place in the Army. A fully qualified chaplain cannot just go through a credentialing process and then be hired independently by government institutions. The power of placing chaplains on active duty is entirely in the hands of ecclesiastical authorities of each and every denomination. This is another troublesome policy. The ecclesiastical endorsing process protects the integrity of the faith that is represented in the chaplaincy, but it also guarantees discrimination against men and women who do not fit the endorser's criteria for ecclesiastical leadership because of their gender, race, or sexual orientation.

The Full Gospel chaplains with whom I visited were godly folk, but the conference introduced me to political loyalties that were not in keeping with chaplain professional ethics. During the day, there were all kinds of sweet conference programs to assist chaplains with family counseling and scripture classes. Each night, there was a different propaganda film and a different political diatribe. The first alleged Mr. Clinton was a womanizer and murderer of at least 26 law enforcement agents who were knowledgeable of his personal scandals. The second agitated for the Christian Right's responsibility to defend against the federal government's war against Christianity as evidenced in the film's footage of the Waco massacre. This film was essentially a justification for militia defense organizations. The third was a paranoid prophecy about the Church of the Latter Day Saints' devious plan to take over America. I asked questions about the appropriateness of these films for indoctrination of military chaplains. Needless to say, I wasn't considered a good candidate for Mr. Ammerman's endorsement as a Full Gospel chaplain.

When I returned to Fort Polk, I continued to search for a Christian faith group. Soon, I joined the First Christian Church, and requested consideration of endorsement from the Louisiana Disciples of Christ Ministry Group. At the same time, I had this nagging feeling that if I was going to change, I should return to the Catholic Church. Soon after I announced the Church of the Full Gospel was not a good fit for me, Chaplain Travis reneged on his commitment to support my soldier ministries.

My own commander, Lieutenant Colonel Tucker, supported attempts to engage the single soldiers, from nursing home visits and bingo parties with chair-ridden residents to the annual food drive for poor families in Leesville. Most of these events occurred after soldiers were released from work to at least provide an alternative to the almighty beer and dirty dancing girls during the soldiers' free time.

We did all these things as a separate squadron, though. Rarely was it possible to collaborate with other chaplains to set up programs that could compete with Billy Goat Hill for the soldiers' off-duty time and energy. It was never easy to get married chaplains to participate in night and weekend programs that were focused on single young adults. Married chaplains would take ten or more soldiers on Duty Days with God, that is, provide soldiers with the opportunity to go to the lake or to a football game during the work day. When I organized my first battalion retreat, scheduled on a weekend rather than the duty day, a company commander pointed out that it was unusual in the Army for voluntary religious programs to be held after duty hours.

"I just resent those Duty Days with God," he complained. "They don't pray, they don't study the Bible, they don't learn about morals or faith. They just swim. Or Fish. Or play volleyball. I'm ordered to cough up soldiers for the chaplain's Duty Day With God so the chaplain can look good. Meanwhile, I have missions to be accomplished, and my soldiers are using religion as an excuse to get out of work."

Another captain complained about duty day programs.

"Do you see these soldiers in the chapel on Sunday morning? No. I go to church every Sunday. Walk through the barracks, and you won't find a soul awake before noontime. They are sleeping off their Saturday night party. Duty Day With God — it's a hoax to make it look like the command is doing something to take care of soldiers. You watch. You hold Duty Day with God on a weekend, and no one will come. Soldiers don't care about religion. No one here works on Saturdays and Sundays unless we have an alert. As far as I am concerned, except for prayer breakfasts, they can exercise their free right to worship as they please on their own time!"

Despite the predictions of my fellow captains and senior sergeants, that no one would come to retreats or programs that were on the soldiers' time, I held my single-soldier retreats on weekends anyway. Surprisingly, soldiers signed up for long weekend excursions. I took them to New Orleans. All of my retreats required participation in Spiritual Autobiography classes, where soldiers and spouses first made drawings, and then wrote about their faith, their hurts and pains, their dreams, their hopes.

The spiritual autobiography technique is tremendously effective, especially with reticent or emotionally disturbed people. One or the other categories could

Did You Say A Retreat In New Orleans?

RSS Soldiers signed up for quarterly spiritual autobiography retreats.

describe a lot of junior active duty soldiers. I learned the process from Dan Wakefield, author of *The Story of Your Life*, who in turn, was trained by Reverend Carl Scovel of King's Chapel.

All of our squadron retreats and functions were interfaith — not exclusively Christian. To avoid imposition of Christian theology on nonbelievers or those of other faiths, I often used expressive art and music exercises to help soldiers name their spiritual needs. These techniques work well with young adults, because of the intuitive focus on their inner thoughts and feelings. Essential to the success of experiential faith sharing is a ground rule that no criticisms or psychoanalysis will be proffered. All expressions are to be treated with the utmost respect and reverence.

Can you imagine a former Latino gang member drawing a scene from his childhood, then writing a poem about his favorite uncle, whose loss he never mourned before? Or a man drawing dark images, and talking in words for the first time about the sadness he has carried for years because his brother and two best friends were killed in an auto accident? Men are too often conditioned to suppress their grief and sadness. They wind up expressing hostile, often violent anger instead, because aggression is considered manly, but non-violent emotional expression is deemed prissy. Young men and women who could not talk about their sadness healed some of their pain by drawing images or writing a poem or song that captured their sorrow. The more consistent this pattern seemed to be, the more I was convinced that soldier development had to encompass more than teaching shoot-to-kill combat skills. Primary and secondary education, for that matter, needed more emphasis on artistic creative expression for all our youth. Studies are proving that children who play Mozart achieve better math scores. Children who can draw and sing read better. I'll bet our kids would be committing less crime and violence if they were required to show up for an after school arts program or chess club. I really believe that our young people should be required to do all these things in school and training programs, whether or not they are talented. They may never earn their living making art. They will be more expressive, well-rounded human beings, which is a good enough benefit.

These same spiritual autobiography techniques work well with unit spiritual leadership retreats. When Stephen Covey's texts on principled leadership and the spiritual autobiography process are both used, it is possible to hold a leadership discussion of the role of spirituality in military leadership, without imposing any one religious point of view. Instead, the workshop is centered on developing the sense of meaning, purpose and integrity in each individual, allowing them to draw on their own rich heritage.

Sexploitation and alcohol abuse were the crux of most of the barracks disciplinary problems that drained the energies of leaders at Fort Polk. Soldiers who hope to avoid trouble will often hang out in their barracks. Their rooms are stockpiled with wall-to-wall stereo equipment, televisions, and all the alcohol they can afford to buy. Under BOSS policies, soldiers were free to have as much liquor in the barracks, as much sex, as much company as they wished. Traditional fraternization policies were set aside to make way for BOSS, although the laws were never changed to accommodate the policy relaxation. The more casual the relationships between junior and senior enlisted soldiers, however, the more likely the erosion of professional respect. This was true at Fort Polk, in Korea and Fort Hood. It's still true. And, it will always be true. There's much truth to the saying: familiarity breeds contempt.

DUIs or violent assaults were the only drinking related crimes that could destroy the career of a young soldier. Lesser acts of indiscretion would merit enrollment in an expensive rehabilitation program. The sick truth is that the Army first subsidizes the soldier's alcohol dependency, then pays to treat this same dependency. Usually, soldiers are sent for three or six weeks of in-patient treatment. Often, soldiers are admitted for five days to an in-patient psychiatric unit for attempting suicide during a drunken binge. Afterwards, the Army assumes the cost of sending young adults to weekly psychology appointments just long enough to preclude another embarrassing or criminal display of alcohol abuse. Meantime, the Army continues to subsidize the soldier's heavy alcohol consumption with tax-free deeply discounted alcohol prices.

Although the early BOSS policies precluded commanders from prescribing limits to the drinking of young single soldiers, the commanders I worked with were smart enough to teach responsible drinking habits to their troops. Living conditions for single soldiers were not conducive to sensible drinking habits, but at least the RSS commanders tried to instill responsibility. Many of the company commanders I worked with had incentive programs to discourage alcohol-related problems. Ken Feiereisen, for example, commanded a maintenance company the size of half a line battalion. By promising his soldiers a long weekend pass for every quarter the unit was free of a DUI, he was able to prevent DUI incidents in the unit for more than 580 days. DUIs, however, are only a fly on the ear of the elephant named Substance Abuse in the military. The chronic over-consumption of booze by emotionally undisciplined soldiers will continue to have its effect on a certain percentage of troops. Leaders must spend significant amounts of un-clocked time undoing the consequences of heavy drinking.

Three problems that creep into alcohol-focused parties repeatedly waste resources and the time of Army leaders. First, the problem of fraternization. Second, the problem of aggravating or setting off the beginning of the genetic disease, alcoholism. Third, the problem of psychological disintegration, which often happens in young men and women when they live in stressful, isolated, overwhelming, circumstances.

When Army leaders, sergeants and officers are active sponsors of drinking clubs, I think parents have good reason to be angry with the Army. Alcoholism is a progressive disease that is often triggered in young adults when they are encouraged to drink heavily. Command sponsorship of drinking clubs does not happen very often, but when it does, it is usually an act of misguided paternalism. Sometimes, lieutenants or sergeants take control of drinking buddy groups because they fantasize they can maintain control and keep everyone out of trouble. Of course, the more you work with people who abuse alcohol as a group, the more you realize that the thinking is muddied, the supervision is usually non-existent, and the emotional swings of the group are a poor substitute for intimacy. Parents who allow their children to smoke marijuana at home, because they feel they are in control if they know exactly what their children are consuming, often express the same misguided paternalism. Outside counselors can see from afar that no one is in control — the marijuana is a symptom of deeper problems.

A handsome, Caucasian middle class soldier was assigned to our medical troop. This man was extremely well-liked, even though he was addicted to alcohol, drugs, gambling, and some would argue, women. Sergeant F's platoon leader was a lieutenant young enough to be his baby brother. The soldiers response to F's death showed that fraternization issues made the handling of Sergeant F's addictions more complicated. The men and women from this troop were best buddies in the bar room as well as the company day room. Sergeant F was caught several times under the influence of drugs. Because he was such a great soldier, more than once he was placed in extensive rehabilitation by his commander. Sergeant F stubbornly clung to his addictions, nonetheless, so he had to be removed from the Army. Days before he left the 2nd Armored Cavalry Regiment, Sergeant F attempted to rob a local motel at gunpoint to settle his debts of several thousands of dollars. He was surrounded by six or more law enforcement agents. Sergeant F turned the gun on himself and committed suicide. This man was loved by his fellow soldiers. His best drinking buddy was his platoon leader.

General Magruder rightly insisted that we could hold no military ceremony for this sergeant who died while committing a crime. The Medical Troop was in an uproar, however, because they loved their deceased friend. With the blessing of both the Deputy and Installation Chaplains, I held an informal memorial service, not to glorify Sergeant F's deeds, but to help the troops grieve the loss of their friend.

In my reflections, I talked about our need to recognize Sergeant F's problems for what they were. If we wanted to show our love for Sergeant F, we would need to turn away from the addictions and guns that destroyed his life. He had so much potential, but his choices destroyed him. Chaplain Pedder, the deputy installation chaplain attended this informal service to lend support and to make sure the tone was appropriate. Chaplain Travis did not attend. The troop commander and my executive officer, then Brent Edmister, felt that my comments about Sergeant F were appropriate. We simply could not ignore the fact that Sergeant F's death was a warning sign to all of us. Sergeant F's young lieutenant and other close drinking buddies were incensed that I could speak so frankly about the reasons for his demise.

All of Sergeant F's drinking buddies, to include his platoon leader, agitated to have me chastised for naming the crimes and addictions that brought F to his death. After our service, Sergeant F's lieutenant and others went back to his hometown and participated in proper military burial ceremonies. Sergeant F, though he died committing an armed robbery, was buried with a military 21-gun salute, with 2nd ACR soldiers wearing Class A uniforms to perform honors at his graveside. Sergeant F's drinking buddies complained to his family that I failed to provide a proper military ceremony at Fort Polk. They did not tell the family that General Magruder forbade the rendering of such honors for soldiers who died committing criminal acts. Sergeant F's family contacted the post to register their complaints about the service I did.

Two weeks later, when Specialist M was killed in a gang shootout, Chaplain Travis attended the memorial service. Travis was incensed and sided with the black gang members that I should never have taken a stand against the guns that were proliferating at Fort Polk. By this point, Chaplain Travis was threatening daily to destroy my career. Chaplain Travis took a call from the family of Sergeant F, and encouraged F's sister to write a congressional complaint against me. The Inspector General, during its investigation of the service I did for Sergeant F, reviewed the film of our informal grieving service and insisted to my command that I acted appropriately, given the tragic circumstances under which F died.

The lesson that was missed when Chaplain Travis sided with the troops: fraternization, guns and glamorization of alcohol consumption had gotten out of hand under the BOSS rules. The Army's new tolerance for fraternization was reeking havoc, destroying lives. Most military fraternization is not about sex between soldiers. Fraternization is a crime in the military, especially when it is same gender. The real danger of fraternization is the blurring of boundaries that

Fort Polk's Deputy Installation Chaplain, Curt Pedder

Chaplain Pedder became Vice President of Citizen Soldiers to Restore Military Integrity.

makes it impossible for supervisors and leaders to objectively monitor and lead their soldiers.

Fraternization always creates problems in military units, but especially when the fraternization is associated with drinking. While many co-workers can separate their professional life from their social relationships, not all can, and there's no way to predict who will lose their bearings. The influence of alcohol makes it difficult for junior and senior people to maintain their judgement about boundaries with their bosses, too. Mixed-gender fraternization can have no value. Same-sex fraternization usually blinds the supervisors to criminal and violent behaviors of a drinking buddy.

Mixed-gender fraternization is worse because it happens far more frequently. At every post where I have been assigned, military police, military attorneys, and wise commanders have made the correlation between excessive buddy drinking and allegations of sexual assault. Men and women would go to the bars together, or visit in each other's room and drink to the point of obliteration. Later, a woman would often accuse a man of date rape or sexual assault. According to the military code of justice, a man can rob a bank while drunk and be sent to jail, but a woman cannot give consent to have sex — even with her long-term boyfriend — when she is drunk. Although feminists hail this policy as a victory for victims, it is just another instance of infantalizing women, holding them to a lower standard of personal responsibility. Men are held accountable for crimes committed while drunk because it is assumed they must always be in control of their mind and their actions. Women are not deemed capable of such self-control.

When I taught sexual ethics classes to soldiers to reduce the incidences of sexual irresponsibility in their commands, I pointed out to soldiers that fraternization policies are the salvation of healthy relationships in any military unit. Fraternization rules were developed long before gender was an issue in the army. Traditional leadership theory maintains that a leader, a boss, a supervisor will have difficulty maintaining a climate of fairness, impartiality, and good discipline if he or she gets too cozy and familiar with the hired help. When fraternization policies were enforced in the all-male army, they were mostly used to stem drinking-buddy behaviors. In the mixed-gender army, one can never assume there is such a safe thing as a drinking-buddy of the opposite sex. The consequences of such a relationship could lead not just to unseemly allegations of fraternization by jealous peers, but to allegations of alcohol-induced rape — if not by one's partner then by outsiders who are using sexual misconduct cases as leverage to achieve other goals.

I repeatedly taught soldiers that ethical decisions had to be made independently of personal gain.

"The Army has checks and balances. If you do the right thing, you will get your rewards. You may not make general, but the Army will take care of you."

My soldiers insisted that the Army had changed. I was teaching the post-My Lai ethics paradigm that the Army developed to teach soldiers to do what is legal, ethical, moral and correct whether or not a supervisor supported you, using legal avenues of dissent whenever a senior leader pressures you to do something wrong.

In one Maintenance Troop ethics class, Sergeant First Class G insisted, in front of more than 200 soldiers, that I needed to see the new reality. I commanded in 1985 when leaders were rewarded for moral courage and risk taking. In 1994, surely, you would be punished for doing the right thing.

"What's the worst that could happen? You'll retire as a colonel or a master sergeant," I would ask. "You make it sound as if you will be murdered or disappeared if you uphold the law. Most likely, you will just lose a medal. Isn't it more important to maintain your integrity?"

"But ma'am," a junior soldier would retort, "A medal is worth promotion points!"

"Ma'am if you go against what the others are doing, you'll pay a big price!"

"So you mean peer pressure is a valid excuse for doing something wrong? I know what peer pressure feels like. I know, for example, how much pressure soldiers put on each other to get drunk. I go to parties, and someone is always trying to put a drink in my hand. Here Chaplain, have a glass of wine! Who's in control when that happens?"

"So, Chaplain," a grinning mechanic waved his hand, "How much did you drink?"

"Nothing." Gasps from the troops. " Don't get me wrong. I like to have a glass of wine, but when I go to military functions, I'm on duty. People still talk to me about their problems. And the only way you can take charge of your drinking, anyway, is to fill your own glass, buy your own."

"Like, how can you go to a party and sit there like a dweeb..."

It's not an overstatement to suggest that My Lai and the Aberdeen scandal were both rooted in this kind of moral cowardice. How can we correlate the relationship between war time genocide and rape with the mere fraternization and drunken debauchery that creeps into undisciplined garrison bases like Aberdeen? The more I have witnessed, the more I am absolutely convinced the correlation boils down to the slippery slope of what sociologists call "rape prone" ideation. At the interpersonal level, the slope begins: Never hold to your moral or ethical standards if you fear your peers might label you a dweeb. Never do the right thing if your superior invites you to participate in crimes or behaviors that are immoral. Your boss writes your report card. If your boss says to participate in a consensual gang bang, by God, you do what you need to do to get a good report card! You will recall after My Lai, Lieutenant Calley was court martialed for his participation in a massacre, despite his defense that he was just following orders. Generation X soldiers don't even know what My Lai represents. Our moral preoccupations have drifted so far from that national tragedy. Sergeant G's warning to me about the Real Army did not make sense to me until years later. He was right. The Amy may be using chaplains to preach ethics, but the Army is practicing utilitarian survivalism. Do whatever you need to do to get ahead.

Surely, the single soldier's existence wasn't all that terrible, was it? Is it possible to be a single soldier in the BOSS Army and stay out of trouble? Yes, it is. Many a young commander believes he can keep his male soldiers out of trouble by keeping them in the field. If he just trains them hard, and concentrates on what these young men joined the Army to do: play with guns, hug the mud, and conquer the elements for weeks on end for the sheer thrill of it. You can keep the single male soldier out of trouble for a year by keeping him in the swampy boondocks — out in field training. The worst that might happen: a prostitute might sneak into a medical van and infect fifteen or more of your men with STDs. When this happens, middle-aged physician assistants pace back and forth, screaming, "They were in the field, for God's sake!"

Extensive field training does not work as an antidote to trouble for female soldiers. Guaranteed, the pregnancy rate will spike to register women's protests when a unit stays out in the field for ten days at a time. Extensive field training does not work at all for married soldiers. I recall the first time a lieutenant from the Cav begged me to speak to his all-male combat engineer company on domestic violence prevention.

"Our unit is 98 percent married," he complained. "Yet, when we come back from the field, the blotter reports skyrocket! These men are married, and here they are beating up other men in the bars, and beating their wives up at home!"

Why in God's name were 98 percent of the combat engineer company-level soldiers married in the first place?

Unquestionably, in a properly structured training atmosphere, the military can be a vehicle for overcoming all the ghosts of one's past from character weaknesses or flaws to serious anti-social behaviors. For generations, young American males have been plucked from troubled childhoods, thrown into harsh living situations, disciplined by overbearing father-figures, stripped of their homeboy identities, and miraculously, over the course of a brutal nine or fifteen week period of basic training, turned into upstanding American citizens. We don't have those ideal training circumstances anymore.

Then, new enlistees were beholden to their sergeants for most of their first enlistment contracts. They earned permission to go out on the town, to start college classes, or even to marry. "If the Army wanted you to have a wife, they would have issued you one," was not just a cold adage. This was sound military training policy for first term soldiers. Although the Army of the '90s is saturated with real world missions, training and character formation is not the primary mission of commanders and sergeants who command deployable units.

The most tragic error Army generals made in the '90s, however, was to use the institution of marriage to mask the deep developmental issues that crippled our young soldiers. There is no time in the training units to transform our troubled youth into rock solid human beings. The myth that eroded the Army's commitment to the single soldier is that married soldiers are less of a disciplinary burden than single ones. Several military generals even testified to this myth before congress when the Marine Commandant insisted the time had come to ban marriage for first enlistment contracts to give soldiers a chance to grow up before they take on family responsibilities. Army generals sincerely expressed their belief that although American soldiers married years younger than their civilian counterparts, they were better, more stable soldiers because of their marital relationship.

Tell that to the company commanders who must intervene whenever family violence erupts in the throes of infidelity and substance abuse! When married soldiers go out to the field, even for a few days, their spouses often spin out of control .

Tell that to the first sergeants who spend hours with angry wives who want their husbands disciplined for picking up another woman at a bar!

Tell that to the first sergeants who sit with forlorn suicidal young soldiers whose wives took the family credit cards, racked up thousands of dollars of debt, and ran off with their boyfriends, leaving the soldiers to face discharge due to their indebtedness!

When I shared the first draft of this book with CBS *60 Minutes*, I pointed out four areas where the married-soldiers-are-better-behaved-myth needed to be reviewed: domestic violence, alcohol related violence, sexual misconduct, and psychological disintegration. Although the producer, Tom Anderson, said my book was too broad for him to reduce to a 15-minute segment, *60 Minutes* did do a segment on domestic violence in early 1999. As I pointed out in the draft that Tom Anderson read, short of murder, the Army does not treat episodes of domestic violence as a crime, but as a psychological pathology. When a man beats his wife, he is sent to counseling. When a man beats his buddy or his girlfriend, he is charged with assault. Although the Army spends hundreds of millions of dollars each year on domestic violence prevention and counseling, rates of violence have never gone down. In their segment, CBS cited statistics that showed the military's rate of domestic violence is five times that of the civilian sector. If it is true that 10 percent of the civilian population is afflicted with domestic violence, wouldn't that mean that potentially 50 percent of military families are also afflicted? The Army is failing soldiers miserably by promoting convenience marriages. Immature relationships are neither convenient for the couple nor for the Army.

In January of 1994, Chaplain Travis, Colonel Molino and Al Bailey asked me to talk to their air defense artillery battery on the morning that a husband and wife killed their child during an argument. That morning, the couple fought about whether the male soldier was going off to a girlfriend's or to a rapid deployment exercise.

Much later in 1994, Chaplain Travis sent me to a Command and Control Squadron staff briefing to cover for him. The commander, Lieutenant Colonel Al Bailey confronted me as soon as I sat down at his conference table. I was the only woman in the room.

"Chaplain, the *Army Times* here says that every week, on average, one soldier kills a family member. What can we do about this?"

One Fort Polk officer's wife killed her spouse of 22 years when he initiated divorce proceedings to start life over with a pretty young German girl. The 2nd ACR's first squadron lost a child when the parents killed their small child during an alert. We were losing one family member per month to family violence during the stress of our deployment exercises.

In my own squadron, I encouraged couples to go to hospital social workers to talk out their problems, or go to private counselors instead of acting violently towards their family. I thought Travis took me to the air defense battery to encourage the men to prevent violence in their families. I thought he wanted me to do the same throughout the regiment wherever he sent me to meetings in his place. Yet, when I returned, Travis ranted, "You need to get off your feminist NRA agenda, and get out of the counseling business and start being a combat chaplain." This was a complete turnabout from what he had promised to Colonel Molino and Lieutenant Colonel Bailey.

Why the sudden change? Travis began to attack all of the Army's domestic violence programs as useless. He was also troubled by the advances made toward his teenage daughter by school classmates. He threatened shotgun violence to stop the boys. When I recommended a sexual harassment suit instead, he blasted me.

Chaplain Travis wanted nothing to do with domestic violence cases, which is why he brought me in on every case he felt uncomfortable handling. If I could, I would avoid domestic violence situations, too. I have stayed away from my mentally ill brother, who attacked me more than once. I went to court to have him hospitalized after he tried to kill me in 1976. The court judge read out my brother's long history of violence, including breaking a psychiatrist's nose, and hurting a lot of people. Not until my brother killed his roommate was he institutionalized in a hospital for the criminally insane.

I knew exactly why Chaplain Travis never wanted to respond to domestic violence emergencies. Even when you think you are completely healed from the attacks of a loved one, at some deep level, the feeling of terror returns with every plea for help by the victim. But when a soldier brings in his wife, and begs to be put in confidential counseling before he hurts her, you have to respond. You can't just tell the soldier to get lost. You can't just tell spouses to leave. Chaplains have to work with the family, the command and the social workers to get families into treatment. Besides, the Chaplain Corps volunteered itself for the mission of domestic violence and workplace violence prevention. I know from my own personal experience of going to a family priest when my brother tried to kill me. If the priest or the chaplain does not respond in some helpful way, and leaves the victim to the whim of the violent person, that ambassador for God might just as well have said, "God is dead." I came to realize my career as a chaplain was dead if I were to continue responding to domestic violence situations after Chaplain Travis ordered me again to "get off my social work agenda and become a combat chaplain."

Before Travis became my chaplain supervisor, I wrote an article for the post newspaper to encourage men and women to think differently about violence in their lives. General Magruder sent me a personal letter of thanks for the article. In some command meeting, the article was recommended to leaders as a model of prevention. I counted on General Magruder, as I counted on Colonel Molino and my squadron commander, Ed Tucker to be faithfully committed to the prevention of domestic violence. When Travis realized I received two letters from General Magruder, both encouraging me to speak out against domestic and gun violence, he was embittered beyond any hope of reconciliation.

The cynicism shared by Chaplains Travis and Chilen, however, about the ability of chaplains to help violent Army families was born out statistically. More than 7,000 soldiers were assigned to Fort Polk when I lived there. There were 22 chaplains assigned, a full team of domestic violence counselors, and full in-patient and out-patient psychiatric units at the hospital. The problem was never brought under control, but not for lack of trying. Spousal abuse will never be eliminated so long as soldiers are encouraged to marry to get out of the barracks, and so long as the amoral bar-hopping culture of promiscuity is the only social outlet available to the single and married soldiers alike. You can put a chaplain in every household. Although it will never be right, husbands and wives will still erupt with violence when they suspect infidelity.

Domestic violence is not the only tragedy wrought by untimely military marriages. Marriage by 19-year-old untrained privates will never be a short cut to maturity. Most tragically, the young men and women who leap into marriage to avoid the awful pain of loneliness and training failure are no less susceptible to suicidal thoughts than barracks rats. They get suicidal when their marriage goes badly. Or, they disintegrate when they believe they do not have the strength to cope with the military and at the same time, the demands of a young pregnant wife.

In 1994, a young man married a homely, controlling woman soon after he became the commander's driver. One afternoon, our chapel line rang incessantly. We were in a staff meeting. Chaplain Travis ordered me not to answer the telephone. The phone would not stop ringing. After about 20 or 30 rings, I walked out of the meeting to respond to the call, for which Chaplain Travis never forgave me. This woman was frantic because every night her husband was expressing his desire to drive off the road on his way home from work. Her calls to the company's first sergeant went unheeded, because she was perceived as brattish — willing to go to any lengths to get her husband home for dinner.

The engineer commander, a handsome, green-eyed former Marine, depended on his driver for his midnight trips to field sites. The single commander was in charge of an all-male company. He reveled in tactical training. The commander trusted my intuitions, so he sent his short, insecure and inarticulate driver to me for pre-screening. The commander did not think his soldier had a suicide problem. He thought the soldier had a marriage problem. After a long conversation with the soldier, I could see that he had both. I called his boss at about 6:30 P.M. The captain answered his own phone — a sure sign he was single, not attending to the post's family life emphasis by going home at 4:30. I recommended that the soldier be sent for psychological counseling first thing in the morning because he was really depressed. He simply couldn't juggle the equally pressing demands of his commander and his wife. The next morning, the counseling department confirmed the persistence of our soldier's suicidal tendencies. The psychiatrist helped the engineer commander to teach the young man how to juggle competing demands.

One could argue that the hectic pace of the commander triggered depression in his married subordinate. One could also argue that if the old rules prohibiting marriage during first enlistment were in place, the young man might have grown out of his insecurity and learned how to juggle his job before taking on other life responsibilities. This man was one of dozens in our squadron who proved that marriage simply cannot compensate for deep-seated insecurities that our soldiers bring to the Army. When these soldiers marry, they have more, not fewer problems. It's just that some commanders choose to ignore the violence, suicidal thoughts, drunkenness, and sexual misconduct so long as the behaviors are happening out of sight.

The benefit packages offered to married soldiers is so great that soldiers with real debilitations are being recruited because they can get help for their problems in the Army as nowhere else. One cook in the 2nd Armored Cavalry Regiment was an overweight, very dirty, schizophrenic with a wheel-chair-bound husband and five children. The Army guarantees special support to families with "exceptionalities." This woman could not handle two competing demands at the same time. If her squad leader said, " Private C, come over and peel these potatoes," and then a minute later, "C, I changed my mind. Come over to the sink and wash the fresh spinach," C would spasm with fear and anger. This woman did not acquire her schizophrenia on active duty. She was recruited from the backwoods of Pennsylvania, lured into thinking she could provide family stability as an Army cook. She, too, was suicidal more than once, even as the psychiatric unit processed her out of the regiment and into the Veterans Medical Care system. Before she left, I had to go down to the dining facility more than once to give the mess sergeant opportunities to vent his frustrations that his soldiers were so crippled they could not do the basic job for which they were hired.

Men and women often marry friends or companions to share their military benefits with those who are less fortunate. These soldiers personally benefit from the Army's generosity because the marriage frees them to move out of the barracks. The extraordinary benefits give them heroic status when they sincerely try to lift another ready-made family out of poverty. More than one soldier at Fort Polk married a woman who was ten or more years older than he. The women often have had two, three or four children with emotional and physical problems. The Army Family Action Plan demands that commanders help such families gain full access to the hospital, counseling center, and social work programs.

Once, on my way to Sunday morning services, the command called me to the home of a staff sergeant. This man's wife had beaten him up several times over the weekend. She stuffed him in the trunk of her car. She moved her boyfriend into government quarters and beat up on him as much as she beat her husband. The staff sergeant was found by the military police next to the lake surrounded by empty beer bottles. The police took him into custody when they discovered he mixed pills and alcohol in an apparent suicide attempt. When we went to this soldier's home, his wife was throwing things about wildly. She beat up on her husband when his commander brought him to the house. She was wildly incoherent, manic, weepy. Because the soldier's suicide attempt was a mater of record, the entire chain of command was called to respond. The Army had, after all, zero tolerance for suicide. It became apparent that both the soldier and his wife were suicidal. We took them to the community hospital. When the young woman called her father, he exasperatedly said that his daughter was schizophrenic, but she was not being treated by the military as if she was mentally ill. We saw that first hand.

I never did get to church. The lieutenant colonel psychologist who was on call that day refused to come to the hospital to evaluate this couple's situation. My chain of command was livid. The emergency room staff and the psychiatric staff believed the wife, at least, should be admitted. They prepared her room. The psychologist absolutely refused to come in to evaluate this case.

After many hours of waiting in the emergency room for an emergency psychiatric evaluation, the company commander finally talked to the psychologist who still refused to come to the hospital.

"Sir, I will have to make a memorandum for record. I have to disagree with your decision. I will make a memorandum for record of my disagreement."

The next day, the psychologist and Chaplain Travis were demanding that I be punished for insubordination. Neither one realized that I never talked to the colonel. Our company commander had talked to him. At one point or another, my entire chain of command was involved in the process of getting this suicidal and violent spouse hospitalized. The only reason the colonel would not do the emergency psychiatric evaluation was that the golfing weather was perfect.

There was no consistency to the level of care this psychologist gave or the moral standards for which Chaplain Travis chose to scapegoat me. About the same time, a female soldier who was pregnant, with a $180-a-day cocaine habit was under this psychologist's care. The command had already spent more than a year helping this woman try to regain custody of the two children she lost due to her drug habits and negligence. She had already been caught in the barracks with a nine-millimeter gun laying in her barracks room. For either of these two crimes, a male soldier would be put out of the Army. Despite the fact she could not meet child support payments for her first two children, she was pregnant again. I supported the command group's decision to have this woman discharged from the Army. A male soldier would have been jailed or discharged for just one of her repeated offenses. Lieutenant Colonel F took her under his wing, and worked with a circle of people to keep the woman in the Army. This, despite the fact that three nurses complained that she was having various male visitors sneak into her room at all hours of the day and night for intimate visits. How else was she to pay for her lines? Once again, Chaplain Travis and Lieutenant Colonel F attempted to censure me for "meddling in medical affairs." How dare I support the commander's decision to discharge a cocaine-addicted single parent to the Veterans Administration Hospital system?

In April, 1994, the 2nd Armored Cavalry Regiment flew to Fort Chafee, Arkansas to rehearse for a possible mission in Haiti. Three episodes relating to that deployment ruptured my relationship with Brett Travis even further. We went to the field for ten days to practice the exercise. The National Forest where our soldiers train in Louisiana is astonishingly beautiful. White wild stallions roam the forest. Our water purification experts can fetch their own catfish for nightly fried dinners. The blackened night skies gleam with millions of stars that sparkle at the tip of your nose. Chaplains can do their best counseling in these conditions. Soldiers are away from their families and Billy Goat Hill. They reflect on their life experiences at a much deeper level. Given the fact that at any one time, not more than 150 out of my 800-plus troops were in the field, some chaplains would accuse me of spending too much time in the field. I never missed an exercise — even at the platoon level — if it would give me good soldier contact time.

During our preliminary ten-day field exercise, the wife of one of our mechanics was about to die of breast cancer. My commander and my executive officer, Brent Edmister asked me to go to Alexandria to provide chaplain support to both our soldier and his dying wife. My driver and I drove an hour to the hospital, and spent the day with this man. When we returned to the field at the end of the day, we were told Brett Travis stopped by to observe my work. He was livid that I was not in the field. Major Edmister pointed out that if Travis had called to coordinate his visit, I could have arranged my hospital visit around his schedule. Travis felt combat chaplains had no business going back to garrison hospitals — especially to visit family members. Although Major Edmister defended his choice to split my time between the field and the garrison, Travis fumed.

While we were at Fort Chafee, Colonel Molino's vehicle broke down. The Regimental Support Squadron Maintenance Troop overhauled it while Colonel Molino, Lieutenant Colonel Tucker, Major Jayne Carson and I sat in an Expando van. We shared a gourmet lunch of hot Meal Ready-to-Eat (MREs) and peanut butter crackers. Colonel Molino asked me, as he did once before, how we could reduce the number of unplanned pregnancies in our command. He then asked me what the stressors were that caused so much child abuse and so much psychological disintegration among our military spouses. He knew I attended all of our squadron's family support group meetings, all of the regimental and post-wide officer wives' meetings, and all of the chapel-based family meetings to which I was invited. With Major Carson and Lieutenant Colonel Tucker nodding in approval, I shared a number of family concerns that came up time and again.

First, I noted that the clinic appointment system was broken. There was only one phone line on which to make clinic appointments. The telephone lines were interminably busy. When you finally got through, the receptionist would state that no appointments could be made for three weeks or another month because the doctors were going on deployments or to their residence programs. When you got into a specialty clinic, you would find doctors sitting around, studying for their boards, seeing one or two patients in an afternoon. In desperation, families sat in the emergency room night after night to get relief for their babies' ear aches or other aggravating trifles.

Second, there was no such thing as proactive dental care — even for deployable soldiers. When you called to make an appointment to have your abscessed tooth treated, invariably, you were instructed to call back the following Tuesday between 7:00 and 7:30 A.M. This would go on for months. You skipped physical training to make the appointment, and the receptionist would repeat her instructions week after week, "Call back next Tuesday between 7:00 and 7:30 A.M."

Third, our soldiers and officer wives were frustrated that they were treated callously when they asked for treatment of pre-cancerous symptoms. More than one soldier and family member was laughed off or treated callously when they presented symptoms that warranted a cancer screening. More than one died or was only diagnosed when their cancers were in advanced stages.

Finally, our community hospital had no ability to care for high-risk pregnancies. When pregnant women went to our emergency room with symptoms of miscarriage, they were treated very cavalierly. Curiously, these contract doctors who would tell these women not to get so emotional about the loss of a six or eight week pregnancy were the same men who believed that abortion under any circumstances was nothing short of murder. Our hospital doctors would minimize the complaints of women who were carrying their second or third high-risk pregnancy. The wife of one of our Regimental Support Squadron officers gave birth to a stillborn baby in her seventh month. She went to the hospital three or four times, begging the hospital to help her. She knew days before that something was happening to her child. She was sent home each time without monitoring. This woman tried to obtain her hospital records to document the fact that the hospital was fully cognizant of her high-risk status, but the hospital claimed to have lost her records.

I was called by the hospital chaplain's assistant to help an enlisted man from a male combat battalion. His wife went to the hospital several times to beg for medical support. She was treated like a ditzy, attention-starved wife. After several weeks, the doctors finally examined her and discovered her child had died in utero. The woman ran away from the hospital when the doctors insisted she would have to go through labor. I went to the woman's home, prayed, did grief rituals and sat with her for hours before she finally agreed to return to the hospital to deliver her stillborn first child.

Colonel Molino took notes about all these medical situations. Then he asked me, as others did, how we could reduce accusations of sexual assault. I had not yet been called to the emergency room for a single accusation of rape that was anything more than a false allegation — usually to procure a morning after pill. I said the problem of false allegations would never go away so long as women were denied the right to obtain confidential abortions in military hospitals. I was not advocating abortion. I pointed out repeatedly that the military's prohibition against abortion was resulting in two tragedies: false allegations of rape as well as the abortion itself.

Colonel Molino closed the meeting by saying, "Chaplain deYoung, when I usually meet with my officers, I have a long list of things for them to do. Every time I visit with you, you give me a long list of things to do!"

He instructed me to get on Colonel Dunn's calendar to share with him the concerns of the female soldiers and spouses who were not receiving adequate gynecological care at Fort Polk. Colonel Dunn was the hospital commander. I agreed to represent all of the women in the 2nd Armored Cavalry Regiment by raising the concerns that surfaced repeatedly in our family support group meetings. This tasking outraged Chaplain Travis, despite his own frustrations with the hospital's treatment of his wife.

The third occurrence that outraged Chaplain Travis still frightens me when I recall it. Somewhere in the middle of our Arkansas deployment, a STRAK staff sergeant from Maintenance Troop chased after me.

"Ma'am, Ma'am. We need your help."

This man took his five-foot African-American female soldier to the medics after she doubled over with cramps. The woman was crying in agony. The sergeant took her over to the medical tent.

"Ma'am, when she got on the stool, the lieutenant physician assistant verbally abused her. He yelled at her and screamed at her. Ma'am, this isn't the best soldier in my squad, but that should never have happened!"

During my next visit to the medical troop area, I talked with the regimental surgeon, a sweet doctor who completed medical school but who never did a hospital residency. The lieutenant who allegedly abused our female soldier was painted up in clown makeup. None of the medical staff were busy training or treating soldiers. They were playing. I took the medical troop commander aside and let him know about the complaint I received.

"Well, you know, chaplain, she's female, under 40, not fat and she's fertile. There can't possibly be anything wrong with her."

The captain said military medics are supposed to screen symptoms through such analogues. They don't test, they don't examine. They run down checklists.

As a peer, I beseeched him, "You know, all over this regiment, soldiers are talking about the medical tent as a place where they'll be abused. Don't you think it's better to test first, then let the commander discipline the soldier if she is a malinger? Two of the physician assistants have had soldiers removed for malingering after it was proven the soldiers were not really ill!"

I asked the captain to just check into the situation to make sure the other soldiers felt safe going into the medical tent. He promised he would.

Another soldier from the chemical troop was being treated in the medical tent for some kind of rectal infection. The medics described his treatment.

"His butt was packed."

The doctors would not let me visit with him. When our field training was over, the doctors flew back to Fort Polk, but sent this man home on a twelve-hour bus ride. All of us who rode the bus were crammed into children's seats with our knees up to our chins. The soldier was taken to the hospital shortly after we returned to Fort Polk. He almost died from an infection. For more than a day, my command was in the throes of medically retiring the soldier until his condition finally stabilized.

When we returned to Fort Polk, our female soldier who had been verbally abused by the medical team expressed her fear that she was being retaliated against because she sought medical treatment in the field, and because she and her supervisor registered a complaint against the physician's assistant. Her mother called me on a Saturday morning.

"Chaplain, my daughter, she's been having those pains ever since her baby was born two years ago. The pain makes her cry, Chaplain. Why are they punishing her for goin' to a doctor?"

I asked Lieutenant Colonel Tucker, the squadron commander, to look into the accusations of poor medical treatment and retaliation against her. He consulted with Colonel Molino, then appointed a female officer to investigate.

The regimental commander sent me to meet with Colonel Dunn, the hospital commander on or about June 6, 1994. Colonel Dunn welcomed me to his office for a conversation about the medical concerns raised. Before the briefing, defensively, I gave him a quick review of my own training at HVP and work experience. I also insisted that I was not trying to usurp the judgement of doctors about the medical decisions that were made.

"I was a graduate of the Hospital of University of Pennsylvania Medical School," Dr. Dunn said quietly. "And so, let me just say, I know that you are not naive!" Dunn was gracious and receptive to our concerns. He listed many administrative changes he was in the process of making. He asked me to report that he had assigned a nurse administrator to fix the hospital's central appointment system. He promised to change some of the pharmacy and Ob/Gyn policies. He thought it good to send a gynecologist down to the troop medical clinic twice weekly to provide timely PAP smears for soldiers and spouses.

Both Dr. Dunn and the Emergency Room staff were legitimately concerned with the inundation of families in the ER for minor problems that could most likely be resolved with home remedies. He asked me to encourage the family support groups to bring out his community nurses to teach the families about homeopathic care for minor sniffles and scrapes. The medical system was clogged with family members who had problems that did not require a physician's care, which made it impossible to give adequate care to the more seriously ill. I agreed to bridge the relationship between the hospital and our military families by facilitating nurse practitioner workshops for our spouses.

Dr. Dunn supported plans to provide birth control education and improved access to birth control. He said he was not in the professional position to endorse the right of a woman to have an abortion at a medical facility. He fully understood the negative social by-products of denying desperate women choices. Dr. Dunn assured me that he would review medical procedures regarding a woman's privacy when she asked for permission to go to a civilian doctor for an abortion.

Most surprisingly, Dr. Dunn scoffed when I recounted the complaints of the physician assistants and doctors that women were abusing the system with excessive sick call.

"Your numbers are not out of line or disproportionately high..."

His rational response convinced me that he was working to rid the medical team of hostility, to provide better care and to rethink the balance between soldier care and family care. Some things were just out of Dr. Dunn's hands, however. The shortage of doctors, the proliferation of ready-made families in the junior enlisted population, and the extraordinary increase in single-soldier pregnancies and pregnancies by junior enlisted spouses put excessive strain on the system

Meantime, Chaplain Travis began to busy himself collecting evidence of my incompetence — despite the fact he had just given me a stellar report card when my primary raters changed from Major White to Major Edmister. He screamed at me that I had better "call off the medical investigation" or he would end my career. I was shocked. I reminded him that chaplains don't control investigations, commanders do. Chaplains are supposed to notify commanders of ethical, moral and morale issues that are detrimental. Chaplains were also supposed to help keep the command free of unethical pressures to cover up investigations. Chaplain Travis' threats against my career escalated.

Colonel Molino stopped the ruckus between Travis and myself for a while, but he left our command about July 7, 1994. Before he left, he gave me a signed

2nd Armored Cavalry Regiment poster with his handwritten note, "Chaplain Marie, you have done so much for our troopers. Thanks!" He also called me to the parade field to give me one of his limited regimental coins. These actions simply enraged Chaplain Brett Travis.

Within days of Colonel Molino's departure, Travis arranged for a meeting with myself and the two new, highest-ranking chaplains on post: Chaplains James and Chilen. Both of these chaplains issued grave threats that my career was in serious jeopardy. I asked them if they realized that Chaplain Travis was threatening my career because I had blown the whistle on the perceived medical abuse by our medical troop lieutenant. They did not ask any questions or express concern about Chaplain Travis' ongoing threats to end my career. Chaplain Chilen repeated his threat that he would not support my continued stay on active duty. I began to cry, which prompted Chaplain Chilen to suggest I was extremely hypersensitive, perhaps narcissistically so. Actually, I was crying with despair that for the third time in my life I had deluded myself into thinking the Army was an honorable, ethical institution where I could serve people with dignity. Worst, I believed that the chaplains, as they claimed in their regulations and manuals, were supposed to provide moral leadership, not mask corruption and bad treatment of soldiers.

By the fall of 1994, Chaplain Chilen managed to alienate almost every faith group on the post, to include his own Catholic community. He was, according to the post Director of Religious Education, a member of Opus Dei. He did not believe women should participate in any kind of liturgical leadership. He eliminated the contract for the Catholic female choir director. Except for the general's wife and other high-ranking officers' wives, he discouraged women from reading or distributing communion during the Mass. He wouldn't allow the Catholic priest, who was supposed to be the post Catholic chaplain, to run the parish. Instead, he reserved that role for himself and his male companion, a retired Spanish-speaking priest.

Chilen also tried to eliminate the African-American Full-Gospel service by removing the extremely charismatic African-American pastor and putting in a white Southern Baptist. The Southern Baptist, Don Caruthers, was an extremely sensitive and good chaplain. He was upset because he was removed from the mainly white Protestant service to cover a denomination that was Pentecostal, a shouting and falling-out congregation. I was tasked to preach to the vacation bible school class. It was hoped I would fail this assignment, because the vast majority of participants were fundamentalists, who are taught to shun Unitarians. In one sermon, I did a call and response with the kids, where I compared our need for Jesus to the need to have a good thick crust as the foundation of a delicious, gooey pizza. If you didn't have that crust, you were just going to have a sticky gooey mess on your hands. Life was like that, too. Our squadron dentist was an evangelical Christian. His wife came to me at the next family support group meeting and said her son just loved my sermons.

"Chaplain, I know you're a Unitarian, but my son said, 'Mom, she LOVES Jesus."

The main post chapel program was dominated by fundamentalists and conservatives, too. Chaplain Chilen assigned me to Chaplain John Powers, and later to Chaplain Roos for additional duties. Both of these men were extremely supportive of my work with the teenagers at the chapel. To their surprise, I was more conservative about youth activities than the average Christian. I did not think we should let our kids go off with soldiers, or to the theatres where, unsupervised, they could sneak into adult films. My new executive officer's wife was the post choir director. I sang in her choir on Sunday mornings, since Travis banished me from his pulpit for the second time. So, assigning me extra duties did not have the effect intended. Chaplain Chilen hoped to document that I could not work cooperatively with fundamentalists. The key leaders at the chapel supported my work and basically set aside the Unitarian label when they evaluated my work.

Finally, Chaplain Chilen wanted to end a weekly children's bible program, called AWANA (Approved Workmen Are Not Ashamed — based on a quote from Timothy). This program, although sponsored by fundamentalists is the most wonderful children's program. There are dozens of games and activities. The kids wear scout-like uniforms. They earn badges and medals as they memorize different sections of the bible. Chaplain Chilen wanted this program shut down because Catholic children wanted to participate. There was no Catholic alternative that was as much fun. The families who ran AWANA, to include my executive officer, Brent Edmister and his wife Linda, were incensed and fought to keep the program going. Chaplain Chilen put me in charge as the chaplain sponsor. He removed Don Caruthers, who was absolutely adored as the previous chaplain. Chilen hoped the fundamentalists would be so incensed at a Unitarian being assigned that they would protest. If they did protest, Chilen would have grounds to shut down the program. The kids at Polk needed this program, whether Catholic or Protestant. It was one of the healthiest activities available. They came in to the Chapel Center screaming with laughter. They left with blessed smiles on their faces. I met with Karen, the AWANA lay commander. We both agreed to cooperate in making the program a success for the kids and not to participate in the religious antagonisms that Chaplain Chilen seemed to foster. I was their chaplain adviser until I left the post.

Despite the fact that my work at the post chapel went well, and my commander and key leaders valued my work and our relationship as a community, Chilen and Travis continued to harass me and threaten my career.

When things got bad, I went to the Inspector General. The first time I visited the Inspector General, he ridiculed every concern I raised. The second time, at least half the other chaplains, all male, and dozens of congregants had registered similar complaints. The IG called in a Southern Baptist from the

Regimental Support Squadron Chorus

Company commander Captains Mitchell, Anderson and Feiereisen and soldiers visited nursing homes during the Christmas holiday.

Third Army to handle all of our complaints. This man reiterated, time and again, that Chaplain Chilen was considered the finest chaplain Third Army ever had. What was our problem? We met privately for a long time.

"Chaplain deYoung," he asked me. "Where do you see yourself 20 years from now? You could have a wonderful career as a chaplain. You can't be alleging racism and sexism and religious discrimination!"

Even after I elaborately described the threats and retaliation Travis and Chilen made, the chaplain asked, "Where do you see yourself 20 years from now?" I considered this question another corrupt threat.

"Sir, I was a real officer before I became a chaplain. I was trained never to respond to a problem based on my career aspirations, but based on what is right. I'm old. Don't worry about my career. But Don Caruthers is a fine, Southern Baptist chaplain. Worry about him. He is a good combat chaplain, and Chaplain Chilen is pushing him out. Caruthers can go to war as a combat chaplain. I can't. You need him more than you need me. I hope you will listen to those guys if you won't listen to me."

Four majors in my squadron were up for promotion in the same year. To give each the best opportunity for promotion, the executive officer changed three times during my tenure. When Brent Edmister left, Chaplains Travis and Chilen had the opportunity to carry through on their threat to destroy my career. On my final evaluation, both Brent Edmister and Ed Tucker gave me stellar ratings. Chaplain Travis wrote words that suggested I was the Army's worst chaplain ever. Both Brent Edmister and Ed Tucker advised me to protest the rating, which I did.

That process was convoluted and extremely painful. I experienced my own version of "data drag," which male soldiers experience when they try to defend themselves against criminal charges. I had to write to Department of the Army to get the secret and unsupportable charges that Brett Travis leveled against me to justify his false accusations. The documents did not reach me until after my rebuttal was over. One of the chaplains retrieved the post chaplain files, however, which documented the fact that Tyree, Copeland and others from the regiment refused to work with me. Chaplain Roos documented the fact that Chaplain Travis insisted he was morally obligated to put me out of the chaplain corps because of my Unitarian background.

Colonel Skip Sharp, the new regimental commander, did not care at all about the medical, family or ethical concerns that were at the heart of the disagreement between myself and Travis. Whereas Colonel Molino wanted religious tolerance, no gun violence, responsible drinking, positive activities for soldiers and families, and an end to domestic violence, Sharp made it clear he did not intend to focus on these things. He let Lieutenant Colonel Tucker know that he didn't want to hear anything about the whistle-blowing retaliation Travis conducted against me.

To defend myself I copied all the allegations that Travis had leveled against me, but for which he had never counseled me or presented me or my commander with any previous evidence or accusations. Based on the notes taken, and the supporting statements of my own commanders and Chaplain Roos, Colonel Sharp's investigating officer finally instructed Chaplain Travis to at least neutralize his comments.

Eventually, he did. With the help of their wives, Brent Edmister and Ed Tucker strengthened their comments in my evaluation. My raters suggested I needed to leave Fort Polk, or I would not survive Chaplain Travis. It was clear to both of them that both Travis and Chilen were hell-bent on putting me out of the Chaplain Corps.

Throughout all this, I became close to many families in my squadron, at the post chapel community, and ironically, even in the medical community. I sought comfort at the local Disciples of Christ Church. I preached there more than once, and visited church members in their homes. On post, my squadron had regular parties. We worked together to make the best of this stateside hardship assignment. We did our best to care for the young mothers and single soldiers. We went off for glamorous outings together in the local botanical gardens. Not only did we go on unit picnics together, we spent many evenings together in each others' homes.

Eighteen months after I arrived at Polk, it was clearly time for me to move on. My last Christmas there epitomized the mean-spiritedness that had infected some of our chaplains. For as long as I can remember, the Army has always compensated families by allowing generous time off after field problems, and during the Christmas season. The United States Army comes to a standstill from about the 15th of December through the New Years holiday every year. Nothing substantial gets done from Thanksgiving weekend until after January 1. Soldiers are released for block leave. Each section is reduced to a half-day or a day-on/day-off cycle for more than two weeks.

Unless strong single soldier programs are in place, Rapid Deployment Forces like the 2nd Armored Cavalry Regiment are ripe targets of opportunity for troublemakers during long holiday breaks. Only a small percentage of soldiers are allowed to go on leave because the rest are still on two-hour recall for world-wide deployment. Soldiers who have families can spend the time shopping, caring for children. Soldiers in the barracks are free to wreak havoc or find some outlet that can lessen their loneliness. In my first year, Colonel Molino asked his commanders to create special programs for the single soldiers to give them alternatives to what traditionally had amounted to a two-week drunk for barracks rats.

One city-wide project that I helped coordinate was founded and sponsored by Chaplain Kurt Pedder and the local ministers from Leesville: Operation We Care. This Thanksgiving and Christmas food basket program served needy families, guaranteeing all who qualified a fresh turkey with fixin's. To inspire the generosity of school children and local churches, the Leesville ministers depended on the cheerful labor of Fort Polk soldiers to help move, sort, pack and deliver all the food baskets. In 1993, the Leesville ministers' association invited chaplains at Fort Hood to provide music for their annual ecumenical kick-off service. At Chaplain Pedder's suggestion, I put together a music group. I gladly coordinated some choral music for Operation We Care.

This one program, Operation We Care, was the singular effort by local Christian (but not Catholic) organizations to bring all of the fractious groups together in Leesville. It created the kind of peaceful harmony that a sudden snowfall can bring to a rough-and-tumble, big-city neighborhood. Almost everyone united behind Operation We Care. The arch rival Baptists and Pentecostals. The poor and the affluent. Families and single people. To my delight, Operation We Care was the one program that even welcomed the participation of single soldiers.

With Chaplain Northrop's blessing, the group I put together sang at the Leesville service in 1993. We also sang during the weekend telethon to raise money for Operation We Care turkeys. We could never count on the same people participating because we were part of a rapid deployment force. Since we could deploy anywhere in the world on a moment's notice — especially to Fort Polk field sites — we learned how to substitute for each other just as spontaneously.

Music wasn't the only RSS contribution to Operation We Care. Soldiers from my squadron joined me to assemble foodstuffs and distribute baskets at the community center where town folk worked for days to create well-balanced meals for poorer families.

As the time came to plan for Operation We Care in 1994, Chaplain Chilen argued that the Army should not participate in the Leesville program, because Army soldiers shouldn't need food baskets at Christmas time. Actually, the program had a reputation for sending back 20 baskets per battalion each year — about 150 baskets to Fort Polk families.

By Christmas 1994, troopers in my squadron were emotionally invested in a number of community programs that we ran. We were going to participate in Operation We Care, then I was given direct orders by my chaplain supervisor, Brett Travis for me to discontinue my participation in these local volunteer church efforts that I did during off-duty hours.

For years before this sudden edict, and before I ever volunteered to help, the Army had provided five-ton trucks to gather the food, and soldiers to load the trucks and to deliver the baskets. Out of nowhere, Chaplain Chilen refused to provide any support whatsoever in '94. He eventually reneged when a local minister got in touch with the matriarch from one of those five families and had her whisper in the ear of someone in the General's office that he could expect a visit from her soon. Chaplain Chilen could read the writing on the wall. Knowing that he was going to be professionally embarrassed if he continued his present course, he soon reversed himself. He allowed my squadron's participation in Operation We Care. But I was not to have any public role in its operation. Was this restriction because I was a woman, a Unitarian, or both? Or was it because he knew that I had a lot of people power in the Leesville area because I worked with all the faith groups and in as many programs as necessary to keep our soldiers viably engaged?

Chaplain Travis insisted I was not permitted to participate in Operation We Care as part of my official duties. The religious program does not belong to the chaplain, however. It belongs to the commander. My commander still wanted RSS soldiers to get involved in community service, even if Colonel Skip Sharp didn't care about such things. Tucker permitted me to go on leave, that is, on vacation, so that I could continue to work with my soldiers in ecumenical and team-building efforts through my local church, the First Christian (Disciples) Church in Leesville. When Travis found out I was exercising my free right to religion and working through my local church as a volunteer during my off-duty hours, he insisted I return to active duty so that he could supervise my volunteer work.

We proceeded to put together the volunteers and the music that my RSS choir was asked to sing. The last gig was on cable television. It was one of the finest memories I had of the town folk who lived outside Fort Polk. Pastor Dub Williams from the Pentecostal Church made the same jokes as the year before about never expecting to see "ladies in the CAV! Do y'all wear those combat boots?" We tried to match the humor of the local gospel quartets, but Cajun humor takes a lot of learning. A young medic sang a sweet tenor solo both in the kickoff church service and before the television cameras. The Christian Motley Crew's lady lieutenant, a graduate of a New England military academy, played a mean fiddle solo. Plus she accompanied us during carols like Silent Night.

At our last telethon, Chaplain Lou Roos, the Fort Polk Protestant Pastor, asked me to present a check to Operation We Care representing the donation of

Fort Polk parishioners to this family support program. Sadly, for giving me that visibility, and for supporting my successful leadership of two programs Chaplain Chilen had instructed me to manage, Chaplain Roos took a lot of abuse and formal retaliation from his two chaplain raters, Chaplains James and Chilen.

Chaplain Roos and I both suffered for our stubborn participation in Operation We Care. Our young soldiers benefited, though, so it was worth it. During the 1994 Thanksgiving-Christmas family stand-down at Fort Polk, our young single soldiers got their picture in the Leesville paper, cockily driving their five-ton into the grade school playground to pick up the groceries. That's the kind of 15 minutes of fame we should do everything in our power to provide for the young of America, particularly the soldiers. They get so much more satisfaction out of their sudden celebrity than do the victims of gun violence. They are alive to read, clip, post and mail their newspaper stories to their mothers.

Chaplain Chilen worked hard to decimate my career for being so involved in social ministries, but since I had stepped up my programs, we had not had another soldier or family member death by accident or violence. Before I left Fort Polk, Sergeant Mac, a mechanic who was gruff but very compassionate about soldier problems, came to see me.

"Ma'am, I hate to see you leave. You will never know how many lives you saved on this post. But you saved a lot of lives."

The post family life chaplain whispered to me at my chaplain farewell luncheon, "Don't ever change, Marie. Don't change."

My commanders could never figure out what Chaplain Chilen had against me. Catholic soldiers in our command finally learned that Chilen was angry that I argued false accusations of rape would only stop if women were allowed to have confidential abortions in military hospitals. I never encouraged any woman to get an abortion. In fact, one of the trumped-up allegations Chaplain Travis coordinated with the hospital psychologist was that I allegedly interfered with a woman's right to choose abortion. I never did that either. I simply sent a woman to the hospital who made a false allegation of rape to get a morning after pill. I believed then, and I believe now, that a woman who accuses more than one man of raping her to get morning after pills needs psychological counseling.

Ironically, it was not only abortion that Chilen opposed, he also opposed emergency financial care for poor military families. Show me a pregnant woman who is financially desperate, and I will show you a woman who is a high-risk candidate for abortion. Through regimental channels, Chilen said that I disrespected his authority when I asked him to provide $150 emergency chaplain funds to a family for a medical emergency. In that case, a hospital doctor called me personally to get a not-too-bright private from Fort Polk to Brooke Army Hospital in San Antonio, Texas. The soldier's baby had gastrointestinal bleeding. Shortly before the doctor called me, two patients died from gastrointestinal bleeding that was not adequately treated by Fort Polk doctors. This doctor wanted the baby to be tested right away. He did not feel it was enough of an emergency to warrant a helicopter ride, but he didn't want the baby to wait ten days for the technician to show up at Polk.

When I called Chaplain Chilen to solicit emergency funds, he inquired icily, "Why does this family need money? The Army pays his food bills. He has a free apartment and free utilities. What do you mean he doesn't have any money to travel?"

We had to get the soldier on the road. When Chilen continued to insist the soldier should not need help from the emergency fund, I responded,

"Sir, I'm sorry I bothered you. I don't want to argue with you. We have to get this soldier on the road this afternoon. General Magruder doesn't want any more car accidents. I'll ask our soldiers to help out. I'll use my credit card if I have to. We have to get this soldier out tonight. The doctor just faxed me a letter stating the emergent need for this test."

Chilen frostily said, "Fine." Then he hung up. I asked the soldier's supervisor to go down to the motor pool to pass the hat for our hapless young man.

I asked the first sergeant if he could send another soldier on permissive temporary duty to do the driving. With the help of soldiers in the unit, we got the soldier and his baby on the road.

Many officers on the base complained more than once that Chaplain Chilen, who earned about $70,000 per year as a colonel, lived in a large government house with his male companion, another retired priest. Although non-married adults are not allowed to receive military benefits or housing, the commander wrote a letter authorizing Chaplain Chilen's companion full use of Army housing and benefits. I did not know this until a few days before I left Polk. I wouldn't mind sharing our bloated officer's benefit package with Chaplain Chilen's companion. I can understand his angry attitude towards any expression of support for a woman's right to choose for herself whether to keep or abort her child. But it was revealed to me that Chaplain Chilen's blinding hatred of me stemmed from my insistence that one way or another we were going to cough up $150 to help a dumb, broke private get his baby to the hospital for a life saving test. When my commander revealed this to me, I was confused enough to put off conversion to the Catholic faith or any Christian faith that seemed to demand such blinding, illogical obedience. It took me some time to realize that one man's leadership style does not represent the faith, or Christianity as a whole.

At some deep level, however, I knew that Chaplain Chilen's complaint that most of our soldiers' financial problems were self-inflicted were true. Most of the time, the chain of command bailed the soldier out of troubles. Sometimes, the soldier's lifestyle choice was so dysfunctional, even the most fatherly first sergeant couldn't help.

You could cynically argue that Chaplains Travis and Chilen were right about one thing: the mission to de-glamorize alcohol, guns and sex is an impossible one in the BOSS Army. Perhaps they were right. We cannot influence the behavior of soldiers. They are going to do what they are going to do. If that's true, then what do we pay leaders for? Why do we pay huge sums of money to put chaplains in every battalion? It is simply not true that soldier behavior cannot be modified. Experience proves otherwise. In the military, leaders change the behaviors, attitudes, and lifestyles of their soldiers every waking hour. Whatever behaviors the leaders choose to modify, they have it in their power to change by example, exhortation, and use of disciplinary measures designed to proscribe undesirable traits. Even the liberal church realized it had to restore its commitment to moral education in the youth.

As one minister put it, "By not directly teaching our young moral values, we created a vacuum. And in that vacuum, we inadvertently taught our young moral values — only they turned out to be negative values."

The key to positive change is identifying and rewarding positive social behaviors and de-glamorizing the destructive behaviors such as heavy drinking and promiscuity.

At Fort Polk I discovered the chaplains did not have the answer to the Army's moral and social crises. It was not safe for commanders to delegate their moral authority to the Chaplain Corps as it existed on Fort Polk. After consulting with several officers and chaplains from other posts, my conscience directed me to pierce the veil of illusion that made Fort Polk such an unsafe place for soldiers and for family members. I wrote General Magruder and the Chief of Chaplains, General Donald Shea. I thanked General Magruder for his generous support of my ministry during my 18 months at Fort Polk. I felt that he needed to know that his command climate was dangerous because of the repeated retaliations and career threats that were leveled by Chaplains Chilen and Travis, and some of the doctors in the medical community when certain troublesome healthcare practices were questioned.

I stated that according to chaplain regulations and guidance from my commanders, I brought several dangerous medical situations to the attention of our command and the hospital commander, Colonel Dunn. My commanders were most appreciative of the systemic issues that were raised. Indeed, Dr. Dunn took corrective actions to improve the healthcare delivery system once family concerns were raised. The chaplains, however, engaged in ongoing, hostile threats and acts of retaliation.

General Magruder called me to his office for a meeting with the post Inspector General. When I recounted the situations that sparked our crisis, he instructed the Inspector General to finally get to the bottom of my concerns.

I met with the IG, but this time, he did not toss off my complaints. He wrote out my concerns and then opened another investigation.

Before I left Fort Polk, I had many wonderful farewell gatherings with my soldiers. I coordinated an RSS spiritual leadership retreat where several officers helped me provide a day-long conversation among 35 officers. The next day, we held another conversation among 30-or-so senior sergeants. We used exercises to emphasize that soldiering was not just about a job, a skill, or a paycheck. And leading is not just about who's boss. That last retreat left me with the confident hope that the key leaders in my squadron were deeply aware how much power each had individually to divert young men and women who were so pigheadedly bent on self-destruction. They still had the power to mold the hearts of our young, even if the Army made this task more difficult. At the end of this retreat, the senior non-commissioned officers gave me a sterling box by which to remember them. My commander, Ed Tucker gave me a commendation medal. He recommended a meritorious service medal, but Colonel Skip Sharp downgraded it to the standard.

We had a command farewell during which we could laugh at the many crazy family and training situations we had shared during our 18 months together. The officers' wives gave me a Louisiana cookbook with a personal note from each woman. On my last Sunday morning, the post chaplain, Chaplain Roos honored me by thanking me for my work with AWANA and with the teenagers who attended Wednesday night bible studies. He gave me a gift on behalf of the congregation, and then allowed me to share some parting thoughts.

Towards the end of my tour, the Supply and Transportation Troop held a formal cavalry renewal of wedding vows for one of their sergeants who was already married for twelve years. His wife wanted a church wedding. She was as stunning as a young newlywed bride. One of the S and T lieutenants, an OCS graduate, had grown quite friendly with me. Less than a week before I left, his baby almost died. I drove to the Shreveport critical care center to be with his wife. Mrs. P. talked for hours about how many times she took this baby to the Fort Polk Emergency Room only to be treated with disdain. The baby had multiple birth defects. Thank God, this woman insisted that her baby's blue lips needed medical attention. The baby was medically evacuated to Shreveport. I was awestruck by the tenderness this man and wife showed to their paralyzed baby. We prayed for the baby's recovery. The baby came home finally. A day before I left Fort Polk, this family asked me to baptize their baby. I will never forget the reverence with which we shared this moment.

I was called down to the Non-commissioned Officers' Club for a meeting on my last working day. I was greeted there by a room full of soldiers, spouses and officers from all the troops with whom I served. They gave me little gifts by which to remember them. The chemical troop, known as the Chem Dogs gave me a pencil holder, a droopy dog. They signed the cup, "The 87th Chemical Company thanks you for your moral and spiritual support."

Even though I received lots of heartfelt affirmations from my squadron community, by January of 1995, I was really hurting. I had thought I was going to climb to the mountain top on eagles wings, but found myself, like Sisyphus, constantly pushing the rock up the hillside. In all of this insanity, I found God at Fort Polk, through the kindness and compassion of the many who refused to give in to the culture of retaliation and despair. The Fort Polk Christians made a Christian out of me.

The day that movers packed up my household for Korea in January 1995, an RSS officer's wife knocked on my apartment door. Despite extensive counseling after she lost her baby during childbirth and long prayer sessions with her pastor, she felt a need to hold the Army accountable for the mistreatment she received, which she believed contributed to her baby's death. She was still angry that the hospital would not release her medical records.

By this time, the medical treatment of soldiers and family members had reached crisis proportions. On that same day, a hospital nurse knocked on my apartment door to tell me that the hospital would finally have to take seriously all of the complaints about the mistreatment of family members. She said that a twelve-year-old child was taken to the emergency room by his parents, both soldiers who worked at the hospital. The ER nurse who treated the asthmatic child kept yelling at the child to "Shut up and take your medicine." The nurse gave him nine or ten inhalation treatments, when only one or two are supposed to be administered at a time. The child panicked, and begged the nurse to stop the treatment. "Shut up and take your medicine!" The nurse yelled again. The child died from cardiac arrest.

When Mrs. K, mother of the stillborn child, came to share her grief with me, and her need to hold the Army accountable, I felt it would be obscene to discourage her. I went to the *Army Times* newspaper and gave her the telephone numbers for lawyers who specialized in wrongful death lawsuits for military family members.

On my very last day at Fort Polk, I was called back to General Magruder's office for a follow-up meeting. Chaplain Chilen was with me. The General asked the IG to run down the list of situations that contributed to the rift between myself, Travis, Chilen, and some of the doctors at the hospital.

I asked for him to review the psychiatric admissions procedures and to establish a policy of round-the-clock psychiatric evaluations for our suicidal or violently mentally ill soldiers and family members.

He said, "Would it satisfy you to know that Lieutenant Colonel F has been asked to retire immediately?"

All's Well That Ends Well

This Toujour Pret photo of the 2nd ACR leaders was given as a farewell gift to Colonel Molino. (Holding the emblem: LTC Ed Thomas Tucker, RSS Commander and Colonel Molino, 2nd ACR Commander. Major Edmister stands to the left of Tucker. Major Jayne Carson stands far right, second row. Top row: OCS graduates 2LT Perez and the author.)

I asked him to make sure that soldiers and family members were not retaliated against when they raised complaints about medical treatment. He assured me he was handling that.

I asked him to declare the command's commitment to religious pluralism. He vowed to do that.

I asked him to put in place formal military ethics training for the officers and the chaplains, since the behavior of both chaplains and some hospital staff were countermanding the Army's official policies and standards of conduct.

I thanked him on behalf of family members for encouraging improved medical care for female soldiers, access to birth control, and improved care for family members. I did not ask General Magruder to admit personal knowledge of the hospital breakdown. Surely he was familiar with this problem. One evening, when I went to the hospital to visit 82nd Airborne soldiers who were injured in a drop, I watched Mrs. Magruder leave for a helicopter ride with the 82nd commander to get medical treatment at a "real" army hospital for her own problems. Junior enlisted wives needed the same serious attention, but until this investigation was over, they weren't getting it.

General Magruder advised me that I would be transferred to the 19th TAACOM (Theatre, Army Area Command). I would become the deputy command chaplain, which was a lieutenant colonel's slot. I was still a captain. Magruder turned to Chaplain Chilen and instructed him not to call, write, or telegraph in any way his feelings or attitudes about me or my work as a chaplain. Chaplain Chilen promised to comply.

Once again, General Magruder thanked me for my hard work as a chaplain and for the many courageous sermons and stands I had taken.

"A word of advice, Marie. If you want to stay in the military, you must learn how to handle these matters differently. You must try a different approach."

Well, that was advice I had heard from Lynda in years past. Now I was hearing it from my favorite general. By and large, he was extremely appreciative of my ministry. He gave generous praise whenever I provided an invocation, a sermon, or a memorial reflection. He called me a leader when I came to the rescue of a visiting priest who had not been properly supported by the fundamentalist chaplain assistants. He took action to solve the grave problems I brought to his attention. And, he sent me on my way to have a hopefully much brighter experience as a junior chaplain. By February 9, 1995 I would report to the 19th TAACOM as the Deputy Command Chaplain.

I thanked General Magruder, then returned to the squadron to thank my commander and my friends — the officers and enlisted with whom I had served. I typed a few letters of recommendations for soldiers, then said, for the last time, "Tojour Prets!"

CHAPTER 14

Land of the Morning Calm

God and the Chief of Chaplains saw fit to reassign me to the Republic of Korea. Not without a struggle, though. My chaplain supervisors did not want me to leave Fort Polk with Unitarian Universalist chaplain credentials in tact. All of my commanders and the Inspector General realized, however, I had to leave the base immediately if I was to survive chaplain politics.

Instinctively, I knew that Korea would be difficult, but not a hardship for me. Korea would be a healing experience. I wanted to serve the Army in Korea because my father and my ex-husband served in that great country. I'm a half-hearted abstractionist. I don't learn best by reading or memorizing theories. I learn by walking around in other peoples shoes. I knew that if I moved to Korea, I would learn much about my father, my ex-husband, and of the Americans who served in the Korean Conflict.

In 1993, Chaplain Pedder had sent me into the backwoods of Louisiana to celebrate women's contributions to the United States Army. I spoke in Alexandria at a Veterans Day service, during which I extolled the sacrifices of men and women from the time of the American Revolution to the present day. Women thanked me with tears in their eyes when I mentioned the forgotten sacrifices of our Korean War veterans, noting they were usually not remembered in the annual litany of sacrifices of our soldiers. The following Memorial Day weekend, I evoked images again, particularly from the Korean War, of men and women who were forgotten, but not without valor. Women and men approached me with tears to thank me for honoring their voluntary sacrifices.

These moments made me realize our family had done a great disservice to my father and other relatives who served in Korea — but who were treated as if their service was as routine as driving a taxicab. I wanted to learn more about the war that nobody talked about — not in school, not in military training, and certainly, not in the family.

Before I was even conceived, my father served as an enlisted signal corps soldier in Korea. I sometimes think I would never have been born if it was not for the Korean War. Twentieth century wars have brought together the most unlikely couples. In the old movies, war time love matches are divinely inspired, driving soldiers to super human feats of heroism and chivalry. And the lovers live happily ever after. In real life? Only when I became a minister and privileged to the stories of so many did I discover that war shapes lives in unimaginable ways, and it often destroys the best of men and their families, especially those whose lives were melded together by wars that were so irrelevant to the families into which they were born.

The Korean War, or as it is dubiously called, the Korean Conflict, was the first American war that seemed to be at once necessary to the survival of democracy yet irrelevant to the Americans who sent men to fight there. My year in Korea convinced me more than ever that if that war never occurred, I would never have been born.

James Peter deYoung was like so many Korean and World War II veterans. Once he returned from the war, all he ever wanted was a quiet, stable family life. He met my mother in a small town during his Army training. My father was exceedingly handsome and slender. My mother promised all the joys of family life. They married to secure their dreams. In their wedding pictures, my mother has an ecstatic look of triumph. She obviously clinched the most handsome guy on the training base, and he looked exceedingly proud to have this gentle Irish lass with soul-piercing eyes as his new bride.

Shortly after, my father went off to Korea for the rest of his Army enlistment. My pregnant mother stayed with her family in Tuscarora, Pennsylvania, while my father fought in Korea. My brother was born while my father was overseas. I was the first born after my father's return. I don't think much time elapsed between his return and my conception.

James Peter deYoung's longing for real family was typical of so many GIs then and now. The guys are almost robotic in their relentless capacity to somehow intertwine fantasies of combat heroism with dreams of perfectly stable, loving families as their rightful reward. Neither will materialize for the unstable men in real life, but that doesn't stop the Army from promising both heroic adulation and old-fashioned family living to the underprivileged to fill its ranks.

The better soldiers, and my father was one, at least achieve a lifetime of stability, if not of real happiness and security. The most secure, the most well-raised, will come home from war with dark secrets. Stories, images, and horrors that will change them, separate them from their families with whom they will never unburden themselves.

Like so many veterans of the Korean War, my father's service went completely unnoticed and unappreciated in my family and community. This was partly his choice. James Peter deYoung never talked about his war time service. He never displayed military photographs of himself or his wartime buddies. I only saw a picture of him in Army fatigues after my grandmother's funeral. Jim had the slender figure of a soccer player. His buddies snapped a photo of him patrolling down a Korean dirt road with his rifle pointed out. Though smiling, he was obviously out of his element.

Whenever the movie *Pork Chop Hill* played, my father would encourage his children to gather round so they could understand what the Korean War was like. When my baby sister Alice was born, my father took charge of the kitchen for a week while my mother was in the hospital. One day he made Korean fried rice with all the leftovers in the refrigerator. We hated the rice, because it was not like Chinese fried rice - it wasn't crunchy with scallions and celery or browned with soy sauce. The night before our youngest sister was brought home from the hospital in 1964, my father took us to a Chinese restaurant to celebrate with real fried rice, for which we forgave his innocent attempt to bring Korean culture to our lives.

I never saw my father's version of fried rice again until I lived in Korea. Korean rice is different from Chinese or Indonesian fried rice. The rice is klumpy, and still white after it is fried. Vegetables such as carrots and peas are mixed in. No wonder American kids don't like it. Fried rice is supposed to be a treat. We don't eat peas and carrots as a treat. Whatever made my father think we could possibly enjoy such stuff? Of course, what he hoped to do was share a part of his life that we knew absolutely nothing about. Now, I regret I was not old enough or worldly enough to ask him about his life in Korea. Whenever a plate of Korean rice is set in front of me, I think of my father. How did he learn to make it? Who cooked this rice for him? What were the Korean people like? How in God's name did he survive an experience like Pork Chop Hill?

If it is true that immature women often marry their fathers, I certainly married the better parts of my father when I married Al Doeve. As an Indonesian-Dutch immigrant to the United States, he felt compelled to volunteer for the United States Army during the Vietnam war. The Army obliged Al by sending him to Korea. Like my father, Al had a strong distaste for guns and war..

When I met him, he declared himself a pacifist and filed for conscientious objector status, which he obtained after his tour of duty in Korea was over.

Although we are not at war with North Korea, assignment to the Eighth United States Army is still just one step away from war, for the Korean conflict was never formally ended. Assignment to this remote country will inevitably alter a soldier. Americans put their lives on the line in a country that is both beautiful and terrifying in its fratricidal history as a divided, conquered but proud and ethnically pure nation. I knew I had to spend some time in Korea if I was going to close the chapter on my life as a daughter and wife of veterans of the Korean Conflict.

I never spelled out these reasons to my colleagues or superiors. It proved not to be necessary. When it came time to choose, I asked one last time for Korea. General Magruder and General Shea were kind enough to arrange for my transfer. And so, without ever having the opportunity to talk to my dad again, I was able

Young Lovers

Alice Marie Coleman and James Peter deYoung are triumphant on their wedding day.

to tend, for the first time in my life, to the unanswered question of why Korea was an important, if absolutely unspoken, influence on my father and on the entire unfolding of our family life. How did Korea shape the changes in my husband's personality, and how did it intrude into my marriage?

Why was America still there, after all these years?

In early February of 1995, I boarded an evening flight that would stop in Detroit and continue on to Seoul, Korea. The 14-hour flight was uneventful. The in-processing for soldiers assigned to the Eighth Army begins at Kimpo Airport. Since I was to be an assistant command chaplain, I was given royal treatment by Sergeant DeGlopper and his assistant from the 34th Support Group in Yongsan. The men walked me through the various inspection points and carried my bags to their sedan.

They arranged for me to stay in the Dragon Hill Hotel for my first night — a luxurious military hotel that serves as a grotto for Americans stationed all over the rock. I did not appreciate the gesture at the time, but I was later to realize that accommodations at the Dragon Hill are very hard to come by. Here you could watch cable television, bathe in steamy hot water, pick up great literature, buy stunning Oriental paintings, and jog on high-tech treadmills with headsets to pick up the latest news from CNN or C-Span. You could splurge on the most exquisite fresh shrimp and cantaloupe. Whatever you needed to remind you that you were not just a grunty soldier but a human being from the most privileged society in the world, the Dragon Hill Hotel was the place to get it.

Father Louis Schmidt, the command chaplain for the 19th TAACOM had been without an assistant for some time. On the last leg of his two-year tour, he was advised that he would go directly from one overseas tour to Germany for another three-year tour. Very few Protestant chaplains would suffer the indignity of two back-to-back overseas assignments, but Catholic priests are often forced to do this, because the priest shortage is perpetually acute. The men who comply quickly learn they must leverage their sacrifices for other forms of support — or they will burn out. Nobody wants to be useless to God and country. Louie Schmidt was no exception. He gracefully complied with the extended overseas tours, but insisted upon administrative support. He was granted his wish for transitional assistance in the form of one chaplain captain — me.

Within two or three days of my arrival, I moved to the Army's Religious Retreat Center in Itaewon. This beautiful compound is set on the side of one of Seoul's mountains. A Buddhist temple straddles the other side. The Retreat Center was a gift to the United States Army for its intervention during the War. I had a few more days to acclimate myself, after which the entire Unit Ministry team would gather at the Retreat Center (RC) or their bi-annual training meetings.

I learned at once that Koreans think of their mountains as sacred places. There are many sacred mountains throughout Korea where the people walk to regain their serenity, communicate with their ancestors, and generally partake of the spiritual forces that descend upon those who climb to the mountain top. The mountains in Korea look exactly like the mountains in upstate Pennsylvania. Even after he became an agnostic, whenever we drove to Tuscarora as a family, my father would break from his quiet reflections and chant, "Here we are! We're in the mountains! This is God's country!" I could never understand the incongruence of his beliefs until I walked up and down the sacred mountains in Korea. The Korean people teach us well that in the mountains, God speaks to the loneliest aching souls.

Chaplain Schmidt soon introduced me to his sergeant in charge, Sergeant Park, a Korean-born former Republic of Korea army soldier who thought of himself as a Presbyterian evangelist, and the ideal link between American and Korean augmentee soldiers (KATUSAs).

Sergeant Park did not have any relationship with his subordinates, or with the chaplains in the 19th TAACOM, for that matter. He was almost 50 years old, and quite traditional. He drove the chaplain's sedan back to Taegu on the final day of our conference and loaded it with goodies for his family and my two bags. Chaplain Schmidt and I took the free Korean train from Seoul to Taegu as part of my orientation.

After my horrendous experience with Chaplain Chilen, who made it his business to put myself, a few other Protestant chaplains, and many Catholic women volunteers out of the religious programs, it was quite a shock to encounter Chaplain Schmidt's warm inclusive style of ministry.

Louie was near mandatory retirement age. His total focus was on the Catholic community and on the social well-being of the command group he

Blessed Be God

Chaplain Louis Schmidt presides at the Ecumenical Seder at the 20th Support Group Chapel.

served. The 19th TAACOM, although a mammoth theatre-wide organization in wartime, was a paper tiger in peace. Each section at the headquarters was only one deep. Our operations were entirely notional. We reviewed plans. We created new scenarios or support systems. We monitored the work of subordinate units in the field to test existing or future operations orders. Mostly, we partied and waited our time until we could go home to the U.S.A.

The 19th TAACOM was not without a mission during Louie Schmidt's tenure, however. He was part of General Brown's command group that confronted the ugly possibility of war due to the North's famines and nuclear inspection standoffs. For years before, nothing had happened at all in the 19th TAACOM. One senior sergeant showed me all the plans that he assembled in the war room that should have been there since the Korean War. Until the 1994 scare, plans were non-existent — at least in the secure offices where they should have been on file.

Father Schmidt was the gentle cajoling party spirit who spiritually motivated all of Brown's commanders and section leaders to quietly and doggedly change the TAACOM culture from a gaggle of clock watchers to a coherent team of planners and analysts. By the time I got there, most of the work had been done. My job was to help Chaplain Schmidt finalize the unit ministry team plans and to support the 22 chaplains who were spread from Pusan to Camp Red Cloud, Pyongtaek and Waegwon.

On that first train ride with him, the unbearable loneliness of a Korean tour was palpable in his every word. Despite his valorous efforts to maintain dignity and joviality, Father Schmidt's loneliness was real. He would look out the train window and stare into the smoky gray skies, then squint as he panned the ossified mud fields. I could not imagine why he would tolerate another overseas tour when he was obviously devastated by the isolation Korea had brought. But his disciplined tone suggested he had learned decades ago that most places in the world were, when you got down to the heart of it, very lonely for leaders and for priests.

Chaplain Schmidt looked out over the crusty brown barren fields as he pointed out the contrasts between the modern cities and the straw huts that still housed thousands of people on the perimeter of every city along the railway tracks. He imparted lessons about food choices. He expressed his gentle frustration with the language difficulties of his staff. Our sergeant in charge and his secretary were wonderful people, but neither could write or type in English. Even when Chaplain Schmidt's letters and documents were perfectly drafted, somehow, pigeon English was injected into the final draft by the NCOIC or his secretary. Even after Chaplain Schmidt corrected the errors, new ones would pop in. It was almost impossible to get out a correct English document, despite the sincerity of the staff. Thus, my first task was to monitor all the documents that flowed to ensure minimally professional standards of English. I did not signal my displeasure that I was being tasked to do a sergeant's administrative work. If I was going to be a weenie paperwork supervisor full-time, however, I knew I wasn't going to last long as a chaplain.

As I stirred my instant Korean espresso, Louie Schmidt ventured into his frustrations about the relationship between Sergeant Park, his non-commissioned officer in charge and the 20-or-so chaplains in the 19th TAACOM. Sergeant Park served as the sergeant in charge of all the chaplains during the Basic Officers Course. The Chaplain Corps should never have put sergeants in charge of commissioned officers, but indeed, they committed this fatal flaw during my course as well.

Sergeant Park saw himself as the supervisor of chaplains, which was deeply resented by all. Not only because he was a sergeant, but because he was highly judgmental of American ministers, despite having no professional or personal credentials by which to be so condescending. Park was a fundamentalist evangelist, a preacher-wanna-be. Who knows why he never pursued a Masters of Divinity, because his education would have been completely subsidized. Presbyterians in the United States go to extreme lengths to educate Korean men for the pastorate — and they produce many fine Korean Presbyterian pastors, too.

I don't know what Park was like at the basic course, but chaplain captains in Korea who suffered his supervision at the Chaplain School were extremely resentful that Chaplain Schmidt deferred all management problems to Sergeant Park for adjudication. It was now my job to mediate between Sergeant Park's history of verbal abuse and derogation of the chaplains. We had to resolve the chaplain management problems that had been left to Sergeant Park's discretion.

I could see that Chaplain Schmidt was extremely pastoral but equally conflict-avoidant. He wanted peace, harmony and kindness to prevail. He would come to the rescue of any soldier or young officer to prevent their career failure.

He wanted competence in his office, but just didn't have the heart to take on the hard management problems directly. As long as he was without an assistant command chaplain, he let a sergeant fill the role — giving Sergeant Park the opportunity to relive his glory days as a tyrant supervisor of officers whom he deeply distrusted and disrespected.

After we reached our headquarters, Chaplain Schmidt made it clear we would have absolutely no privacy, so he covered the difficult subjects, unburdened himself, on this train with dozens of anonymous Korean civilians as trustworthy observers. He had one more concern — soldier misconduct. Chaplain Schmidt described the classic social dilemmas American soldiers created for themselves which were disheartening to him, but all-too-familiar to me during my two prior tours on active duty. Father Schmidt was at an age when the world should have been a more uplifting place — more focused on the spiritual, the good, the beautiful, the true. The reality he confronted in Korea was misery.

Korea was a nasty place where soldiers lapsed into the four big addictions (women, alcohol, drugs, gambling) with the same compulsivity you would only expect in America. Schmidt recognized that punitive strategies against behaviors born of human frailty were futile in such a far-off and forgotten place. He was realistic enough to know, nonetheless, that these kinds of indulgences could no longer be tolerated in a sophisticated anti-American country. The political reality was such that one incident reported on CNN could incite a riot, or even an international cry for U.S. withdrawal from Korea altogether. Indeed, before my tour was over, the Okinawa rape case exploded in our faces.

As Louie continued to confide some of the scandals he was manipulating behind the scenes, I wondered, as a junior captain, what I could do about the sex, wine, women and criminal indebtedness? Schmidt had no answers — only an attitude of compassion towards those who succumbed to the temptations.

Louis Schmidt exuded kindness, in stark contrast to Chaplain Chilen. I wondered if God intended for me to be placed in his care to be reminded that most ministers and priests really devoted their lives to healing and spiritual comfort — not to consolidation of power. Schmidt seemed to be a good priest in every sense of the word. In this one afternoon, I felt myself being tugged back to the church, but I said nothing. Later, I asked him if he would be offended if I attended Catholic masses during my tenure. He was horrified when I pointed out not all chaplains could morally tolerate religious crossover — they wanted their services to be denominationally pure, and they wanted incompatible denominations to be cleansed from the Army ranks. Schmidt's services were open and welcoming to all. American or Korean. Soldier or civilian. Catholic or non-Catholic. Private or General. Gay or straight. Children or elderly. I found myself joining his Catholic community, since, once again, I was excluded from most of the regular Protestant preaching schedules because of my denomination.

The next five months were spent rewriting the Chaplain handbook, visiting all of the chapels run by the 19th TAACOM, and generally having a good time learning about Korea and socializing with the officers and wives who lived in Taegu.

There were financial improprieties in the 20th Support Group Chaplain Fund that could easily have been avoided if the chaplain who managed the fund complied with the guidelines given by the command auditors. Those two men refused to comply at first, because the guidance was administered in a punitive disrespectful way by Sergeant Park. As it turned out, the captain who managed the fund seems to have been one of Park's students. The mutual antipathy between these men was beyond dispute. More than $40,000 was described as missing from the fund, however, so the auditor's guidance could not be ignored just because Sergeant Park was functioning as a deputy command chaplain. When I took over, there was still a brouhaha, but the chaplains from the 20th Support Group soon complied when I staffed the problem horizontally and vertically until General Brown had enough knowledge to throw his weight behind immediate resolution.

General Brown came to me privately and informed me that the previous chaplain in Seoul was a fallen down drunk Catholic priest who managed to ignore his responsibilities to the point where hundreds of thousands of dollars were embezzled from the chaplain fund.

"That Chaplain Billy Fowler has done a wonderful job of straightening this out. I don't want any repeats down here in the 20th."

Chaplain Schmidt instituted a chapel visitation program. For more than 18 months, he traveled with his sergeant to every chapel to make sure the facilities were clean, accessible and filled with programs and activities. He also wanted to be sure the chaplains were visible and available to both soldiers and commanders. By the time I arrived, Chaplain Schmidt was eager to delegate the visitation program to me. Sergeant Park had gone out on his own, but once again, a number of chaplains were alienated by his verbal abuse and put-downs of their work. I saw the program differently than Sergeant Park. Our subordinate chaplains were isolated, considered rabbit feet by most commanders — talismans to ward off death, corruption, and poor morale. I felt our visits from the TAACOM should be helpful and supportive of their tribal spiritual leadership.

At first, Sergeant Park and I traveled together. We took the train to Seoul once. Another time, we took the train to Pusan. We drove to Waegwon with the two chaplains who pastored the Camp Carroll community. Eventually, we met Chaplain MacGregor at Camp Red Cloud. Chaplain MacGregor drove us more than once to Camp Page and Camp Eagle on the Eastern Corridor. During our first trips in late February and early March, the Korean countryside was

You Call This A Hardship Assignment?

As Assistant Command Chaplain, the author traveled to remote locations to support the soldiers and chaplains. During Easter weekend, she flew to Korea's beautiful Chejudo Island to perform a soldier's wedding and lead Easter Services. (Pictured here in front of flowers.)

depressingly bereft of living plants or color. The skies were dull brownish pewter, thick with smog. Despite the fact that Korea was now considered a first-world economic power, you would never have known it by the unrelenting stretches of impermeable crusted winter dirt.

During one or two trips, Sergeant Park wanted to share the wonders of Korea with me, so along the way, we stopped for tea and soup and kimbob. Wherever we could select tree-lined bus routes, we did. The Korean War devastated the countryside and mountains. To recover, the country carefully planted evergreens and flowering trees to protect the soil and restore a measure of beauty to the land.

The lessons of the Korean War began to speak to me as I ventured from camp to camp. In every headquarters building, there were candid shots of American GIs and of the Korean countryside during the War. Even in prosperous times, Korea was a painfully frigid and depressing place to be in winter. I could not imagine how all those young GIs and nurses survived in tents where the winds can knock down your equipment and freeze your bones in ten minutes flat.

There were many pictures of Korean families expressing their gratitude to our soldiers by bringing them hot, steamy plates of rice and fresh vegetables. You could see the affection-starved souls of our men in these images. The humanity of the Korean people was so beyond question that soldiers came to believe their mission to save the Koreans from communism was sacrosanct.

Korean children smiled just as angelically in the War as they do today. It was not difficult for me to understand how that craving for family would impel a man to sacrifice part of his life heroically for people who did not look like him, dress like him, eat like him or live like him. The GI's craving for family also fueled his dream that he would be rewarded some day with the same kind of simple comfort – a tender wife and adoring, happy, playful children crawling around his legs.

In 1995, American GIs came from poor family backgrounds just as my father did, except not only were their families economically poor and emotionally broken, their cities were ruined, too. These GIs were no less inclined than the GIs who served in the Korean War to gaze longingly at the chirpy, laughing little boys and girls who walked freely in their city streets. Korean children exuded contentment and well-being early in the morning and late at night as they ambled from home to tutors to school to tutors and back home late each evening. They gave our disadvantaged young adults something to hope for.

If the American Army is going to be the re-mediation program of last resort, then every GI should be required to serve one year in Korea. No guns are allowed. The society is extraordinarily devoted to education. Traditional Korean culture is available in every town. There are cultural activities; classical music and art museums are a short cab ride away. When our GIs see the photos of a country that was laid to waste, completely leveled during the war in the early '50s, but yet a prosperous, relatively crime-free, well-educated society today, they know the American way leaves a lot to be desired. It is unthinkable for Koreans to leave their children illiterate. We think nothing of letting children pass from grade to grade without learning how to write their names. It is unconscionable for Koreans to have guns in the home. We literally defend to the death our right to conceal handguns. Korean divorce is almost unheard of. In America, fidelity in marriage is laughable. Korea stirs up deep longings in the young GI who knows that life can be much better. They get their first taste of it in the Land of the Morning Calm.

The 19th TAACOM headquarters is broken up into little compounds in one vicinity of Taegu. Most of the office buildings were on Camp Henry. Some enlisted soldiers and the guesthouse residents lived there. Single officers lived at the top of the hill on Camp Walker. The junior officers' club was situated at the head of the BOQ complex. Dozens of family bungalows and a few barracks buildings dotted the base of the camp.

This enclave, the Taegu Country Club, had a supermarket, theatre, the only medical and dental clinics available to soldiers, a heli-pad, a Burger King, a theater, a small department store, a recreation center for teens, a gym, and an Anthony's Pizza.

The Senior Officers' Club hosted most community functions. The TAACOM sponsored People-to-People dinners, giving soldiers and civilian employees a chance to learn about Korean culture. Ladies wore traditional flowing costumes and performed fan dances. Lengthy friendship speeches were proclaimed by General Brown and his Korean counterparts. Every word was re-uttered by an English or Hangul translator for those who could not understand the primary language of the speaker.

There were banquets and breakfasts and dances and all kinds of classy Hails and Farewells to make the time fly by at the TAACOM. Even the officer wives' group held elegant little parties in their bungalows or at the Club to keep up the spirits of all.

Best of all, Taegu teemed with culture. You could jump in a cab with three other people and attend the classical symphony or a concert by solo artists — usually by musically gifted blind students. Not since San Francisco had I lived on an Army base where it was so easy to gather a half-dozen soldiers together and take them to the arts center or to a concert.

Apsan, Taegu's sacred mountain, towered next to Camp Walker. On Saturday mornings, the best rejuvenation was a leisurely climb up the sculpted paths of Apsan. When the azaleas blossomed, and the scented wild flowers beckoned, God's presence was unmistakable. There were Buddhist meditation temples at several points along the climb for those so inclined.

The Deputy Chaplain slot was about getting paper work properly shuffled and personnel and spiritual support to our men and women in the field. I was in the peculiar situation of serving a group of majors and captains who outranked me. The Army depends on position authority to get a lot of administrative work done, however. I changed the name of our field visits from "command chaplain inspections" to "technical support" visits. By April, I had managed to form a good rapport with a number of the chaplains. Several of the chaplains asked me to preach at their chapel. This was a thrill. I can now say to my sisters' grandchildren that as a token female chaplain, I've preached in Pusan, Waegwon, Pyongtak, Uijongbu, Seoul and Tongduchon. More than once, I flew to Chejudo to preach and do a wedding there. Later, when I joined the Second Infantry Division, I preached in other towns.

Chaplain Tyson called me from the Eighth Army Headquarters and asked me to preach at the quarterly chaplain training retreat at the end of April, 1995, which would be focused on preaching. This respite allowed me to visit with the 40 other chaplains in country. Although we were busy preparing for General Brown and Chaplain Schmidt's change of command, I needed to spend time with my peers. Chaplain Tom Norton, from the Army's War College Department of Ethics, taught the sessions on preaching. He was recommending ways to bridge sermonic themes with popular culture when he mentioned he loved to preach the Gospel using Willie Nelson Texts.

"I've never been able to preach to the tune 'You can't hang a man for shootin' a woman who tried to steal his horse!'

The male audience hooted with laughter.

Around that time Timothy McVeigh and other Army renegades had blown up the federal office in Tulsa, Oklahoma. By then I was passionately convinced that what we preached had a direct correlation on whether or not our soldiers blew up buildings or beat their spouses. We could inspire soldiers to resolve their frustrations civilly and work out their family problems amicably.

The next morning, I preached at our chaplain's worship service before class. The sound of 40-or-so men singing gospel hymns in a resonant chapel was very moving. I was aware of their discomfort that I, the token female had been given this special privilege — the opportunity to preach to a community of preachers. I thanked Chaplain Tyson for giving me the opportunity to demonstrate what a sermon from a token female would sound like. They laughed. Then I began.

"You can't hang a man for shootin' a woman who tried to steal his horse!" They howled with laughter. I continued.

"You can't! You can't hang a man for shootin' a woman who tried to steal his horse!

Why? Because Willie said so. Because Paul said so. Because Jesus said so."

In that sermon, I proceeded to challenge the chaplains to compare the gospel of Jesus and the examples of Paul and Willie to the cultural assumptions that were killing our soldiers, our family members every day. Jesus taught us to break the cycle of violence. Paul, who confessed his murderous nature, repented in time, and became Christianity's strongest advocate for gentleness, kindness, and forgiveness in the name of Christ. Even Willie, who, admittedly not a saint, wrote divine songs about tender forgiveness of love gone awry.

I pointed out that back in America, we assumed that men had a right to defend their property with guns. Jesus called us to respond differently. In the Army, we often believed that cheatin' spouses deserved to be shot. Jesus challenged us to confront our own sins rather than cast stones at others.

I read dramatically from a prepared text, during which the men laughed, and at times sat in dead silence. I begged them to help us to turn the Army's culture around. We chaplains had the power to turn military society from a world where violent gun retaliation was acceptable, to one where our men and women were careful guardians of safety, and our homes and bases were free of domestic violence — if we preached the gospel of Willie, Paul and Jesus.

We returned to our preaching class after a rousing Baptist hymn. No one discussed the sermon. Afterwards, I went shopping with one of my Fort Polk chaplain friends. We bumped into Chaplain Norton. He expressed delight that I was able to address these themes. He volunteered to look at a sexual ethics curriculum I wrote in response to Colonel Stewart's pleas that we get sexual misconduct under control in the 19th TAACOM.

The male chaplains stayed clear of me for the rest of the day, but they were intensely engaged with each other. I thought they were uncomfortable hanging around a single woman. The next morning, a Catholic chaplain sat at my breakfast table. I think his name was Chaplain Santos.

"Chaplain deYoung, you raised a very important theme yesterday. May I give you one piece of advice? Don't tell jokes before a serious sermon like that. It detracted from the importance of what you had to say."

I got defensive. He put up his fingers.

"Just listen to me. The men were talking all night about this. Some of them are very angry with you for speaking out against guns and violence. Some of us agree with you. This is the most important issue. I buried 14 soldiers at my last assignment back in the states. Every one of them died from a gunshot. Believe me, this is something the Army has to deal with!"

I thanked him for his encouragement, and promised not to mask my nervousness with jokes the next time. The fact that the men were earnestly discussing the problem of gun violence gave me great hope.

During another one of our chaplain retreats, I met with the late Chana Timoner, a rabbi from New England who joined the active duty corps from the same reserve command I did. She was having major health problems, so she was on her way back to the states. She wanted to have lunch. We sat down at the Dragon Hill.

She asked, "Have you ever had women make false allegations of rape before? I have never seen this kind of pattern before. I've had three women on one base make false accusations. And one is a prostitute!"

This was a theme I would discuss with Chana on more than one occasion. At that time she was serving an aviation battalion. Aviation units are notoriously amoral in the practice of sexuality. Amorality would work legally, if not spiritually and medically, if there were no laws on the books prohibiting adultery, promiscuity, pandering and prostitution. The Army's legal prohibitions against these lifestyle choices have added false allegations of rape to the host of emotional, spiritual, and medical problems that occur in sexually undisciplined communities.

By and large, there were far fewer disciplinary problems at the 19th TAACOM Headquarters, but there were a few. The headquarters first sergeant beat someone up in the bar after he was verbally antagonized. The command glossed over his lapse. In our remote mixed-gender posts, the allegations of sexual assault and the incidences of unplanned pregnancy were even higher than at Fort Polk. Every week General Brown was briefed about the 19th TAACOM sexual assault trials. Some of these involved brutal assaults of women. Most were drinking-buddy situations gone amuck.

Colonel Stewart, the Deputy Commander of the 19th TAACOM expressed his desire to turn this situation around. I devised job descriptions for another chaplain slot in the 34th Support Group. The Black Gospel congregation was the largest congregation in all of Korea. Yet the chaplain who served this community was only designated pastor as an extra duty. There were several full-time protestant and Catholic chaplains assigned exclusively to their congregations. Meantime, the gospel pastor was assigned to a battalion that was sliced and diced all over the TAACOM. Colonel Stewart approved the new chaplain slot.

After a long philosophical chat, I asked him if I could share the curriculum that I worked up for the 2nd Armored Cavalry Regiment, which, even by Chaplain Travis' standards, had gone far to reduce episodes of misconduct, if not unplanned pregnancies. He thoroughly approved of the curriculum. Chaplain Schmidt then helped me to circulate the curriculum to the Eighth Army, because Lieutenant General Timmons was desperately trying to reduce the ugly episodes of misconduct by using preventive measures like putting locks on the doors of female soldiers. The locks and other measures assumed that women were being attacked against their will. We knew that the dynamics throughout the Army were far more complicated than that. Women and men indulged with no fear of consequences and with no regard to anyone's emotional, spiritual or professional well-being. Then, when something went wrong, the sexual misconduct allegations would fly.

My course was selected by the Eighth Army Chaplain, Pete Christy and by Lieutenant General Timmons to be used by chaplains throughout Korea as a prevention class. My friend John Molino adapted the book, *Sex in the Forbidden Zone*, which was also used to good effect. The Promise Keepers was also offered as an alternative. Although preferred by the vast majority of fundamentalists, this course had no appeal to women because it implicitly argues women have no place in the Army — they should be home tending the hearth, while men practice authority in both the home and the community.

I went back to Seoul to teach "Sexual Ethics: Your Choices, Your Life!" at the August chaplain retreat. Chaplain Hoffman, from the Chief's Office was there to hear the presentation. He publicly praised it, referring time and again to the underlying ethical principles that would protect men and women from hurtful exploitation.

In mid-spring, I began to travel from post to post with other officers rather than Sergeant Park. He resented my authority in the Command Chaplain's office. He especially resented that I was able to work through conflicts with a number of chaplains in the field whom he was not able to bring under his control. The fact that captains and majors refused to bow to him damaged his esteem. Most importantly, I wanted to use the cheapest mode of travel to our government, which was the Korean public trains or buses. And, I wanted to keep the focus on chaplain support rather than inspections and supervision.

Sergeant Park wanted to use the government sedan to travel, which was deemed an extravagant expense by the command. When traveling by Korean trains, the U.S. only paid $15 or so round trip from Taegu to Seoul. When driving the government sedan, Sergeant Park could pocket more than $250 in travel expenses for each trip. Meantime, Chaplain Schmidt wanted to take Sergeant Park back to the United States for the Chief of Chaplains Conference in May of 1995.

Before the Chief's Conference, the 19th TAACOM's Executive Officer came to me and complained there was no reason to send Sergeant Park to the Chief's conference at a cost of thousands of dollars to the command. There was no reason for the command to send Park, but he had a reason to go. Sergeant Park's son was at Annapolis. He had already worked out arrangements with Chaplain Schmidt to leave the conference to visit him. Sergeant Park was already in the habit of refusing anything I asked him. More than once, we straightened this out with Chaplain Schmidt. We both recognized that Sergeant Park was undergoing an extreme identity crisis — he still thought he was the boss of all the chaplains because he was a CHOBC NCOIC and he had functioned like the Deputy Command Chaplain for so long.

Neither Sergeant Park nor Chaplain Schmidt would consider dropping him from the attendance list, even though Chaplain Billy Fowler, the colonel from the 34th Support Group, should more properly have gone. When the Executive Officer adamantly said we would have to cut the fat out of the budget somewhere, I drew up revised travel plans for the rest of the fiscal year to cover the deficit that was projected. I staffed the memo to the Executive Officer, which he signed to acknowledge that Sergeant Park could travel to the states if and only if the Chaplain section cut the rest of its travel budget to the bare bones.

Park and Schmidt went to the states. I continued to travel on the trains or with other officers on the C-12 planes that didn't cost our department anything if we took the stand-by seats. I visited with a very depressed chaplain whose battalion lost a soldier due to murder-suicide. Patriot Battalion soldiers are the most over-deployed Army personnel. They go for six-month jaunts to Korea, then to Saudi Arabia, then to Kuwait, then back to Korea. This particular soldier, having discovered that his wife was unfaithful, obtained permission to return to the United States less than a month after he arrived in Korea. He flew home, purchased a handgun, went to his wife's home, shot her, and then turned the gun on himself. Weeks later, one of the EUSA generals boasted at a Chaplain meeting that there were no suicides among US soldiers in Korea. Well, that was not entirely true.

When Chaplain Schmidt returned from the Chief's conference, he delegated his authority to me once again, because he needed to prepare for his departure to Germany. As soon as Sergeant Park returned, we reviewed the budgetary constraints we were under. We resumed travel. Park traveled independently, many times to Seoul to do spot audits of the chaplain funds. I helped a number of chaplains to prepare for their return to the States and by preaching and providing on-call weekend coverage.

A number of enlisted soldiers called me to help them get transferred from one in-country assignment to another. Every time I asked Sergeant Park to handle enlisted matters, which was his primary responsibility, he would shout, "You treat me like dog meat!"

As we prepared for a whole new chain of command, from General Brown down to the Sergeant Major, the junior officers were keeping a hectic pace. Most of us did physical training from 5:00 to 6:00 A.M., so we could get into the office, check our overseas e-mail, and get on the road to do site visits. The new company commander wanted all of the headquarter captains and majors on the physical training field with his privates. There was only one way for this to work. Either we did physical training at 5:00 A.M. so that we could do our jobs for the rest of the day, or we went to enlisted physical training at 6:30 and reported to work at 9:00 A.M. like the privates. Then, we would not be able to get our overseas calls and e-mails transmitted. We would not be able to take a cheap train to Seoul or to Pusan. The 19h TAACOM would revert to what it was before General Brown established active management goals: the place where officers whiled away their hours until their hardship tour was over.

There was another budget crunch. While trying to resolve a dispute, I discovered that Sergeant Park was charging our command for hundreds of dollars of travel every time he took the government sedan to Seoul. He had his travel orders changed time and again to permit this. During that year, we were putting infantrymen and signal soldiers in jail for selling a few hundred dollars of commissary supplies to the local Korean black market. One sergeant, who deployed to the Honduras, the Gulf, and Somalia before taking a hardship tour in Korea was in the throes of divorce. The Criminal Investigation Division rigorously investigated his Basic Allowance for Quarters (BAQ) payments with the intention of throwing this man in jail for allowing two or three BAQ checks to pass to his wife after the divorce was finalized.

Sergeant Park, meantime, was justifying both the use of the government sedan to drive to Seoul and his payment of about $250 for each round trip. Furthermore, Sergeant Park was arranging for our Republic of Korea (ROK) liaison chaplain to collect hundreds of dollars every time he visited another base to offer prayers and bible studies for the KATUSAs, too.

Because I put my word on the line to send Sergeant Park to the United States in exchange for a bare bones in-country travel budget, I attempted to put a stop to it. Because Sergeant Park alienated himself from all the chaplains by his seemingly scrupulous inspections of the chaplain fund accounts, I insisted we hold ourselves to the same standards of financial conduct. Sergeant Park's response was that I treated him "like dog meat!" He refused to accept my authority on this or any other issue.

"You think this is stealing? You should see what the others are doing! Up and down this command, I know — they tell me! Sergeant Majors are doubling their salaries! All up and down this hall! All up and down this command! They double their salaries!"

Yes, I could see this was happening. But were chaplains supposed to follow by example or attempt to set the moral standard for the command? Furthermore, I was appalled as I traveled around Korea to our camps in the Division and in the Eastern Corridor that the remote posts were short of supplies, gear, bedding, and even essentials like fresh vegetables. How could we justify this "doubling of salaries" when soldiers in the Division didn't even have enough sheets and blankets to take care of their soldiers in the tank battalions? How could we say it was okay to make money from the black market, and watch bright juicy oranges walk out the front door of the clubs while soldiers in remote towns hardly ever saw fresh oranges?

We had two or three sessions where Sergeant Park adamantly refused to conform to the TAACOM's travel policy. He finally waved his arms at me, "You say no TDY? Fine! No TDY! I no travel!"

In retrospect, his insubordination could not have been more perfect. Frankly, what would the point be of sending a sergeant out to monitor funds management when fraudulent financial claims would be filed?

On the day General Sullivan became the new commander of the 19th TAACOM, Lieutenant General Timmons stopped me as I was about to welcome my new boss to Taegu. With the fire of John the Baptist, Timmons pointed to me and demanded, "Chaplain, how am I supposed to reduce sexual assault in my command?"

We stepped off to discuss the course I sent forward for his review, and my concerns that the BOSS Army policies were making the sexual misconduct and alcohol abuse problems more difficult to eliminate.

Sometime earlier that day, General Luck came over to my new supervisor, Chaplain Glenn Fasanella and myself. Luck put his arm around my shoulder and kissed me on the forehead. He had recently heard some healthy lifestyle messages I had given as part of my radio messages. General Luck had a reputation for hugging all his guys, and his gesture did not have anything but a kind feel to it.

I thought my reputation in the 19th TAACOM was rock solid. Because of my work in supporting the chaplains throughout the TAACOM, and because I helped a number of commanders with their sexual misconduct situations, as well as for the curriculum I had written. I received extraordinary ratings from both Chaplain Schmidt and Colonel Stewart before they departed the TAACOM.

But they were now gone. Soon, I had to resolve the travel dilemma with Sergeant Park. Also we had to establish new lines of authority with our new command chaplain, Glenn Fasanella. Chaplain Fasanella embodied all the complaints that decent women have when they say that women are held to a higher standard than men. He had had a severe car crash ten years before. He could never do physical training. He worked at the Pentagon for most of his career. He was extremely indecisive. Chaplain Fasanella vacillated on every issue that confronted us during the first weeks of his command. First, he wanted me to function like the deputy. He wanted clean financial records, no fraud or misuse of government funds. He drew up his proposed organization, brought Sergeant Park and myself in to explain it, then proceeded to tell us how leadership structures were really supposed to work in the Army. Sergeants were supposed to report to and support officers, not the other way around. Then, Sergeant Park went into the kind of weepy tirade he had performed for Chaplain Schmidt and myself on more than one occasion.

Chaplain Fasanella stated that the misuse of TDY funds was an important issue of fraud and abuse that our section would have to address. Yet, he was complicit in the practice of TDY fraud. His wife was going to take over as the number two financial manager for the 19th TAACOM. She was, in his modest estimation, the Department of Defense's TDY queen.

In the midst of all this, I went to Seoul to conduct business with chaplains. As required, I signed into the Chaplain Retreat Center in Itaewon, because a stay there would not cost our command. There was a change of command at the Retreat Center, and with it, a change in the standards of conduct. The new chaplain who commanded the RRC was in the hospital with a serious ailment. The RC was being run by a non-commissioned officer. As I walked to my room in a corridor filled with private retreat rooms, I was amazed to find a group of soldiers running up and down the halls in towels, flashing each other. I went to the non-commissioned officer in charge, Sergeant Z, and complained about this lapse of propriety.

"Ma'am, this is the BOSS Army! This is the new army! There's nothing we can do about that! The soldiers are on their free time. That's just the way the Army is these days..."

I was furious that the chaplains were challenged to help the command reduce accusations of sexual assault and misconduct, yet, we were condoning an atmosphere at our retreat center that contributed, even aggravated all the Army's problems. I checked out of the Religious Retreat Center. I went down to the Dragon Hill Hotel and paid for a room out of my own pocket. Chaplain Fasanella encouraged me to turn in my receipts for this stay at the Dragon Hill. I declined to charge the government for my stay at the Dragon Hill, and thereby, lose my right to speak to the underlying problems in our command.

After Chaplain Fasanella consulted with the 19th TAACOM financial managers, he discovered that indeed, TDY fraud was a command-wide problem. He returned to our office, and advised me he changed his mind. Strict adherence to the Command's travel regulations would no longer be a goal for the Command Chaplain's office. When I objected to the futility of this position, Fasanella gently chided,

"Marie, you have so much potential. Do you realize you could be the first woman Chief of Chaplains?"

Chaplain Fasanella did not know me well enough to realize this was the worst possible tack he could have taken. I quickly disabused him of my desire for that auspicious role.

Chaplain Fasanella asked me to meet him the next day. He gave me a lengthy letter of concern chastising me for my abrasive and confrontive leadership style. I was to cease and desist from my inquiries about Sergeant Park's misuse of command funds. I was to do physical training with the privates. I was to hand over the deputy command chaplain's authority to Sergeant Park until the Lieutenant Colonel who should properly have been doing my job, was installed as the new deputy.

Sergeant Park's refusal to abide by any travel policies that would require him to use public transportation like the rest of us, and his refusal to treat any chaplain under the rank of colonel with respect, was a widely known problem. Singling me out to do physical training with the enlisted soldiers was obviously an act of gender discrimination. Most of the captains whom I worked with in our headquarters were like myself. We knew financial fraud when we saw it. We knew a cover-up and retaliation when we saw it. On the advice of at least half-a-dozen friends, I went to the Judge Advocate Attorney and to the 19th TAACOM IG.

The head JAG discussed several incidents of chaplain misconduct that he had to handle over the years — both in Korea and at Fort Hood, where he put one chaplain in jail, and fully intended to put two others in jail.

When I visited with the IG, I was so blindingly angry, that I sat and let one invective fly after another. He calmly proceeded to explain why I was right, and why Chaplain Fasanella would have to reverse himself. The IG thought he could mediate the situation. I knew that would not happen. Chaplain Fasanella already made it known to both of us that he would write me a career killing evaluation if I stayed with him. The IG and the JAG recommended that I move up to the Second Infantry Division.

This prospect delighted me. My first five months with the 19th TAACOM were complicated, but rich with cultural programs and social encounters with a number of career officers and sergeants. There was always a party to go to, a picnic in this-or-that colonel's backyard. Whenever I went to the remote Army camps in Korea, I felt our soldiers were being neglected. The contrast between our Taegu country club and the camps we supported was great. All the power, and too many chaplains were concentrated around the flag pole.

Before I left, the new Deputy Commander for the 19th TAACOM sat me down in his office. He charmed me with his elegant description of life as a lifelong Army bachelor. He encouraged me to use my time wisely in the Division. Then he slipped me another letter of concern about my leadership style. When I shared the facts with him as I understood them, he had no knowledge of the TDY fraud issues. No knowledge of Sergeant Park's disrespect to me and other officers. No knowledge of the fact that I was being singled out falsely as an officer who didn't do PT. I ran every morning with Captain Keith Street. The colonel had no knowledge, and he was too new to realize he was being used by Chaplain Fasanella to retaliate against a whistle blower. "I did not realize these issues were involved in this matter," he said

This sweet, elegantly-spoken man, thought I was being reprimanded for my gruff mannerisms, as evidenced by the stream of obscene invective I had let fly behind closed doors. I suggested that Sergeant Park, whom the commander highly esteemed because he ran with the company every day, didn't do "jack shit" in the office. Chaplain Fasanella was censuring me for using words that male chaplains, priests and even General Edwards used in public staff meetings. Fasanella thought four-letter words were unbecoming to a female chaplain. Since this experience, I have ferociously argued to women that they ought never take the risk of thinking they will be treated as nonchalantly as men regarding the use of obscenities in the military. At that time, I simply did not think that language was nearly as worthy of censure as obscenely fraudulent conduct. To me, participation in financial fraud while soldiers did without fresh food, winter boots, blankets and other basic amenities in the most forward deployed combat division in the world was obscenity.

When the new deputy commander drew his meeting with me to a close, it was clear that the 19th TAACOM would limit its concern to language, not deeds. I consulted with my friends in the 19th TAACOM. I consulted with my friend from the Chaplain School, Father Ed Kelley. Then, I visited a JAG lawyer in Seoul. She helped me file a formal complaint alleging 1) TDY fraud, 2) command knowledge of that fraud, 3) retaliation against me for surfacing the waste, fraud and abuse issues, and 4) discrimination against me as a female officer. How was I discriminated against? As my male peers explained to me, the male Korean sergeant was permitted to repeatedly disrespect me because senior chaplains believed "we couldn't expect an older Korean male to respect the authority of women." I also detailed the situation about Sergeant Park's misuse of funds. Finally, I noted Chaplain Fasanella's confirmation to me that not only Sergeant Park was participating in the fraud, but sergeants and officers across the TAACOM participated.

These charges were investigated, but of course, by Chaplain Fasanella's new peer colonel from the 19th TAACOM. The woman was very friendly to me. I socialized with her more than once after her arrival. The fact that she was internal to the command and Chaplain Fasanella's peer did not deter me from registering my ethical concerns. I filled out a lengthy statement. Ed Kelley was kind enough to listen to me as I tried to sort this thing out. He carefully read my statement when I saw him up in the Division. I did not feel quite so insane for making this issue a thorn in the 19th TAACOM's side so long as there was a chaplain in the division who could confirm to me time and again that basic supplies like blankets and beds were not adequately stocked in his division.

I have no knowledge of what happened to the investigation or to the chaplain assistants who were party to this fraud. I assume that nothing was done to stem the greed. I do know that within a year or so, the 34th Support Group Chaplain Fund was investigated for major fraud. A naive Sergeant Craft was court martialed because the fund's massive theft was uncovered during his tenure. I am unequivocally certain the problems were always there, but were glossed over by Chaplain Fasanella.

Although I did not admit as much to the colonel who seemed to care about me when he offered his sweet letter of concern, I knew in my heart-of-hearts that I needed to change my style if I were going to survive the Chaplain Corps. I needed to change not because I feared my career as a chaplain would not survive. My OCS training still challenged me to put ethical concerns before my own advancement. Ever since my confrontations with Chaplain Travis and Chilen, however, I had occasional attacks when I ran that scared me. Some of that was due to anti-histamines, which I took to breath easier in Korea. Still, the attacks would sneak up on me, even when I wasn't feeling any professional stress. If the job conflicts were inducing physical symptoms, I needed to find a new way to handle the conflicts. All of the issues I had been addressing were worth fighting for but none of them were worth dying for. So, changes I would have to make.

Once I filed an official complaint for the 19th TAACOM to investigate both the fraud issues and the command chaplain's practice of retaliation against me, I simply severed all connection with chaplain politics and the flag pole. I packed up my boxes of books and arranged to have my stuff moved to the Division. I gave my guitar to a young chaplain assistant. He drove me to the train station, and I started my new life the minute I purchased a one-way ticket to Seoul.

My outspokenness always came at a price. It was time to pay the piper. With this move, I felt that the trade-off for raising these issues would work to my favor. I would be much happier. I was about to join the Second Infantry Division, to be the first woman chaplain for the 44th combat engineer battalion: Broken Hearts! The only downside to the move was that once I signed into the division, I would lose my freedom to travel throughout Korea — unless the destination was reachable by Humvee.

CHAPTER 15

Broken Hearts Are Second to None

My new BOQ apartment was twice the size of the studio provided to officers in Taegu, but one hundred times as filthy. It was caked with mud from the Korean countryside. There were no Ahjimahs, or lady housekeepers, which accounted for the black scum in the bathrooms, and layers of dirt on the walls, furniture, windows and floor.

As I wandered around looking for mops, clean rags, soap and wax, I recalled a childhood biography of Daniel Boone, particularly a chapter about the dramatic civilizing effect women had on pioneers. When Daniel's wife joined him, she insisted on decorating, tidying up, and preparing sit-down meals. My sister used to make her husband shed all his filthy field gear, and shower on the lanai before she would allow him to enter her Hawaiian home. Now, as women crept into the 2nd Division, would we ruin everything for these happy, smelly engineers by turning their BOQ crash pad into a home? I decided not to worry about the men, just my own need to make myself a cozy home, however temporary.

By scrubbing walls and bathroom tiles I allayed my nervousness about my new assignment. That first night, my new chaplain boss loaned me a clock radio, which I plugged into six or seven outlets before I could finally pick up the AFKN radio station. It was 8:00 P.M. Time for "Morning Edition." Our time zone was eleven hours ahead of the States. Tomorrow's U.S. news was always aired the night before.

On my first full morning at Camp Howze, I visited with my new chaplain supervisor, Chaplain Rolando Castillo; my executive officer, Major Rovero; and the battalion commander, Lieutenant Colonel Harold Chappell. The Division required three or four half-days to in-process. I had one-and-a-half days to sign in before taking my mid-tour leave. In-processing was held at Camp Casey in the mornings, an hour drive to the east in Uijongbu. My friend Ed Kelley took some time off to be with me during these excursions. I spent the afternoons getting to know Camp Howze and the three Protestant congregations I was to pastor.

Soon after I settled in, I began to do physical training at the same time as the battalion every morning, but on my own. I no longer had primary responsibility for site visits and data analysis. In this new assignment, my sole purpose was to be a troop chaplain. You can only minister to the troops if you make it a habit to be with the troops. On Fridays, Major Rovero pulled the staff officers together, or we joined the rest of the battalion for fun runs. On the other days, I knew I could never keep up with the guys in the line companies, so I just ran the steep Howze hill like everybody else. Our informal trail blazed through heavily-manured farm plots, overstuffed food shops, and local bars. At 6:00 A.M. very few Koreans were on the cobbled streets. The women who pulled weeds from their crops would wave and greet all who passed each morning.

From the day I arrived until the day I left, the guys from the 44th Combat Engineer Battalion never harassed me for running at my own pace. When you do your best, the men encourage you — no matter what your age or gender. Once a young engineer cheered me on as I ran five miles,

"Ma'am, Oprah Winfrey ran her first Marathon when she was 44 years old. You can do it too!"

But, to receive sustained encouragement, a little bit of humility is essential. Running five miles at your own pace does not make one qualified to be a combat engineer or a Navy seal. It makes you physically fit, and capable of understanding the pain and demands required of the grunt. I didn't mind admitting my limitations so long as my co-workers accepted them.

Bragging about abilities one does not have will inevitably result in a contest. Between men, such contests are just horseplay. Women aren't always prepared to handle the physical challenge, however, when they assert their physical superiority. One of the 19th TAACOM sexual misconduct cases stemmed from a barracks party in Korea, where a woman bragged to an infantryman that she was as capable of ground combat as he was. Her confidence was derived from the fact that she completed the Army's sanitized, almost commercial airborne school and because she lifted weights. The infantryman pulled out his knife, put her in a chokehold, and asked her if she was able to get out of the situation. If two men had done that to each other, no one would ever have heard about the situation again. The woman charged the infantryman with assault, however. He was convicted. If that conviction was necessary to protect female troops, so be it. It should also have signaled the futility of the Army's plans to assign women to such rough and tumble units. If they can't handle horseplay, do we want to endanger them by putting them in close combat situations? Can we use our judge advocates to prosecute enemy soldiers who put women in chokeholds?

I never presumed that my physical fitness was the same thing as combat readiness, but I ran anyway, to earn the respect of my battalion. By running on my own each morning, I was able to make eye contact with every company, every platoon as we crossed paths. We'd shout encouraging slogans to each other and call out each other's names. The young men, even the young officers liked the attention I paid their troops. Soldiers who planned to drop by the chapel would nod or wave their hand as they ran past me to notify me of their intentions. These same guys would not be caught dead going to a psychologist, but in the most macho of deployed units, a visit with the chaplain is about as normal as

First Class Leadership Brings First Class Results

Lieutenant Harold Chappell and Major Rovero —
Commander and XO of the 44th Combat Engineers.

spending time with a weight trainer in the gym.

My very first run at Camp Howze threatened to end disastrously. I got completely lost. After running out the post gate, I followed Bravo Company as they ran through the narrow streets that led to a flat amusement park. Bravo darted off. I just ran straight until I saw them again running along a manmade lake. Women were tending to their beautiful lettuce leaves, and little poodle dogs barked as I plodded patiently along. Pet poodles were a sign of wealth to these remote villagers. They were not penned up, destined for slaughter in a kaekogi, or dogmeat factory. The run along the lake was a much-needed religious experience for me. Fog rolls lay gently above the water, adding a touch of mystery to this alien land. Flowers and plants perfumed the wooded path alongside the lake. But suddenly, I was lost. Camp guards told me I'd never get lost if I just ran to the end of the lake path and came back the way I started.

I reached the end of the path without a problem. But, on the return trip, I crossed a bridge, and realized for the first time the road forked into two unrecognizable paths. An elderly Korean woman laughed and jogged along side of me, teasing me in Hangul about running. She imitated the airborne shuffle, and panted with fake exhaustion. She obviously thought it ridiculous that I would choose to be a soldier and choose to run so far. Ahjima kept laughing and telling me things I couldn't understand. She pointed me in a direction that had a steep hill. As I glanced up, Colonel Soo, the Brigade commander clipped down that hill, so I thought I could trust Ahjimah's directions.

"Kamsahhamnida!" I thanked her. She pointed again to the hill.

"Nay! Nay," which means, "yes" in Hangul. Her golden tooth gleamed as she chased me up the hill chuckling.

After about two miles of rolling hills, I came to MSR-1. What to do? Run all the way back the way I came, and complete a ten-mile course for the first time in my life, or just run an extra three miles along MSR-1 back to the post? No contest. Continue on. Eight miles was my natural running limit. I knew for certain I'd rather be run over by a truck than run the extra two miles a turnabout would require.

The run on MSR-1 was the only close encounter with death I ever had in Korea, or in the Army, for that matter. Trucks honked their horns as they passed on the breakdown lane at 70-mph, barely skinning me as Korean custom requires. I ran past a guitar factory where I hoped I could soon buy a new guitar. Finally, beyond acres of flat farms, I could see a tall KIA building, the manufacturer of Korean cars that stood next to the gate of Camp Howze. Killed in Action? Is that what KIA stands for? I wondered. What a great name for Korean automobiles! I turned the corner and ran to the Howze gate. Home at last, Thank God. The guards smiled and nodded. I didn't tell them where I had been, because any sensible soldier, even a private, would have chewed me out for being so stupidly reckless as to run up MSR-1.

Colonel Soo, on the other hand, was so impressed when he saw me running, that he came down to my office that afternoon to introduce himself and welcome me to his brigade. Soo took pride in his teaching. He was always encouraging his people to develop their thought process. Colonel Soo was friendly and kind, but I sensed that he was going to be a really tough commander to work with. He was. He broached his immediate concern soon after he took a seat on my couch — the safety and well-being of the women assigned to his brigade.

"I worry about them when they go to the field. I don't like seeing the men and women in the same tent over at the construction sites. I need to know if our PX is stocking items that women need. You shouldn't have to go to Seoul for some of your basic needs. Captain B pointed out that the PX only carries queensize panty hose. These kinds of things we can fix. Do you know any female soldiers who wear queensize pantyhose? Why does the PX buy queensize pantyhose? Where's their thought process?"

I laughed and complimented Colonel Soo for his bottom-line commitment to the integration of women.

"Sir, you have at least 700 male engineer soldiers up here, don't you? Remember, they like to wear pantyhose for road marches — it cuts down on the friction, and on the possibility of blisters. But, I agree, all twelve of the women here should be able to get pantyhose that fit so they can wear the dress uniform."

I knew there were only four or five women in our battalion, and another four or five at the brigade headquarters living on Camp Howze. The Construction Engineer Company at Camp Edwards had five or six women, including a female executive officer. There were a few women at the Medical Treatment facility at Camp Edwards, including the officer in charge. Otherwise, female soldiers were scarce on both posts.

I hoped I wasn't assigned here as the token female, who was only brought on the team to smooth out all the sexual harassment and sexual misconduct episodes. My first couple of days, as I climbed the Howze hills, I was pleasantly surprised by the respect men accorded other women who appeared on the slopes. I was able to relax.

"Sir," I tried to reassure Colonel Soo. "I don't think you have any problems here. The men treat women with respect wherever I go. You seem to have trained them right!"

Most impressive to me was the professional demeanor, the squared-away attitude projected by the young men and women of the 44th. Pride was everywhere. Courtesy was the norm. We were far away from the powerful flag pole commands. Yet, the enlisted soldiers glowed with a high sense of purpose that was nowhere to be found down in the Taegu Country Club. Now that I had two major flag commands under my belt, I was ready to interpret. For all the comforts, lapses of protocol, indulgence in fraternization and favoritism that you expect while working at a large flagged headquarters, the collegial atmosphere always had a downside. At the TAACOM, there was never a sense of esprit de corps, common purpose, or deep satisfaction in the junior ranking soldiers that I witnessed at Howze — or throughout The Division.

Howze belonged to the elite of Korean society. Beautiful stone paths were set, gardens gracefully planted. Pine and chestnut trees firmly gripped the mountainside. Some time back, an American general used federal funds to install wonderful ponds and meditation temples, for which he was punished. Hopefully he only got his wrist slapped.

No matter where you lived and worked on Camp Howze, it was guaranteed you would have to walk up and down the steep hills five to ten times per day. The officers and Charlie Company lived at the top of the hills, but we worked at the base. Headquarters Company worked at the base, but frequently had to interface with the Brigade staff, which was halfway up the hill, or do physical training at the gym, which was at the top.

Howze is the only Army base I know where soldiers did not ask to go to the medical clinic to avoid physical training. The clinic was at the very summit. Once your heart rate was up to 120 from the steep hike to the medical clinic, the worst part of the run was already over — there was nothing left to avoid. My father was wrong about the ability to lose one's thick thighs by trekking up and down steep hills. I spent six months on those hills, long enough to reach the scientific conclusion that thunder thighs have nothing to do with lack of exercise or mountain climbing — they are a genetic trait. Asian women are just born lucky in that regard. But the hill climbing made us healthier in every way — physically, spiritually, but best of all, recreationally.

Unlike Camp Casey, which was flat, drab, overcrowded and under-civilized, the natural beauty of the sculptured Howze hills made it feel homey. Paved roads made it easy to get about the Howze Hill, but the male engineers revealed all the traits of grunt infantrymen in their commuting habits. They stayed on pig trails believing they saved themselves extra steps and steep climbs. Really, they just preferred walking through the woods. No one hassled them on the pig trails. The young lieutenants did not require salutes on these hidden dirt paths, either. The pig trails had the bonding effect of a tree house or a fishing hole for these guys.

Whatever fears I had about acceptance of women in the Division were dissolved when I met my new battalion commander. Harold Chappell was a West Point graduate. Before taking the 44th, Chappell served with the National Training Center Staff and the Tenth Mountain Division. When he finished commanding the 44th, Chappell was headed for the War College in the summer of 1997.

Chappell stood tall over his battalion. He overshadowed the brigade commander, Colonel Soo, too, but he was careful not to allow his height to suggest arrogance or superiority. At first, Chappell's stiff demeanor felt like coldness, distance. I didn't think he was going to like my friendly style. He turned out to be a charismatic leader, and a strong, funny, positive influence on his troops.

Over time, Chappell proved he was not only a great tactician and trainer, but he genuinely cared about his soldiers. Harold Chappell wasn't a chatty guy, but he wasn't aloof, either. I soon grew to appreciate the fact that he would listen to everyone, withdraw and reflect, and then issue decisions that balanced fairness and compassion.

Until I arrived, there was only one woman officer on Chappell's staff, the S-4. She was soft-spoken, a terrific logistician and a good athlete. We both did PT on our own most of the time, because the men worked out at a much more rugged pace, with which neither of us could keep up. In every other respect, she held her own without trying to out-guy the guys. Chappell did not patronize her or fail to address problems in her Area of Operation. I noticed she was easily accepted by her male peers not just because of her competence, but because her husband served as an officer in another part of the division. Generally, women have an easier time if their husbands are also in the same area or branch. Just before I left, another female lieutenant was rotated in and the S-4 returned to the States with her husband.

The new female lieutenant had a more difficult time with her male peers. She was more aggressive, more sexy, single, and vulnerable to the confused dynamics that wreak havoc when a female soldier vacillates between being a tough guy in uniform and a sleek, seductive lady off duty. She would out-shout, out-cuss, out-macho her peers while in the baggy, battledress uniform. Then, at socials she'd come with her beautiful hair down her back, dressed in a skin-tight, spaghetti-strapped, low-cut dress with a mid-thigh slit up the side. In grunt units, you pay your dues at social events by putting money in a jug, guzzling from a Grog Bowl, or by doing pushups. The lady lieutenant was not prepared to do pushups. The dimension of sexuality introduced an awkwardness you don't find in all-male units. As I watched this dynamic play out over the months, I grew in my conviction that near combat units should revert to all-male composition. The prospect of having one siren in the midst of 35 to 600 men who have no legal or ethical way to act on their aroused sexual feelings and desires just causes unnecessary and expensive problems.

Soon after I arrived, Colonel Soo had an officer's call at the Oak Club, on the highest peak of the Howze hills. To get there, you had to climb up at least 200 steps beyond our BOQ, already a steep ascent. When Chaplain Castillo and I arrived, there were about15 brigade and battalion officers. I was the only woman. The men were perfect gentlemen, recounting family stories, then as is customary, they complained about Colonel Soo as soon as he went home to his family in Seoul. Some of the guys played pool, others watched sports replays. After everybody loosened up, a major turned on the laser Karoake player. Each of us took our turns singing love songs and country classics. Chaplain Castillo, a faithful priest, sang songs like "Love me Tender, Love me True." I sang the one with the line, "He thinks he'll keep her," which scared the brigade executive officer, an extremely conservative West Point grad, whose wife left active duty to raise the family. That song was played on country radio every morning back in Louisiana as 6,000 soldiers drove in to physical training. The other dependable favorite: "Prop Me Up Beside the Jukebox When I Die."

Sassy satires and soft love songs help the troops bond as they gear up to roll in the mud and break sweat together. The songs blare on the radio and on loudspeakers as soldiers run up and down a designated running path. But in the states, the men go home to their wives and girlfriends. At this remote Korean outpost, singing tender love songs in mixed company complicated things.

Social indiscretions could adversely impact the unit — no matter how sexual or asexual the context. Colonel Soo was perpetually worried about in-discipline, even between men. He placed a general ban on fraternization even between same-sex soldiers in the brigade, but Army-wide BOSS policies were still too lax — they permitted relationships between soldiers who worked in different commands. There was a lot of tension between junior officers who wanted to stretch the fraternization policies as far as the law would allow and the more conservative senior leaders. More experienced officers knew that liberal interpretation of fraternization policies would eventually put the Brigade on the nightly news with some wildly inflated accusations of misconduct.

On principle, let alone fear of media distortion of a soldier misconduct case, Colonel Soo was right to try to curtail all fraternization, because it is almost impossible in the best of circumstances to maintain good morale on an isolated post. Ours was the most forward deployed division in the world. Same-sex fraternization can be just as distracting, and downright destructive as romantic fraternization. It is very easy for commanders to take a stand and enforce fraternization policies between junior soldiers and senior leaders. It is almost impossible for leaders to control romantic entanglements. This has tragically caused military leaders to turn a blind eye to heterosexual sex in the workplace.

In one example a female captain from the medical command in the Western Corridor fell in love with the company commander at Camp Edwards. These two made a charming, cute couple. Despite their best efforts, the dynamics went wildly out of control. The woman started a relationship with one captain, broke that off, and then continued with another. Hostility seethed between the two young 20-something studs. Their objectivity was often blurred in handling professional responsibilities. At the medical clinic, soldiers couldn't consult with the female captain in confidence. They knew she reported everything back to their commander in an effort to help the soldiers, of course.

Officers and sergeants in the company could not shake the perception that their male commander was very passive. They complained his girlfriend was running the company. No decision seemed to be made without her input. Those who were affected by the day-to-day decisions were often exasperated by the indiscretions of the lovebirds. Outside of a television MASH episode, none of us could ever recall seeing a medical doctor in an engineer commander's office before. The strangeness of this female doctor's obvious participation in the company commander's every decision was almost comical, but the consequences were disruptive.

In a war situation, the fear is that soldiers who are in sexual relationships will be preoccupied with their own needs, and oblivious to the survival of the fighting team. Often, chivalrous critics of women in combat units think the reason for preoccupation is out of concern for the woman's safety. Actually, the sexual preoccupation is entirely of a selfish nature, with no regard for the well-being of anyone — just a comforting distraction from the soldier's duties, family troubles, or personal identity crisis. Soldier-lovers are detrimental to the unit far sooner than the moment the fighting starts. The starry-eyed seldom focus on their duties or their other teammates even in peacetime.

The construction company men and women all slept in one big open room or one big tent when they worked in the field. In garrison, they were still an undifferentiated mass. They migrated to the dining facility for day meals, and drifted over to the club every evening. The club was the company's living room, where the commander and his girlfriend, and all the soldiers and their girlfriends drowned out their loneliness with loud country and rap music and as many beers as necessary to numb the ache in their hearts. The commander and his physician girlfriend called the unit family and resisted efforts by senior officers and noncoms to break the company out of its paranoid tipsy stupor.

When Private A was discovered dead in his room, the Construction Company was paralyzed. The commander, a sensitive but insecure young man, could not hear or think through all the responsibilities that were his to fulfill. In shock, and overwhelmed with his own emotions, he wanted to withdraw his whole company from public view. In his mid-20s, the captain was a buddy to the troops, just a few years older than some of his privates. He and his girlfriend modeled the weakest of coping styles for the troops. They were just getting through the year.

There were some leaders who hoped Private A's death would expose the passivity of the commander, and lead to his removal. There was no reason for this to happen, however, because the captain, in his own way, accomplished an awesome amount of repair and reconstruction. He was a good enough captain.

Lieutenant Colonel Chappell, the consummate mentor, chose to use the tragedy to teach the young man how to separate himself from his soldiers as an act of caring leadership. The company first sergeant, a man with at least 18 years of soldiering, also stood up and presented fatherly, teaching support to the commander and the troops.

Our memorial service for the soldier proved to be the structural activity that lifted the company out of its shock and disbelief. In preparation for the service, the company commander and I did the standard critical incident debriefings in each platoon. Brigadier General McNeil flew to Camp Edwards as soon as the death was announced to provide a strong presence to our commanders and soldiers, and I believe, to affirm the leadership of the entire brigade. This company had developed a posture of isolation and victimization that our battalion commander wanted dissolved. While we gathered readings and rehearsed the memorial service, the division psychiatrist conducted a psychological autopsy, interviewing all members of the company, the leaders, and some of the medical staff at the Camp.

We held the memorial service on Camp Edwards, but the Edwards chapel only held 25 people, so we took great pains to convert the Camp theatre into a chapel large enough to hold the company. The soldiers, stupefied by A's death, wanted to show their grief and solidarity. They scrubbed the theatre and swept down the pavements outside. They tidied up the club next door, and set up a coffee bar for the two generals who would fly in for the memorial service.

Even the company's mascot, a large brown Doberman could participate. We were prepared to let the dog take his customary place in the center aisle, next to the first row.

The first time I preached at Camp Edwards, this dog drifted in, sat for awhile, then drifted out like a sergeant major doing spot checks here and there on the troops.

"I guess he doesn't like my style of preaching!" I commented to the soldiers in the pews.

The dog was everywhere — the club, the dining facility, the motor pool, and the barracks. When the troops mobilized for an alert, the dog would go crazy, zig-zagging down the street, wailing his feelings of abandonment. The soldiers kept a coffee can in the dining facility to collect money for his food and other creature comforts. Technically, this was illegal. By recording this for posterity, I know I take the chance of spurring some bureaucrat to do a spot inspection and bring the dining facility manager up on charges for mismanaging funds in the DFAC. But the dog was a source of comfort to the crusty old first sergeant as well as the youngest private. He transmitted no diseases, induced no hangover or altered state, and demanded no child support payments. That dog couldn't save every soldier from self-destruction, but I believe he had a positive effect on most.

The Division sent one of their band horn players to play "Taps." There was no musical instrument in the theatre, so I provided my electric piano for the hymns. The company's executive officer played while different soldiers led the singing.

All of the military honors were paid to Private A, including a 21-gun salute. Private A's closest friend shared his own awareness of the deceased man's dark side. He shared his lessons learned. A's instructor from AIT provided some fatherly comments about A's potential. Colonel Chappell read from scriptures. All the soldiers who sat in front of me were like orphans in this distant country — weeping as much about their own feelings of abandonment as about the loss of a fellow soldier. I meditated upon the source of our strength as soldiers and as men and women of faith to see us through the darkest hour.

General Tommy Franks concluded the ceremony by saluting and coining the private as a final tribute. I had never seen a general do that at a memorial service, especially when it was obvious the soldier had self-destructed. General Franks communicated volumes of love and concern to the soldiers in that room with that gesture. As dull as dog-eared Franks was in his official training tapes mandating careful cold weather training in Korea's harsh winter climate, when the General saluted Private A, the sense of redemption he communicated electrified the company. The unity, their sense of purpose was rekindled in that final farewell.

A few days after the memorial service, General Tommy Franks, and General Timmons from Eighth Army reiterated their policy that sergeants should visit all soldiers every single day. In less tragic circumstances, when the generals in Korea issued this edict enlisted soldiers would openly rebel that Army BOSS policies forbade sergeants from visiting their barracks rooms. Yet, when General Franks restated his position that all soldiers should be visited, and barracks rooms looked at on a daily basis, there was not a whimper of complaint.

Thousands of miles away from home, the young troops, by their acquiescence were willing to admit that they were still kids in need of adult supervision.

After Private A's death, the Camp Edwards community was much more receptive to the programs and support offered by the chapel, the sergeant major, and even the division mental health department. I arranged for a mental health counselor to work out of the chapel office one day a week to help soldiers with anger management and depression. During field problems, whole platoons would attend worship services, a highly unusual military occurrence in peacetime. For Thanksgiving and Christmas, the soldiers visited with orphans and provided a Christmas party for the kids. The commander held a Christmas tree lighting ceremony that made the Camp feel like an American town.

Camp Edwards had the highest concentration of women in the Engineer Brigade, and the greatest number of sexual misconduct incidents. None of the other companies in the 44th were tied up with soldier-to-soldier sexual misconduct issues while I was with them. Edwards, the mixed-gender Mecca continued to have problems with sexual misconduct, though, even after the infusion of leadership and intervention by the Division Mental Health Department. When you put men and women side-by-side in remote, difficult situations, you will have many problematic sexual relationships. Unless, of course, you just laid the bodies out side-by-side in a graveyard. Even then, I am not sure earthbound spirits would abide by fraternization policies.

Shortly after the memorial service, I was called to the camp in the middle of the night because the first sergeant suspected a rape. Parents were calling from the States. A soldier confided to the first sergeant that one of her female soldiers seemed to have been raped by her boyfriend. The attractive, drunken, underage woman talked obsessively about her boyfriend with whom she had regular sex and to whom she was engaged. Her friends believed she was being abused, but the young woman denied everything except her obsessive need to be with her fiancée. The two were having a property dispute. The young man tried to set strict spending limits on both of them, so they could save money to get married. The woman denied her fiancée raped her, but we were receiving calls from her parents back in the States alleging abuse. I referred her to the Domestic Violence counselors at the 121st Hospital in Seoul the next duty day. Both the young infantryman and the female soldier were ordered to stay away from each other until he completed an anger management class, and she completed counseling to deal with her drinking and sexual obsession.

A month or two later, the same young woman was caught with another male soldier from the company having adventurous sex in her barracks room, while still engaged to her jealous infantryman. The first sergeant fumed, because he had taken such extreme precautions to safeguard this woman from what he thought was an abusive boyfriend. The battalion started proceedings to send the young girl home. The company spent an absurd amount of time trying to appease this woman's family, to ensure her safety, and to provide psychological help for her. They didn't have time to constantly clean up after her sexual adventures.

This woman could easily be one of the veterans who claims now that she was raped and the Army did nothing to help her. I have never seen a situation where an Army woman alleged rape and the Army did nothing to help her. I have seen other women act like this girl, who spent months manipulating her family and her commanders into thinking she was a victim to hide her binge drinking, wild spending, and promiscuity. Sincere sergeants and commanders invested vast quantities of time to protect her — only to realize they were duped.

It is impossible to avoid these kinds of sexual peccadilloes when women are in remote areas or hardship assignments with predominantly male units. There are men and women in every unit who are unprepared to accept the discipline, the harsh realities of soldiering. Most often, immature men can be mentored, trained out of their juvenile attitudes. As long as women are afforded the "abuse excuse" to deflect from their own misconduct, you can predict two outcomes. The immature women will use the abuse excuse, and thereby avoid an opportunity to learn from their mistakes. And, the unit will be demoralized both because of the special treatment conferred upon a soldier who does not add value as a combat multiplier, and because of the excessively harsh treatment of the men accused of sexually abusing women.

For the most part, Lieutenant Colonel Chappell inspired his battalion to transcend our hardship tour by teaching them to be proud of their mission and the heritage of our battalion, the 44th. There's no such thing as zero tolerance for misconduct, however, if you want men to follow you into battle. You have to accept that occasionally, soldiers are going to fail in their personal conduct. Chappell understood that. He modeled self-control for the soldiers, and taught that they could manage themselves to avoid an awful lot of trouble.

Chappell's best talk to the soldiers described his own path from being a private to a West Point graduate, to a battalion commander.

"Nothing comes easy," he counseled passionately. "We're not going to come up to your barracks room and spoon feed you. If you want something out of life, you have to go after it. I was a private in Germany."

The soldiers were all ears when he announced this fact for the first time.

"I took classes. I didn't waste my time doin' drugs. Drugs were there for the taking. I went to West Point, and I had to work really hard. Even my wife has had to work hard. We have three children. She has earned her Bachelor's in management. It's not easy. We had to pull together to work this out. I could never quit my job to get my master's. I had to go to night school and on weekends. That's what the American Dream is all about. If you want somethin' you work hard, and your dream comes true!"

College enrollments went up after that speech. After he exhorted the soldiers to manage their drinking, to be in control always, there were no more alcohol-related incidents to drag us out of bed in the wee hours of the morning.

Each month, we had a battalion run. Anyone who could crawl was required to start the run. Even the Construction Company from Camp Edwards was required to participate. Chappell headed the run, even when he had a bum leg. To my surprise, I was able to keep up for most of the four to six miles, because he set the pace to keep the 500 soldiers together the whole way.

In December, we had a fun run that started at the bottom of Camp Howze. We headed straight to the highest peak, wound around, and then ended at the bottom of the camp, so that we would all have to walk up the 70-degree slope to shower and dress for the duty day. Colonel Chappell was a good sport and let folks like me run past him on the steep incline. All the engineers, including Chappell took off like jackrabbits, though, once they reached the summit.

Both the brigade and the battalion commanders supported prayer breakfasts to help individual soldiers draw on their faith as a source of strength while so far away from their loved ones. Colonel Chappell would beam, cheering our young soldiers as they sang their hymns. The cooks were honored for all they bestowed on us each day when we dropped by begrudgingly for our "three hots."

For all the holidays, Colonel Chappell came to chapel in his dress blues, and ate with the officers and soldiers at the dining facility. He took great pride in encouraging his cooks to win the Connelly award for regular meals. On Thanksgiving and Christmas, the cooks were chefs. They worked round the clock to make gorgeous ice sculptures of swans. The female chefs baked and decorated prize-winning cakes. The gravy masters would grin as you asked for a second or third scoop. They would insist you try the au jus on their prime rib. They won the Connelly every holiday I was with the 44th.

Chappell joined us as we played with the Korean orphans with whom we shared each holiday. On Christmas Day, the soldiers from Camp Edwards organized a big party for the orphans. They dressed up a GI as Santa Claus and had carefully wrapped presents for every child who sat on Santanim's lap. I took great pride when the cameras from AFKN captured our day and aired the singing and gift-giving on the AFKN news. A number of sergeants bought huge turkeys and all the fixings, then prepared another homemade dinner for their men in the barracks.

The first time Korean orphans were brought to the base, I was surprised to find many men and women were angry that the children were allowed on post. They could not bear to be without their own children and families for such a long period. They felt that the presence of Korean children was only a cruel reminder of their loss. But once the children began singing sweetly, the hardness melted. As one soldier commented, "At least I have two children to go home to.

These children don't have any families." One sergeant came to the altar and knelt in prayer after our first worship service for the children. He began to sob and sob. After a while, I sat with him. His brother was killed in an accident just before he came to Korea. The sergeant, who had piercing green eyes said he was always a faithful Catholic, but he had not been able to forgive God for his brother's death until he came to church that day. The children tenderly invited him to unburden his anger and grief so that he could come back to the church to find comfort in his talks with God.

During Thanksgiving weekend, our battalion held a football tournament where I learned first-hand the myth that men lose more time due to sports accidents than women lose due to pregnancy. For two days, our men were out on the fields, exhausting themselves with round robin games. Not a single woman, enlisted or officer, volunteered to play in these flag football games. We were extremely content to watch from the sidelines.

By the end of the weekend, about seven of our soldiers, including my executive officer, were in the hospital from injuries. Most were released and put back to work in a few days. Men can break a bone in a football game, but if they are supposed to go to the field, the company just takes them along, because they can watch phones, and do light chores until they heal. Pregnant women cannot work at all in the field, in the motor pool, or in jobs that require heavy lifting, etc. They stay behind to watch telephones that never ring when the unit is out in the field.

No matter how hard commanders try to protect soldiers from their personal weaknesses or vices, the choice to indulge or not always belongs to the individual. At Camp Howze, where the soldiers were challenged to live highly disciplined lives, I realized that more soldiers want to make healthy choices than we might assume. The 90s soldier very often struggles to be faithful to his wife out of a strong need for family stability. Men and women who struggle to be faithful to their spouses or partners back in the states, are sometimes ridiculed by peers or by their bosses for being so puritanical. Usually the taunting friend wants to seduce a soldier into having an affair. Sometimes, promiscuous men and women try to alleviate their own guilt by encouraging the most pure to have an affair with another married soldier, or a fling with a prostitute or bar girl.

The untold Army story, the unsexy story that will never play in the modern media is that a lot of men and women do remain faithful, and they have some healthy ways of getting through a hardship assignment. Throughout the Division, you can find men who work long hours, seven days per week, as their way of coping. Others do arts and crafts. Colonel Soo maintained all kinds of activities that were not profitable (profitability is a legal but stupid requirement to maintain activities on Army bases) to ensure that engineers had alternatives to bars and bar girls.

At Camp Edwards, one sergeant opened the alcohol-free activity room night after night. He painted ceramic vases and cookie jars while soldiers watched movies and played poker, so that others could see him having a good time, staying connected to his family back home. By November, he made Christmas presents for all his kids and the rest of his big farm family.

We left the Camp Howze post chapel open all night. I would check on it every now and then, because I was aware that men, even chaplains, had run a prostitution ring out of this chapel not too many years before. Whenever I would stop by, at 10:00 A.M. or 2:00 A.M., I would find men playing either the piano or the organ. One young brilliant organ builder spent his spare hours tuning my pianos and organs, then playing the five easy pieces he knew.

A soft-spoken lieutenant would play Chopin waltzes late at night and on weekends. This man, like many of the lieutenants who took their mentoring responsibilities very seriously, believed he should model the whole person as a leader. In the field, he was task oriented, no-nonsense. When he tickled the ivories in our chapel, you wanted to lilt down the aisle in a waltz. It was hard to imagine the same man at his day job with mud caked fingernails, setting up explosives with his men to shape the battlefield for freedom.

Movies were shown for free on Camp Howze. The reels ranged from tender relationship themes to the action-packed kill-and-thrill adventures. The relationship movies were great sources for sermons, because they provided illustrations I could use that were relevant to our lives. But the parallels were not so personal that I would violate the confidence of anyone who came for counseling about problems that were similar to the movie.

Two men facilitated a Promise Keepers group on Camp Howze. These men were rigidly fundamentalist, expecting all women to be subordinate or submissive. I was responsible for supervising this group. Chaplains supervise all religious programs within their unit. On occasion, a male soldier would come and complain that the group was sexist. Once one of the leaders, Sergeant A, came to me to confess his rebellion against my role as pastor of the Protestant congregations. Another soldier pointed out passages in the Bible where God selected women to be prophets. Sergeant A recounted his reading of the story of Deborah.

"I guess I just didn't know my Bible well enough. There are times when God speaks to women. It is not for me to judge."

His sincerity astonished me. Sergeant A was a very gentle man. He facilitated the Promise Keepers not because he wanted to oppress or dominate women, but because he desperately wanted to save his family from the ruination secular values seemed to guarantee back in our homeland.

I do not think the Army should spend a dime to subsidize Promise Keepers, although a fortune was spent in Korea and in the States to send soldiers to Promise Keeper rallies. But I have been ambivalent about the participation of men in this movement. I see too often that the men are so blinded by the pain of their family histories that they lead from that place in their hearts which is embittered. At other times, the men sincerely use the group to overcome their own temptations to drink excessively or to objectify women. With moderate Promise Keepers leadership, the guys can nurture each other through really rough times. The problem is that the Promise Keepers leadership is rarely moderate.

I visited with the Promise Keepers group on occasion to encourage them to be less judgmental and controlling of their wives, and more open to a marital partnership.

"If you take the promises in Promise Keepers seriously, you will have to leave the Army," I advised.

The men stared at me in shock.

"Look. You want it both ways. You want to be able to go off for six months at a time, a year at a time. Play in the woods. Play with your machine guns and your track vehicles. How can you be so completely in charge at home if you are never there? Army families don't survive unless the men learn how to trust their wives, and to give them control of a lot of the family responsibilities. You have to be at home to be the head of the house. So, either you go back to backwoods Louisiana to pump gas seven hours a day so you can be in charge of your family, or you learn how to trust your wife to take care of the family while you are off in a foreign country for a year at a time!"

Most men in the Army understand the need for flexibility and mutuality in marriage. They are able to sustain their marriages without Promise Keepers. The four or five men at Camp Howze who clung to their rigid notion that men must always be in control sought refuge for their rigidity in the Promise Keepers group. They paid a steep price for their rigidity. A particularly zealous young sergeant was handed divorce papers upon his arrival in the States. One year of intense rhetoric and marital separation proved to be too much. His wife fell in love with the man in whose care the sergeant placed her.

Another Promise Keeper, Sergeant P, obsessed about his need to refrain from drinking and promiscuity. Sergeant P talked about his fears at every Promise Keepers group, every Bible study, and every church service. The young man had a wife at home. At 20 years old, she was caring for their three children. She was extremely needy and incapable of handling the yearlong separation from her husband. One night, two or three months after Sergeant P's arrival, I received a call from our organ repairman, who was on staff duty at the battalion headquarters.

"Ma'am, you need to go to the Troop Medical Clinic. Sergeant P jumped out of the window. We think he broke his neck."

Sergeant P called his wife. She confessed to him that she just made love to another man because she was lonely. Sergeant P, a Pentecostal, went into an angry trance. He ran to the third floor of his barracks, jumped out the window.

He fell to the ground without a scratch. Sergeant P ran back up to the third floor and jumped a second time, only scratching his forehead. Another soldier who saw him jump both times came over and got him medical help. But not before Sergeant P jumped the third time from the third story landing!

I went to the TMC, but couldn't find Sergeant P. He had already been transported to the Western Corridor Clinic for x-rays. When I called the duty officer who was with the soldier, I was told, "Oh, don't bother, Sergeant P is just drunk. He didn't get hurt. He's just drunk."

I mentioned to the duty officer that to the best of my knowledge, Sergeant P did not drink. I was sure that he had gone into a Pentecostal trance. In my hospital ministry, I had seen Pentecostals fall to the floor over and over again wailing and moaning to express their grief and anger when a loved one dies. Inner city hospitals accept this spiritual practice, and usually call in a chaplain to modulate and subdue the tone of the trance with petitionary prayers. The Army is so accustomed to this spiritual and deeply Pentecostal practice that special non-denominational Gospel services are held to allow for such expression in Sunday worship.

Because Sergeant P's falling out was an expression of primal rage, and his own doomsday fear of family disintegration was finally realized, I asked the duty officer to make sure the sergeant received a psychiatric evaluation. Sergeant P was transported to the 121st hospital, where I saw him the next day. The psychiatrist said that Sergeant P's blood test confirmed he was not drunk. He had gone into an angry trance. The hospital kept Sergeant P for four or five days to teach him some anger management skills.

Anyone who has worked in an Emergency Room or an Operating Room will tell you a certain cryptic humor is necessary to maintain sanity among the hired help. Sergeant P was released. Both his psychiatrist and his social worker told him that I, as his chaplain, had all the resources necessary to guide him if he ever was troubled again. Sergeant P would visit me whenever he was angry, or desiring a transfer back to the states, or threatened with economic doom. He was a sweet, but unstable man. I felt like I was back at Oakland Army Base, in another dubious situation. Without a Master's in social work or psychiatric credentials, I was designated to be Sergeant P's primary counselor. This is all the psychiatric support soldiers are guaranteed in combat units. If soldiers can't get direct support in deployed units, and they can't get direct support in garrison, why do we keep social workers and psychiatrists on staff? My cryptic humor helped me cope with the repeated irony of our soldier's predicaments. Whenever P's case was discussed with the Docs or my chain of command, I alleviated my own feelings of inadequacy by referring to him as Superman.

We had many other soldiers whose wives were unfaithful during their hardship tours. One gentle soldier, the grandson of a preacher, came to me to reflect on his marriage. He was soft-spoken. A medic, and quite a healer. The young man would reflect on his own failings, and discern ways that he could show more concern and tenderness for his wife. He was able to talk to his grandfather openly about his crisis.

A surprising number of young men and women had the maturity to recognize that their marriages were worth salvaging even after such a devastating experience as infidelity. We would make appointments at four in the morning, so they could call their spouses back in the States to work through some of their painful conflicts long distance.

Some of the men would ask to go home on emergency leave. We had to screen the men before sending them stateside. The Army already documented the alarming statistic that a soldier kills a family member at the rate of once per week. The issue, in our experience, was usually infidelity.

Because of the high correlation between infidelity and domestic violence in the military, I counseled commanders and soldiers to evaluate each situation carefully before permitting a soldier to go home. At Camp Edwards, we had a soldier whose wife was committing adultery in government housing at Fort Hood. Another Fort Hood soldier literally moved into the family apartment. Commanders at Fort Hood would do nothing to stop the adultery or to move the adulterer out of our soldier's apartment while he was in Korea.

Richard was soft-spoken, but while grieving his wife's unfaithfulness, he talked often of his desire for revenge. Some people still think violence is a legitimate way to handle relationship disputes. I encouraged Richard to go through the Mental Health Department's anger management class to help him cope with his crisis, but discouraged him from going home until he could accept his situation. I advised the command not to approve his leave. Later, when Richard found out that I encouraged a few other more stable soldiers to go home to face their wives directly in the midst of infidelity, Richard confronted me.

"Ma'am, I heard you told the medic he should go home to work out his problems with his wife. How come you wouldn't let me go home?" He asked as he drove me to a field-training site.

"Richard, I don't make these decisions. I only advise soldiers and commanders. But you tell me why I recommended that you stay here to cool off when that man moved in with your wife?"

"Because I would have killed her," Richard chuckled. "And I would have, too. Now, I'm just going to file for divorce. She ain't worth it."

Although I tried to be discreet about the early morning long-distance couples counseling I conducted between soldiers and their stateside spouses, we had to log calls, and get control numbers for each. After handling another young private's case, where the man threatened suicide unless he was allowed to go home for the birth of his first child, Colonel Soo stopped me on the street.

"Chaplain deYoung, how come all these soldiers talk to you? I don't get it. All these soldiers want to talk to you. Is it because you're like their mother?"

The Brigade Sergeant Major stood by with a tight-lipped smile.

"You're like their mother and all these soldiers come running to you. I can't believe it!"

He grinned from ear to ear as he barked his observations to me.

Colonel Soo never failed to show appreciation for women when we did our jobs. There is no question that women can complete non-combatant professional responsibilities as well as men. It is thrilling to have opportunities to demonstrate one's competence in places where women have not dared to tread in the past. I made myself useful in the 44th, but there were limitations to what I could do because of my gender. I never once saw another woman in the line units from the level of Tank Task Force down to my line companies when they were in the field. Every tiny chance I had to prove myself, I would go out to be with the grunts. But I couldn't help notice just how much more efficient, how much more comfortable, how much better the combat units function when they are all male.

There's no sexual tension. Not an ounce of angst is spent to resolve gender conflicts. The conversations have a hard edge. The men focus on tasks and mission. Until they hit the chow line or their cots late at night, they are all business. When women are part of any unit, the operation tempo is slower. There is always sexual tension, even in the high-speed units. There's male and female PMS tension. There's gender rivalry.

No one on active duty ever wants to believe that war could be imminent. Military leaders have wisely taken precautions since 1994 to update plans, however, to properly position equipment and personnel, and to have the capacity for response to an impulsive North Korean attack. Early 1995 rumors of food shortages leaked out. North Koreans suspended the Armistice Agreement that summer. North Korean soldiers penetrated the Republic as far south as Kunsan at various times. To top it off, the North was destabilized due to the continuing famine and the military's rebuff of Kim Jung Il's leadership.

As the threat level increased, Second Infantry Division alerts were treated as go-to-war exercises — to a point. Vehicles were loaded. Base security was established. Not all the commanders wanted to run through a full mobilization each time an alert was called. Driving in Korea was such a flirtation with death that the Division imposed strict accountability standards.

The Second Infantry Division had an accident rate that was four times as high as any other military unit in the world. In the tritest of accidents, Korean drivers would nick mirrors off the left side of our vehicles. Whenever a military road accident occurred, the entire chain of command would have to report to a general officer and give a detailed explanation of the cause of the accident, risk assessment, as well as plans to prevent recurrences.

Common killers were Road Terminators, big Korean trucks that would take sharp mountainous curves by driving in the lane of opposing traffic. American drivers never win in confrontations with the Terminators. Between Terminators and the Mirror Nickers, General Tommy Franks soon issued an edict that the Second would hereafter be known as the Right Lane Driving Division.

Some commanders were so fearful of being called on the carpet because of an accident that they would not take their vehicles off post for alerts. Rollouts, or practice deployments, were simulated or notional. Everywhere, that is, except for the 44th and the 72nd Tank Task Force. Lieutenant Colonel Chappell sternly believed he had to model strength for his junior leaders and officers, and insisted that we would "train as we fight." Chappell articulated his concerns at every leadership meeting, battalion orientation, awards ceremony and site visit. We would all be toast if we weren't fully prepared to secure the base and execute our mission, assuming of course, we survived the fan of artillery fire.

We rolled out carefully for that first alert — a simple convoy to Camp Edwards and back, but a most necessary exercise to prepare for war. Equipment must be used and tested regularly. It's amazing how many soldiers fake vehicle maintenance if they think their vehicles will never be used!

For a while, there was a rash of break-ins in community buildings at Camp Howze. Someone broke into the Officer's Club, grilled some frozen hamburgers, left dirty dishes, empty beer bottles and grease on the grill. Colonel Soo went into a rage. He imposed a post lock-down. Twenty-four hour roving guard duty. No one was exempted. This went on for days. The culprit was never caught. Eventually, Lieutenant Colonel Chappell persuaded Colonel Soo to end our group punishment. Then, another break-in. This time the devious fellow broke into the gym and took a hot shower. We theorized he was one of the soldiers who went AWOL to stay with a Korean sweetheart. Colonel Soo fumed and refused to end the roving guard or the lockdown. After several more days of nightly patrolling up and down the post, Soo finally relented as Lieutenant Colonel Chappell insisted that the problem was under control. Our battalion-wide lockdown was lifted. A bunch of us went into Seoul on Friday night for the first time since the lockdown had been imposed. Elated by our brief respite, I returned on the last bus from Yongsan, just in time to meet the Engineer Brigade curfew. As the bus pulled up to the gate, a KATUSA came on board:

"Identification, please. You come on post, we have LOCK DOWN!!!"

"Jesus Chriissttt!"

"What the f——?"

"Ill Byung Kim, what the hell happened??'"

"Sorry, burglar is back. Please you come on post, you cannot go off. If you want to be free, get off here!"

"Oddishee, you goin' back to Seoul?"

The bus driver stared at us as if we were idiots. He pointed to the bus stop just across the street from my chapel, where he fully intended to park his bus for the night.

"Oddishee, take us back to Seoul. What the f——-!!"

Those were not my expletives. I was just as angry as everybody else, but I kept my complaints to myself. Seems the culprit broke into our Post Exchange this time and stole things like T-shirts and sports equipment. Colonel Soo was using old-fashioned military discipline and peer pressure to break the backs of the creeps who were violating post security and military law. We were all sick of the discipline. We fantasized mutiny.

After several more days of the lockdown, I took advantage of my status as a short-term acting engineer brigade chaplain and went to visit Colonel Soo. The colonel barked his angry frustration to the visitor who preceded me. When it was my turn, Soo waved me into his office with a smile. Colonel Soo's office overlooked the command road. His view included a backdrop of hardy pine and chestnut trees. He had many vases and works of art given by Korean nationals in gratitude for his service. Colonel Soo was Chinese American. The decor in his office was as soft and serene as he was hard and brusque in his manner.

We chatted about his beloved daughter and wife for a few minutes, and then the Colonel listened to my pleas to end the lockdown. Soo was very frank. He insisted that this disciplinary technique was absolutely necessary because he didn't want the Army turning into a bunch of thugs. Colonel Soo lamented the change in American society, how one had to be armed to the teeth to feel safe in cities like New York. He vowed he would never let the Army turn into such a hellhole.

Colonel Soo softened up after we talked awhile. We talked about all the great things his soldiers were doing, how you cannot use group punishment to great effect for more than a short period. Finally, Soo agreed to end the lockdown, but as we spoke, we were notified that an infiltrator made it to Camp Edwards from North Korea. The Camp Howze Korean National security analyst came into Colonel Soo's office and briefed that our new threat level was very serious. Colonel Soo couldn't end the lockdown after all, but he agreed to communicate his pride in the goodness of our soldiers, and to let them know he would call off the lockdown as soon as the threat level subsided.

That morning, three infiltrators were captured at different points around the South. Korean security forces killed the one who made it to Camp Edwards. Of course, the Koreans were the real security forces on base, not American GIs. We could not have captured the infiltrator with our flashlights and unloaded rifles.

The engineer troops forgave Colonel Soo once the infiltration happened. The Division put soldiers on roaming guard duty for awhile. We targeted our sarcasm and ridicule at division leaders now. Soldiers marched up and down the hills of Howse, round the clock. They joked about the futility of GI guards carrying unloaded rifles and flashlights for safety's sake. Everybody knew that very few commanders trusted their soldiers to handle live ammunition outside a tightly supervised range. An untimely death would be a career stopper for the commander. How could we stop North Korean commandos?

As paranoid as our guard duties seemed, and as exhausting as they were, because round the clock duty meant sleep deprivation every night, they pulled the troops out of their complacency, loneliness and self-absorption. Army grunts will endure any hardship, any schedule, if they think it is mission-essential. The cohesion began to build.

My driver and assistant was a tall, handsome, Korean KATUSA, Il Byung Choi, that is Private First Class Choi. By regulation I was supposed to have an American, but chaplain assistants were notorious for having their assignment orders to Korea deleted, leaving the chaplains who accepted hardship tours high and dry. There were never enough American assistants (or chaplains for that matter) to go around. I was blessed when PFC Choi was assigned to me. He was very proud of his computer literacy and his ability to handle funds. He set up the chapel and translated for me whenever I had to counsel Koreans who were in a relationship with one of our soldiers.

Private First Class Choi loved to drive our Cut Vee because it gave him a little extra status. EUSA did not permit KATUSAs to drive American vehicles, because the Korean government jailed them if they had accidents. I needed to visit soldiers in the field. I could have played the game, "No driver, no go to the field," but I think those who play that game need to be removed from the active duty roster.

Choi finagled with the KATUSA Sergeant Major Kim, and earned permission to drive for me. He was by far the best assistant I ever worked with on active duty. He was a lot of fun to travel with, too.

We visited the engineers' field sites together. I was the only woman out there besides Ahjimah, which in Korea means Miss or Missus. Every unit hired an Ahjimah to carry Ramen noodles, bulgogi and rice to the field. The Ahjimahs had camouflaged tents to match American field gear. Ahjimah would follow the convoys out to the field site, and pitch her tent right at the edge of the company's perimeter. In her warm, steaming tent, she would have huge hot pots of water prepared to cook noodles. Ahjimah precooked rice and bulgogi, then warmed platters for the men. Soldiers would trade their MREs for Ahjimah's fresh hot spicy food. The guys would pay $3.00 for a box of Korean cookies that would only cost them a dollar if they had planned ahead and bought their cookies in the town. They didn't seem to mind paying extra, so long as Ahjimah relieved the stern training atmosphere with her kind chatter, mothering slaps, and her raucous laughter.

When I found out that this or that Ahjimah had supported the same company for 25 or 30 years I would tease the guys.

"Well, now I know that you are not against women in combat after all. Here we are on the front line, and Ahjimah rolls out as part of your company convoy."

Of course, the men never anticipated a live battle. They expected Ahjimah to flee to her hometown if that happened.

Who knows if Ahjimah would stay around for a live battle? I think she would, and I surmise she did during the Korean War. I had seen Ahjimah's platters before. It took me a few months to recall where. This was the Korean rice my father cooked to celebrate my sister's birth.

Ahjimahs are honorary members of their units in Korea. Congress could pass strict laws against Ahjimahs. But I can guarantee you that as long as American soldiers are allowed to use their wits, and women are not paid adequately for doing other legitimate kinds of work, these women will be in close proximity to field soldiers.

When PFC Choi and I visited our engineers, who were scattered over the countryside, we would stay overnight as warranted. In one of my first visits, I stumbled out to a Porta-Potty in the dark, only to encounter a man who was using the facility with the door wide open, probably because the putrid smell would have suffocated him if he closed it. After that, I always found an indoor bathroom while driving from one site to another so I could tidy up in privacy.

Choi and I were prepared to pull up a cot and stay with the guys when they asked us to. Sergeant Ski was the first sergeant to ask, "Chaplain, are you gonna stay with us tonight? You can use that cot over there. Go see the guys at the range and come back. We'll be ready for ya'." Ski kept his squad organized throughout the night. Repairing their tracks. Pulling guard duty. I wandered about and visited all the other squads in the company until bedtime.

My first night in a tent with the combat engineers was luxurious. The tents were heated with big barrel stoves. Ski summed up the routine for the next morning: First he would make cocoa, then the guys would go out for stand-to, they would do hygiene, and put polish on their boots to keep them from cracking. Ski fussed about in the tent, which was surprising, because outside the tent, he was a mean sergeant. But he made the guys think their tent was as cozy as a ski-lodge. I walked down to the camp's entrance, where there was an indoor bathroom and prepared myself for the overnight. On the way back, soldiers paused and joked about the cold, their Ramen and Cheese noodles, Slicky Boy, and the Porta-Potties. Some were surprised that I would actually stay the night. They were not used to seeing chaplains in the field — not even men.

After I left the Army, I bumped into one of the privates from the 44th while attending church at Fort Hood. The private told his engineer friend, "She's really awesome. She stayed out with us when it was freezing cold..." It doesn't take much to make an impression on these guys — they stayed out in the freezing weather for weeks at a time, so an occasional night on a cot next to the tent heater was no significant accomplishment. Staying with the engineers helped me to earn their trust rather quickly. If a first sergeant invited me to stay overnight with his men, Choi and I would stay. If it seemed inappropriate because of the round-the-clock missions, then Choi and I would just travel from camp to camp, visit all the soldiers in the field, and return to the garrison.

After my first week with the Broken Hearts, Il Byung Choi said, "Ma'am. I am very surprised by you."

"Oh, yeah?" I thought he was going to comment on my religion.

"Yes, you are woman. I thought no one would come to your office because you are woman chaplain. But I was very surprised. In one week, you visited with more soldiers than other chaplains visit their whole year. You are a woman, but the soldiers talk to you. I was surprised. In Korean, we say, you have a very wide footprint."

PFC Choi made it extremely easy for me to do ministry, and he had a very wide footprint in the battalion, too. He was a healthy, normal young man, but as a Christian Presbyterian he lived above reproach, unlike our American chaplain assistants, who were required to live by no moral or religious code. Choi cared about our soldiers, both American and KATUSA.

Choi drove Korean style at first, but because I was most afraid that he could be jailed if there was an accident, I insisted he had to drive American style. "Chun chun hee! Chun chun hee!" is the instruction every officer must know in Korean. Slow down! Slow down!

Once, PFC Choi raced to the central intersection of a small village only to come to a crashing halt within inches of an elderly woman who was feebly crossing the street.

"Chun chun hee!" I almost croaked.

Choi's pride was hurt such that I might not be able to heal the breach between us. Suddenly, I thought of a way to explain our differences as a cross-cultural phenomenon.

"In America, we don't race to a stop sign and slam our brakes at the last minute." With my hands, I drew a musical square wave. "We gradually slow down, glide to a stop, just to be sure, in case the brakes don't work, that we won't hit anybody. Please, you are a wonderful driver. I'm afraid if our brakes

29 Chaplain Assistant Extraordinaire

Saying good-bye to Corporal Choi (far left).

Airborne Chaplain Forever!

Chaplain Fowler was the most vigorous, dedicated chaplain to serve in Korea.

fail you will go to jail. I don't want you to get in any trouble."

Our Cut Vee was pulled out of the salvage dump and reassembled with scrap parts taken from other vehicles. Although the Cut Vee was trustworthy, and one of the more dependable vehicles on post, I was not lying when this face-saving explanation came to mind.

Later that day, Choi showed emotion, as he rarely did. On the way back to Howze, he turned our conversation to the driving issue.

"Ma'am, I have been thinking about what you said about the American way. I think it is better." He had tears in his eyes. "When I was a boy, I was on the side of the road, and a car came racing by and I was hit and I was in the hospital for a long time. This is why I am only an average student. This is why I am not at the University. Because I missed a whole year of school, I can never go to the special university. I think the American way to stop is better. I will do better."

After that, Choi commanded the vehicle without my interference, and I concentrated on map reading. I read the Hangul names of the towns on our map and matched them to the Hangul signs on the road. Because so many roads are created overnight, our Army maps are totally inaccurate. We had lots of fun trying to find the ROK Army posts where Charlie Company parked itself most of the time to avoid garrison details. We navigated the tank trails, riverbeds, and other work sites of our construction engineers. We were at our most adventurous when we tried to find the Tank Task Forces supported by the 44th. When all else failed, PFC Choi would get out, ask a local farmer in Hangul how to get here or there. Then, he would joke with them about the American lady Moksanim for whom he was driving, and we would be safely on our way.

Compared to Americans and the KATUSAs, ROK army soldiers have a very harsh life. They get paid pennies a day. Occasionally, when the weather was really foul, Choi would ask if we could stop and pick up this or that ROK soldier who was standing out in the pouring rain, waiting for a bus. I soon realized Choi was not only acting in kindness, he also got a kick out of explaining to these soldiers that he was driving for an American lady Moksanim. Their eyes would get wide. They'd smile, wrinkle their foreheads in puzzlement, and shake their heads and laugh. We would drop the soldiers outside the gate of their post, and continue on to our next engineer company.

Choi was a Christian. Not at all interested in weapons and fighting. None of the American assistants assigned to me liked to handle weapons or play war games, either. But American assistants are not required to be religious, or to uphold standards of conduct that are befitting the Chaplain Corps' program. Consequently, most of the American assistants don't want to be involved in church services, or counseling efforts. They don't want to work at night, or stay in the field too long. They are as likely as any other soldier to be alcohol abusers, or wife beaters, or prostitutes, or promiscuous, or criminals, or gang members. One Catholic priest summed up the problem the Chaplain Corps has with American chaplain assistants before he left active duty. American chaplain assistants are too often retreads who do not want to be soldiers. They just want an easy high-paying job. You cannot get an easier, high-paying unsupervised job than being a US Army chaplain assistant.

KATUSA chaplain assistants are specially selected because of their model character, their Christian faith, and their family connections. Choi was the most pastoral assistant I have ever seen. He ran a Bible study for the KATUSAs. He set up all my religious programs. When we organized prayer breakfasts, or parties for local orphans, or unit retreats, Choi helped me to plan and execute the programs for combined KATUSA/American groups.

Il Byung Choi helped me organize all those nighttime soldier activities I could never expect American assistants to help with. Our last event before I returned to the States was a Coin and Covenant Banquet. More than 50 single soldiers and a few wives gathered at the NCO club for dinner and a pep talk by Chaplain Colonel Billy Fowler on the importance of faith. He encouraged soldiers to make positive commitments to get through a hardship tour and the hardships of life. We also arranged for Chaplain Park, the head KATUSA chaplain of the 2nd Division to speak, which was not usually done. Many KATUSA soldiers attended this free bulgogi feast. Choi was so enthusiastic about the success, he asked me to come visit his parents after we returned Colonel Fowler to Seoul. We drove Colonel Fowler back to his house on the Army base in Yongson. After Mrs. Fowler and Billy Fowler said goodbye, PFC

Choi burst out with his request, "Can we go now to Yoeedo?" I had never seen him so excited.

"The big church that everybody talks about?" I asked, thinking Choi was referring to the world famous Pentecostal mega-church.

"No Ma'am, Yooeeedo. It is where my parents live."

"Yooeeedo is a place?"

We were driving a camouflaged Cut Vee, so I tried to explain to PFC Choi this might be against policy. Choi could not understand why Americans had laws against driving a government vehicle to a private home when we had just dropped off a Colonel at his private home on an army base.

"Are we going to make this Top Secret?" I asked, thinking the visit to his parents would be very important to our relationship, and to Choi's sense of fairness. The United States Government paid him twelve dollars per month, but we got more for our money than what we paid three American soldiers. He laughed. That was our code for "Don't tell a soul unless you want the lady Moksanim to go to jail." The regulations strictly prohibited social use of the vehicles. I had to think of this as official business.

"Top Secret, Ma'am." Choi drove us across the bridge to Yoeedo. We drove down a wide boulevard, and pulled up to a very tall Apartah.

"This is it?"

He nodded, secured the vehicle, and led me up to the entryway of his home. The exterior was gray drab. Once inside, I marveled again at the Korean taste for beautiful hardwood floors and ceilings, and lovely vases and Korean sculptures.

Choi's parents met us at the door, fully surprised, but happy to see their handsome son. Although most KATUSAs lived an hour or so from their families, they were not allowed to go home for six or eight week periods as part of their training discipline. His mother went to the kitchen and prepared sliced apples, sliced oranges and tea for us. PFC Choi showed me his room, and all his special interests. His sister came out to visit with us for awhile. We chatted about Choi's accomplishments. I boasted to his parents about his field exploits, our adventurous drives, and his extraordinary success at building the bond between KATUSAs and American soldiers. Choi minimized every sentence by tucking his head down and shaking, "No!" But his laughter gave away his pleasure that his parents were being honored by his work.

As much as I hated to leave, we knew we could not stay the night, because the Division still had a curfew. Although we were on a mission, it would be obvious that we had overstayed our time in Seoul and missed the deadline. Choi's parents bowed. We bowed. They bowed again, and we bowed again. We went to the door, put our shoes back on, and took a couple of top-secret risks on the way home to beat the curfew.

There are many other soldiers from the 44th Combat Engineers who will have a place in my heart. Chaplains are assigned to the Headquarters company of the unit they will serve. Headquarters units seldom go to the field as often as a line unit or a service support company, such as the medical or supply and transportation companies. Headquarters companies usually send a small slice of cooks, mechanics, and other support workers to augment each company in the field. It usually takes two or three field trips to get a support unit's headquarters element to function properly for a major exercise. However, because of First Sergeant Pearson, the 44th Headquarters did everything right the first time.

I will never forget First Sergeant Pearson's road march out to a field site where our Headquarters Company was required to sleep on the ground in temperatures less than ten degrees. When we executed our annual Cold Weather Training exercise, Pearson modified his plans to meet the much lower field standards required of the Headquarters, but the experience was still tough. Fun, too. When darkness came, we marched about five miles to a secluded field site. Pearson had given us classes on how to lay down our mats, sleeping bags, ponchos, poncho liners and waterproof bags to seal ourselves from the cold. Both PFC Choi and I set our mats next to each other, cocooned ourselves, and fell into a deep sleep. We had to get up at 5:30 in the morning. We were both so toasty we didn't want to leave our bags. Finally I persuaded Choi to get up by telling him the truth — we were going home in a vehicle as soon as we could pack our gear and hop on the trucks.

First Sergeant Pearson took great pride in his ability to lead soldiers — to make men out of boys. Pearson never married. His oath of office was like a priestly vocation for him. He was a top athlete, a superb engineer, and truly magnificent in reaching out to young men from all kinds of backgrounds. Because Pearson's love of soldiers was so great he could bring together the most diverse group and make it all work out.

When Pearson first took over the Headquarters Company, the older sergeants almost rioted because he made them take down their nudie photographs as long as there were women assigned to the battalion. My sense is that Pearson would have banned the paraphernalia even if the company was all male, because he was constantly trying to teach his soldiers not to debase themselves. That is not to say that he was unwilling to acknowledge the soldier's urgings. Pearson prided himself on his relationships with all the barkeepers so that he could count on the women to call him anytime one of his soldiers was in trouble, or about to lose control because of girlfriend problems.

My favorite commander was Joe Hanson, the Bravo Company Commander. Joe pushed himself to the limits, because he served a high-profile tank commander, Lieutenant Colonel John Antal, the 72nd Tank Task Force Commander. Antal was a historian, and very Patton-like in his leadership style.

He had written many historical articles. Antal's vehicle was the most dramatically camouflaged Humvee I ever saw in Korea — pine brush sticking out every which way, with leaves and pinecones stuffed in here and there. High art. It looked great in the woods, but very silly on the highway and on the snow-covered mountains.

One morning, while visiting Bravo Company, we could not return to Camp Howze from the field as planned because the roads were Red, too icy for safe travel. Captain Joe Hanson was maniacally happy as he invited me to shadow him on the tank trails while he planned his company's breaching operations for the next day. I jumped in his vehicle, left Choi to fellowship with the KATUSAs, and shadowed Joe as he drove up a steep hill, scoped out the plan of attack, and drew a diagram of the course of action. He instructed his driver to take us down to the valley so that he could recon the points where mines would be placed, obstacles blown up, etc. Joe was like a kid playing with spaceships and transformers on that brilliantly white plain.

Joe was an especially mature commander. He left his wife back in the states, and suffered the same hardships and deprivations as the men in his company. His days were as long as mine. When I left the chapel after the evening soldier programs, I would stop by the gym to relax with a few nautilus exercises. Joe was often just getting there himself, after he had done all his counseling and planning for the next day. The only time Joe left his troops to the care of the first sergeant was when his wife came over for mid-tour leave. As soon as she arrived, Joe introduced her to the company, all the officers and the battalion staff. Captain and Mrs. Hanson presided over the barracks until just before Christmas. He and his wife, a bunch of soldiers from our chapel program, Chaplain Castillo and I climbed up and down the hills of Howze the night before Christmas singing carols.

My friend, Ed Kelley was the Catholic Chaplain for the Division and for the 72nd Tank Force. We often arranged to hold Protestant and Catholic services at the same time so that we could cover his tankers and Bravo Company engineers on one afternoon. Joe Hanson had a hard time slowing down for this worship, but when Lieutenant Colonel Antol made it his business to support our services, the engineers paused, too. It was fun to link up with Ed at Tent City and during our monthly chaplain meetings on Camp Red Cloud, too.

Although the life of KATUSA and ROK army soldiers was much more harsh than that of our American soldiers, the Korean military system has some strong cultural traits that I think our Army would truly benefit from. Very few women can be found in the ROK Army. I did not find any woman KATUSA. Korea has compulsory service, like most countries in Europe. ROK army soldiers are very tough and disciplined, but the bonding between men is phenomenally tight. I don't think American soldiers have been that close or patriotic since the early part of Vietnam.

American soldiers have to adapt to Korean leadership styles and Korean problem solving styles. Whenever my computer broke down, I asked the best technician to fix it. If the technician were an American, he would sit down, and play with the computer like a toy until he mastered the problem. The best Korean technician will go get at least one other Korean. They will discuss, analyze, and slap each other on the back until the problem is solved. Group solutions seem to be preferable to individual ones.

In the winter, my assistant developed a strong sense that a particular American soldier was harassing the KATUSAs in our company. Corporal Choi gathered the KATUSAs to discuss the problem. He collected a list of episodes that would be called racial harassment if these things happened to American GIs. Before he had a chance to go to the sergeant privately, the sergeant picked on him in the dining facility. Choi responded with a few choice expletives and confronted him publicly. The whole dining room was stunned, because my assistant was usually angelic in his demeanor.

Choi came to me in shame, and confessed that he might have brought dishonor to our work. The whole thing was reported to me by another friend of Choi's to protect Choi from an unfair complaint. Choi's friend was afraid American soldiers would set Choi up for a beating from Sergeant Major Kim, the top enlisted KATUSA soldier. When Choi finally came to me, I asked him if he needed me to help him resolve the matter. Corporal Choi insisted that he should try to work out the problem with his American brothers, and to demonstrate that Koreans and Americans could work together as brothers.

The men talked out their disagreements over the next few days. Choi would report new understandings about how KATUSAs needed to adapt to the American Army culture. He would gleam as he boasted his success in convincing the sergeant to accept other Korean practices, such as deference to the hierarchy within the KATUSA system, and respect for the senior leaders or the older persons in the unit. Very often, American soldiers go through elaborate rituals, even fisticuffs to establish the authority of the leader. Korean culture is extremely hierarchical. Young soldiers accept the authority of their leaders without question. Choi taught us all the measure of wisdom in Korea's approach to authority.

The KATUSAs thought the American preoccupation with equal opportunity laws was quite overdone. When Choi and I visited Charlie Company, we found ROK army men gathered around, cooking their own meals with big pots and pans. Fresh bulgogi and rice. Kimshee everywhere. The KATUSAs who worked side by side with Charlie Company had to eat Meals Ready to Eat, just like the American GIs. One young man, guarding bullets at the range, teased me about the foolishness of the American Equal Opportunity program.

"Ma'am, I would like to register a complaint," he said as his buddies laughed. I encouraged him. "Ma'am, these MREs they are discriminating. You see, we Koreans, we must have kimshee and rice. There is no MRE with Kimshee and rice. Therefore, I must register a complaint to you for Equal Opportunity!"

His Korean buddies beamed with laughter.

The contrast between commanders who honored the rules of the unaccompanied tour and those who did not was definitive. Although all soldiers assigned to the Division were supposed to stay for one year as unaccompanied soldiers, too many of our essential leaders mocked this standard. When they brought their girlfriends and spouses, however, their work and our morale suffered. Joe Hanson was extremely focused on building his combat team throughout the year, so he asked his wife to remain stateside. However, the other two line commanders were not able to devote as much of their creative energy to the enormous task of leading a forward-deployed company. The other line company commanders brought their wives from the States to our remote post. Apartments outside Howze were extremely primitive, often lacking heat or running water. Despite the hardship to the families, many soldiers brought their wives to Korea, either because they could not handle the pain of separation, or because they did not trust their wives to remain faithful back in the States. Or both.

The Army continues to take a weak leadership stance in handling the thousands of wives and families who moved to Korea during their spouses' tours. Apple Blossom Cottages were subsidized throughout Korea to provide these spouses with an opportunity to do their laundry, cook a hot meal, or just spend a few hours in a civilized living room. Chaplains were given proponency to manage an Army Community Services Program called the Outreach Coordinators. These coordinators were spouses hired to identify the needs and obtain support for families who lived on the economy. In 1994, the Chaplain Corps managed a $150,000 program to pay outreach coordinators. The hidden expense of this program is shocking. Social workers, chaplains, Army Community Service managers, the Family Advocacy workers all have responsibilities to family members who don't belong and should not be in a forward-deployed division. Additionally, soldiers are assigned to coordinate evacuation missions, to inspect local building operations, to monitor housing arrangements, and to care for families who should not be there.

Camp Howze, the sacred mountain five miles from the DMZ, home of the combat engineers, a prime target for North Korean Artillery fire, provided a modest castle for wives who had no business being in Korea for more than a mid-tour vacation with their husbands. One of the commander's wives was the Howze Outreach Coordinator. Upon my arrival, the headquarters company commander complained bitterly that this woman was recruiting spouses to stay in Korea after meeting them during mid-tour vacations.

"Keep her out of my company!" He was surprised that I didn't attack his lack of compassion for family values.

The Chaplain Corps, perpetually aware that its spiritual mission is antiquated and undesired by the military, is always taking on social taskings that make the command look good. Many of the projects, such as taking unaccompanied soldiers to visit and play with orphans, are worthy projects and compatible with the intense missions and demands placed on deployed soldiers. When the chaplains eagerly assumed responsibility for running the Apple Blossom cottages, they not only erred on the side of selfishness (many chaplains, including the Division and Engineer Brigade chaplains who preceded me brought their wives to Korea), they also erred on the side of stupidity.

When Second Division country becomes so safe that we can ensconce American families throughout the Korean villages, it is time to bring American troops home. It has never been that safe. As the Division was gearing up for a real North Korean threat, the wives outside the Camp Howze gates raged that their husbands were not free to come home for dinner, or to play with the children. Many officers had their wives living with them in the BOQ. Two commanders from my battalion brought their wives up to the Q whenever their spouses wanted to escape the cold misery of village life. It was impossible to convince one of these commanders that it was not fair to discipline an enlisted soldier who brought his Korean girlfriend into the barracks if his own wife lived in the BOQ!

Those who endure hardship tours without their spouses seethe with resentment that the Army accommodates the weakness of some of its officers. The injuries are magnified when the spouses, especially commanders' wives, fight with their husbands into the wee hours of the morning. Our thin walls left no conversation to the imagination. Imagined infidelities were lorded over commanders who had to work past suppertime.

College educated women, who could only fill their days in Korea by working illegally as English teachers, often conjured soap opera fantasies about the debauchery their husbands would engage in if they weren't monitored closely. True, every company had its prostitute junkie. Most of the soldiers in the 44th Engineers, however, either by command directive or by personal choice were relentlessly focussed on building a war-fighting machine. A few of the single officers used to sit and watch porn movies together. If anything, the tendency to sublimate sexual energy by drinking excessively was the greatest danger our unaccompanied troops faced.

The spouses in the Division came to believe they had enormous power because General Franks' daughter was living in the barracks with her husband on Camp Casey while other officers had to double and triple up. The same dynamic that spouses have used in the States to acquire disproportionate command attention and resources surfaced over time — Pillow Power. The women wore their husbands' rank. Indeed, upon visiting spouses at Camp Casey, Mrs. Shalikashvili promised the wives she would take their plight to Washington to advocate for greater resources for wives who were breaking the deployment rules in the first place.

The Camp Howze Outreach Coordinator was despised because she exploited pillow talk politics to an extreme. She often verbally confused the wives' Chain of Concern with the Division's Chain of Command. One minute she would threaten, "Mrs. Flowers is going to hear about this. Then, "Mrs. Luck will be furious when she finds this out!"

While the men were in the field, this coordinator would use Army funds to take our enlisted spouses to the non-commissioned officers' club for dinner. Needless to say, in an almost exclusively male environment, ten to twelve wives gathered in a bar room creates tension. The outreach coordinator was extremely upset when I responded to the concerns of conservative spouses and soldiers by refusing to use government funds to pay for the next outreach meal. As far as I was concerned, the savings was not just the $100 or so for the meals each month. It was a savings in leadership time spent by squad, platoon, and company leaders to assuage the fears and anger of the soldiers who lived harshly out in the field while their wives were possibly being tempted in a barroom at government expense.

The Chaplains in the Division went to great lengths to appease screaming family members, and thus earn points with their commanders. The previous year, the engineer brigade chaplain obtained more than $22,000 from the Division Chaplain's Fund to fly about 24 soldiers and their spouses down to Chejudo for a marriage retreat that had no program besides R&R. A year later, I was still hearing about the misuse of funds for such activities. When I refused to subsidize my Outreach Coordinator's plans to take families on another outing, the Chain of Command threats erupted again.

One night, after the coordinator participated in a NEO, a Non-Combatant Evacuation Operation, she came to my office in a state of panic and depression.

"As we waited for the vehicles to take us to the airport," she sobbed as she complained, "and as we were boarding the planes to Japan, I realized that we would never get out of Korea alive if there was a real war!"

"Yes, that is most likely true." I responded.

"The roads will be impassable. We'll never make it to the airport!"

"Do you see why we discourage spouses from moving to the Division area? We know the roads will be impassable, as the Koreans will panic and block up the roads in their own attempts to flee!"

"Why didn't anybody tell us this before we moved here?" she asked as she heaved sobs with her own belated recognition that the Apple Blossom was an outrageous program.

"We try to discourage spouses from moving to Korea. That is why I encouraged J to go home when her apartment was stripped of heat and plumbing in November. All the spouses would be safer if they moved back to the states!"

"The Army should have informed us directly of the risks we were taking. Right now, the threat level is high. My dogs won't get out. I won't get out...."

Since the Army evolved into a welfare society, family members and soldiers have grown more accustomed to blaming the Army for their own poor choices, and then expecting the Army to pay for damage done. Perhaps a bit too directly, I decided to push this coordinator to think through the ethics of the Apple Blossom movement.

"Look," I started. "First of all, your husband commands a company where he must counsel soldiers to handle their loneliness and their spouse's absence in a disciplined way. The soldiers look at our officers and see a lack of discipline. Why should enlisted soldiers be held to a higher standard? Second, what about the wives and children who stay in the United States? God forbid, if we should ever go to war, a whole unit will be detailed to help women and children evacuate — women and children who should not be here in the first place! How is a wife going to feel if she finds out that her husband was killed because there weren't enough soldiers on line to defend a position — when she finds out the men assigned to fight were detailed to evacuate spouses? How is a wife going to react when she finds out that her husband's gunnery partner fled his fighting position to ensure the safety of his family — and her husband was wounded or killed for lack of fire support? Is it really fair to divert our soldiers to protect families who should not have been in the Division in the first place?"

She responded with a cold stare, a quiet brood. The coordinator repeated her complaint that the NEO exercises were futile — they would not work if war broke out. We never spoke about the matter again. I continued to encourage this woman and other weepy, angry, fearful, dependent spouses to move back to the States. By the time of my departure, our battalion was down to two American spouses.

The Division Chaplain cautioned me not to speak too loudly about the spouses who moved to Korea.

"You realize that some of our chaplains brought their spouses to the Division?" Chaplain McLean, a tall handsome Methodist reminded me.

In my usually direct manner, I responded to his rhetorical question.

"Yes, and I know that General Franks' daughter is living in the BOQ with her husband at Camp Casey. Unaccompanied officers are furious that they must live three to a room, when the General's daughter is taking up half of an apartment."

The Division Chaplain and I never spoke about the Apple Blossom problem again. He did, at one chaplain gathering suggest that I was obviously suffering from menopause, and thus, could help the male chaplains who had to cope with wives in similar situations.

Before I left Korea, a senior chaplain at EUSA asked me to write up my concerns about the Apple Blossom program as an anonymous paper that he would float for review. It did not surprise me that this senior ranking man agreed that chaplain support of the Apple Blossom movement was a very bad idea. Why did he not use his rank to make the points himself in a formal decision paper with his signature on it? I have always been disappointed when the chaplains earn rank to "speak truth to power" and then stop short of doing so, for fear of losing their chance at the next rank. In the end it was clear to me, the Apple Blossom Cottage industry was one of the illusions that could make commanders and chaplains feel good about taking care of the Army Family.

During the Christmas break, the Dallas Cowgirls travel throughout the Division to dance for the lonely American GIs. The brigade sergeant major used his connections to bring the Cowgirls to our Camp Howze Gym. For the holidays, a couple of the GIs brought their wives from the U.S. The wives were considering a move to the village. The brigade sergeant major stopped me one morning.

"Ma'am, do you think it is sexist to bring the Dallas Cowgirls to Korea?"

"I'm not a football fan. I don't know."

"Ma'am, a lot of the wives are complaining that the Army is sexist because they say the Dallas Cowgirls dance like strippers."

"Sergeant Major, as far as I am concerned, the wives are out of line. They don't even have a legal right to be here. They can take care of their husbands' needs whenever they want to, but the rest of these guys are starving for feminine contact. What's the harm? If the wives don't like it, they can go home!"

"I'm not going to respond to that!" He grinned.

"Well, I've never seen the Cowgirls dance." It was my turn to generate a little heat. "I hear the guys complaining because they are required to come to the gym for this event. They want to have fun, but they don't want mandatory fun!"

"They don't have to stay, but I had to pull in all my favors to get the Cowgirls to drop here. We can't get all of them. But they are going to fly in, and do part of their routine, then sign autographs. The guys just love them."

The sergeant major was about to take his next assignment as the top enlisted man in the Engineer Corps. Ordinarily, I did not have much influence on this man. He would smile and say nothing whenever Colonel Soo asked me questions.

"So, what's the problem Sergeant Major? Are female soldiers complaining?"

"Well, there are a few women who have made comments."

"Look, Sergeant Major," I stared him in the face. "You have almost 700 men up here and what, a dozen women who have the legal right to live in this community? These men get out there every day with their lean, sexy bodies and do PT. We women get to look at them every day in their shorty shorts, flexing their muscles. I think the women have the better end of this deal, because we get to dance with the cowboys every day... I don't think a 30 minute show is too much for female soldiers to put up with...."

The sergeant major chuckled.

"I never thought of it that way."

I am sure he had, but if he had said it himself, he would have to worry about a sexual harassment complaint. I promised him I would attend, although until that moment, I had no intentions of watching the Cowgirls, any more than I would ever watch a football game on television.

We were marched into the gym that afternoon for mandatory fun. We waited patiently until we could hear the chopper whirling above. The men started to cheer as if they had just seen a spectacular touchdown.

A young Crow Indian mechanic started to fume as he sat next to me.

"Ma'am, my fiancée is not talking to me. Why did the command require us to be here? My fiancée does not approve. She wants to call off the wedding..."

"But you don't have to stay. As soon as the sergeant major gives the signal, you can just get up and leave. They need a body count to justify the drop onto this post."

"Yeah, there's gonna be a body count. You know, when they require you to attend something like this, its just no fun."

"Well, if your fiancée was back in the States, would you have come?

"Hell, yes. But I don't enjoy this stuff no more when she's around."

"Well, you go back and tell her, the chaplain said you are both lucky, because you can be together over the holidays. The rest of these men have nobody to cuddle up with this Christmas..."

Our proud Crow Indian stayed for the show. I performed his wedding ceremony a few weeks later. My assistant, now Specialist Choi, couldn't help me because he was away for the weekend, celebrating the Korean New Year.

"Ma'am I must bow to the parents, then bow to the grandparents. It is very, very nice. They give me a lot of money! Just for a bow!" Choi was living on $12 per month. I couldn't let him miss this opportunity to earn some spending money.

Some volunteers helped me with our mechanic's wedding. First Sergeant Pearson and several soldiers from the company did the shopping, baked cakes, prepared lasagna, and set up a nice buffet. The electricity went out the night before the wedding, so a man who volunteered to cook in the dining facility was unable to until the morning of the wedding. The dining facility cooks prepared the wedding feast on the side as they put together greasy burgers and

butter soaked grilled cheese sandwiches for the soldiers who stuck around
Howze that Saturday. We delayed the wedding service just long enough to get
the cakes out of the oven.

As soon as the best man could make it from the kitchen to the chapel, we
held our first formal wedding of the year in the Camp Howze chapel. It took
some time to calm down our soldier, who was madly in love, and full of
unreasonable expectations and fantasies about what his wedding was going to be
like. He wanted a mellow, Monterey California wedding to happen in an uptight,
unsophisticated, and unprepared Army post — all with just a few weeks notice.
First Sergeant Pearson was the father of the groom as well as the father of the
bride that day as he calmed his angry, disillusioned soldier, and gently
encouraged the man to make the most of his decision. In Korea, you must do
things the Korean way, or you are bound to be unhappy. You just live with the
power outages, and the bureaucracy. It was hard for Americans to just let go.

There were two or three other untimely engagements of male soldiers
during this year. None of the men married, though. Korean bureaucracy has its
merits. With every lovesick young man who asked me to help them to marry
their sweethearts, I could not help but realize that American GIs were just as
dreamy and unrealistic about marrying during a deployment as my father was
when he was a young GI about to be shipped to war. The intensity of feelings of
patriotism and loneliness and heroism and insecurity and infatuation and
tenderness get so mushed up when young men are sent off to such extreme
circumstances. We need to find a better way to encourage young men and
women not to complicate their lives by sweeping their first sweetheart off her
feet and promising heroic love for all times. But then, if my father followed the
advice I would give to young people today, I would never have been born.

These are different times. We were at war when my father served in Korea.
We are at undeclared peace now. More risks had to be taken then. More care
should be taken now. The Army is often forced into bad social policy with
leftover Vietnam aphorisms like, "Old enough to die, old enough to drink. Old
enough to shoot, old enough to marry." Our mechanic was much older than the
average soldier who madly proposed to a barmaid after two or three dates. I
couldn't help but think, however, that our soldiers are not rational enough to
listen to advice when they're stuck in a country they don't understand far away
from the home they love. They should postpone their weddings until they are in
the States where they can control things.

Back in the States, our Crow Indian would have made one trip to City Hall
to get a license instead of 20 or 30 trips to our Embassy and Korean
bureaucracies. His family would be joyously present, instead of the surrogate
Army. He could have controlled the catering, the honeymoon, the gown and tux
situation. In Korea, everything is out of the soldier's control. Even the ovens.

They work when they want to work. Not always when we need them.

In the winter, I received orders to return to the United States. Our battalion was going to be without a chaplain for nine months. Whether or not it was in his best interest, Lieutenant Colonel Chappell supported me in my bid to stay in Korea. We tried to have my orders deleted. I even called the Chief of Chaplains to beg him to leave me in Korea. Chaplain Don Shea took good care of me at Fort Polk. He was kindly honest when I asked him about the roles Catholic women could play in the Corps. None. Perhaps he would stretch himself and remember what it was like for 700 soldiers to be deployed halfway around the world without a chaplain. The Chief was sweet, but uncompromising.

"The engineers didn't do their homework. They didn't give us the manpower slots in time."

"But sir," I begged. "I wrote up the paperwork. Colonel Soo approved the new slots. They are going to be on the books in September. Can't I just stay as an overfill?"

"No, this problem goes back in history. The engineers have refused to pay for their chaplains. Now they have to wait. I don't have enough chaplains to go around. By the way, you are doing very good ministry there. Thanks for all that you are doing."

The Chief of Chaplains had been very good to me. He sent me to Korea when I needed to get out of Fort Polk. I could not argue with him about my own request to stay in Korea. I could not have my way every time. The politics of the situation made me extremely angry, though. There were senior chaplains sitting in offices all over the United States doing nothing. There were captains all over the United States doing garrison ministry that could easily have been done by civilian pastors — if that ministry needed doing. As far as I was concerned, the only reason chaplains were paid exorbitant salaries and kept on active duty was to provide religious support in remote deployments like Korea. Now, my battalion was going to be without a chaplain for nine months. Just like so many others in Korea, the real reason slots were left unfilled was because chaplains preferred to stay in the States with their families.

I did not have a right to complain about my situation. I found a unit, the 44th Engineer Battalion that made me very happy. I had the same kind of professional satisfaction I enjoyed at OCS and while working for General Stanford and Lieutenant Colonel Siegling. Under LTC Chappell and Colonel Soo I was able to live fully in the Army as it is supposed to be. At the same time, I had more conviction than ever that many gender policies needed to be changed. Deep in my heart, with all the experiences I accumulated there, I came to believe that in wartime, women just don't belong in this kind of unit.

Although Chaplain Shea did not say it, I am sure he believed the 44th Engineers was no place for a female chaplain. Moreover, if we were at war, I would have totally agreed with him. I just did not want to leave at that moment because I really had fun with the Engineers, and they needed me as a chaplain, if only temporarily. When the Chief of Chaplains speaks, however, his word is final. I had to say goodbye to my engineers. That is why rituals and ceremonies were invented, I suppose. To make the goodbyes easier to say. It was not easy to take my leave from the men and women who served with the 44th or with the Engineer Brigade.

Lieutenant Colonel Chappell and the Executive Officer, Major Rovero paid a hoohah tribute before I left. In our last battalion formation, he gave me an Army Commendation medal for the work done. Next, he gave me one of General Tommy Frank's personal awards for excellence — a starter jacket with the Second Infantry Division logo and an embossed symbol recognizing me as part of the team.

That Second Infantry Division jacket is ugly as sin. I can't wear it anywhere in the States. The soldiers in our 44th Engineer Battalion cheered when I was given it. It will always hang in my closet. Someday, when I am too old to care about appearances, I will wear it to a Veterans' Day parade. If the gender policies I advocate ever go into place, no one will believe I earned it myself. I might be tempted to trade that jacket someday, but I would never trade the six months I spent with the Broken Hearts. The 44th Engineer Battalion was not just an adventure, it was a kinship experience for me. I had a chance to learn what my male peers endured in combat units. I was able to walk in my father's boots to a certain extent. The mistake my father's generation made was not to honor the service of Korean War Veterans, not to redeem the sacrifices he and thousands of others made. The Broken Hearts from the original 44th Engineer Battalion were pained by their wartime separation from their families. In a way, I came to understand that many of the Korean War veterans were Broken Hearts. Their hearts were broken when they returned to their families and their country only to find their sacrifices were made in vain. I don't think I earned my 2nd Infantry Commander's Excellence jacket. But in honor of all those forgotten veterans, including my father, I will keep it to remind myself that the price of serving your country well in combat should never be a broken heart.

CHAPTER 16

The Army Is Not Our Family

I could not escape the journey home. As much as I wished to remain in Korea, to minister to troops isolated in the Western Corridor, just miles from the DMZ, I was legally bound to arrive at Fort Hood, Texas on February 22, 1996. Orders were orders.

I arrived at the Headquarters building about 15 minutes before my leave expired. As if I were still a private, I decelerated my pace, stopped for a cappuccino, and allowed myself to be distracted right up to the last minute of freedom. Why did I dread taking this new assignment? The post welcome sign was friendly enough — "Welcome to Fort Hood: the largest Army base in the whole world!" That was it! To live and work on the largest army base in the whole world. That was something to dread. The Fort Polk Inspector General once encouraged me to stop ruminating about the systemic problems that plagued the Army. "You can't fix any of these problems, so you may as not well ponder them," he urged. Rumination is the curse of my core personality. I don't believe I will lose this tendency even in the advanced stages of Alzheimer's.

"Largest Army Base" triggered a premonition that would become the grist of my ruminations about Fort Hood. Simply stated, the most egregious planning error ever made by the United States Department of Defense was to assemble 45,000 soldiers on one huge mega-post under the military and civil leadership of a few dual-hatted generals and sergeants major.

The largest army base in the world came into prominence after the Gulf War. The Second Armored Division, "Hell on Wheels," moved to Hood from Fort Polk in early spring of 1993. For years, the Fort Hood housing shortage was pathetic for single soldiers and family members. Single soldiers were crammed four into one small bedroom. Families lived in hotels. I jogged every morning with a female warrant officer who lived in her car with her son during her first three months at Hood until affordable housing became available.

The consolidation of two divisions on one post created misery for most soldiers. Not everyone suffered the onslaught of soldiers, however. The '92-93 Base Realignment and Closures (BRAC) move created a sudden construction boom in the local Texas economy. Carpenters and plumbers happily could not keep pace with the influx of families. That changed by the time I arrived in February '96. Wherever I hunted for an apartment or small house to rent, the towns were glutted with spanking new houses that had been erected in fewer that ten days per unit. Who would risk purchase of such flimsy homes, especially after moving from Fort Polk where similarly pasted-together government houses were condemned for habitation less than 15 years from when they were built?

Family life was complicated for Fort Hood soldiers, but it would not provide the greatest challenge. The most serious affliction on the post was the total abandonment of the single soldiers, particularly the fighting men, in favor of a privatized family agenda. Will it ever be safe in American society to warehouse so many single soldiers in such anti-social living conditions? Families could have the house of their impoverished dreams, but what about the single soldiers? A few new barracks were built like economy motels. Every soldier had private access to his room from an outside staircase, with no responsibility for reporting to a CQ (Charge of Quarters), or participating in community life. In most of the old-style barracks four men were still stuffed in a room, with dingy lights, rusty furniture, and dank smelling bathrooms.

Did the Pentagon or the Army ever think twice about the wisdom of concentrating so many soldiers on one post, isolated from the civilian culture for three years? The post had more than two fighting divisions, staffed predominantly with men. What scared me about Fort Hood was the men. No less than 30,000 trained killers would be harbored there. Why so much testosterone was contained and pressurized in such an arid, undeveloped location was a mystery.

Were there ever strategic advantages? Hardly. To send a division overseas, vehicles and equipment must be railed hundreds of miles to a port, off-loaded, then on-loaded to ships. Was the purpose to synchronize training and deployment activities, or to streamline acquisition procedures, thus reducing duplication and wasteful expenditures on equipment, parts or construction? Such a purpose reveals profound ignorance of the psychology of command. We will never chasten commanders to buy or build less. We will never persuade commanders of competing divisions to share resources and personnel. Logically, the commanders staff and equip their units based on real deployment scenarios. Two divisions don't go off to the same theatre — they deploy one at a time and their missions accommodate American commitments in diverse parts of the globe. So it is ridiculous to believe that the two divisions were consolidated on one base to save a few jobs or the cost of a few tanks here and there.

Why the crush of soldiers, organizations, and divisions in one rural community? The only observable reason is political — economic pressure. The move was made to help build up an artificial rural economy — an economy that was already falsely inflated as long as it was the home of one full division. Killeen and Copperas Cove ballooned into permanent cities but the cities' only dependable income came from services and goodies panned to soldiers.

With only one division, their economic bubble burst during the Gulf War. The cities surrounding Fort Hood almost went bankrupt. The First Cavalry Division was mobilized to Kuwait for almost a year. Too many soldiers sent their spouses and children back to their permanent homes. Most of the businesses and landlords in Killeen and Copperas Cove suffered from the sudden and prolonged evaporation of military dollars. Their pain was so acutely felt that in the next BRAC move, politicians managed to finagle the relocation of a second division from Fort Polk to Fort Hood, to mitigate the consequences of another sudden mass mobilization.

The theory that another division would save the local economies was premised on the already questionable assumption that only one division would ever deploy at a time. When the Army was a fat hippopotamus, there were thousands of people who stayed in garrison during mobilizations. Soon after the Gulf War, however, we only had ten divisions standing in the active force. All ten were quite busy deploying to real war zones, hot zones, or simulating extensive deployments in rigorous field training and practice deployments. When Hell on Wheels was moved to Hood, it was already far more likely that a serious military conflict would require deployment of all active forces and then some.

Without a doubt, troops were ultimately moved to Hood to shore up the local economy. A mighty strange reason to crowd 45,000 predominantly male soldiers onto one Army post. But that was indeed the rationale for making Fort Hood the testosterone capital of the world.

Déjá vu! Once again, political decisions were made to benefit the civilian sector, but without regard for the soldiers who would serve at Hood. Once again, soldiers would be confronted with the big Army lie. New recruits were promised adventure, strict discipline, hardcore training, dormitory housing and the pride of living in safe, value-based communities. Instead, they would be assigned to an Army post in the middle of Nowhere, USA. Their neighborhood would be permeated with the culture of drugs, gangs and guns. Their units had no money to train, so soldiers would have too much time on their hands. The communities surrounding Fort Hood would love soldiers mostly for the easy profits to be made in the sale of cars, stereos, alcohol, drugs, and women's bodies.

That said, it didn't me take long to realize in those blazing hot months of '96 that Fort Hood was not just in the throes of drought induced brush fires. The entire base, this mammoth "platform projectile" for the Army of the 21st Century was in the throes of spiritual drought and a bonfire of insanity. Even the smallest units there were like piles of kindling wood, just waiting for the right crack of lightening, or the toss of a lit match to roil in fire.

Naivete does not color my perception here. I am keenly aware men have always had barracks brawls over their women. Soldiers have always sneaked alcohol to obliterate their loneliness. The difference is that the Army brags that drugs were rooted out of the barracks and out of the soldier's lifestyle. With an antiquated, inefficient testing system, little intelligence is needed by soldiers to outwit command efforts. Fort Hood 1996 was rampant with marijuana, coke, mushrooms and the legal drug of choice, aerosol paint inhalants — not to mention alcohol abuse.

Manicured prettiness of Hood's landscape belied the social chaos Hood engendered. Its orderly lawns and super one-stop social service systems could fool any news reporter or Senate Panel of Investigators but they did not dampen my dread of what I faced.

I began in-processing the morning after my arrival at Hood. Our personnel managers advised us of the post's routine gun sweeps. In the last inspection of privately owned vehicles, Fort Hood military policeman confiscated almost 300 guns. We were told barracks would be routinely swept with military police dogs to curtail illegal drug activity. Sighs of relief wafted to the ceiling. I sat with a cluster of experienced captains. We wanted to believe we did not have much to fear on this well-policed installation, besides the bats that flew in our rooms each night.

Those gun collection statistics belied Hood's safety record just as Fort Hood's majestic highway entrance deflects the newcomer from the danger of dwelling among so many trained killers. Childcare centers and shopping malls grace the entrances of the main post. Dun-colored family bungalows stretch for miles along the post perimeter. What you see is closely manicured lawns. What you get is a highly organized culture of guns and gangs.

Even the water towers, traditionally red-checkered landmarks that guide disoriented soldiers to a new base were disguised with innocuous images. I was to work in Fourth Infantry Division. The unit patch, a cream-colored diamond with ivy leaf vines sprouting in the center was painted onto our water tower. No wolf howl or battle cry could be invoked with such a New Age insignia. What did the ivy represent? No wonder hardcore soldiers from First Cav substituted the moniker "Untrained" for the Fourth Division! At least the trefoil on my 2nd ACR patch shouted with the motto, "Tojours Pret!" Always ready. What war cry would a patch of ivy leaves inspire?

Military Police reassured newly arriving officers that Hood was strictly monitored. That, and the ivy leaves present on every uniform, lulled me into momentary quiescence.

Before long, the wakeup alarm rattled. I begged the division chaplain not to send me to aviation, because the aviation battalions are notoriously undisciplined and arrogant. I was sent to the 404th Aviation Support Battalion. Within days, I received a call from the mother of an AWOL soldier from my new battalion. She desperately depended on the Army to reform her only son, who had abused substances since his adolescence. The private deserted rather than face charges for use of marijuana. Later, the young man called me, and asked if he could be returned to the unit. He feared a long jail sentence for desertion. The first sergeant balked when I asked if there was potential for this young man to be reintegrated.

"Ma'am, he won't go to jail for desertion. That's only in wartime. I am just about ready to drop him from the rolls. Tell him to wait three more days until I drop him from the rolls — then he will be discharged administratively. Yeah, he will have to turn himself in to get the paperwork finished, but he won't do no jail time. He'll be out in days!"

I braced myself as I fulfilled my promise to this soldier's mother.

"First Sergeant, he says he doesn't want to quit the Army. His mother says it is his last chance for rehabilitation. Do you think he can change?"

A volcanic eruption blasted the wax out of my ears.

"He's not going to change, Ma'am," the first sergeant screamed with exasperation. "He's been using marijuana since he got here. I've talked to his parents hundreds of times. They are part of the problem. They keep giving him money, bailing him out. He's lied to his parents. He lied to me. He's fooling you! Listen, these kids are only four blocks from the biggest marijuana store in Killeen. Drugs are all over this post. They just walk right outside the gate, and they can get whatever they want."

"Top, you make the decision, not me. But what do ya' mean, they're getting pot right outside the gate — aren't those places off limits?"

"Sure they are. So when the military police start cruising through, the soldiers weasel their way down to 6th Street in Austin to get their lines."

"But our undercover agents are supposed to be down in Austin, preventing that kind of transaction, too!"

My questions, as ridiculous as they were, seemed to be therapeutic for the first sergeant. Cynical irony calmed him down to a hushed staccato.

"Right. CID! Ha! They're down there using, just like the rest of the soldiers. Then they turn around and bust a few..."

I heard similar complaints about the military police in Taegu, Korea. Much of CID's time was spent investigating black market sales by soldiers, yet their own sergeant had a $50,000 gambling debt, a girlfriend, and a bad case of judgement whenever he left his wife to go drinking with the girlfriend. She put him a few thousand in the hole after every binge.

The Headquarters Company first sergeant sighed with exasperation as he reminded me that he was going to soon be free of all this wasted mentoring of soldiers.

"Get him out of the Army, ma'am. That's all we can do. Get him out."

He fulminated about the exorbitant waste of training dollars the Army spent on soldiers who were not fit to serve. Training standards were such that you couldn't turn a kid around anymore.

Then Top lapsed into the fatherly figure that first sergeants used to be. He asked me to reassure the private's parents that the soldier was okay, despite his decision to go AWOL.

"I already did that, Top. I promised them I would ask you for a second chance, which I just did. You know what's best!"

I didn't want him to think I was a Pollyanna, ready to undermine all his hardcore disciplinary tactics. We both knew successful rehab was the rare exception on active duty. A soldier had one chance to reform. He would be discharged from active duty if caught using drugs again. Very few men had the ego strength or career vision to be motivated to stay clean after their first rehab treatment. They usually need two or three treatments before they are free of their dependencies. So many old-time soldiers brag about their own growing up experiences in the military. Two or three trips to the brig before they would finally let go of their rebellious attitude and accept Army discipline as a way of life. Anymore, one trip to the brig means discharge when your time is done. One trip to rehab and a soldier would be tossed out if he got in trouble again. There simply wasn't the time, the money or the programs to invest in soldiers who needed extensive remediation. So why was the Army still advertising that it could make men and women out of bad boys and girls? What's the point of spending $40 thousand or more to train a mechanic only to reject him as a conduct failure?

The 404th Aviation Support Battalion was a high-tech maintenance unit. Soldiers repaired Apaches and combat helicopters. Dopers who were caught lost their job classification if they had high tech jobs like missile or helicopter maintenance. Most took their chances because the Army's system of drug testing was unreliable. Urinalysis tests for a few drugs like pot and coke are the Army's flimsy legal tool to identify soldiers who are drug abusers. No testing for other drugs of choice, so it doesn't take long for the dope heads to find out which drugs were beyond the threat of an Article 15. Most believed they could clean out their system of non-addictive and "harmless" drugs such as marijuana. After all, only ten percent of the soldiers assigned would be tested each month. As a result of the next pee test, three or four soldiers from the 404th came up hot. All were Chaptered out of the Army. Rehabilitation was not an option.

Married soldiers were just as likely to use illegal drugs as single soldiers. One of the most handsome 404th helicopter repairmen ever to land on planet Hollywood came up hot. His sweet, homely, freckle-faced wife was about six months pregnant. The young Sergeant J knew that he could not work as a helicopter repairman, even if he went to drug rehab. In recounting his fatal career error, Sergeant J asked, "Would you want your helicopter repaired by a dope head?" How could such an astute, attractive soldier be so foolhardy? A momentary lapse of technique impelled me to lash out at Sergeant J, wondering what he would do to support his wife.

"Ma'am, there's a lot of guys using down there. The only difference between them and me is I got caught. I knew we were due for a test, and I just wasn't careful. They usually tell us in advance, so we can stop in time."

Tipping off soldiers that drug tests were imminent was a clear violation of the drug testing regulations, but soldiers expected it at Fort Hood.

"Fourteen days. That's all you need to get all the marijuana out of your system." Sergeant J was the most charming abuser I ever met. He beseeched me to counsel his wife, to help him beg for her forgiveness. I agreed to facilitate a session between them.

Mrs. J demurely followed her husband into my office for their first session. Her tears flowed as soon as the office door closed behind her.

"J, I know they're all using. But you promised me you would stop. I left you before and you promised me you'd stop."

She dabbed her watery eyes with military tissue, ash colored and scratchy as it always is. J's commander sent him to my office to save his marriage, if not his career.

"I know honey. You mean the world to me. I just used it that one weekend when I went fishing with the guys."

J could melt an ice cube on an Arctic plane with his soft smiling pale blue eyes.

"You always leave me alone on the weekends." Mrs. J. would not relent. "You promised me you would stop before. You promised me you wouldn't smoke at home. That's why you go fishin' — so you can do dope! I'm goin' home to my daddy's. He just said whenever I'm ready... J, you just don't care anymore!"

"That's not true, baby doll. I just need to relax. The job is so stressful. With the baby comin' and all."

He patted her large tummy until her tears dried. She started to coo softly. J wanted a second chance. He could have gotten that chance. His supervisors said his work was stellar. His wife was madly in love with him. They grew up in the same town together. Their roots were as deep as an oak tree — such a contrast to the typical military couple who met in a bar or at a dance and married four weeks later. With all of J's recommendations from supervisors, sergeants, and even his wife, I promised I would go to bat for him, to ask the battalion commander to consider rehabilitation and then transfer to another MOS. In Sergeant J's case, he would have gotten his second chance. Except for this hot pee test, it was generally believed he walked on water.

But a couple of days later, Sergeant J stopped me before I made a fool of myself, and told me not to bother.

"Ma'am, there's one thing. I better tell you one thing."

Was he going to reveal he was gay? He sweated so much, I thought he might. Nothing so irrelevant to his legal troubles as that.

"Ma'am. I already went to rehab. If this test shows I was usin' I am out of the Army."

J wept the tears of Judas as he begged forgiveness from his wife, who was about to become the homeless, uninsured spouse of a total Army loser.

The Army had spent at least a $100,000 teaching this man how to be a helicopter mechanic — a training expense that was going down the toilet because he couldn't control his marijuana cravings. And the Army was unwilling to pay the cost of a six-week rehabilitation program. He had done that once, only for three weeks. Now, by regulation, he would be forced out on his ear. Did that mean that the Army would be safe, that he would never touch a helicopter part again? God, no! J enlightened me as he consoled his wife.

"Baby doll.... You know I can get a contract in our hometown. Bell Helicopters is always hirin' enlisted men. Five years as an Army mechanic. I can make more money and be home at night. I won't have all this Army stress... just do my job...." He convinced his wife that they were better off leaving the Army.

I was appalled. I blasted him.

"What makes you think you can take a civilian helicopter repair job and still use weed?"

"Ma'am, I ain't using weed no more. I stopped. My son means too much to me. Did you know we are goin' to have a son?"

"That's right chaplain," Mrs. J interjected. "There's always jobs at Bell. I hate the Army. We'll make it. I just need to deliver this baby... cause we won't have no insurance for awhile."

It did not occur to me that J might have intentionally gotten caught so he could passively work his way out of his Army contract to a civilian job. Not until more unrepentant, almost gleeful soldiers were pushed out for smoking weed did I suspect this game. Women get pregnant to get out. Men do drugs. They are not addicted. If they want out, they do drugs. By God, the modern Army puts them out. So long as they pass the drug tests at Bell Helicopter, they can make what seems to them a fortune.

If that was Sergeant J's intention — to get out of the Army before his contract was up to secure a job with a civilian contractor, he forgot one thing. In his five years he had become a proud soldier. It was as much a part of his being as the anticipation of fatherhood. That this part of his identity would be ripped from him upon disciplinary proceedings never occurred to Sergeant J until the day his son was born. Not as humiliating as an old-fashioned defrocking in front of all the soldiers, a technique which just might cause the nice-guy-recreational-user to know the difference between entertainment and career suicide. His supervisors were discreet, almost protective of J. They withheld all disciplinary proceedings for almost three months to insure that Mrs. J would have proper medical care for delivery of their baby.

Sergeant J rushed into my office the afternoon his son was born. I don't think the man knew what a natural high meant until he had gone through the birthing process. Euphorically, Sergeant J described the moment when his son's head appeared. His wife's tender cry of joy. His first lifelong gaze into the miraculous. Then, he burst into tears of profound grief. Sergeant J wept for awhile. He knew his moment of reckoning had arrived. As soon as his wife gave birth, Sergeant J's commander convened disciplinary proceedings. Sergeant J was going to be censured that afternoon, and would shortly be booted out.

J left my office a sergeant, humbly prepared to face his commander. He returned a private. Thank God, he truly understood that despite his destructive choices, his wife and a son still loved and depended on him. All of us believed that he would do well in time. If he hated the Army so much, why did he have to let all of his hard work go up in smoke? Why couldn't he have just finished out his contract, then take the civilian job with no shame to follow him? The cliché, "you can't save everybody," is undoubtedly true. But do you have to lose so many in times of prosperity and peace? Who could save these youngsters?

When I walked around the hanger to visit 404th soldiers at the request of their sergeants — thus reducing the time soldiers spent away from their job for stress counseling, I saw bright, challenged young men and women. Sexy in their flight suits. Proud of their technical skills. One woman named all the parts of the helicopter laid out on a mat. I asked if she was waiting an equipment inspection.

"No ma'am. We're not being inspected." She reassured me. "We just keep it this way so we won't miss a part, or a sequence."

The mechanics in the hangar bragged they had had no accidents or mechanical failures since the battalion was mustered. They were proud of their track record.

For many of these soldiers, the Army was clearly their ticket to a good life. Their backgrounds were harsh. They came from towns where McDonalds was the brightest job prospect for those who stayed local. You would think that fact would inspire appreciation for the worldly opportunities that the Army provides. Yet, at Fort Hood, the amount of chaos young soldiers achieved in their private lives was inversely proportionate to the extent they pulled themselves together on the job. Whatever happened to the American Dream? How come soldiering wasn't helping these kids to live better lives?

Was the Army the problem, or was the Army stuck with a whole generation of aimless, self-indulgent drifters? Drug abuse was happening in the best of units, the worst of units. Chaplain influence was non-existent. You could hire three chaplains per battalion. No impact would be felt so long as the Army exploited the myth that the military could only be a reflection of the broader society as its excuse for avoiding the tough work of disciplining young soldiers to meet the standards of the profession of arms.

Some commanders did try. Some chaplains did try. The problems were too entrenched to make any difference.

General Coffey was the commander of the 4th Infantry Division for the first half of my year at Hood. Coffey wanted to stop the fratricidal gun deaths. He wisely issued an old-fashioned command directive asking every soldier in the division to register all of the guns in their private arsenals — whether they lived on or off post. I was horrified to see the e-mail traffic openly deride this wise man. Colonels. Sergeants. Majors. Privates. Email was circulated with nanosecond speed castigating the general as one of those liberal federalists you just had to watch out for! I finally saw how Chaplain Brett Travis garnered so much passive support at Fort Polk when he censured me about my anti-gun homilies. Modern soldiers, mostly from redneck militia country were not like the intellectual, disciplined warrior of my father's day — or my husband's, either. My father and my former husband saw guns as extraordinary tools to be used under the most strictly controlled circumstances to defend the nation against foreign aggressors. The men I served with in the modern Army, from Chaplain Travis to my own commander of the 404th Aviation Support Battalion were their guns. Their masculine identities, their sense of survival was so caught up with their right to own guns, they could not feel masculine or safe without private arsenals.

Rebellious soldiers at Fort Hood lobbied the NRA to come to their aid. The NRA waged a public campaign to cast General Coffey's policy as nothing short of diabolical. General Coffey, old-fashioned commander that he was, invited every soldier in the Division to participate in a heart-to-heart dialogue about gun culture. I tried to round up other chaplains and officers to attend the dialogue with me, but no one would go. The 404th commander chided me for supporting Coffey's policy. I was obviously just a dumb liberal Northerner for thinking that our men were dangerously over-arming themselves.

At the appointed hour for the General's talk, I raced over to the Division Headquarters. There was no meeting. Was I fooled? No. I raced to the back of the headquarters and I saw a military vehicle taking off. I waved down the driver.

"Do you know where the General is supposed to talk to troops about his gun registration policy," I asked.

"Chaplain, I'm going that way. Hop in." General Coffey invited me into his limousine.

During the short ride to the post theatre, he quizzed me about my own feelings.

"Chaplain, if a soldier called you, and he said he was going to commit suicide, would you want to know if he had weapons at his disposal?"

"Sir, I would ask him what he had with him right that minute."

"Why?"

"Sir, that's standard suicide prevention. If the soldier has a weapon, you don't talk about his problems until he puts the weapon down. If he has pills, you ask him to put the pills down, tell him you are uncomfortable talking while he's holding that gun."

"Chaplain, if you were going to a home where there was domestic violence, would you want to know how many guns were in the house?"

"Sir, I think every sergeant or chaplain or policeman would want to know. You don't want to walk into an ambush. Our soldiers kill their spouses, then they kill everyone else in sight."

We talked about his policy. I thanked him for taking such a courageous position. He was a bit downtrodden.

When we arrived at the theatre, electricity sparked. Usually, when you walk into a theatre filled with grunts, glum silence prevails. Grunts are not talkers. But General Coffey agitated these men in the most hurting part of their souls — where they felt insecure about everything — their manhood, their capacity to control their environment, their world. There was a mob of angry, sneering joviality. They came to pay the general his comeuppance.

The general asked the men all of the questions he asked me. He asked them, man to man, what they felt like when they had to go to their soldiers' homes during a domestic dispute. Did they want to know what weapons were stowed away, where the danger lurked? He asked them about suicidal soldiers — would they feel safer going to a young despondent private's home if they knew what kinds of weapons the soldier was holding?

He paced back and forth across the stage as he explained his motivation for the gun registration policy. General Coffey sounded like Colonel Dunn, my engineer commander, and Colonel Soo when they kept saying they felt responsible for the criminal culture that was taking control of the Army.

"When I was a commander at another post, two of my soldiers got into a fight downtown. They killed each other in a gang fight. Because one was killed on each side, the downtown authorities didn't want to pursue the matter. Now, I knew we had soldiers in our command who were part of the fight. There was nothing I could do about their participation because the civilian authorities would not prosecute."

There was dead silence. Coffey's experience mirrored my own. General Coffey's frustrations mirrored the experience of every sergeant, every captain in that room who was responsible for the young soldiers who filled the ranks of the '90s Army. I don't know what General Coffey is like on a day-to-day basis. That afternoon, he was tall, strong, but most of all, fatherly. Without bringing in the Bible or Jesus, he preached the most important sermon I had heard since General Stanford's quarterly soul talks with the troops. Coffey envisioned a new reality for us that was a throwback to the past. He wanted us to have all the caring responsibilities we now had for soldiers, but with the real authority to protect our young from their own mean, violent, angry bent. He wanted us to be the best, not the dregs.

The general opened the floor to questions and comments. A few soldiers stood and voiced their sacred commitment to their right to bear arms. Coffey pointed out that his policy did not in any way take away a soldier's right to bear arms. The training sergeant major from the Engineer Brigade stood up and rattled off a long list of guns he had in his arsenal. He was obviously a plant. His litany was typical behavior of gun fanatics — to deny the public's right to know what they owned, but then to brag endlessly about their collections. When he finished, he twinkled as he defied the general,

"Sir, what right do you have to make me register my guns. What I own is my business and nobody else's!"

The general suavely walked across the stage in silence. He turned to the sergeant major and softly replied, "But you just told me what you have." Coffey made it clear he would modify his policy now that he had constructive feedback from his leaders.

The anger dissipated eventually. The Division Sergeant Major asked all the enlisted with rank of sergeant and above to remain in the theatre. The rest of us could go back to work. Sergeants were leaving the Army in alarming numbers. The general wanted to talk with the non-commissioned officers about their reasons for quitting. The sergeants took turns repeating their complaints with vary little variation.

"Sir, with all due respect, you can't discipline soldiers anymore."

"Sir, this is the stress card Army. These soldiers hold up stress cards when you tell them to do something. In Basic Training, they hold up yellow cards. The sergeant can't discipline them, they can't demand any more work."

"Sir, you can't teach soldiers anything anymore. They know it all. They don't want to learn. You can't grow them up. We're not allowed to keep them late when they screw up."

"Sir, we're not training enough. Too much time spent on family. Too much time doing details. The Army's no fun anymore."

On the ride back to the Division Headquarters, the General asked me how I thought it went. I thanked him again for his strong stand against gun violence. I thought the soldiers understood his safety concerns. I asked him if he would keep his policy in the face of the NRA campaign.

"Chaplain, the politics... I may not be able to continue this."

For all I know General Coffey thought I was a fluff chaplain. This was the only opportunity I had to see him in action, because he was to move on to his next dream assignment. I was beginning to see patterns in leadership, though. Coffey was a troop commander, par excellence. I have never seen a general besides General Timmons in Korea take such a powerful stand against the social trends in the Army. Neither man bowed to the political reality that the larger culture was dictating norms in the Army. They both used their might to insist that the Army had a professional code that demanded adherence — regardless of America's tolerance for social deviance.

I had no other opportunities to speak with commanders at higher levels about the behavioral trends that were endangering our troops. At my level, there were company commanders who believed they could shape the ethos in their companies by keeping troops attuned to a larger-than-life mission. Even in our aviation battalion, taking soldiers to the field to keep them out of trouble was the classic response of well-meaning commanders. Hood soldiers took their drugs with them, however, or they had them delivered at checkpoints on the road. A Harvard-educated chaplain who became a Foursquare fundamentalist worked to be released from his active duty commitment upon my arrival at Hood. Chaplain P publicly stated the immoral presidency of Mr. Bill Clinton as his reason for departure. When 15 men from his support battalion were caught using marijuana out in the woods, he confessed the futility of his ministry. Hood soldiers were out of control.

Recreational drugs were the least of Hood's problems. Gang violence and retaliation for adultery consumed inordinate amounts of time — both work time and the private time of every leader in the chain of command. One mechanic, an Eagle Scout from the northern mid-west who married the girl of his dreams was devastated when his wife began an affair with a man she met at basic training. Upon her return to Fort Hood, she announced her intention to divorce Sergeant D. No amount of comfort from his parents, his co-workers or his boss could allay his grief or his obsession with the wrong committed against him. His wife believed Sergeant D would maintain the tender demeanor of a soap opera character. She expected him to acquiesce to her indiscretions. Oblivious to Sergeant D's grief or anger about her new love she wanted peaceful camaraderie between her two lovers. Upon return from a field training exercise, Sergeant D looked across the motor pool parking lot to discover the lover of his wife waiting to pick him up in the family car. D howled in front of his peers and junior soldiers, chased the cowardly lover down the street, jumped him and proceeded to stomp on him until he was pulled away from his competitor by his friends.

Perhaps the command could have overlooked D's impulsive violence if he had expressed his rage in the parking lot of a local saloon. Violence would not have helped mend his relationship with his wife, but his buddies would have made a pact of secrecy to avoid disciplinary measures against D. Nobody wants to rat on a lovesick buddy. D's private life unraveled before him and he retaliated with violence at his workplace. Commanders could not hide from D's in-discipline, no matter how sympathetic they were toward his justified anger.

The wheels of military justice were set in motion. Sergeant D was sent to me for preliminary counseling. He was placed in an anger management class. His arch rival was also a soldier. Despite soothing, sympathetic support from D's platoon sergeant, his first sergeant, his platoon leader, his commander and counselors from the helping professions, D would not relinquish his obsession with having his wife-stealing competitor brought up on charges of adultery. After all, the Code of Military Justice strictly forbade adultery. D didn't mind being punished so long as the adulterer would be punished, too.

D's demand for justice illuminated the fundamental flaw of the military justice system. Decisions to prosecute are strictly arbitrary — a commander's prerogative. The wife-stealer belonged to a unit in the First Cavalry Division. His commander had no intentions of losing "a good soldier" just because he was the culprit in a public, adulterous affair. Thus, three soldiers from three different companies were engaged in a corrosive, illegal twisted affair. Unless all three were given cease and desist orders, and instructed to keep their private lives out of the work place, all those in close proximity to the affair would waste precious time attempting to separate the illicit lovers from a justifiably angry soldier.

How do you tell a church-going, God-fearing Eagle scout sergeant that the military prohibition against adultery is unenforceable if the offending culprit is otherwise an asset to the command? Why couldn't the lovesick soldier accept the stark reality that adultery charges were only leveled at soldiers whom the Army wanted discharged, but for whom commanders had not built a properly documented case of professional incompetence that would withstand an appeal? Supportive counseling and anger management classes do nothing to quell the rage of a soldier who believes the Army's core values and code of military justice are arbitrary.

My days in the 404th were filled with acrimonious marriage situations like this. It had been many years since I worked for General Stanford. The Army unveiled its new Domestic Violence Prevention program when he became my boss. As Stanford conveyed his personal commitment to this program, he piously intoned, "I can control sex in every bedroom within this command. I can stop domestic violence. I will stop domestic violence!"

Generals believe they have God-given powers to create social circumstances that will eradicate every social plague they encounter. Generals in the '90s were still promoting the myth they could curtail domestic violence through the sheer force of their personalities.

The tragedy of our times, however, is that they have been reluctant to enforce traditional standards of discipline and morality for fear of ridicule by the media or censure by Congress. As long as the military sets up the expectation of providing for the Army family, then condones adultery and other acts of misconduct that destroy the family, you can count on one thing. Domestic violence will happen. It will happen in big ways. Generals don't have the power to stop domestic violence, especially in a culture that lauds marital infidelity and promiscuity. How can you enforce a legal code that has an absolute standard of morality in a society that considers immorality a private, non-criminal matter? Angry spouses go to the media to voice their frustrations over shabby housing or inadequate day care facilities. Angry soldiers write to Congress. One politically incorrect decision, such as censuring a woman who has children out of wedlock, or censuring men who have affairs and a General's next star would be given to his gutless competitor who tolerated everything and offended no one. The Army was filled with generals like this. They were called diplomats, a euphemism that fell short of the true accolade — a soldier's soldier. General Stanford never had godly powers to stop domestic violence, but he and other generals like him were partly right.

That morality can be legislated is a myth. The most effective tool a commander has to curtail adultery and other immorality is his command authority. If the commander expresses intolerance for immorality — particularly acts committed in his working environment, barracks, or family housing for which he is responsible, then the instances of brazen indulgence in these family-destroying activities would be significantly curtailed. Never eradicated. There are a small number of people who are compulsive sexual addicts or thrill seekers. They only get pleasure when they know they are flaunting the rules and in danger of being caught. So, catch them and punish them.

The vast majority are more inclined to live up to the moral standards a commander establishes, because they take pride in doing the right thing, being good soldiers. Whatever the commander defines as good, the soldiers will abide. True, the fact that the locus of authority is external means that soldiers are not very well-developed. You have to start somewhere. In a culture that reflects chastity and fidelity as abnormal traits, the external authority has got to strongly assert the opposite before the virtues of chastity and fidelity will take root in a military community.

In my experience, the vast majority of soldiers who participate in adultery, promiscuity, pandering, prostitution, and even fraternization were soldiers who had never been taught these things are harmful. Yes, harmful — to one's psychological well-being and to the well-being of the family and community. When teaching military ethics to companies of soldiers, I often pointed out that the Code of Military Justice is an elaboration of the Big Ten. Any soldier who abides by the Ten Commandments will never have trouble with military law. Often, students balk that the separation of church and state precludes any reference to the Big Ten. Further, they point out that the military, nor the government has any right to impose morality on individual citizens. They often believe they could win the argument in a court of law, should their behaviors ever be subject to court martial. That mistaken assumption, the heart of so much of our societal disintegration, is also the heart of the social chaos that dominates the Army today.

The Uniform Code is, by necessity, a moral code. When soldiers are taught the purpose of the code — to enable the unique society of soldiers to unite in the deepest bonds of trust, camaraderie, and service to each other, they accept the notion that there should be a public standard of morality in the Army. Every soldier can tell you of a buddy who lost his wife to a best friend while the soldier was off on a deployment. The cumulative anger from these betrayals has a delayed but lethal effect on the bonds of community so necessary to survival in combat. Command intolerance of adultery could inoculate a large percentage of soldiers against the temptation to exploit the vulnerability of lonely spouses. Should intolerance include jail time for the offenders? Certainly not. But in other professions, when personal behaviors intrude and disrupt the workplace, termination is in order. Adultery should either be a career-ending behavior for everybody or it should be scrapped from the code altogether. Commander's shouldn't arbitrarily use adultery as the only sling available to slay the Goliathan incompetence or misconduct of their bad soldiers.

At Hood, I was to relive again and again, the paralysis of commanders in the face of bold and selfish immoral conduct when it came to private acts between two consenting adults. The trouble is, in the Army there is no such thing as private, consensual behavior. As Sergeant D's situation illustrates, things like adultery are never private. The act of adultery hurts the soldier, the family and the morale of a unit. Time wasted by commanders, sergeants and counselors to respond to allegations of adultery or the accompanying domestic violence is costly to both the unit and the taxpayer. Every moment spent by a commander or first sergeant soothing a soldier in the throes of self-destruction is a moment diverted from real training, and real development of the warriors who have the trust of the American public to save the world with military force. Every moment spent by a leader untangling the damage caused by affairs and promiscuity is a lump of taxpayer dollars tossed down the sewer pipe.

The paralysis was a top-down leadership problem. Lacking the courage to impose a standard of morality on the troops at Fort Hood, generals lathered away the symptoms of domestic violence, angry spouses, gangs and drugs. They responded to immoral and illegal conduct with a wash of programs that would not change personal behaviors or strengthen the military family or the fighting force.

General Schwartz's edicts focused on quality of life for families. Perhaps the General thought the adultery epidemic at Hood was due to the strenuous work schedules and field training requirements. His response was to curtail the work schedules and length of time spent in the woods training to fight. Thus, married soldiers were instructed to go home to their families at 4:30 P.M. The III Corps General mandated weekends off even during field training. His priority was unequivocally the satisfaction of military spouses. This policy had been in effect for two years when I arrived at Hood.

There seemed to be a belief that lavish family support programs could substitute for the healthy conformity to a moral code. Hundreds of millions of dollars were spent at Fort Hood building childcare centers, renovating family quarters, detailing soldiers to clean up family housing neighborhoods or to play traffic guard for school-bound children. No whine from a military spouse was ignored. Televised town meetings were held to temper the dissatisfaction of military spouses.

General Schwartz actually instructed soldiers, spouses and leaders to call his office personally if soldiers were ever abused with an extended duty day or weekend work. This pacifying technique contributed more to the erosion of discipline and the waste of manpower than anything I have ever seen in business or the government. If a supervisor wants a soldier to copy a 50-page manual at 4:28 P.M., his private points out such a tasking violates the general's policy of sending soldiers home at 4:30. The supervisor attempts to enforce his tasking by demanding the soldier stay until the copying is complete. The private files a complaint with the Inspector General. Or his spouse calls the Three Star General's abuse hotline to complain. Although unions are legally prohibited in the military, married soldiers had the most powerful union organizer to protect their benefits: the three star commanding general of the Third Corps.

Is it any wonder that soldiers lined up with bar girls, prostitutes and pregnant women to marry, to fall under the protection of the nicest family man the Army has ever known?

Rates of domestic violence or extramarital affairs were not diminished by this generous gift of time off to military families. The problem, as usual, is that most of the soldiers were not mature enough to handle their family responsibilities, let alone the job for which they were being paid. No amount of advocacy for private time, no commitment to work release standards could ever compensate for the pathetic circumstances under which most soldiers got married. Weekly family time off will never compensate for the lack of relationship skills necessary to sustain an intimate relationship. No amount of swaggering and boasting by a General that the Army cares for its families could ameliorate the pain and suffering that amoral and truly immoral sexual behaviors bring to the home.

One young man from the 404th, JW, was sent to me for emergency counseling. JW married young. His supervisors worried he would quit the Army without completing his contract, and thus lose his housing and college benefits. JW was known as a good soldier until he started fighting with his wife. JW was in the throes of despair about his marital discord. Lovesick soldiers may report for duty each day, as JW did, but their minds are usually stuck in the last barroom argument or bedroom spat with their lover. They sit under a foggy cloud as long as they feel out of control in their relationships. Supervisors don't hesitate to send the lovelorn to a chaplain, because these soldiers drain the mission, and are often dangerously distracted.

Proud of his career, JW was willing to do anything, up to a point, to allay his supervisors' concerns. He brought his wife to my office for marriage counseling. This couple had three lovely children who were very affectionate and chatty with both parents and myself. The crux of the conflict was presented by JW. His wife, KW sported a silver bell on her tongue. She danced nude in a bar in another city, almost two hours away from base. JW did not object to the dancing, as it brought their family three or four thousand dollars extra income every month. What he objected to was her flirtations with other men in his unit. And, he objected to the time she spent away from the family, commuting an hour to and from her job each day. Neither JW, nor his wife would admit that the dancing itself might have ruptured the trust, the bond in their marriage. Nor could they see misplaced priorities in their desire to earn cash at the expense of marital concord. They were both enamored of the cash — her dancing brought in double what JW could earn as a soldier.

Now the Army paid JW a salary, provided him free housing, free medical care, subsidized child care, tax-free shopping centers, subsidized grocery stores and recreational facilities. This couple had three beautiful, but noticeably neglected children. Why in God's name did they need extra cash each month? KW insisted that she would not quit dancing, even if her husband forbid her to. She came from a broken family. She would not surrender her financial independence, despite her husband's ability to provide for the family. No fundamentalist, no Promise Keeper or James Dobson was going to deprive KW of her feeling of control that came not from the dancing, but from bringing home so much money.

If traditional military values were being upheld in this command, a sergeant could have told JW that he was bound to uphold the UCMJ, and therefore, he ought to refrain from pandering his wife's body, even if her reason for dancing nude was to quadruple the family income. But in 1996, traditional military values and virtues were discarded. The military believed that adaptation to the amoral culture was necessary to retain good soldiers. JW didn't want his wife to stop dancing nude. He wanted her to earn her $4,000 more efficiently, so that she could be home to cook his dinner and spend time with the children.

Welcome to the New Army! Welcome to the X Generation, whose role models include prostitutes that market their books about use of prostitution to pay for Ivy League education on worldwide television. At Fort Hood in 1996, nude dancing was considered a legitimate business activity by military legal authorities. Thus, leaders could not (or would not) question the moral or psychological consequences of JW's family decision to engage in the nude dancing industry for profit.

As a military chaplain, I could point out to this young couple that they were compromising the intimacy, trust, and mutual regard so necessary to an enduring marriage. I could not say that JW's economic exploitation of his wife's body was against the military code of conduct. The command abrogated the military code of conduct when the Fort Hood Judge Advocate General Corps endorsed such activities as nude photography and nude dancing as legitimate business enterprises in a free market economy.

Would the Army's generous housing benefits hold this family of five together? Would the childcare programs and subsidized shopping centers lessen their marital stresses? Would the Thursday afternoon free family time, the mandatory weekends off permit this family to develop the intimacy necessary to endure the hardship of long deployments or the trauma of war? Not so long as the couple continued in their pact to set aside not just the Army's moral code, but the one they brought from their fundamentalist churches in favor of the financial bonanza nude dancing afforded them.

Was their legitimate business enterprise really of no consequence or cost to the Army? JW's tolerance of his wife's nude dancing cost the command plenty. JW and his wife may have pocketed 3,000 dollars every month, but the vehicle maintenance shop lost the concentration and productivity of a mechanic. JW and his wife may have developed a business plan where he could start his own company after three or four years, but he was building his enterprise at the expense of taxpayers. Needless to say, command tolerance of his activity had a ripple effect on the choices made by other soldiers, too. Why should other soldiers live morally upright, professional lives when the Army allowed some to build fortunes from illicit professions that were actually in violation of the UCMJ, if not the civilian standards of conduct and business?

**You've Got A Truck! Next Year,
We'll Budget For The Canvas**

This trusty Humvee provided transport to field sites at Fort Hood. There was not, however, enough money in the equipment budget to canvass the cargo section.

Because soldiers were given so much family time, the single soldiers at Fort Hood lived in an incubator for crime, addiction, or at the very least, self-destructive lifestyle decisions. Fort Hood, with its ultra-concentrated population of trained killers, was just one more post where single soldiers were left to fend for themselves during family or Phantom Time.

If appearances count for anything, you could only conclude nobody cared about the single soldiers in the barracks. Our 404th soldiers lived three and four persons to a single room. Room lights were as dim as a dormitory in a third world country. One light fixture per room. Rusted metal furniture. No place for soldiers to sit but on their bed. In these overcrowded, mildewed barracks, the air-conditioners and the vents were inoperative. The pee smell from the toilets could only be surpassed by open sewers.

General Schwartz met with the 77 chaplains assigned to Fort Hood to discuss his vision for Army families. I asked him directly what he planned to do about the substandard housing for single soldiers and the lack of programs to mentor first-enlistment soldiers to successful completion of their tours. I pointed out what the general knew. The only way soldiers could escape these living conditions — worse than they would experience in any federal prison - was to participate in self-destructive actions. Female soldiers copulated as necessary to earn the right to a private apartment upon verification of pregnancy. Men caroused in the bars to escape their loneliness, and frequently married bar girls whom they believed they loved. The general said he had a small amount of money for the next fiscal year. He planned to renovate some of the barracks. When I raised my hand to ask a follow-up, he drew the question and answer period to an abrupt halt and left the room.

There was no comprehensive plan to care for single soldiers. Given this fact, it was still not beyond hope to encourage single soldiers to rise above the squalor of barracks life. You could, if you devoted your time to it, steer soldiers away from the fatal mistake of getting married or having a child out of wedlock to flee the barracks. The successes are unforgettable, but unfortunately very rare.

One African-American senior sergeant called me from the 404th hangar and asked me to talk to his young subordinate. When Sergeant D called, he patiently explained to me his fear that his young, brilliant soldier, a white man from the back woods of Arkansas would get married to bolt the barracks. I went to the hangar. We sat down on folding chairs next to their inventory. After we joshed about vacations in the Ozarks, where the conflation of a gas station, a whitewashed Baptist chapel and the surreptitious parking of a lone police car constituted a bona fide town, we got down to counseling business. Sergeant D sat quietly and let me talk to Specialist T for a bit.

In a nutshell, Specialist T was too sensible and disciplined to be living with the BOSS Army barracks rats at Fort Hood.

"I don't have anywhere to go. I just have a bed. The soldiers are always drunk. They're always loud and doing things I just don't want to have any part of it. There's no where to think. I have an archeology text on my desk. I can talk about microbes and I can talk about Walt Whitman. The guys make fun of me. They think I'm just stuck up. The girls are telling me I'm gay because I won't sleep with them!"

Specialist T should have gone through college on full scholarship. His dad was a dirt poor gas pumper in the Arkansas Ozarks. Though he was a towering, blond, green-eyed man, he had no confidence that he could overcome his family's hillbilly image. T found a young Hispanic single mother whom he befriended. He spent most of his weekends with her family. The family was religious. They were decent. They didn't drink. I never asked T if he was a Baptist, but regardless, he didn't want any part in the devastation wrought by other soldiers' binge drinking.

"Specialist T, do you love this woman?"

If there was a real love relationship, I might have offered pre-marital counseling, but I would have encouraged him to slow down and sort out the possibilities.

"No ma'am. It's not like that. We're just friends."

"When were you planning to get married?"

"Next Thursday. I have to get out of these barracks."

"You know, if you didn't have so much potential, I would just let you make up your own mind."

Specialist T smiled. He admitted he was ashamed of his father's poverty. He didn't think he could overcome the stigma of his backwoods Arkansas heritage. We talked for quite a bit about his interests. He made a follow-up appointment to visit with me in my office. He came back to see me twice. We made progress in that short time.

Unfit For Service

Cramped living space. (Fort Stewart, Georgia, 1997.)

"Your father raised you right. So, I can't figure why you turned down a scholarship to college. You hate being a private. That makes me really worried. Do you know that if you marry this girl, you will have financial obligations? You may never get through college because of those family obligations. Why aren't you taking classes here on post? The Army will pay 75% of the tuition the whole time you earn your degree on active duty — then you can save your benefits for graduate school — for your Ph.D.!"

But ma'am, I can't afford the textbooks. I can't afford the 25% balance of tuition."

"How much are we talking about?" Specialist T needed 90 dollars to buy books and pay the balance of tuition.

"Has anybody talked to you about Officer Candidate School?" I asked.

T brightened.

"Specialist T, you are really, really smart. When I came into the Army, my friends said I would never be happy as an enlisted. You don't belong in the enlisted ranks. I went through Officer Candidate School. You belong in the officer corps. You tend to see the big picture most of the time. Maybe you should think about Officer Candidate School. Have you ever talked to your commander about your career?"

"No, ma'am."

"You need to make an appointment to see your commander. Let Sergeant D get you in!"

Sergeant D was grateful I encouraged T to consider OCS. About a week later, after the young man canceled his plans to get married, Sergeant D called to thank me. Actually, Sergeant D deserved the thanks for mentoring his talented soldier. As promised, I contacted T's company commander, a major who was about to leave Fort Hood.

"You know, Sir, this young man has a lot of potential. Army Community Services won't give him a loan because he just wants to use the money to take a college class to better himself. He's not pregnant. He comes to work everyday and does his job."

"I know what you mean, Chaplain."

"He didn't run up an outrageous phone bill. He didn't run up his credit cards. Since he's single, with no dependents and he has potential, the system won't help him."

"Chaplain, he's the kind of soldier the Army wants to keep!"

"If I can come up with the money to get this young man into a college class to pull him through the summer, will you have a heart-to-heart talk with T about seeking an OCS or even an ROTC commission?"

"I will do everything I can."

The commander spent time mentoring this young Arkansan. Specialist T finished his class with a 4.0. I assume by now he is on his way to becoming an officer or a successful civilian.

Not enough soldiers get the attention and support that Specialist T got. Fewer were responsive to the gestures made by leaders to help them move ahead with their lives. I've been in the Army long enough to know that his intelligent responses to a horrific living situation were admirable, but exceptional. Very few of the barracks rat stories worked out so successfully.

Within months after I arrived at Fort Hood, the female chaplain who served the Combat Engineer Brigade was selected to be an evaluator at the National Training Center. Jim Crews, the 4th Infantry Division Chaplain, asked me to provide chaplain coverage for the entire brigade. This would have left the 404th Aviation Support Battalion with no chaplain. The 404th commander was livid when this decision was made, because I had just established myself and cultivated ties with all the companies and staff. It was finally negotiated that I would work for Colonel Dunn, the Engineer Brigade Commander. I would provide primary chaplain support to his brigade headquarters, the 299th and 588th engineer battalions and backup coverage to the 404th. I kept my tiny office in the aviation headquarters, but moved to the DISCOM chapel to do most of my ministry. Colonel Dunn generously insisted that I stay with him long enough to be rated as a brigade chaplain. By this time, I was a chaplain with three years as a captain. I would receive my second rating in a chaplain leadership position. The change was good for me, but not just because it afforded me another opportunity to have my work evaluated by officers I respected. Colonel Dunn was also a member of the Protestant congregation, so I counted on him to support our chapel programs just as I could count on my engineer commanders in Korea.

As much as I still don't think women belong in combat engineer units, I just love working with combat engineers. Fort Hood engineers promised no respite, however, from the social anarchy that has traditionally been a lifestyle choice for aviators. The social chaos was just as great in the engineer units as in the 404th. There was such an intensity to the training pace and such an improvement in the barracks quality of life, however, that the new and added responsibilities were welcome.

My primary rater was Lieutenant Colonel Mark Soltero. He was a stickler for staff PT. All of us were required to report to the Brigade Headquarters for warm up exercises and a daily run or game of sports. Once we ran about two miles as a group, we were free to run at our own pace. I was living in Copperas Cove at the time. I started out the door more than one rainy morning to drive ten miles to our PT field. The thunder cracked, the rain poured in torrents. Only once did I make the mistake of assuming Lieutenant Colonel Soltero would cancel PT. I went back in my apartment and rode my stationary bike. When I got to the staff meeting, Mark Soltero said he missed me.

"Sir, it was pouring rain!" I thought I would be clobbered by his engineer standards.

"Chaplain, it wasn't raining here on Fort Hood! Don't assume because its raining in your neighborhood, its raining in Fort Hood!"

Right he was. The next morning, I bravely ventured to Fort Hood in the pouring rain. To my amazement, the storm stayed on our side of the highway right up to the 4th ID entrance gate. But Battalion Road was as dry as desert. God played very cruel jokes on the soldiers when it came to weather conditions during the physical training hour.

Sometimes we played soccer, volleyball or touch football. Once, I invited the officers to my house for a morning run up and down the Copperas Cove hills. Mark Soltero did not expect oldtimers like myself to run like jackrabbits. He worried that we would have heart attacks if we did not maintain fitness.

Colonel Dunn did not exempt himself from this daily rigor. He stood next to the flagpole in front of his headquarters. After we saluted Old Glory, he got down and pumped out all those exercises that are supposed to prove we can leap tall buildings in a single bound, and then ran the full length of Battalion Road at a clip that put many a junior soldier to shame. As part of my farewell from the Engineer Brigade, I was finally awarded the Army's PT fitness badge — the emblem you get to wear when you max the fitness test. I was really proud of that badge, but I owed it to Lieutenant Colonel Soltero and Colonel Dunn because they made physical training a necessary but fun part of our daily lives together.

Daily exercise proved to be the one structured routine that was life-giving in an otherwise debilitating work situation. The engineers needed a chaplain, even a female chaplain, because their soldiers were drowning in social problems. As one first sergeant reminded me repeatedly, the combat engineer MOS drew men with the lowest IQs in the Army. So, here you have a professional occupation where you train soldiers to blow up bridges and buildings by day, but by night you send them out to minefields that are planted with gangs, drugs, prostitutes, guns and saloons.

It took me some time to realize that a soldier's professional occupation could become a metaphor for how he chose to self-destruct. We buried two soldiers who were very hot headed, rebellious young men. They could not accept the authority of their sergeants. They both married women whom they adored, but of whom they could not expect fidelity. Both were torn between their parents and their spouses. Both changed their insurance policies to divide their $200,000 life insurance benefit equally between their parents and their spouses. Both proceeded to die in violent automobile crashes. The first fell asleep at the wheel less than ten miles before he arrived at his parents' home for a vacation. The second was burned beyond recognition in a car with three other people on his way to his wife's family. Both family situations required delicate mediation by command family assistance officers. Both memorial services required delicate handling.

In neither would I glamorize the soldiers' deaths or suggest that their crashes were God's will. Memorial services are for the survivors. I strongly urged the young men who attended that God had a very different plan for the young men who died in accidents. God has special plans for all of us, and we must be attentive to the ways in which God plans for us to share our gifts in this world. General Kern thanked me on more than one occasion for these remarks.

We handled one case after another of young soldiers from backwoods Texas or Louisiana, who married the girls of their dreams, only to discover they were sleeping with many other men in the battalion. One sergeant married a woman who would come to counseling sessions with her blouse unbuttoned almost to her navel. More than once I asked her to button up. The man was crazy about her. She was crazy about dozens of other soldiers — or she was crazy about the benefits earned from her intimate association with them.

There were soldiers in every battalion — engineers, infantry, and the 404th — who were sent to me to help them with spouses who were too debilitated to live on an Army base. One young man married a chronically depressed woman who had five boys from age six to fifteen who were all on medications for one mental illness or another. Men who married into situations like this cannot usually go to the field or do minimal duties each day. This soldier worked hard. He was a leader in the field. We loved him, but he was the perfect example of the Army's failed Exceptional Family Member program. He felt it was important to help other young fatherless boys, and so, he married a woman almost old enough to be his mother so he could be a father figure to her boys. An inordinate amount of command time, hospital resources, and housing space was shifted to help him accomplish his goal. He took these responsibilities on because the Army provided benefits he could share. The fact was, he could never deploy to a foreign country. He could not go to the National Training Center because he needed to be near his family to keep them stable.

Another young man was forced out of the Army for making the same decision. He was so obsessed with care for his family he neglected his work duties altogether.

There weren't many women in the Combat Engineers. In one battalion, two junior enlisted women were assigned. They both got pregnant to get out of the barracks. The one fell in love with the sergeant major's driver. When she became pregnant, he refused to marry her. Her first sergeant arranged for special duty, eased work requirements. The woman agitated every helping agency, every doctor to get permission to be removed from the Combat Engineers. When her doctor denied her medical reasons for a transfer, she filed an IG complaint against her first sergeant, the man who invested days in trying to get her work and home life to a point where she could succeed.

The other woman married a soldier from the 588th Battalion. She did not love him. She just wanted to move out of the barracks. As soon as they moved into an apartment, she began an affair with another soldier. She was going to divorce JO, thinking she accomplished her purpose for marriage — she had an apartment. When she was informed she would have to move back to the barracks if she divorced she resolved her dilemma by getting pregnant by her new boyfriend. All while she was still married. JO was still madly in love with her. He refused to give her a divorce. She filed domestic violence and stalking charges against him. This was a classic example of the paradox of sexual misconduct allegations in the United States Army. This woman, who committed acts of adultery, and who put herself in a state of non-deployability by becoming pregnant, was never charged for her sexual misconduct. When her husband refused to divorce her, and he continued to spy on her to prove the infidelity, he was charged with domestic violence and stalking. This man worked hard as a mechanic. He was always worldwide deployable. He was treated like a criminal. Yet, this young lady was selected for commercials to recruit women for the Army. If the commercials were even slightly honest, they would have played the theme, "Be all you can be: pregnant and hassle free!"

Although the Engineers were focused on the exciting high-tech Advanced Warfighting Experimental Exercise, there were still problems with gangs and guns in the battalions. One soldier in the 299th was caught with a gun in his room. By all accounts, he was playing with his piece while talking to his girlfriend. He accidentally shot himself in the foot. He could have gotten two years in prison. When his commander called me to the hospital, I stayed most of the night to talk to him. This man sounded the fear of most soldiers when he justified having his gun in the barracks.

"Ma'am, it's not safe in the clubs. It's not safe around here. You have to have your protection..."

This man was three months from completing a spotless enlistment. His sergeant major was furious with him, because he worked so hard to develop him. The soldier was ashamed and afraid to talk to the sergeant major. We prayed together, read the Bible, and I counseled him more than once before the sergeant major decided to punish him with all kinds of extra-duty and pay reductions.

Another soldier was identified as a white survivalist. He had been in trouble earlier for hanging a Confederate flag and other white supremacist things in his room. His African-American commander defended him as his best soldier. This young man went AWOL after his girlfriend miscarried. When he was brought back to the unit, his battalion commander begged him to let go of his survivalist associations to choose the Army. His first sergeant and a major from the battalion sent him to me for counseling. The young man was inarticulate, but he hit the bull's eye when he described his own motivation to stray.

"Ma'am, when I came into the Army, we worked together like brothers. Now, nobody trains. Nobody takes care of each other. When I was down in Panama, we went on expeditions for days. We helped each other to survive. We were brothers. Here, every man is selfish. You just get what you can for yourself. You just worry about your family. Nobody cares about us. Nobody cares about mission!"

The Third Corps Sergeant Major complained that soldiers on Fort Hood were available to work less than 22 hours per week by the time you released them for the weekends, gave them comp time for night duties, sent them home for family time on Thursday afternoons, sent them for parent teacher conferences, released soldiers at noontime for pay day activities and sent them to the schools to be crossing guards. Of course, you had to add the days in spring and fall when the command shut down to clean up the post family housing area. You had to add the four-day training holidays that were given to protect family time. If soldiers had babies to care for, this time off was a celestial blessing. But if soldiers were single, lonely, without an identity, and angry at the world, is it any wonder they take comfort in the militias and gangs who promise to be their families to fill the void?

I sent this young white survivalist to a Catholic priest to help him get to the root of a lot of his religious anger. He was raised Catholic. His parents marriage fell apart. He blamed the church. This young man was eventually allowed to leave active duty. I found it extremely ironic that his African-American commander continued to defend him.

"He's just mixed up. I know I could work with him."

Months later, when I returned the 404th Aviation, I could see the structure of the gang problem with a new clarity. Not only were our single soldiers left to demonic forces for vast quantities of time. Not only was their living situation akin to the ghettos they left behind in the American City. The soldiers were prey to gang forces because they were denied the one thing that made them join — community. In the BOSS Army, there were still no CQs. The barracks were designed like cheap motels. Soldiers come and go anonymously. Anybody can walk up to your door to sell you tickets to a church barbecue or to blow you to pieces.

More than once, angry civilian lovers or gang members walked up to soldiers bedroom doors and shot them dead in their rooms. During my last field problem, the 404th narrowly escaped that tragedy, but we were still left in ruins. A female soldier from one of our companies was pregnant and engaged to be married to a soldier from another company. She was having casual sex with a third soldier from our headquarters company. When her fiancee discovered the infidelity, he arranged for an ambush of our headquarters soldier. This man had a strong gang background. He beat off his attackers and fled to our battalion headquarters. For the rest of the evening, the battalion commander, three company commanders, the Executive Officer and myself were holed up. Worse, these thugs, who were model soldiers by day, continued to chase each other with tire irons for the rest of the weekend. Worst of all, when the female complained to her sergeant that her fiancée was angry with her for sleeping with another man, her sergeant wound up with a major sexual harassment complaint that was investigated by CID. He told her that she needed to change, to give up her whoring.

When CID was called to investigate our barracks gang rumble, they came and confirmed the danger. When the MPs were called to provide security, we were advised we would have to provide our own security in the barracks. The MPs, much like police in an urban ghetto, had their hands full. There was no way to provide security for that building, given its physical design and Army weapons policies. Every gang member, every street-wise scorned lover knows this. That's why 16-year-old girls and gang lieutenants feel they can walk up to a private's room and shoot with impunity.

The barracks building designs and the social priorities at Fort Hood, and I might venture to say, on most modern Army posts, will always favor the gang lieutenant, the destructive ring leader. On that night, when the MPs told our battalion commander we would just have to fend for ourselves, I finally understood why the young soldiers on our post felt they had to have their guns to protect themselves. They were on their own.

I wholeheartedly understood what I had previously intuited. That the most egregious mistake ever made by the Army was the decision to expand Fort Hood during a peacetime economy into a city of 45,000 predominantly male, oversexed, under-challenged, under-supervised, uneducated and uncultured soldiers.

The second most egregious mistake ever made by the Army was the refusal at Fort Hood, as on all other Army installations, to look at the systemic policy failures, to look to the cultural poverty of amassing so many warriors in a single location.

The third, most ridiculous, as well as painful, mistake made by Army leaders was to assign the task of transforming the culture to the chaplains. The superabundance of white, fundamentalist right-wing chaplains renders the sociological task impossible, however half-heartedly chaplains may volunteer for the role of savior. To be fair, the legacy of resorting to religious coercion to excise the pathologies of an oversized military community is not a short-lived consequence of the groundswell of Christian Coalition during this past decade. Indeed, the first great general of America's Continental Army, George Washington insisted that chaplains were required in his Army to minimize the debaucheries that inevitably emerge in predominantly male military societies.

Washington's men, however, do not seem to have been afflicted with the social pathologies of our present American society — drugs, gangs, and a pervasive contempt for family values. Washington's men could be easily subdued with a prayer or an hour-long hell-fire and brimstone sermon. The soldiers in today's Army do not fear the fires of hell. Less than ten percent of the soldiers attend worship services, so they won't even have a chance to hear about hell fires. The soldiers in today's Army are on fire and they often burn with uncontrollable rage. The chaplains were asked to be moral forest rangers. The 70 chaplains assigned to Hood were expected to produce the phoenix that would rise out of the ashes of each act of self-destruction wrought by the angry young men. Ever in search of a mission to justify positions in the amoral, secular, and perpetually downsizing Army, the chaplains once again grabbed the fire-fighting mission, without ever intending to heal the calamities before them.

It is understandable that male chaplains would wholeheartedly appropriate the philosophy of the Promise Keepers in an effort to contain the social volatility at Hood. Fort Hood is not only situated in the hills of Central Texas — it's at the heart of the Texas Bible Belt. Thus, it is not surprising that the 70-odd chaplains assigned to this purgatory would embrace the tenets and leadership tactics of the most notorious national fundamentalist men's group to transform the hearts and minds of Fort Hood's men. Fort Hood chaplains somehow became the Promise Keepers personified. Before too long, however, they were exposed as the Promise Breakers. Despite the chaplain's investment of thousands of dollars into fluffy events like Promise Keeper Rallies, they had no influence whatsoever on the command climate that encouraged sexual immorality. They were complicit in the culture of violence and promiscuity.

The Chaplain Corps has doctrinally constructed the Unit Ministry Team, which consists of the chaplain and the assistant. Chaplains must go through graduate training, professional licensing, moral scrutiny, and chaplain training in order to assume the moral and spiritual leadership role in the Army. Chaplain assistants have none of these requirements — especially the legal and moral responsibility to set the moral standards for the command by their example. Yet, under the doctrine of Unit Ministry Team, chaplain assistants are treated as if they can be confidential counselors and trained professional ministers in the unit. Because of this ambiguity, the Chaplain Corps has woven a web of immunity that makes chaplains and chaplain assistants unaccountable for conduct that is unprofessional, illegal or immoral. Complicity was the most indelicate reason for withholding the moral leadership role from the Chaplain Corps, however, particularly the chaplains at Fort Hood. Fort Hood chaplains were active participants in the sex industries and escapades that so destroyed soldiers, their families and their military units.

During August 1996, a young female chaplain assistant was sent to me for a period of rehabilitation. The 4th Infantry Chaplain NCOIC gave me a packet that was supposed to describe her misconduct. There was nothing substantial in the file. The master sergeant attributed the young women's conflicts to the immaturity of her chaplain supervisor. He couldn't handle female assistants. I discovered later that the master sergeant removed all of the documents that certified substantial misconduct by this young woman.

I was led to believe there was a sexual conflict between this young, blond attractive female and her African-American chaplain supervisor. Since that chaplain and his subordinate were practically the same age of 29, I accepted the argument that the conflict could be diffused by moving her to our unit, where there is a sufficient difference in both experience and age to avoid a reoccurrence of that conflict. For about one week, this lady worked diligently to prove that she was a good soldier. I felt fortunate that L would even come to the field. The other female assistant in the DISCOM was pregnant, unable to go to the field with her chaplain. In the 404th, the pregnancy rates skyrocketed once we started regular field training. In the FARP (Forward Area Fefueling Point) platoon, we had 12 out of 15 female soldiers pregnant. That ratio prevailed for all of the sections that required women to go to the field sites even for two or three days. The fact that L wanted to spend time in the field with soldiers seemed to indicate I would finally have an assistant who took her job seriously. Within days of our deployment to the training sites there was a downhill slide.

We went to the field for five days with our battalion. As the company commander said later in a disciplinary meeting, L was Jekyll and Hyde. Out in the field, Hyde made her first appearance. Whenever we visited a group of soldiers L confabulated all kinds of stories that placed her in dangerous or sexual situations. She claimed to be a horseback rider and a skydiver who had broken many bones. Then a hiker whose father spent six months in the States and six months in the Soviet Union. Later, during an investigation when L needed the support of soldiers in the unit who were Puerto Rican, L claimed her father was from Puerto Rico. When I pointed out the contradiction, she told a third variation. Her father was in Russia, and her stepfather was in Puerto Rico. L claimed to be a long distance runner, and a weightlifter. She claimed to be registered as a Gulf War Syndrome victim. A few weeks later, I checked L's physical training scores, because she was not taking her PT tests as required. Her test scores revealed she could not do a two-mile run in the time required, which for a woman her age, was 23 minutes — a speed that would cost any man his job. She barely did enough push ups and sit-ups to pass.

Every soldier must take a physical training test within 30 days of assignment to a unit. L never took a PT test during the three months she was assigned to the 404th. She kept getting doctor's excuses to avoid taking the test. Whenever the company-training sergeant would schedule L, she walked off the job, went over to the Troop Medical Clinic and induced the medics to give her another profile. If a man tried that twice, his commander would put the soldier out of the Army. Truthfully, if an ugly, but otherwise technically qualified woman soldier tried that, she would be harassed into quitting.

Specialist L had a knack for inducing men and women to set aside every standard, every test, and every disciplinary action. Her familiarity with men in high places just seemed to put her beyond any supervisor's reach. In the office, in the chapel building, L flirted with men, married and single. During our first field problem, she described herself in a situation where she and another soldier got a swimming pool, in the middle of a major training exercise down in El Paso, Texas, and sat in their bikinis. This last fib was to several black men, who stood licking their lips, even after I interrupted L and pointed out that such an event could never have taken place in the middle of a training exercise.

When we walked away, L expressed her contempt for the black men who licked their lips, and how they always hit on her. I pointed out she had flirted with every one of them. I stated clearly that her behavior was unprofessional, not to be repeated, and that she had to stop flirting with men. I told L to stop fabricating stories. She insisted that the pool story was true, and that she was given permission by her first sergeant to get the pool and the bikinis. I pointed out to L that the men in this company were experiencing a high rate of misconduct charges. At that very moment, seven different black supervisors were accused of sexual harassment or assault. All the accusations came from women with whom they'd had private relationships — some sexual, and some not. I did not want L to experience harassment, or sexual assault. Neither did I want her to distort her own solicitations into criminal charges against the men, as other women in the battalion were doing. At the rate this battalion was proceeding with harassment charges, there would be no black men left to lead the enlisted troops.

Strangely, L began to lie about completion of her duties. She was to set up field telephones. She insisted they were broken. She insisted she didn't know how to set them up. Her previous Signal Battalion supervisor later told me he set up a special class to ensure her competence in this basic responsibility. L refused to assemble the heater in the tent. She stayed with her friends until bedtime, because their tent was heated. L dragged when we were to walk from site to site to visit soldiers in the base camp. She insisted she had an injury that prevented her from walking.

Three days into the field problem, L refused to drive. She wanted to stay back at the Personnel tent with her friends. The behaviors of most of the women in this tent were extremely provocative. The battalion commander complained about used douche bags outside the portajohns and his observation of men and women walking around the tents and outdoor area in their underwear. L was obviously caught up in the activity. After a major confrontation, where I insisted L would have to drive me to various field sites, she yielded. She lumbered out to the vehicle as if she were exhausted, and slowly put the truck in gear. We went to the FARP, where helicopters perform hot fueling exercises — fuel is obtained while the helicopters are still running. Hot fueling is a latent pyromaniac's delight. The potential for a wild fire is very real. One flick of a lit match, and the whole operation can go up in flames. There was an accident. During recovery, L sat with a black man, who was slightly injured in the accident. The FARP platoon leader, a West Point graduate deemed the soldier was not injured enough to be taken to the emergency room. He was not a medic or a combat lifesaver. After an intimate conversation, where L and the injured soldier were oblivious to the efforts of the unit to restore order, L planned to drive the soldier somewhere, under the auspices of taking him to the hospital.

L allegedly had combat lifesaver credentials, but she never produced her credentials or equipment to be useful in situations like this. Nevertheless, she insisted as the only combat lifesaver in the platoon that the young man should be taken to the hospital. FARP leaders squabbled — senior sergeant versus lieutenant. I pointed out that if L took the injured man to the hospital that I should go along. How else could we quickly verify the man's ability to return to work, and eliminate the fear of accountability that the man "could be suffering a concussion" as L insisted. There were no signs of concussion — the black soldier and L, when not under the scrutiny of supervisors or myself, smiled, preened, moved closer to each other. Since there were no medics in the battalion, anywhere on the field, it seemed safer to just take the man to the hospital, have him checked, and then return him to the field. We did that.

L was furious that I came along as her supervisor, thus arousing my suspicions. Once again, the woman who hated the flirtations and sexual gestures of black men singled out a black man to conduct an intimate, flirtatious conversation within the middle of a work crisis. Once again, the woman who spoke contemptuously of black men because they hit on her had no fear of going off alone with him in a military truck. What this potential victim of harassment or sexual assault resented was the presence of her supervisor.

Later, while initiating disciplinary procedures against L for refusing to drive, refusing to put up the tent heater, refusing to set up the communications lines, and her other duties, I contacted the Signal Company first sergeant for whom she worked before becoming my assistant. L boasted to our men that this first sergeant allowed L to parade in front of her peers in a bikini during the Roving Sands exercise. The first sergeant adamantly swore that L was lying. He punished L and the friend for appearing in clothing that was too sexually alluring, a fact that was confirmed by L's previous supervisor, Chaplain M. In fact, the Signal Company's first sergeant punished his whole company by taking away their right to wear civilian attire during a one-day stand-down. He insisted he included counseling statements for that misconduct in L's rehabilitation packet, but they were mysteriously removed from the packet given to me.

If any male soldier had committed the continuous pattern of in-discipline that L committed, he would have been thrown out of the Army. The sergeant major of the 404th battalion was furious that L was even permitted to serve in our battalion. He demanded to know how she was sent over without her accompanying disciplinary packet.

"Watch your back, Ma'am. She's a liar. She is a compulsive liar, and she is doing things that have no place in your section."

The 404th sergeant major persisted in his demands to see L's disciplinary packet. I went as high as the Third Corps Sergeant Major for the Chaplains. He said the entire record was sent to the Division. The Division NCOIC lost the damaging information. The Division NCOIC was protecting other female chaplain assistants, too. During my last field trip with the 404th, the executive officer for one of the Apache battalions demanded to know why his male chaplain could not get rid of his female assistant who was sleeping with everybody in the battalion and then some. When I went to the chaplain to ask him why he tolerated her misconduct, he exasperatedly said his hands were tied.

L kept disappearing from the work site. With the guidance of my sergeant major, I wrote up a number of disciplinary counseling statements. I took these to my supervisory chaplain and to the Third Corps for review. My supervisory chaplain approved the disciplinary actions, but he said he had to stay out of the situation.

"I can't afford another Equal Opportunity case right now."

I was to learn later that this kind man was used by the Chaplains to cover up chaplain misconduct elsewhere in the command.

He was given a female sergeant who was a full-blown alcoholic, but a very hard worker. The woman worked along side my friend Ed Kelley both at Fort Hood and down in Guantanamo. She'd had sexual relationships with a number of male chaplains, white and black. They usually plied her with alcohol, then "made her feel like a woman." At the same time, an African-American chaplain was running a swinging club out of the Black Gospel congregation. This chaplain, Lieutenant Colonel Manzy was put in jail, thanks to the prosecution of Lieutenant Colonel Manuel, whom I'd gotten to know in Korea. Many chaplains and JAG officers revealed to me that there were a number of chaplains complicit in this sexual scandal. Only one, the African-American was jailed. This racial pattern of selective prosecution persists to this day. The female alcoholic who was transferred to the DISCOM was eventually put out of the Army by my supervisory chaplain. She was, afterall, promiscuous, alcoholic, but most of all, no longer doing the job for which she was paid. She retaliated by filing a gender discrimination claim against him. She also filed many complaints to CID against the chaplains who used her sexually, but none of these men were ever held accountable.

When I sat Specialist L down in the presence of our company commander to counsel her about her misconduct in our battalion, she was like a siren. She had a lie to cover every situation.

At the end of our first session, the commander said, "Chaplain, she has two personalities. She changes right before your eyes."

In pressing the matter further, the company first sergeant insisted we needed to get Specialist L out of the Army. No man could commit even two of the infractions this woman committed without being charged for misconduct. We pressed on.

At that moment, there were seven men in one company who were being held hostage to female complaints of sexual harassment. When a male sergeant attempted to hold female soldiers accountable for missing duty, not cleaning their equipment, or disappearing from the job, the women filed sexual harassment charges. According to Army policy at the time, all disciplinary actions against the female "victims" ceased when they filed harassment charges. The men's professional careers were ruined.

Chaplain involvement in sexual misconduct was not a thing of the past when I attempted to discipline the woman who was sent to work for me. The DISCOM chapel had a female NCOIC during my last days there. When she realized I made the decision to put Specialist L out of the Army, she begged me not to.

"Chaplain, you don't know. This is nothing. What L is doing is nothing compared to what the chaplains and assistants are doing all over this post!"

Maybe L's behavior was nothing to her but I wanted no part of the sex industry in my ministry.

When it became apparent to L that she was going to be discharged from the Army for patterns of misconduct that were beyond rehabilitation, she filed a sexual harassment complaint against me. Of course, the charges were unfounded. But our battalion commander realized that dozens of his soldiers were implicated in sexual misconduct with this woman, including some of his favorite male chaplains. The 404th Battalion Commander declined to have her discharged from the Army.

I was revolted. I knew in the depths of my heart that the Chaplain Corps was corrupt. I knew that the many policies that had been designed to help soldiers and families were absolutely counterproductive. I just could not imagine the Army would ever recover from the social chaos if we allowed all these forces to work against each other. Everybody was suffering.

I resigned my commission.

My brigade commander and General Kerns, the new 4th Infantry Division Commander asked me to reconsider. They valued my work as a chaplain. I knew that my work was completely wasted in an Army that had allowed its personnel policies and its moral code to go to the dogs.

The Aberdeen Scandal broke in the media. I began to call television producers and newspapers to ask them to look more deeply into that story. I visited with Tom Anderson from *60 Minutes*, and shared with him a structural analysis of the policies that were contributing to the Army's complete collapse. There was no rape at Aberdeen. There were orgies. Women are not being harassed and exploited by men. They are Queen Bees, running lucrative sex industries and exploiting sexual harassment laws to protect themselves from criminal sanctions. Furthermore, the single-soldier pregnancy policies and the promotion of convenience marriages by first-enlistment soldiers was creating all kinds of violence, legitimate workplace hostilities, and social chaos. Tom Anderson understood my points, but he insisted the story was too big for a 15-minute segment.

"You should write a book."

I started an organization, Citizen Soldiers to Restore Military Integrity, to encourage other soldiers to register their legitimate frustrations with their congresspersons and the media. I began to visit Army bases to discuss the situation with other soldiers and chaplains. I attended part of the Aberdeen Trials, where I discovered that the woman who accused Sergeant Simpson of ten counts of rape was actually my assistant's partner in sexploitation at Fort Hood. I visited with the female captains of the 404th shortly after that trial and confessed to one that I felt it imperative to let Sergeant Simpson's defense attorneys know about R's behavior at Fort Hood.

"Chaplain, don't worry. That woman hasn't done a day's work since she joined the 404th. She has four different men up on rape charges. Yet, the medical clinic supervisor is demanding that I put her out of the Army. Do you know, chaplain, she visits the clinic every week. Every week with a different STD?"

I confirmed this fact with the medical clinic NCOIC, who faxed me copies of the regulations that stipulate that soldiers who have repeated STD infections should be discharged. After all, they are missing whole days of work every week when they come to the clinic to treat their self-inflicted diseases.

Over the months, the media blitzed stories about women who were being raped in basic training, women who were being harassed and abused. I discovered when I went to the trials of many soldiers that most of the reporters, from Jaime McIntyre to Dana Priest sat in the courtrooms day after day. They did not have a clue about the real sexual dynamics, the real problems that were tearing the Army apart, not to mention the families of the men and women who live under mountains of bad policy.

In my early advocacy days, I was so angry, at times I was positively foul mouthed. I realized that Tom Anderson was right. I had to write a book. With the moral support of my family, I took my first professional sabbatical to write this story. My sister Lucille and her husband John Puccio faithfully encouraged me to take all the time I needed to flesh out the experiences of those of us who have lived in military society, only to experience family breakup or career heartache.

If I have one dream, it is that our society will finally wake up and realize that the Army is not the place where we can "Be all We Can Be." The Army can no longer be the repository for all of society's damaged children. The Army cannot be the salvation of parents who never taught their kids to stay away from guns and drugs. The Army cannot be the place where men and women go to find their family of last resort.

The Army is an institution designed to project an organized killing force to defend our country against all enemies, foreign and domestic. Only persons of well-developed character, well-formed personalities and habits of discipline should be recruited and retained to do this terrible, morally comprising work.

We should not expect Uncle Sam to fix all our broken children. We should do that ourselves — back in our cities and small towns where we should invest in our children's well-being so that they have no need to turn to drugs, sex and guns as a substitute for the real love and concern of their own parents, schools and religious leaders.

If we are going to have an Army, we must never forget its sole purpose: to kill for the sake of our defense. The Army never was and should never be a substitute for a family.

WELCOME TO

Hellgate Press

Hellgate Press is named after the historic and rugged Hellgate Canyon on southern Oregon's scenic Rogue River. The raging river that flows below the canyon's towering jagged cliffs has always attracted a special sort of individual — someone who seeks adventure. From the pioneers who bravely pursued the lush valleys beyond, to the anglers and rafters who take on its roaring challenges today — Hellgate Press publishes books that personify this adventurous spirit. Our books are about military history, adventure travel, and outdoor recreation. On the following pages, we would like to introduce you to some of our latest titles and encourage you to join in the celebration of this unique spirit.

Our books are in your favorite bookstore or you can order them direct at **1-800-228-2275** or visit our Website at **http://www.psi-research.com/hellgate.htm**

ARMY MUSEUMS

West of the Mississippi
by Fred L. Bell, SFC Retired

ISBN: 1-55571-395-5
Paperback: 17.95

A guide book for travelers to the army museums of the west, as well as a source of information about the history of the site where the museum is located. Contains detailed information about the contents of the museum and interesting information about famous soldiers stationed at the location or specific events associated with the facility. These twenty-three museums are in forts and military reservations which represent the colorful heritage in the settling of the American West.

BYRON'S WAR

I Never Will Be Young Again...
by Byron Lane

ISBN: 1-55571-402-1
Hardcover: 21.95

Based on letters that were mailed home and a personal journal written more than fifty years ago during World War II, *Byron's War* brings the war life through the eyes of a very young air crew officer. It depicts how the life of this young American changed through cadet training, the experiences as a crew member flying across the North Atlantic under wartime hazards to the awesome responsibility assigned to a nineteen year-old when leading hundreds of men and aircraft where success or failure could seriously impact the outcome of the war.

GULF WAR DEBRIEFING BOOK

An After Action Report   ISBN: 1-55571-396-3
by Andrew Leyden   Paperback: 18.95

Whereas most books on the Persian Gulf War tell an "inside story" based on someone
else's opinion, this book lets you draw your own conclusions by providing you with
a meticulous review of events and documentation all at your fingertips. Includes lists
of all military units deployed, a detailed account of the primary weapons used during
the war, and a look at the people and politics behind the military maneuvering.

FROM HIROSHIMA WITH LOVE   ISBN: 1-55571-404-8

by Raymond A. Higgins   Paperback: 18.95

This remarkable story is written from actual detailed notes and diary entries kept
by Lieutenant Commander Wallace Higgins. Because of his industrial experience
back in the United States and with the reserve commission in the Navy, he was an
excellent choice for military governor of Hiroshima. Higgins was responsible for
helping rebuild a ravaged nation of war. He developed an unforeseen respect for
the Japanese, the culture, and one special woman.

NIGHT LANDING

A Short History of West Coast Smuggling   ISBN: 1-55571-449-8
by David W. Heron   Paperback: 13.95

Night Landing reveals the true stories of smuggling off the shores of California from
the early 1800s to the present. It is a provocative account of the many attempts to
illegally trade items such as freon, drugs, sea otters, and diamonds. This unusual
chronicle also profiles each of these ingenious, but over-optimistic criminals and
their eventual apprehension.

ORDER OF BATTLE

Allied Ground Forces of Operation Desert Storm   ISBN: 1-55571-493-5
by Thomas D. Dinackus   Paperback: 17.95

Based on extensive research, and containing information not previously available
to the public, *Order of Battle* is a detailed study of the Allied ground combat units
that served in Operation Desert Storm. In addition to showing unit assignments,
it includes the insignia and equipment used by the various units in one of the
largest military operations since the end of WWII.

PILOTS, MAN YOUR PLANES!

A History of Naval Aviation   ISBN: 1-55571- 466-8
by Wilbur H. Morrison   Hardbound: 33.95

An account of naval aviation from Kitty Hawk to the Gulf War, *Pilots, Man Your
Planes! — A History of Naval Aviation* tells the story of naval air growth from a
time when planes were launched from battleships to the major strategic element
of naval warfare it is today. Full of detailed maps and photographs. Great for
anyone with an interest in aviation.

REBIRTH OF FREEDOM

From Nazis and Communists to a New Life in America ISBN: 1-55571-492-7
by Michael Sumichrast Paperback: 16.95

"...a fascinating account of how the skill, ingenuity and work ethics of an individual, when freed from the yoke of tyranny and oppression, can make a lasting contribution to Western society. Michael Sumichrast's autobiography tells of his first loss of freedom to the Nazis, only to have his native country subjected to the tyranny of the Communists. He shares his experiences of life in a manner that makes us Americans, and others, thankful to live in a country where individual freedom is protected."

— *General Alexander M. Haig, Former Secretary of State*

THE WAR THAT WOULD NOT END

U.S. Marines in Vietnam, 1971-1973 ISBN: 1-55571-420-X
by Major Charles D. Melson, USMC (Ret) Paperback: 19.95

When South Vietnamese troops proved unable to "take over" the war from their American counterparts, the Marines had to resume responsibility. Covering the period 1971-1973, Major Charles D. Melson, who served in Vietnam, describes all the strategies, battles, and units that broke a huge 1972 enemy offensive. The book contains a detailed look at this often ignored period of America's longest war.

WORDS OF WAR

From Antiquity to Modern Times ISBN: 1-55571-491-9
by Gerald Weland Paperback: 13.95

Words of War is a delightful romp through military history. Lively writing leads the reader to an under- standing of a number of soldierly quotes. The result of years of haunting dusty dungeons in libraries, obscure journals and microfilm files, this unique approach promises to inspire many casual readers to delve further into the circumstances surrounding the birth of many quoted words.

WORLD TRAVEL GUIDE

ISBN: 1-55571- 494-3
by Barry Mowell Paperback: 19.95

The resource for the modern traveler, *World Travel Guide* is both informative and enlightening. It contains maps, social and economic information, concise information concerning entry requirements, availability of healthcare, transportation and crime. Numerous Website and embassy listings are provided for additional free information. A one-page summary contains general references to the history, culture and other characteristics of interest to the traveler or those needing a reference atlas.

TO ORDER OR FOR MORE INFORMATION
CALL 1·800·228·2275

K-9 SOLDIERS

Vietnam and After   ISBN: 1-55571-495-1

by Paul B. Morgan   Paperback: 13.95

A retired US Army officer, former Green Beret, Customs K-9 and Security Specialist, Paul B. Morgan has written *K-9 Soldiers*. In his book, Morgan relates twenty-four brave stories from his lifetime of working with man's best friend in combat and on the streets. They are the stories of dogs and their handlers who work behind the scenes when a disaster strikes, a child is lost or some bad guy tries to outrun the cops.

AFTER THE STORM

A Vietnam Veteran's Reflection   ISBN: 1-55571-500-1

by Paul Drew   Paperback: 14.95

Even after twenty-five years, the scars of the Vietnam War are still felt by those who were involved. *After the Storm: A Vietnam Veteran's Reflection* is more than a war story. Although it contains episodes of combat, it does not dwell on them. It concerns itself more on the mood of the nation during the war years, and covers the author's intellectual and psychological evolution as he questions the political and military decisions that resulted in nearly 60,000 American deaths.

GREEN HELL

The Battle for Guadalcanal   ISBN: 1-55571-498-6

by William J. Owens   Paperback: 18.95

This is the story of thousands of Melanesian, Australian, New Zealand, Japanese, and American men who fought for a poor insignificant island is a faraway corner of the South Pacific Ocean. For the men who participated, the real battle was of man against jungle. This is the account of land, sea and air units covering the entire six-month battle. Stories of ordinary privates and seamen, admirals and generals who survive to claim the victory that was the turning point of the Pacific War.

OH, WHAT A LOVELY WAR

A Soldier's Memoir   ISBN: 1-55571-502-8

by Stanley Swift   Paperback: 14.95

This book tells you what history books do not. It is war with a human face. It is the unforgettable memoir of British soldier Gunner Stanley Swift through five years of war. Intensely personal and moving, it documents the innermost thoughts and feelings of a young man as he moves from civilian to battle-hardened warrior under the duress of fire.

THROUGH MY EYES

91st Infantry Division, Italian Campaign 1942-1945   ISBN: 1-55571-497-8

by Leon Weckstein   Paperback: 14.95

Through My Eyes is the true account of an Average Joe's infantry days before, during and shortly after the furiously fought battle for Italy. The author's front row seat allows him to report the shocking account of casualties and the rest-time shenanigans during the six weeks of the occupation of the city of Trieste. He also recounts in detail his personal roll in saving the historic Leaning Tower of Pisa.